BENEATH A
VEDIC SKY

BENEATH A VEDIC SKY

A Beginner's Guide *to*
the Astrology of
Ancient India

WILLIAM R. LEVACY

Hay House, Inc.
Carlsbad, California • New York City
London • Sydney • New Delhi

Published in the United States by: Hay House, Inc.: www.hayhouse.com®
Published Australia by: Hay House Australia Pty. Ltd.: www.hayhouse.com.au
Published in the United Kingdom by: Hay House UK, Ltd.: www.hayhouse.co.uk
Published in India by: Hay House Publishers India: www.hayhouseindia.co.in

Cover design: Julie Davison
Interior design: Karim J. Garcia
Planet Deities designed by: William R. Levacy

Library of Congress Cataloging-in-Publication Data

Levacy, William R.
    Beneath a Vedic sky : a beginner's guide to the astrology of ancient India / by William R. Levacy.
            p.   cm.
        ISBN 1-56170-524-1 (trade paper)
            1. Astrology, Hindu.   I. Title.
        BF1714.H5L48   1999
        133.5'9445—dc21
98-41294

            CIP

Tradepaper ISBN: 978-1-4019-7700-9

10 9 8 7 6 5 4 3 2 1
1st edition, February 1999
2nd edition, November 2023

Printed in the United States of America

This product uses papers sourced from responsibly managed forests. For more information, see www.hayhouse.com.

"If I am asked under what sky
the human mind has most fully developed
some of its choicest gifts, has most deeply pondered on
the greatest problems of life and has found solution
of some of them . . . I should point to India."
— Max Mueller

------------••⊃) ✴ ((••------------

"Make friends with the sky."
— Francis Albert Sinatra

---···꙳···---

*"Always blessings,
never losses."*

— **William R. Levacy**

---···꙳···---

CONTENTS

FOREWORD
BY KIMBERLY SNYDER

New York Times best-selling author of
You Are More Than You Think You Are

When I sat down to review my Vedic astrology chart for the very first time, I had a sense of nervousness. *What would it reveal? Is this stuff even real?* My Ayurvedic doctor had recommended I get my Vedic astrology chart read, and I was intrigued enough to do so. After considering my chart, I was floored. Vedic astrology, as I've come to realize, provides very specific insight based on the unique energy within each and every one of us.

As I went through my chart, a feeling of great energy and power started to rise in me from within. There were unmistakable truths revealed as I reviewed each section of the chart, each house under the influence of planetary movements tracked against the position of the stars, favoring astral positions. My chart felt alive, and from that day forward, it became a tool I had in my back pocket that has helped me to shape my decisions in my career, in my self-care and health practices, in my relationships, and in my personal life goals. It continues to benefit me greatly to this day. I have had my husband's and children's charts read as well, and the insight has benefited us as a family. It informs our lifestyle choices, which sports we select for our children to try, which school systems are best suited to their constitutions, and so on. I cannot overstate the enormous benefits possible from understanding a Vedic astrology chart.

With the momentous increase of interest in yoga and Ayurvedic medicine, the draw to Vedic astrology is also on the rise—and with good reason. Deriving from ancient India, Vedic astrology provides important keys to understanding all aspects of your life: your likes and dislikes, your karma, and your natural inclinations in terms of both your personality and physical health.

What I really like about Vedic astrology is that it never claims to predict your future. In fact, Vedic astrology does the opposite: it helps you comprehend the here and now, and embrace your present self by pointing you to your highest capabilities and truest potential. It guides you to make better decisions from a more expanded place of awareness and understanding.

Vedic astrology not only provides information about your genetic code, but also reveals the energies of your mind and heart. There are large differences between the genetic and physical constitution of your body and the energy of your inner being. This is obvious when you look at how differently two children born in the same family, with very similar genetic inheritance, can vary so greatly in their personality, life, health, and relationship patterns. We are all unique. Vedic astrology helps you to understand why that is.

William R. Levacy's classic manual on the vast field of study of ancient Vedic astrology, *Beneath a Vedic Sky*, is incredibly comprehensive and practically useful. You can study this book and develop your skills to go all the way to becoming a Vedic astrologer yourself, you can use this valuable guide to learn to analyze your own chart for the first time, or, if you're like me, you can use this book to delve deeper into your Vedic chart and glean further information about what makes us tick so we can make better decisions going forward.

Mr. Levacy presents so much valuable information in a succinct, well-organized way that makes the journey through Vedic astrology not only fascinating, but fun too. He guides you to learn key terms, concepts, ideas, and the language of the celestial bodies (Grahas) in an easy, step-by-step way.

In picking up this book, you have already made the decision to move toward a higher understanding of yourself. Welcome and congratulations! As you continue your journey into *Beneath the Vedic Sky*, you will gain powerful, valuable, and life-changing information to guide you for years to come.

With love and best wishes for you on your journey,

Kimberly Snyder

PREFACE

The Purpose of This Book

I felt compelled to write a book on how to effectively use Vedic astrology to become a practicing astrologer. I want to present the basic things that work. My focus is on the main elements of Vedic astrology that I feel beginning students must know to give an effective consultation. My choices of subject matter are based on my experience as a teacher and practitioner of Vedic astrology. These are the core concepts that I have found to work. The other tenets of astrology, which are fascinating but too complex for most beginners, will be the subject of a more advanced book.

Using this "must-know" rule and determining the core competencies of a Vedic astrologer, I have organized this book into what I call "Seven Skills of Vedic Astrology."

These seven skills are:

I. Analyzing the chart by learning the basics of chart interpretation

II. Synthesizing the multiple meanings of a chart into a self-consistent whole

III. Forecasting events or analyzing behavior over time

IV. Applying corrective measures to improve the quality of a chart (and consequently the person's life)

V. Combining charts or comparing one chart's compatibility with another (for example, in marriage, business, family harmony, etc.)

VI. Judging world events or looking at life out in the community and the world, beyond an individual's chart

VII. Using companion Vedic systems to interact with Vedic astrology (Ayurveda for health and Vastu for proper dwellings)

A last piece of advice, based on my own experience, is to enjoy yourself while studying Vedic astrology, do lots of charts, and don't try to understand. Sometimes your intellect can get in the way of a good analysis.

Suggestions for Beginners

If you are a beginner, it may be best to read the book in order. Skills I and II cover all the basics that you need to make sense of a Vedic-style chart. After that, you may add depth and polish to your readings by mastering the second half of the book, containing the rest of the Seven Skills; also see the appendix for further suggestions on organizing your learning process, as well as many other useful supplements. Refer to the glossary as necessary. As a beginner, it would be to your advantage to learn the basic elements of Vedic astrology—Skills I and II.

Following the suggested sequence will help you unfold the knowledge of Vedic astrology in a systematic manner. You'll have the most fun and get results faster overall by focusing mainly on these initial components. If you're in a big rush (I would be!), locate the descriptions for a person's rising sign, Moon, Moon nakshatra, and their Sun—although the Sun sign is not as important as in popular Western astrology. Read these for your initial interest. You must use Vedic chart calculations for this. There are several Vedic astrology software programs available, but you cannot use an old copy of a Western chart that you might have or a Western astrological program (unless it has a Vedic or Sidereal feature).

Don't worry if it doesn't immediately fall into place for you—Vedic astrology is a vast and deep field of study. Just read through it all once, let it sink in, and then you can freely range through the book, studying what you wish to know better. I have employed a table format throughout, for ease of reference and studying.

Using Skills I and II, study your own chart and the charts of family and friends. Let them know that you are a beginning student and ask them if the descriptions that you selected from this book match them. Be sure to stay on the positive side when you make your comments. Don't scare yourself and others by focusing on the unfavorable indications. You'll soon get a feeling for the meanings contained within the chart explanations. Listen to your feelings and let the chart speak to you. Determine the strength of each planet's influence by learning to use the shadbala and sarvashtakavarga calculations; this is where the computer program helps.

Chapter 12 synthesizes the basic skills that allow you to make sense of a Vedic-style chart. Use the Step-by-Step Guide to Analyzing a Chart located there. You will learn how to determine where to put your emphasis when interpreting, especially in situations where meanings seem to conflict. If a characteristic of behavior is repeated several times when looking through the basic elements of interpretation, you can feel certain that that item is relevant to the person. The amount of influence, and whether it's positive or negative, can be determined by using the strength calculation tools (shadbala and sarvashtakavarga) and by following the principal steps of chart analysis. It's okay, as a beginner, to concern yourself with just these first fundamentals of chart analysis and synthesis. Learning to forecast and to combine charts is a more sophisticated study area, contained in Skills III through VII.

After you have acquired an understanding of the basic ingredients of chart interpretation, you can move on to study the material in the rest of the book. After mastery of this book, which focuses on giving you a working knowledge of Vedic astrology, I hope you will be eager and able to tackle even more advanced Vedic astrology works, such as those listed in the bibliography.

Learn the key words given for each of the chart elements. It will help you, at first, to memorize two or three words for each chart component. Think of the feeling and concept behind the statements. Don't be too concerned about learning all the Sanskrit terms at first; rely on the glossary. Eventually, you will benefit by learning these Sanskrit terms so that you can understand works written by other Vedic astrologers, many of whom use them exclusively. Once you do learn to use the Sanskrit, the added bonus is that people will think you're really smart—they won't understand you, but they will think you're brilliant!

As you read and learn, it's okay to jump around some to keep things interesting—but watch that you don't confuse yourself by trying to learn everything at once. You will have to go from child to adolescent to adult—enjoy the process!

ACKNOWLEDGMENTS

In 1983, a friend of mine, Christina Ross, invited me to a class in West Hollywood, California. It was a weekly Vedic astrology study meeting hosted by Phyllis Kneip. Phyllis has been quietly instrumental in giving Vedic astrology a home in the United States. Vedic astrologers come from around the world to teach at her Sidereal School of Astrology in West Hollywood. It was Phyllis, and the learning opportunities she provided, who got me started with the study of Vedic astrology. I thank her deeply.

I would like to thank the many people who have been supportive and a joy to know over the years. My mother and dearly departed father, my brother Ron, his wife Martha, my sister Peggy, Peggy Raikes, Margie Corman, Barbara Bouse, Barbara Foster, Carol Allen, Mary Ann Cooke, Deborah Chodos, Steve Stuckey, Dr. Dennis Harness (and Debra Infante, leading all the American Council of Vedic Astrology staff), Dr. David Frawley, Christina Collins-Hill, Edith Hathaway, Dennis Flaherty, Steven Quong, Dr. Kimberly Hoffmann, Niranjan Babu, Gayatri Devi Vasudev, Sri Vasudev (who protected and guided my friends and me in India), B. "Suresh" Sureshwara, Bill Verkamp, Bob and Alex Bunshaft, Evvy Tavasci, Lynn Perry, Bill Daumen, Drs. Brian and Atsuko Rees, Barry Ross, Les and Nancy Bender, Martha Bonner, Marilyn Rose Utovac, Chakrapani Ullal, and last but not least, the two abandoned cats that I rescued (people say they adopted me), Miss Spoofy and Mr. Spiffy (they are the permanent Shakuna consultants for my readings). I would also like to thank Louise Hay for her vision of a bright and splendid world; and my wonderful editor, Christine Watsky, and her newborn baby, Hannah Lily. A special thanks from myself and all the astrological world to Dr. B. V. Raman, whose brilliant and dedicated work got many of us onto the shining road of Vedic astrology.

I would, finally, like to express my gratitude to Maharishi Mahesh Yogi for introducing me to the vast world of Vedic science. Maharishi gave me the understanding and experience that knowledge is self-unfolding and that consciousness rests at the basis of all acquisition of knowledge.

INTRODUCTION

Foundations in
Vedic Astrology

Vedic astrological chart interpretation is based on a very old knowledge system in India. This system is called the Veda, which translates as "knowledge," and it is the foundation of knowledge in the Hindu culture. In India, the Veda is held as the wisest of all wisdom. The Vedic culture has an amazing repository of knowledge. The knowledge of ancient India, or Bharata, as India was once called, is archived into a set of scriptures or shastras. Vedic knowledge is subdivided into six major branches, or Vedangas. Vedic astrology is one of these Vedangas. Called Jyotish, Vedic astrology represents the "eye" of the Vedas (jyoti means "light" or "eye," and ish comes from the root ishwara, which means "God" or "nature"). The Veda is called apaursheya or "beyond Man"—in its essence, it transcends any specific manifest cultural epoch and the time lines of history. The knowledge of the Vedas, the wisdom of awareness, is open to anyone who is "awake."

Who Started Vedic Astrology?

Vedic astrology comes from an ancient oral tradition. It was first mentioned in writing in the Atharva Veda some 4,000 to 5,000 years ago, in a short text on astrology—about 165 verses dealing with the Sun, Moon, and nakshatras (Moon signs). No signs of the zodiac (Sun signs) were mentioned. However, some researchers infer that descriptions in the Rig Veda give evidence of the knowledge of 12 signs of the zodiac. There are references to wheels with 360 spokes and 12 hubs, and other indications of knowledge of a solar-based zodiac. The Atharva Veda is one of the four major Vedas, the core knowledge system of India. The Mundaka Upanishad, another classical text, declares Vedic astrology to be a major branch, or Vedanga, of the Vedas, the source of pure knowledge.

The system of Vedic astrology is traditionally divided into three elements:

1. Hora, or predictive;

2. Ganitha, or mathematics; and

3. Samhita, or various astrological activities beyond the individual level—for nations, world events, etc.

The ancient sages of Vedic astrology, called rishis, wrote large works on astrology, called horas. Examples are Parasara Hora Shastra and Garga Hora. These original astrologers, or Jyotishis, were considered to be rishis or enlightened scholars. Astrological works based on the writings of rishis are deemed "rishi prokta" (spoken by a rishi). These are the best sources of information and are highly regarded by a culture that puts great faith in its roots and its enlightened teachers.

Current Jyotishis, or Vedic astrologers, derive most of the rules of judgment from the historical Vedic Sanskrit texts such as Brihat Samhita, Brihat Jataka, Jataka Parijata, Jataka Phaladeepika, Saravali, Muhurtha Chintamani, and the like. Additionally, many Vedic astrology interpretation systems have been preserved by a legacy of Jyotish families, passed down from father to child, Master to disciple, over many generations. The ancient sages memorized everything, so little was put into writing. The oral tradition was the convention for learning.

What Is the Purpose of Vedic Astrology?

"The Unborn Lord has many incarnations. He has incarnated as the Nava Grahas (Nine Planets) to bestow on the living beings the results due to their Karmas. He is Janardana. He assumed the auspicious form of the Grahas to destroy the Asuras (negative life energies) and sustain the Devas (positive life energies)."

— Brihat Parasara Hora Shastra

Vedic astrology is an ancient behavioral analysis and forecasting system. It employs a diagram of the positions of the planets relative to the earth and sky, based on the time and place of a person's birth. An astrologer reviews this chart to find information about an individual's concerns and about terrestrial events. The astrologer, depending on skill and clarity of consciousness, makes inferences regarding an individual's disposition and character and may foretell events in that person's life. Using advanced techniques, an astrologer may even forecast events on a community, national, or global scale.

What draws people to astrology through the ages, I believe, is the desire to make the right decisions. Plagued with poor decision-making capabilities, a person can retreat and inordinately reduce their expectations. Taking lower risks, they attain lower results, lower rewards, and, basically, a life of diminished joy. Astrologers help their clients understand whether they are in a slump or a surge and what might be the anticipated duration of either one. Astrologers, as counselors, want to help lead their clients to positive outcomes and to help them build a psychology that naturally triggers life-supporting behaviors.

Ultimately, the best way to get out of trouble is not to get into trouble to start with. Patanjali, the author of the Yoga Sutras, offered a timely aphorism: "Avoid the danger which has not come yet." Vedic astrology offers us a map to guide our life and gives us an analytical time profile of our behavior to help us understand what compels us to act. Vedic astrology helps us determine which behavioral traits to promote and which ones to target for self-improvement.

As a final note, it is not Vedic astrology's purpose to replace an individual's responsibility to decide for themselves what is best. Astrology tells us about the absence or presence of certain tendencies. We may use this information as a tool to form our own decisions and take our own actions. Armed with that, we can move forward joyfully in our lives, anticipating the best and averting the rest.

How Does It Work?

At the time and place of birth, there is a specific astronomical pattern in the heavens. This sky model is recorded from a distinct geographical point. Astrologers document this planet-earth-sky pattern and call it a chart. On the chart, they mark significant features such as the following:

- Where the planets are in the sky—by listing their location in a constellation, or sign of the zodiac

- The location on the earth—by using latitude and longitude; these are called houses

- Which sign is on the horizon, or that part of the sky east of the birth location, at the time of birth—this point is called the rising sign or ascendant

The above are the three most significant components of a chart. As the earth rotates, the signs move through the houses, following the clock throughout the day. The birth diagram is called a horoscope (from Greek horo, indicating time, and scope, meaning to look at). In India, the chart is called the chakra (wheel), Janma Kundali (rising), or Kala Purusha (body of time). In Vedic astrology, a chart is drawn as a square and/or a box of triangles, but in Western astrology, it is drawn as a wheel.

The birth chart diagram is interpreted according to specific rules of Vedic astrology as laid out by the ancient rishis, or seers, such as Maharishi Parasara. Fundamentally, Vedic astrology, or Jyotish, is a system for interpreting how behavior will unfold over time. Modern Western psychology analyzes behavior, but Vedic astrology shows how behavior might change over time. Life patterns seen in the birth chart are matched by the astrologer against the patterns seen in historical rules and records of parallel astronomical information. For predictive purposes, the Jyotishi uses a Vedic planetary almanac, or a computer program, to track the location of planets from sign to sign, and house to house, to locate when circumstances will emerge.

An astrologer determines when a planet will cross a sensitive point in the birth chart, stimulating a specific event. This event, waiting in the storehouse of that person's destiny, occurs as promised in the birth chart, modified somewhat by actions performed in this life. While these events are not necessarily predestined or even required to happen, they show a tendency to do so over the course of a person's life. The chart is a record of that person's karma. The astrologer's role is to match the patterns in the birth chart with the current patterns in the heavens, and to understand the nature of that person's environment. The astrologer consults the records in the ancient texts, much of which is memorized, and then analyzes, synthesizes, and draws a conclusion about the events at hand. The correctness of the reading is directly proportional to the experience and spiritual advancement of the astrologer, as well as to the recipient's desire and receptivity to having their chart read clearly. The reading is a short-term partnership.

Some authors feel that planets actually cause events to happen. They attempt to scientifically verify astrology with references to gravity, cosmic radiation, and the like. While this may or may not be true exactly, I think it more useful to view the planets as indicators of vast emerging patterns more than singular causative agents. To me, that's a bit like saying that the city limit signs for Los Angeles cause the city to exist, rather than to mark where it begins and ends.

As background material, it is good to know that the Vedic texts declare that Vishnu, the great maintainer of the universe, incarnated and reincarnated in cycles born of the essence of the nine planets. Brahma, the creator, acting on behalf of Vishnu, uses the planets in specific ways to disperse the creation around the universe.

How Is Vedic Astrology Different from Western Astrology?

First, let me reassure you. This section may seem rather technical and challenging, but don't worry if you don't understand these challenging terms and concepts. They really don't impact how well you will be able to read a chart, whether Vedic or Western. However, it is useful to know that the systems are different for very specific reasons.

The Vedic system is a more accurate astronomical representation of the Sun's position in relation to the skies. The Western systems emphasize the relationship of the Sun to the earth and the seasons. For this reason, Western astrology can be referred to as "tropical astrology," and Vedic astrology can be called "sidereal astrology." Sidereal astrology simply means that planetary movements are tracked against the positions of the stars, thus favoring the astral positions. In contrast, tropical astrology favors our point of view from Earth, tracking the planets in reference to seasonal points, such as the springtime.

Over the last several hundred years, this difference has caused the two systems to drift apart by about 24 degrees on where they mark the start of an astrological year. Both use the vernal or spring equinox as the start, but in Vedic systems, the vernal equinox currently marks 6 degrees of the Sun in Pisces—this is 24 degrees back from where Western astrologers mark the equinox as the beginning of Aries.

The difference between the Western start of the astrological year in Aries, and the Vedic or sidereal start in Pisces, is called the ayanamsa. Ayanamsa means "division of the year." Unless you were born between about the 15th and 20th of the month, you will find your "Western" Sun has most likely moved back by one sign in a

Vedic astrological chart. Vedic scholars have differences of opinion as to the exact date and time when the two systems started drifting away from each other (the ayanamsa point). The government of India chose the calculations of N. C. Lahiri. Ayanamsas also exist for Raman, Krishnamurti, and Sri Yukteswar. However, they are all close to plus or minus 6 degrees of Pisces.

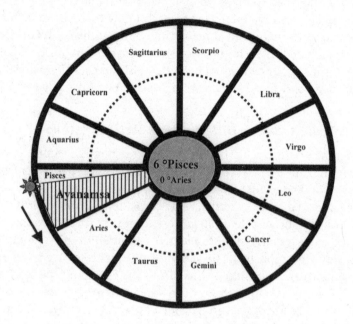

Vernal Equinox

The Sun rises this day at about 6° Pisces, using Vedic, sidereal calculations. The shaded area is the ayanamsa (about 24°), or the difference between the equinox starting point of the Vedic zodiac (about 6° Pisces) and the Western zodiac (0° Aries). In both systems, the equinox point shifts back, or precedes, about 1° or about one day every 72 years. In about 430 years, the Sun will rise in the sign of Aquarius on the morning of the spring equinox, ushering in the Age of Aquarius. The Vedic system adjusts for precession. The Western system does not, and will always indicate that Aries is still at the equinox.

Vedic astrology traditionally uses one house system, called the "equal house" system. (There is another system, called the Bhava Chalita, which adjusts the size of the houses according to the latitude of the birth place.) In Western astrology, there are numerous methods for dividing up the earth's latitude and longitude and forming the astrological land and time divisions called the houses.

Vedic, sidereal astrology also incorporates star signs based on the movement of the moon—about one day per Sun sign. These 27 moon signs are called nakshatras. Vedic astrology also divides the ecliptic, or the Sun's path, into 15 additional divisions, so we not only have the 30-degree divisions of each Sun sign, but further divisions of up to 150 segments. These are called the Shodasavargas. It's like having an additional 15 birth charts to read from. Vedic astrology also distinguishes itself in its predictive tools. Of especial note is the 120-year cycle forecasting system called the Vimshottari Dasa, where each planet is allotted a specific period of influence in the chart and is used to forecast more deeply into the nature of an individual's future. Again, don't worry if these concepts seem bewildering—you can use them to read charts without knowing all the whys and wherefores.

Vedic astrology is also integrated into Hindu societal functions and remains to this day an accepted part of religion and of most daily life. It is not uncommon to see heads of state as key speakers at Vedic astrology conferences. Many modern Indian business managers and computer experts working in the United States still wear astrological pendants to bring them success.

Vedic astrology is also a companion system to Ayurveda, the major health care system of India. In fact, Vaidyas, or "doctors" of Ayurveda, often consult the astrological chart of a client to seek additional diagnostic information. Vastu, the art of architectural measurement and placement (similar to China's Feng Shui), can be linked to the astrological tendencies of an individual's birth chart. (Chapters 19 and 20 will discuss these two systems in more detail.) Finally, Vedic astrology has its roots in consciousness, and so remedial measures can be taken, which can include religious performances (yagyas, pujas, and shantis); gemstones; mantras; charitable acts; gandarvaveda musical renditions; stotras (prayers); vratas (vows); herbs; and mineral concoctions (bashmas). All of these corrective measures are held to counterbalance the negative impressions from previous actions (samskaras). Taking such countermeasures, the client of astrology can not only know what needs to be corrected but how to apply restorative techniques as indicated in their birth chart.

Comparison of Vedic System (Nirayana or Sidereal) and Western System (Sayana or Seasonal)

No.	Rasi (Vedic names)	Signs (Western names)	Samvata (Vedic lunar months)	Nirayana (Vedic astrological calendar)	Sayana (Western astrological calendar)
1.	Mesha	Aries	Vaishakha	Apr 13–May 14	Mar 21–Apr 21*
2.	Vrishabha	Taurus	Jyeshta	May 15–Jun 14	Apr 22–May 20
3.	Mithuna	Gemini	Ashadha	Jun 15–Jul 14	May 21–Jun 21
4.	Kataka	Cancer	Shravana	Jul 15–Aug 14	Jun 22–Jul 22
5.	Simha	Leo	Bhadra	Aug 15–Sep 15	Jul 23–Aug 23
6.	Kanya	Virgo	Ashwina	Sep 16–Oct 15	Aug 24–Sep 23
7.	Tula	Libra	Kartika	Oct 16–Nov 14	Sep 24–Oct 23
8.	Vrishika	Scorpio	Mrigasirsa	Nov 15–Dec 14	Oct 24–Nov 22
9.	Dhanus	Sagittarius	Pausha	Dec 15–Jan 13	Nov 23–Dec 21
10.	Makara	Capricorn	Magha	Jan 14–Feb 12	Dec 22–Jan 21
11.	Kumbha	Aquarius	Phalguna	Feb 13–Mar 12	Jan 22–Feb 19
12.	Meena	Pisces	Chaitra	Mar 13–Apr 12*	Feb 20–Mar 20

Sign starting the new astrological year

The Vedic solar month is reckoned from the entry of the Sun into a rasi, or Vedic sign of the zodiac (the nirayana system). This ingress or entrance is called sankranti and occurs around the middle of the month, not the third week as in the Western sayana system. The difference is due to precession.

You will notice, in the table above, that the two systems overlap around the second to third week of each month (about 15th to the 20th, plus or minus a day or two on either side). If you were born during that time, your Sun sign would be the same in either system; otherwise, your Sun sign will move back one sign in the Vedic system.

Cultural and Environmental Influences on Interpretation

It is important for Vedic astrologers to understand that there are some significant differences between the culture of India and Western culture, especially the United States. I have constructed a chart below to indicate some of the differences in the backgrounds of the two cultures. Both cultures have their pluses and minuses, and some of these characteristics can be seen to some degree in both cultures. While India is the home of the Veda and represents the quintessence of philosophical thinking, it too is modernizing and mushrooming in its own distinct way.

Cultural Qualities of the East	Cultural Qualities of the West
Astrology is linked to religion	Astrology stands apart from religion
Intuition is honored	Intuition is suspect
"Trust me" attitude	"Prove it" attitude
Man is unified with nature	Man stands distinct from nature
Family-centered	Individual-centered
Feminine	Masculine
Releasing	Controlling
God's nature is shown in many forms	One God, one way
Traditionalist; values the past	Pioneer; values the future
Conservative	Liberal
Nature is explained in metaphors	Nature is explained in formulas
Spiritual	Material
Consciousness is at the center	Science is at the center
Knowledge is self-revealing	Knows via instruments and processes
Circular	Linear
Rebirth of the soul	One life to live
Accepts consequences of the past	Blames the past
Marriages are analyzed for success	Marriages are entered into blindly
Low divorce rate	High divorce rate (+50%)
Women work within the home	Women work outside the home
Women are dependent	Women are independent
Women are protected	Women fend for themselves
The elderly are regarded	The elderly are disregarded
Affections are displayed privately	Affections are demonstrated publicly
Don't wander far from home	International travelers, move often
Group or team effort	Individual effort
Educators are supported	Educators seek support
Priests are honored	Priests are questioned

Cultural Qualities of the East	Cultural Qualities of the West
Low technology	High technology
Low rate of change	High rate of change
Life purpose is defined and linked to past	Life purpose is uncertain
High birth rate	Low birth rate
No Social Security other than children	Social Security systems are available
Wet summers, dry winters, hot springs	Wet winters, dry summers, cool springs
Small middle class	Large middle class
Caste system or fixed growth ranges	American dream: anyone can make it
Treats the part in terms of the whole	Treats the part in terms of the part

THE BASICS
OF ANALYSIS

CHAPTER ONE

STARTING WITH CHART FORMATS

You will see that the Vedic charts, which are called chakras or Kundalis, are different from current Western astrological charts. Vedic charts can be created in various styles; this chapter will introduce three of them, which are the most widely used. Throughout this book, I will use the South Indian chart, for reasons described below.

With most Indian astrologers, the convention is not to use the Western glyphs or symbols for planets and signs. Instead, most Vedic astrologers who work in English traditionally use abbreviations of the names. The first two or three letters of the name are most often used; for example, Sun is Su, Aries is Ar or Ari.

North India Charts

Many Northern Indian astrologers use a square chart where each sign is a triangle. You read the chart from right to left, counterclockwise. It is similar to the chart style used by astrologers of the middle ages in Europe. All the houses on angles are in the center of the chart and are readily visible. Gazing upon this mandala-like chart is said by some to be beneficial. In this style, the houses remain fixed in position, and the signs, numbered 1 to 12, are rotated according to the rising sign. The names of the signs are not listed on the charts, just their numbers. Astrologers using this style will often construct a separate chart, marking the Moon as the ascendant point.

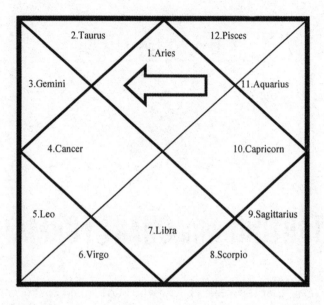

South India Chart

South Indian astrologers, from areas such as Bangalore, Madras, Kerala, or Bombay, use this style. This is the chart style that I prefer, and that I will be referring to throughout the book. It is a square chart where each sign is a box, and is read clockwise from left to right. I like this style because the signs stay fixed, while the houses move. With the signs fixed in position, it is easy to insert data into the boxes of the chart. In the diagram below, I have included with the signs their ruling planets; note that many planets rule more than one sign.

12. Pisces *Jupiter*	1. Aries *Mars*	2. Taurus *Venus*	3. Gemini *Mercury*
11. Aquarius *Saturn*			4. Cancer *Moon*
10. Capricorn *Saturn*			5. Leo *Sun*
9. Sagittarius *Jupiter*	8. Scorpio *Mars*	7. Libra *Venus*	6. Virgo *Mercury*

Bhava Chalita Chart

Some astrologers indicate that you should study the position of signs according to the equal house, or rasi, chart, which is illustrated by both of the previously discussed chart systems. Others indicate that you can also study the position of houses from the Bhava Chalita chart. As you move higher in latitude, you can have instances where two signs (or more) could occupy one house. One house intercepts another's position in a sign. This system is not an equal house system—the houses could occupy a different space than do the signs.

The Bhava tries to deal with this issue by marking house boundaries at the start of a sign and not in the middle or madhya, as is the convention in the equal house system. What you will find is that the house boundaries move back by about 15 degrees. I do not use the Bhava chart, preferring to stay with the traditional equal house system. Some astrologers claim to get benefit from the Bhava by being able to determine what house a planet "truly" occupies at higher terrestrial latitudes. Sri Pati, an astrologer from the Middle Ages, devised this system. It is somewhat similar to the Porphery system in the West.

CHAPTER TWO

PLANETS—GRAHAS

Graha, the Sanskrit word that most Vedic astrologers use to refer to a planet, actually means "that which grabs or holds." Strictly speaking, there is no such thing as a "planet" described in Vedic astrology.

It is interesting to note that, according to current astronomical theory on planetary formation, there are only certain points in the solar system where matter can thicken enough to form planets. These junction points represent the intersection of the pull of the Sun's gravity with the outward tug of diverse spinning stellar dust, gas, and debris. One force is pulling in, the other is pushing out. Somewhere in the middle of this celestial interplay, a planet forms. It's as if these astronomical collection centers "grab" galactic matter to form planets. It may not be so much the physical ball of the planet that causes things but, more likely, the energy coming from that cosmic planetary mathematical/astronomical point.

As mentioned in the introduction, traditional Vedic astrology recognizes only the planets visible by the unaided or "naked" eye (Sun through Saturn), with the exception that the north and south nodal points of the Moon's orbit, where eclipses occur, are treated as planets.

The outer planets (Uranus, Neptune, and Pluto) are not utilized by traditional Vedic astrologers, although Vedic historians note that the authors of Jyotish were probably astronomically advanced enough to have known of them. Most notably, Veda Vyasa, the author of the famous classic, Mahabharata, hints at the existence of outer planets by naming three celestial bodies with coordinates approximating the positions of our solar system's outer planets. You will find that some modern Vedic authors are experimenting by including the outer planets in their work.

Grahas form the center point of Vedic astrology, so know your planets. As we mentioned earlier, everything is oriented to the planets in some way or another. Planets are located in the sky via the signs of the zodiac. Planets are identified in terms of the earth via the rising sign and the corresponding houses. Planets rule signs, are the key to planetary period calculations, and so forth. Learning the meaning of the planets forms the first step on your road to becoming a good Vedic astrologer.

The Meaning of the Nine Planets

The meanings of each of the nine planets are described on the following pages. Each planet is also given "rulership" over a particular sign of the zodiac. That ruling planet will transfer a large part of its influence to the meaning and description of the sign in which it rules—this is a very important point to understand. For example, Mars, a fiery planet, will transfer that fiery energy to the signs of Aries and Scorpio. We see this fieriness translate as energy, enthusiasm—even heat and anger—in Aries and Scorpio-dominated charts.

The Sun (Surya or Ravi)

Signifies: one's own self; royalty; stately appearance; grandness; individuality; self-esteem; one's status in life; will; behavior; body; authority, father, government, employers, superiors; the sustaining center of things; living in wooded areas; resistance to disease; circulatory system or heart; bones and skeletal system; eyesight (right eye of a man and left eye of a woman, according to some); hair growth, baldness; headaches; stocky body frame; heat, fevers, dryness; belly region and digestion; pitta or fiery Ayurvedic constitution (see chapter 19)

Occupations: military and commercial leaders; directors, doctors, politicians, scientists, technical interests; public persons such as entertainers

The Moon (Chandra or Soma)

Signifies: one's own emotions (heart); mind; mother; understanding; royal favor; affluence; intuition; instinctual behavior; subliminal self; memory; imagination; fertility; femininity; fluids and watery things; sensitivity; sweetness; fullness and emptiness (high tide and low tide), desire for change and new experiences; rapid actions; receptivity; feelings and emotions; resource gathering, and hoarding of supplies for home; water; bathing; sleeping well; kapha (earthy) or vata (airy) Ayurvedic constitution

Occupations: activities related to groups or families of people; female pursuits; nurturing or nursing; educators; training of beginners (such as children); tutors; public relations; psychic abilities; liquids; beverages; sea products; water-related or seagoing industries such as Navy, Merchant Marine, Coast Guard, etc.; cooks, food preparers; visually oriented jobs—art, film, etc.; sweets; food; clothing; homes and shelter; hotels; activities that can turn around quickly, such as import/export

Since the Moon is such an important component of Vedic astrology, it is important to be familiar with a little bit of lunar astronomy.

Movement of the Moon

The Moon transits one sign of the zodiac in about 2½ days (30 days divided by 12 signs). The Moon moves 12 times faster than the Sun. From one night to the next, at the same time of the evening, the Moon's position lags relative to the Sun about 12 degrees to the east. The Moon moves through all 12 Sun signs in about 27.32 days (one sidereal month, or starting and returning to a marker star) and about 29.5 days from one new Moon to the next. The Moon does not orbit the earth in an exact circle and is not precisely linked to the solar day. The Moon's path is slightly different and its daily motion causes it to take about 30 days to go around the earth. The Moon will become full and empty 12 times to complete a year. This makes 360 "moon" days (or nights) and makes a lunar year. So we have 365 days of the Sun (counting during the days) and 360 nights of the Moon (counting during the nights) to make one year.

Cycles of the Moon

A **Waxing Moon,** or the bright half (Shukla Paksha), is strong and benefic. It is moving from New Moon to Full Moon (Purnima) during its first 14-day subcycle. The Moon begins to get stronger and more favorable at about 72 degrees away from the New Moon position, moving toward the Full Moon (opposition of Sun and Moon).

Generally, events that happen during the bright half of the lunar month get more favorable support than during the dark half.

A **Waning Moon,** or dark half (Krishna Paksha), is weak and malefic. It is moving from Full Moon to New Moon (Amavasya) during its second 14-day subcycle. The Moon begins to weaken and become unfavorable when it approaches within 72 degrees of the New Moon position (a conjunction of the Sun and Moon). A weak Moon is called Ksheena (emaciated). Some say it is at its worst when the Moon is within 24 degrees or less of the Sun.

Additional information on the Moon, such as tithis or lunar days, lunar months, and ritus or Vedic seasons are too advanced for the scope of this book and won't be covered.

New Moon—starts waxing or bright half of Moon

1	2	3	4	5	6	7
Bad	Bad	Bad	Ok	Ok	Ok	Ok
8	9	10	11	12	13	14
Good	Good	Good	Good	Good	Good	Good

Full Moon—starts waning or dark half of Moon

1	2	3	4	5	6	7
Good	Good	Good	Good	Good	Good	Good
8	9	10	11	12	13	14
Good	Ok	Ok	Ok	Bad	Bad	Bad

Mars (Kuja or Mangala)

 Signifies: one's own courage; initiative; energy; desire for quick action; pioneering spirit; desire; wars and warriors; brothers and sisters; muscular; short body; loans; buildings; wounds; operations; accidents; cutting; burning; engineering and construction; amorality; living in the moment; red eyes, hair, and skin; pitta or fiery Ayurvedic constitution

Occupations: activities related to action and leading or forcing others to do things; pathfinder, innovator, pioneer, military, security, defense, martial arts, police, firefighter, executive actions, director, dictator, executioner, dentists, surgeons, hair cutters, acupuncturists, masseuses; herbal medicines and pharmaceuticals; herbs; cutting; fabricating; industrial or factory work; chemicals, metals, explosives, demolition, weapons, engines, fuels, construction, buildings, real estate, landlords

Mercury (Budha)

 Signifies: one's own mind; quick learning; learning capacity; education; writing; reading; discrimination; logic and reasoning ability; action; speech, communication; one's own intellectual activity; thought; friends, relatives outside immediate family, relatives in general; the urge to think about everything; critical and discriminating thinking; mathematics, logic, science, accounting, astrology, joking, mental disorders, paralysis or nervous system ailments, respiration

Occupations: activities related to thinking, measuring, conceiving, and advising; minister, consultant, teacher, mathematician, musician, writer, engineer, architect, accountant, business manager, analyst of any form, secretary, administrator, librarian, computer worker, communications specialist, speech therapist, language expert, translator, diplomat, technician, designer, psychotherapist, editor, banker, astrologer; works with newspapers, magazines, and other media

Jupiter (Guru or Brihaspati)

Signifies: one's own wisdom, wealth, expansion, knowledge, scriptures, the higher mind, wisdom, optimism, overconfidence, desire to know and improve things, spiritual knowledge, good deeds, worship, charity, fortune (bhagya), sons, education, religion, philosophy, children, wealth, grace, liver, fats, oils, accumulation of fluids, husband, kapha (earth/water) Ayurvedic constitution

Occupations: activities related to wisdom, knowledge, and higher learning; justice; legal counsel, consultant, minister, priest, guru, teacher, educator, tutor, psychologist, astrologer, humanitarian, childcare worker

Venus (Sukra)

Signifies: one's ability to relate; love; the things one loves; wealth, pleasure, comforts, indulgences; vehicles; clothing and accessories; beauty, perfumes, gems, jewelry; sexual pleasure; laziness; vanity; having fun; creativity; art, music, dance, and poetic expression; diplomacy or ministership; creating a favorable impression (this could be extended to signify lawyers); cordiality; receptivity; femininity; objects and affairs of women; jealousy; marriage; social clubs; celebrations and festivals; attractive appearance, good grooming; for men it signifies the wife; vata (air) and kapha (earth) Ayurvedic constitution

Occupations: artist, musician, dancer, actor, poet, singer, creative writer, counselor, diplomat, lawyer, money handler or manager, beauty consultant, dealer in sweets and sugars, silk and fabric merchant, cosmetician, perfume dealer, marriage counselor, advisor to women, metals broker (especially silver), jeweler, florist, clothing/fashion designer or dealer, social director, luxury car salesman, expert in leisure activities, hostess, sex worker

Saturn (Shani or Sani)

Signifies: one's own time and durability; longevity; focus; lessons; justice; the common man; old age; steady and dependable work; livelihood; seeking enlightenment through isolation and restraint; cause of death; adversity

and prosperity; limitations; setbacks, delays; theft, lost things; concentration, introspection, meditation; vata (air) Ayurvedic constitution

Occupations: expert in the affairs of aging and death, coroner, mortician, executioner, farmer, gardener, landscaper, landholder, specialist in antiquarian topics, social worker, manual laborer, craftsman (mason, carpenter, etc.), monk, iron or steel worker, oil and mineral worker, geologist, animal expert or handler, real estate salesperson, land manager or planner, servant (works to keep others organized), timekeeper, punisher (censures others' wrongdoings)

Rahu (North node of the Moon)

 Rahu is the ascending point where the orbit of the Moon cuts across the orbit path of the Sun. It has no mass. It is a mathematical point in space. Rahu is also symbolized as the head of a snake that has been cut in half. The head is where the snake acquires his food, and where he has his poison. Things start out well and strong with this terrifying and sneaky snake, but they fall through at the end, since the snake is cut in half. An ancient story says that Rahu, a demon, crashed a Soma drinking party of the Devas. Demons were not allowed, but through a subterfuge (he asked who was the most important Deva), he grabbed a drink of Soma while the Devas quibbled over who was first in line. Vishnu saw what was going on at the last moment, threw his discus, and severed Rahu's head. Since he had drunk the Soma, he became immortal. Unfortunately, he now consists of his head, still called Rahu, and his new other half, his tail, called Ketu. Rahu/Ketu was not a good loser, and so has spent the time since then interfering with the light from the Sun and Moon (causing eclipses). The Moon is said to be afraid of Rahu and Ketu.

Signifies: one's own material destiny; indications similar to Saturn (but not exactly the same); deals with material karma; toxicity; chronic conditions; qualities to be developed in this lifetime; attachment; foreign influences; deceptions; wittiness; skin diseases; delusions; epilepsy; madness; thefts; land; prosperity; tall people; diplomacy; effects are more beneficial in later life; vata (air) Ayurvedic constitution (since Rahu is said to act like Saturn)

Occupations: unusual activities such as nuclear management; waste removal (plumbers, garbage or disposal workers, chemical or toxic spill cleanup, etc.); body purification specialists; experts in foreign affairs; foreign people or activities; industrial researchers (a.k.a. "espionage"); members of secret government forces or agencies; pharmacists; chemists; drug and alcohol dealers; nutritionists who specialize in herbs; x-ray technicians; alternative/hands-on healers (acupuncture, Ayurveda, etc.); advertising or creative marketing agents; real estate or land agents (similar to Saturn); people who give shots or inoculations (shots are a form of "snakebite"); anesthesiologists; herpetologists. Rahu-based careers usually make more money than Ketu-oriented careers.

Ketu (South node of the Moon)

 Ketu represents the tail of a snake. It wiggles and moves around a lot. Ketu represents nonattachment and is said to be the karaka of moksha, or indicator of enlightenment. Ketu, by all the changes it creates, sets up an environment of unboundedness that leads to enlightenment or liberation. Ketu is regarded as a mystical planet and is an indicator for enlightenment—as such, it is the only planet not given a compass direction. It signifies the direction of "heavenward" or not of this earth.

Signifies: maternal grandfather; indications similar to Mars, but not identical; mystical involvement; unboundedness; cunning thinking; thinking "out of the box"; detachment or separation; lack of material possessions; hypersensitivity; chronic itching; surprises; change; absence of planning; cuts, wounds, accidents; ups and downs; reorganization; short people; a seer; qualities developed in last lifetime.

Occupations: These people are drawn to a lot of occupations. Many of their interests are founded on some spiritual ideal and they will try to find an occupation that helps them realize that ideal. Lots of monks, nuns, and people who have lived in spiritual communities have this position; as well as psychics, astrologers, and mystics of all forms. They usually make quick changes in their careers, often surprising themselves.

Additional Characteristics of Planets

Below, I have tabulated several characteristics of the planets. Many of these designations of planetary meaning were extracted from the Brihat Parasara Hora Shastra. You will be able to use these meanings in a multitude of ways.

The following information represents some of the most important attributes of the planets in table format for easy look-up and study. While there are many more characteristics identified with the planets, I have picked those that I believe are among the most important for beginners to know. The appendix contains many more characteristics of planets, which I highly encourage you to learn if you want to become a thoroughly trained Vedic astrologer. Following the tables is an explanation of each column. Learn them well, since the information plays a big role in determining the value of planets.

Planet	Five Elements (Tattvas or MahaBhutas)	Natural Benefic or Malefic
Sun	Fire	Malefic
Moon	Water	Benefic
Mars	Fire	Malefic
Mercury	Earth	Benefic
Jupiter	Ether	Benefic
Venus	Water	Benefic
Saturn	Air	Malefic
Rahu	Air (like Saturn)	Malefic
Ketu	Fire (like Mars)	Malefic

Five Elements:

1. **Ether** represents creativity, ingenuity, and mental agility. People with a predominance of the ether element make good diplomats, agents, and representatives. They are good speakers and are able to learn amazing amounts of data relating to subjects that capture their interests. They are good planners.

2. **Fire** represents aggression, executive ability, confidence, pride, and insolence. People with fire in dominance are quick-acting and sharp. They like to lead and be in charge.

3. **Earth** represents focus, dedication, and devotion. These people are stable and practical but enjoy luxuries, such as good clothes and living arrangements.

4. **Air** represents mobility and a mental orientation. People with a number of air planets in their chart will be more intellectual and drawn to activities relating to numbers, letters, and other mind-oriented tasks. They are good analyzers and critics.

5. **Water** represents emotions and flexibility of mind. People with many water planets will be intuitive and responsive. They make good counselors and nurturers.

Benefic/Malefic: By definition, each planet is naturally able to bring positive (benefic) results or negative (malefic) results. It's important to remember that even if a planet is deemed malefic, it could be that the negative actions it creates ultimately have a positive outcome. For example, Saturn restricts things but it might be that an activity needs restriction or control and is better off for that. Chapter 12 will explain these concepts more fully.

Planet	Rulerships	Own Sign(s) (Swakshetra)	Exaltation Sign/Degree (Uucha)	Debilitation Sign/Degree (Neecha)	Moolatrikona Sign
Sun	Leo	Leo 20–30°	Aries 10°	Libra 10°	Leo 0–20°
Moon	Cancer	Cancer	Taurus 3°	Scorpio 3°	Taurus 3–30°
Mars	Aries & Scorpio	Aries 12–30° & Scorpio	Capricorn 28°	Cancer 28°	Aries 0–12°
Mercury	Virgo & Gemini	Virgo 20–30° & Gemini	Virgo 15°	Pisces 15°	Virgo 15–20°

Planet	Rulerships	Own Sign(s) (Swakshetra)	Exaltation Sign/Degree (Uucha)	Debilitation Sign/Degree (Neecha)	Moolatrikona Sign
Jupiter	Sagittarius & Pisces	Sagittarius 10–30° & Pisces	Cancer 5°	Capricorn 5°	Sagittarius 0–10°
Venus	Taurus & Libra	Libra 15–30° & Taurus	Pisces 27°	Virgo 27°	Libra 0–15°
Saturn	Aquarius & Capricorn	Aquarius 20–30° & Capricorn	Libra 20°	Aries 20°	Aquarius 0–20°
Rahu	Virgo	Virgo	Taurus	Scorpio	None
Ketu	Pisces	Pisces	Scorpio	Taurus	None

Rulerships: Each planet rules or is the "lord" of a particular sign or signs. A planet that occupies the same sign that it rules is said to be in its own sign or "at home" and will enjoy the benefits that anyone would living within their own domain. For example, when the Sun, which rules Leo for all charts, has moved in the heavens to occupy the sign of Leo in a specific chart, the Sun is then said to be in its own sign, and therefore to have a stronger influence. Rulerships are discussed further in chapter 7.

Own Sign: A planet will not always occupy the same sign that it rules; they are constantly in motion. It is considered very favorable when a planet is found, at a specific time and location in its celestial travels, in its own sign. All planets, except for the Sun and Moon, are assigned to rule two signs. Some authors differ as to what signs, if any, are ruled by Rahu and Ketu. The degrees indicate the position within a sign that gives the planet a strong influence.

Exaltation: This is one of the highest positions for a planet to occupy. It brings very favorable effects, if not modified by unfavorable aspects such as residing in a negative placement or sitting along with malefic planets.

Debilitation: This is one of the least favorable places for a planet to occupy. The planet cannot fully release its positive traits, and malefic planets become worse. The planet can't defend itself well.

Moolatrikona: Gives favorable results to planets, and makes bad planets less bad. This position is stronger than own sign, but not as strong as exaltation, which is the strongest. Rulership shows a constant or static relationship between a planet and a sign, in terms of ownership influence. Moolatrikona and exaltation are dynamic placements determined by the positions of planets in the sky (in signs) at the time and place for which a chart is constructed.

Some authors indicate that Rahu is exalted in Gemini and Ketu is exalted in Sagittarius. Debilitation is the reverse, Rahu in Sagittarius and Ketu in Gemini. Whether they are exalted or not, I have found these to be favorable signs for Rahu and Ketu. Parasara tells us that Virgo and Pisces are ruled by Rahu and Ketu, respectively. He also indicated that Rahu is exalted in Taurus and Ketu in Scorpio and the reverse for debilitation. Some astrologers feel that you can read these nodes backwards, since they have retrograde motion. I believe there is some logic to this and have seen it work.

Parasara indicates that a retrograde planet in its sign of debilitation becomes exalted. If a retrograde planet is exalted, it becomes as if debilitated. There is disagreement among authors on this point, but I have found the rule to be true.

Retrograde Planets

A retrograde planet and its effects is an area subject to a diversity of opinions. Those familiar with basic astronomy know that planets only appear to change their forward motion by standing still for a short while (stationary), then moving backward in their orbit relative to an observer on earth (retrograde), and then returning to their forward motion (direct).

Philosophically, many astrologers interpret retrograde motion as causing more of the planet's effects to manifest. According to the formulas in shadbala (a Vedic planetary strength calculation system), retrograde makes the planet stronger. Note that this does not mean it makes the planet better, nor does it mean the planet is required to be interpreted in a specific way. A planet in retrograde is held by many to exhibit more of what it already has—whether positive or negative. Some state that a retrograde planet causes the influence of the planet to reverse. Some indicate that you interpret the retrograde planet as having the influence of the sign ahead, pulling that influence back into the approaching sign. Ayurvedic physicians report that health problems tend to manifest more during retrograde periods or with people who have strong influences from retrogrades in their charts.

I have found, in my experience, that the loitering retrograde motion throws off the energy of a planet and does not allow it to flow in a normal fashion. The house occupied by the retrograde planet is not allowed to function at its best. There is a principle, given by Maharishi Parasara that supports this somewhat. The sage states that a retrograde planet will reverse the effects of an exalted or debilitated planet.

There is not much written in astrological literature about retrograde planets. I have listed on the following pages some of the effects that I have noticed from my experience. As you know, the Sun and Moon are never retrograde. The nodes of the Moon are almost always retrograde, with occasional states of direct motion and infrequent stationary "motion"—when lingering between forward and reverse. You can see this motion in panchangas (sidereal planetary almanacs or ephemerides), which show true motion of planets.

Mars Retrograde

Keywords: Action in Reverse

Mars is normally the planet of fire, warriors, action, and initiative. When retrograde, Mars becomes less inclined to take action— the person needs to have a "fire" lit under them. Sometimes the person will let a situation get critical in order to use that crisis, either consciously or unconsciously, to drive them to act. These people can be very frustrating in that they will often wait until the last minute to do something. The pressure of being forced to act supplements the weakness of retrograde Mars.

When Mars is retrograde by transit, you should consider it an unfavorable time for actions that need the supporting energy of Mars. It would be an inauspicious time for starting new projects, buying or building a house, activities with the siblings, lawsuits, going to war or entering a competition, marriages, business contracts, starting a new business, buying equipment, working with chemicals and fire, undergoing surgeries or dental work, or the like.

Mercury Retrograde

Keywords: Thinking in Reverse

These people think in a more intuitive manner and are most likely right-brain dominant. Right-brain thinking is more spatially oriented, comprehends through recognizing patterns, and arrives at conclusions without seeming to go through the more observable steps of logic and reason. This does not mean they are wrong. In fact, they are often right, and quickly so. If they are around a lot of analytical people, they have to go back, "rewind," and figure out for themselves how to state what they thought—in terms of numbers and formulas instead of symbols and metaphors. They can drive analytical people crazy because of the seemingly discontinuous manner in which they, the Mercury retrogrades, think. They are not linear.

Jupiter Retrograde

Keywords: Expanding in Reverse

Retrograde Jupiter seems to create bargain hunters. They are always looking for a better deal. Jupiter is the planet of expansion, so when it is retrograde, it motivates the person to try to win back what was lost. Getting a good deal, calling for return of loans, redeeming coupons, getting rebates, and the like all indicate the flavor of retrograde Jupiter. This can be a problem in relationships in that the person is always considering something better, beyond what they have in their current partnership. These persons are often successful in disaster situations—they don't pay attention to how it won't work, they just go ahead. They are also quick to spot an opportunity for profit during times of disaster that others might miss. Conversely, they might smell disaster before others do and get out ahead. A danger with Jupiter retrograde is a lack of timely response to new opportunities. Laziness or too much optimism can lead these people to miss obvious benefits.

Jupiter retrograde becomes interested in projects that have become disregarded or weak. They can still see the value in that event or person, and are willing to take it on for repair and rejuvenation. Since Jupiter is still naturally inspiring, these retrogrades can feel their self-worth expand by helping rejected or abandoned people, projects, and companies become better.

Venus Retrograde

Keywords: Loving in Reverse

Venus retrograde (along with Venus conjunct Rahu or Ketu) can indicate an unusual interest in love. These people don't seem to be stimulated by customary means. Socially, they don't fit into the mainstream. Often people with this position become celibates—or the reverse, sexual "celebrants." They can swing between opposites: averse or perverse. Idealism about love forms to such a high level of expectation that nobody could meet it. The end result is a feeling of not being loved. Often these people turn to religion, because it seems easier to love God—and God does have a lot of love. Sometimes when this Venus is very afflicted, the person could be mistreated in love or have very traumatic experiences with those they love. Venus retrograde people don't always make the best or happiest marriage partners. Finding a fulfilling, lasting relationship is at least a challenge for them. They can be at odds with the traditional philosophical and social aspects of partnering. Sometimes these people prefer the company of their own sex, either through many friends of the same gender or through intimate same-sex relationships. A transit of retrograde Venus can put one's love life into a spin, causing disinterest or increased interest—usually the opposite of one's normal state.

Saturn Retrograde

Keywords: Stability in Reverse

Saturn is a planet of seclusion and renunciation. Often people with Saturn retrograde become more self-isolating, monastic, and even antisocial. They feel like they are alone; no one understands them. Actually afraid of rejection, they act as if they couldn't care less and sometimes reject others first before it can happen to them. Fatalism and pessimism cloud their life. It seems hard for them to go on during certain periods. They can get withdrawn, grim, even depressed. In their isolation, they can become more nervous and fearful—even paranoid or agoraphobic. One good facet is that Saturn generally lets up as a person matures and gains more life experience. So if these people can hold on in their early years, or in the early stages of any life event, they should be okay. We are intended, in this life, to enjoy or to not mind too much—Saturn retrogrades just need to remember that.

Sandhi Planets

Planets are weak when they are located under one degree or over 29 degrees in a sign. These positions take away a significant amount of planetary power. If there are three or more of these sandhi planets, the overall chart gets weakened quite a bit. Sandhi, which means "junction point" in Sanskrit, is like someone moving their home. Their life is in boxes. They are not in their old home, and they are not completely in their new home. Everything is still on the truck.

Combust Planets

Combustion occurs when planets are close to the Sun. There is a range for each planet, but eight to ten degrees from the Sun starts to get pretty hot for all. Combustion is not regarded as good, but I think it is overrated as a malefic condition. It is a C-grade problem that some interpreters raise to an A level. You should note that many good yogas are formed from planets being conjunct with the Sun. These planets are technically "combust" but do well in combination with the Sun.

CHAPTER THREE

ZODIAC SIGNS—RASIS

The general features of each sign of the zodiac follow. These descriptions will aid you in understanding basically how each sign operates. These generic "portraits" list the pure form of a sign. The standard nature of a sign will be modified by planets, favorably or unfavorably. Rarely will you find a completely "typical" sign.

If occupying or aspecting planets (that is, planets whose influences are currently modifying the sign) are naturally favorable, such as Jupiter, Venus, unafflicted Moon, and Mercury, then the best parts of the sign can be expressed. If a planet has high shadbala strength and the sign has high sarvashtakavarga points, then positive outcomes will prevail (shadbala and sarvashtakavarga are strength calculation systems explained in chapters 12 and 13). These benefics, with strong or high "bala" points, will help the sign repel any negative forces that come upon it. Occupying or aspecting planets that are naturally unfavorable or negative, such as Saturn, Mars, Rahu, Ketu, and to an extent the Sun, will promote the more aggressive, weaker, and rougher qualities of a sign. If a planet has low shadbala strength and the sign has low sarvashtakavarga points, the sign will have trouble promoting the favorable forces that describe it or visit it.

The Rising Sign, Ascendant, or Lagna

The rising sign or ascendant is called the lagna or lagna rasi in Sanskrit. Lagna means "attached to" and shows which particular sign of the zodiac is occupying or "attached to" the earth's horizon line for the time and location of a specific chart. Accuracy of the rising sign time is a critical factor in delivering a successful reading. From my experience, I have found that the rising sign contains the largest part of the data relevant to the chart being analyzed. I consider the rising sign to be a miniature biography. It gives an outline of the overall qualities of the chart being interpreted. The rest of the planetary information in the chart—planets in signs and houses, for example—fills in the "body" of this outline. The information on the rising sign can also be used, to a degree, in the interpretations given for both the Moon and the Sun.

You can also regard a sign occupied with four or more planets as having significant influence. You could almost read this highly occupied sign as if it were a secondary "rising sign" of sorts.

In Vedic astrology, when a person is asked to name their sign, they should indicate their lagna rasi (rising sign), since this sign most likely carries the most personal information. As many people know, the popular Western convention is to identify oneself with the Sun sign (which usually moves back one sign in Vedic astrology, as already discussed).

In the explanations of the signs that follow, it is good to remember that:

- *Favorable* traits will emerge if the rising sign's ruler is placed in a favorable sign and house, and the ruler and sign itself is not aspected by unfavorable planets.

- *Unfavorable* traits will emerge if the rising sign is afflicted, for example located in signs of debilitation, an enemy's sign, sandhi, combust, "hemmed in" between malefics, aspected or conjunct with other unfavorable planets, etc.

- A *mixture* of favorable and unfavorable traits emerge if a rising sign has a mix between being located favorably or unfavorably and is aspected similarly.

As we know, nobody is perfect, so you will often see a mixture, but usually the chart will lean toward one or the other, favorable or unfavorable. It should also be noted that some signs have a natural tendency to express more of the negative or unfavorable aspects. Specifically, these signs are the ones that are ruled by the malefic planets of Mars and Saturn (Aries, Scorpio, Capricorn, and Aquarius).

General Descriptions of Signs

It should be noted that the following information given for a sign can apply to the Lagna, the Moon, and the Sun. In fact, according to some established writers in Vedic astrology, meaning can be derived from looking at the Lagna, then the Moon, then the Sun. The strength of each will determine their input.

Aries—Mesha
SYMBOL: A Ram
KEY CONCEPT: Getting things done. Focus is on one's self.

First sign of the natural zodiac. Transfers its influence, and that of its ruling planet Mars, to the interpretation of the first house of a chart.
BASIC NATURE:

Favorable: Self-assertive, full of initiative, pioneering, courageous, enterprising, ambitious, hardy, active; leader in thought and action; forceful character; executive ability; loves adventure; childlike joy; romantic, straight talker, self-sufficient, gets things done

Unfavorable: Adversarial, aggressive; "me first" and "I want it now" attitude; tactless, selfish, impatient, uncooperative, jealous; will cheat to get results; the ends justify the means; intolerant, arrogant, reckless, leaves tasks undone, seeks overly simplistic solutions; saboteur

Taurus Rising—Vrishabha Lagna
SYMBOL: A Bull
KEY CONCEPT: Keeping things stable. Focus is on possessing.

Second sign of the natural zodiac. Transfers its influence, and that of its ruling planet Venus, to the interpretation of the second house of a chart.
BASIC NATURE:

Favorable: Productive; earthy; fixed; skilled at business; harmonious; has endurance; thorough, materialistic, tenacious, patient, hard to provoke, steady, conservative, strong willed; acts deliberately; can concentrate; loves money and food; affectionate, cheerful, ambitious, loyal and true, charming

Unfavorable: Stubborn, inflexible, bound by routines, little originality, boring, greedy, selfish, uncompromising, lazy, self-indulgent, difficult to understand, reluctant, reactionary, ultraconservative, bigoted, intolerant, possessive, jealous, overaccumulates

Gemini—Mithuna

SYMBOL: A set of twins, or a couple—the male holding a club and the female holding a violinlike instrument called a veena

KEY CONCEPT: Making distinctions and communicating. Focus is on thinking.

Third sign of the natural zodiac. Transfers its influence, and that of its ruling planet Mercury, to the interpretation of the third house of a chart.

BASIC NATURE:

Favorable: Literary mentality, quick mind, good with hands, versatile, joyous, inventive, loves diversity, genial, quick at making friends, keeps up with trends, takes care of appearance, talented debater, impressive conversationalist or speaker; good reading, writing, and oral skills

Unfavorable: Indecisive, hasty, changeable, too cunning or clever, "two-faced," caught in conflicts or dilemmas, restless or nervous, capricious, flirtatious; not their best as managers; inclined not to finish things; fickle; bluffs or talks their way out of trouble or out of being responsible

Cancer—Kataka

SYMBOL: A Crab

KEY CONCEPT: Supporting the "family." Focus is on feelings.

Fourth sign of the natural zodiac. Transfers its influence, and that of its ruling planet the Moon, to the interpretation of the fourth house of a chart.

BASIC NATURE:

Favorable: Love of home and family; instinctively a good parent (to everyone); great imagination; supportive, protective, good listener, intuitive, teacher, preacher, emotionally open, appreciates correction, encouraged by kindness, laborious, strong affections, loyal to mate

Unfavorable: Overly dependent or clinging; too available; lack of emotional self-sufficiency; hoarding, hypersensitive, deluded, moody, martyr, worrier, penny pincher; caught in self-pity; feels abandoned or discounted by others; picks dysfunctional friends and partners

Leo Rising—Simha Lagna
SYMBOL: A Lion
KEY CONCEPT: Being the center of the universe. Focus is on commanding.

Fifth sign of the natural zodiac. Transfers its influence, and that of its ruling planet the Sun, to the interpretation of the fifth house of a chart.

BASIC NATURE:

Favorable: Vitality, leadership, generosity, loyalty, "sunny" personality, dignified; responds well to praise; faith in friends; quick to issue orders; skilled organizer; ambition; fame; willpower; large-issue oriented; delegates; romantic; loves deeply; flair for showmanship; dress; self-promotion; greatly honor those they admire

Unfavorable: Vain, arrogant, overbearing, opinionated, boasting, condescending, domineering, obstinate, indifferent; dislikes subordination; not detail oriented; spends beyond their means; power hunter; unhappy if not praised; pompous; intimidating; career pursuits run their lives

Virgo—Kanya
SYMBOL: A young girl in a boat with a bundle of corn in one hand and a torch in the other
KEY CONCEPT: Perfection through purifying. Focus is on serving.

Sixth sign of the natural zodiac. Transfers its influence, and that of its ruling planet Mercury, to the sixth house of a chart.

BASIC NATURE:

Favorable: Analytical, oriented to serving, studious, high standards, purifies and improves things to their ideal state, sensitive, reserved, commercial instinct, detailed, methodical, prudent, hard worker, tidy; skilled in letters, numbers, and measuring; intelligent but in a narrow or focused sense

Unfavorable: Emotionally uninvolved; overreaching; sets expectations too high; worried, frustrated, depressed, skeptical, doesn't believe there is any slack, fault-finding, boring, interferes with others' processes, lonely, monastic, lack of self-promotion

Libra—Thula
SYMBOL: Balance Scales
KEY CONCEPT: Balancing and resolving opposites. Focus is on harmony.

Seventh sign of the natural zodiac. Transfers its influence, and that of its ruling planet Venus, to the interpretation of the seventh house of a chart.

BASIC NATURE:

Favorable: Reassuring, comforting, friendly, adaptable, flexible; can be anything with anybody; sees positive outcomes; states weaknesses in a positive manner; can see both sides of an issue; good diplomat; flair for fashion; balanced; graceful; works to establish themselves in the good graces of others

Unfavorable: Ambivalent, too adjusting or compromising, sneaks away from conflict or responsibility, charmingly manipulative, ingratiating, narcissist, capricious, ineffectual, waits too long to act, vacillates, says "yes" to everybody, chameleon, desperado, dual personality

Scorpio—Vrishika
SYMBOL: A Scorpion
KEY CONCEPT: Obtaining through seducing or investigating. Focus is on the Unknown.

Eighth sign of the natural zodiac. Transfers its influence, and that of its ruling planet Mars, to the interpretation of the eighth house of a chart.

BASIC NATURE:

Favorable: Devoted, supports and nourishes friends, pleasure giving, repairs and resurrects broken people and events, extremely deep level of feeling, highly intuitive, deep spiritual base, healing capacity, gives greatly, shrewd, inspires others to their higher selves, many innate talents, works well by instinct

Unfavorable: Critical, possessive, vengeful, hypersensitive; speaks ill of others; controlling, punishing, overworked; worrier, grim outlook; takes "patients" as partners; becomes victimized in love; gets intimate too quickly; expects others to understand them without setting their expectations up front

Sagittarius—Dhanus

SYMBOL: An archer who is half man and half horse

KEY CONCEPT: Striving for freedom and fairness. Focus is on justice.

Ninth sign of the natural zodiac. Transfers its influence, and that of its ruling planet Jupiter, to the interpretation of the ninth house of a chart.

BASIC NATURE:

Favorable: Aspiring, idealistic, loves sports, courageous, smiles a lot, self-confident, vigorous, thinks and speaks and acts as they desire, loves truth, needs to be told the reason behind things, ethical, humanitarian concerns, benefits from constant mental and physical stimulation

Unfavorable: Religious fanatic, pushy, greedy, delays starting, lacks tact, needs to be moderate, doesn't like to take orders, doesn't like to sit in one place and work, needs frequent changes, needs a free hand, quick tempered; maturity comes later in life

Capricorn—Makara

SYMBOL: A being with the head of a deer and the body of a crocodile

KEY CONCEPT: Prospering through enduring. Focus is on security.

Tenth sign of the natural zodiac. Transfers its influence, and that of its ruling planet Saturn, to the interpretation of the tenth house of a chart.

BASIC NATURE:

Favorable: Practical, cautious, methodical, persevering; organizing ability; their position improves over time; desires fame and name; serves others; not very anxious to get married early; collects old and beautiful things; prefers seclusion and peace; true to their friends and mates, respecting them throughout life

Unfavorable: Suspicious, deals a hard justice, selfish, not optimistic at first, not quick to make friends, success does not come immediately, depressed by obstacles and delays, overstrained, gloomy, worried, overly focused on security, never feels there is enough time, feels they have wasted their life, detached, acts functionally but not affectionately as a parent and a mate

Aquarius—Kumbha

SYMBOL: A man pouring a water pot

KEY CONCEPT: Believing in the Ideal. Focus is on innovation.

Eleventh sign of the natural zodiac. Transfers its influence, and that of its ruling planet Saturn, to the interpretation of the eleventh house of a chart.

BASIC NATURE:

Favorable: Scientific, unselfish, humane, full of new ideas, intuitive, has talent and ambition; prefers both solitude and social activities; has a great desire to study the character and behavior of their friends; prefers those who are equally social, shrewd, studious, kind, sympathetic, and accommodative

Unfavorable: Impractical, doesn't recognize the value of their own talents, unconventional, outspoken, does unusual or irregular things, reluctant or incapable of following a routine, doesn't dress like others, strong likes and dislikes, stubborn, tends toward isolation and depression, doesn't seem to fit in, monastic, too secretive, paranoid, masks their misery with quick laughter or a smile

Pisces—Meena

SYMBOL: Two fish, side by side, swimming in opposite directions

KEY CONCEPT: The stream of consciousness flowing back and forth between heaven and earth. Focus is on believing.

Twelfth sign of the natural zodiac. Transfers its influence, and that of its ruling planet Jupiter, to the interpretation of the twelfth house of a chart.

BASIC NATURE:

Favorable: Mystical, intuitive, inspiring, sympathetic, philosophical, contemplative, wants a romantic or "heavenly" life, good at calming people down and making them feel comfortable, unbounded generosity, socially skilled, polite, modest, charismatic or magnetic, attracted to the concepts of enlightenment and liberation

Unfavorable: Procrastinates, subject to discontinuous and disconnected thinking, lacks confidence, naïve, restless, too utopian, changes point of view to align with others, poor money planner, catches on too late, sensitive to their environment, appears weak or defenseless, thinks about love but doesn't take action, not interested enough about putting in the effort to be successful

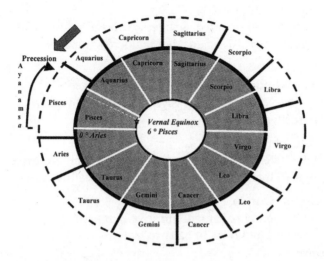

The inner, shaded circle shows the even distribution of each 30° astrological zodiac sign. The outer circle approximates the amount of space each constellation (astronomical star group) covers in the sky. You will see, for example, that Virgo spills over into both of the sign borders of its neighbors, while the constellation of Aries does not fully occupy the zone of the 30° sign of the zodiac and in fact is slightly encroached by the constellations of Taurus and Pisces.

Special Characteristics of Signs—Elements or Bhutas

Count up the number of planets placed in each bhuta (element; also called tatwa). A planet will take on those sign characteristics when occupying that specific sign. For example, if Venus occupies a sign characterized by the element of fire, then that person will have a tendency to love in a fiery manner. If a person has a preponderance or lack of an element, the influence in the person's life will be similarly excessive or insufficient. For example, a person with many planets in earth signs will show more traits of fixity of purpose if the placements are favorable, or they will be stubborn if the placements are unfavorable. If mixed, there will be a little of both purposeful and "bull-headed" behavior. As another example, if you wanted to know something about how a person thinks, you would look for Mercury, the planet of thinking, and which element was represented by the sign that Mercury occupied. So if Mercury was in Capricorn, an earth sign, the person's thinking would be grounded, stable, and practical.

Fire: Aries, Leo, Sagittarius
Favorable: Action oriented, energetic, innovative, takes charge
Unfavorable: Impulsive, rude, hot tempered, impatient

Earth: Taurus, Virgo, Capricorn
Favorable: Grounded, stable, practical, conservative, responsible
Unfavorable: Stubborn, possessive, controlling, averse to change, burdened

Air: Gemini, Libra, Aquarius
Favorable: Friendly, adaptable, witty, intellectual, inventive
Unfavorable: Ineffectual, too mental, overly idealistic, impractical

Water: Cancer, Scorpio, Pisces
Favorable: Feelings-oriented, intuitive, sympathetic
Unfavorable: Emotional imbalance, submissive, slow, ponderous, too sensitive

Qualities of Activity

These qualities reflect the stability of a person, and the amount of change in their life. It also indicates how long events last in their lives. These qualities are considered in prasna (using astrology to answer questions; see chapter 13) to determine the duration of events or the stability of an action or person. For example, a person with a moveable sign in their 4th house might move a lot in their life, or might move at a time when certain planets transit their 4th, or the 4th house ruler is the current dasa or bhukti ruler.

If planets are in the following signs, then the following characteristics are indicated:

Moveable: Aries, Cancer, Libra, Capricorn
Favorable: Likes to move or take action, innovative, full of change, travels
Unfavorable: Irresolute, scattered, hasty, impatient, impractical

Fixed: Taurus, Leo, Scorpio, Aquarius
Favorable: Stable, conservative, practical
Unfavorable: Disinclined to move, obsessive, inflexible, possessive

Dual or Common: Gemini, Virgo, Sagittarius, Pisces
Favorable: Flexible, adaptable, balanced between the moving and the stationary

Unfavorable: Fickle, ups and downs, divided, inconsistent, full of contradictions

Male/Odd/Cruel/Day Signs: Aries, Gemini, Leo, Libra, Sagittarius, Aquarius

Male signs are more action oriented, durable, paternal, aggressive, oriented to taking and leading. Women with a male lagna (rising sign) or with many planets in male signs will be more competitive and masculine in their demeanor. A person with many male planets will tend to give birth to male children, especially if their spouse has male influences as well.

Odd and Cruel signs cause their occupants to be more aggressive and hard.

Day signs are influenced by and more active during the light of day.

Female/Even/Gentle/Night Signs: Taurus, Cancer, Virgo, Scorpio, Capricorn, Pisces

Female signs are more delicate, refined, submissive, providing, and serving. Men with a female lagna or many planets in female signs will show a more refined or a feminine nature. A person with many female planets will tend to give birth to females, especially if their spouse has female influences as well.

Even and Gentle signs cause their occupants to act in a more subdued, submissive, and soft manner. They may allow themselves to submit to the intrusion of a negative person or event, making matters worse for themselves.

Night signs tend to be more influenced by or more active during the night.

Ayurvedic Doshas or Body Constitutions by sign: If planets are in specific signs, as discussed in Ayurveda in chapter 19, then they will exhibit the indicated Ayurvedic qualities.

Level of being or state of existence: Useful in some forms of prasna readings wherein one needs to determine if the subject at hand is in one of these three states:

Mineral (Dhatu): Moveable signs of Aries, Cancer, Libra, and Capricorn

Vegetable (Mula): Fixed signs of Taurus, Leo, Scorpio, and Aquarius

Living Being (Jiva): Dual signs of Gemini, Virgo, Sagittarius, and Pisces

CHAPTER FOUR

HOUSES—BHAVAS

Bhava means "a state of being or existence"; some interpret it as "a mood." Astrologically, a bhava is a "house" or dwelling place for a planet, one of the 12 imaginary divisions of the earth; these sections are somewhat like the slices of an orange. Bhavas are used to calibrate the position of the planets in relation to the earth. In Vedic astrology, one determines the rising sign and that becomes the first house: "the houses are the signs." Each of the remaining houses follow in numerical order, in 30-degree segments, up to the 12th house and the 12th sign. Vedic astrology follows an "equal house" system in that the houses are always 30 degrees in length, even in the higher latitudes where the divisions converge as the geography pulls in at the poles. However, not all Jyotishis use the equal house system; some use Bhava Chalita charts (see chapter 1).

You can significantly increase your understanding of a house by correlating its meaning with what is signified by the natural sign of the zodiac that occupies that position, and with the nature of the planet that rules that house. Houses carry the most specific information in a chart because they represent positions of planets, as marked from one of 12 rotating signs of the zodiac. During the course of the day, each of the 12 signs will rise along with 12 houses and the meaning they carry for that rising sign.

Judging from Karaka Planets

In this interpretive technique, we use the house that indicates a specific behavioral characteristic as an "additional" first house. That is, the house indicating that specific trait becomes as if it were the ascendant. For example, let's say an astrologer wants to know more about a person's mother in their chart. The astrologer would take the fourth house, the house of the mother, as if it were the first house or ascendant, and look for indications about the mother from that point forward. The mother's second house, or accumulation of money house, could be seen from the person's fifth house, which, in effect, is second from the fourth house (2nd from 4th). The astrologer could get information about the mother's sisters (the person's aunts) from the sixth house, which is third (house of siblings) from the fourth (3rd from 4th). Astrologers can use this technique from any point in the chart. More information about partners could be found from counting from a person's seventh house, the house of partners. More would be revealed about a person's father by counting the ninth house as the first house, and so on. Throughout this book, wherever I give significations that I've derived in this way, an explanation will be given parenthetically, such as (3rd from 4th) above.

Benefic and Malefic Houses

Houses are considered either benefic, meaning favorable, or malefic, meaning unfavorable. Some houses are a mixture of the two.

Dusthana or *Trik Houses* 6, 8, and 12 are the most unfavorable houses. Planets ruling these houses, aspecting them, or occupying them are for the most part considered unfavorable.

Upachaya Houses 3, 6, 10, and 11 are called "growing" houses in that one can grow out of the malefic influences affecting them.

Maraka Houses: The rulers of houses 2 and 7 are reviewed to indicate when death or destructive influences are active. Some authors hold that the concept of Maraka applies mostly to one's spiritual nature, rather than physical nature. The 2nd is the house of money and the 7th is the house of sex. There is a spiritual convention that money and sex are not conducive to spiritual growth; hence, planets connected to these houses will "kill" one's spiritual development.

The following list gives several important characteristics of the houses, including whether they are favorable (benefic), unfavorable (malefic), or mixed.

First House—Tanu Bhava, or House of the Body
Keywords: The Physical Self
Position: Favorable
Relates to: The sign of Aries and the planet Mars
Signifies: Appearance, basic disposition, behavior, general well-being, health, head

Second House—Dhana Bhava, or House of Accumulated Wealth
Keyword: Finances
Position: A mix of favorable and unfavorable, since its ruler is not regarded as favorable (a maraka or "killer" planet)
Relates to: The sign of Taurus and the planet Venus
Signifies: General family happiness, food and drink, speech, liquid assets, accumulation of wealth, right eye, face, tongue and mouth, teeth and gums, scriptural knowledge, study, precious metals and gems, concentration, truthfulness

Third House—Sahaja Bhava, or House of Brothers
Keyword: Determination
Position: A mix between favorable and unfavorable; many authors regard it as unfavorable since it represents effort and is the 8th house from the 8th house, the house of death
Relates to: The sign of Gemini and the planet Mercury
Signifies: Siblings, friends, neighbors, courage, physical strength, hearing, ear diseases, salesmanship, art, dance, drama, music, voice, singing, memory, communication, writing, short travels, arms, hands, nervous system, ear, adventure, fun

Fourth House—Matru Bhava, or House of the Mother
Keyword: Feelings
Position: Favorable
Relates to: The sign of Cancer and the Moon

37

Signifies: Mother, knowledge, education (academic), the home, emotions, happiness in general, father's longevity, foundational things, fixed assets, hobbies, leisure time, comforts, houses, boats, vehicles, buried treasures, things from below the earth, chest region (some say heart)

Fifth House—Putra Bhava, or House of Children
Keyword: Intelligence
Position: Favorable
Relates to: The sign of Leo and the Sun
Signifies: Romance, love from spouse or sweetheart, love of God, speculation, spiritual techniques, past-life credit (purva punya), intelligence, discrimination, education (spiritual) authorship, maternal grandfather, pregnancy, mantras, yantras, discrimination, games, amusements and sports, business, government displeasure (especially with taxes and the IRS), stomach

Sixth House—Ripu Bhava, or House of Enemies
Keywords: Service and Defense
Position: Unfavorable, although it can get better over time (upachaya or "growing")
Relates to: The sign of Virgo and the planet Mercury
Signifies: Health or short term diseases, competitors, rivals, opposition, litigation, enemies, intimidation and calamities from the opposite sex, struggles, physical weakness, mental troubles, wounds, injuries and accidents, pets, servants or helpers, employees, cousins, thefts, sexual diseases, poisons, abdomen, maternal uncles, stepmother, healers, digestion, bowels

Seventh House—Kalatra Bhava, or House of the Wife (Partner)
Keyword: Partnerships
Position: Favorable, though its ruler is not regarded as favorable by some, being a maraka or "killer" planet
Relates to: The sign of Libra and the planet Venus
Signifies: Marriage, love affairs (some extramarital), cohabitation, marriagelike relationships, length of mate's life, business partnerships, trade, foreign residence or travel for trade, kidneys, lower back

Eighth House—Ayu Bhava, or House of Life
Keywords: The Unknown and the Chronic
Position: Unfavorable; perhaps the worst
Relates to: The sign of Scorpio and the planet Mars
Signifies: Longevity, chronic ailments, hidden things, scandalous behavior, embarrassment, shyness, accusations, desire for knowledge of the unknown or mystical matters, extravagance, unearned wealth (lotteries, legacies, etc.), worry, sexual energy, vertigo or fall from high places, cheating, homicide, useless ventures, money loss, danger from poisons, house purchased from sale of ancestral home, manner of death, being overlooked, obstacles, unsuccessful attempts, dreams, Kundalini (a kind of energy), wealth of the partner, reproduction and elimination

Ninth House—Bhagya Bhava, or House of Fortune
Keywords: Luck and Knowledge
Position: Very favorable; one of the best
Relates to: The sign of Sagittarius and the planet Jupiter
Signifies: God, guru, philosophy, religion, the father, relationship with father, bosses, ethics, law, dharma (right action), long-distance travel, divine grace (5th from 5th), educational institutions, Gnana (spiritual knowledge), initiation, yogic practices, good fortune, renovation of holy places, connection with Divine powers or energies (Devas), grandchildren, hip area

Tenth House—Dharma Bhava, or House of Right Action
Keyword: Career
Position: Favorable
Relates to: The sign of Capricorn and the planet Saturn
Signifies: Life purpose or career, fame, father's reputation or position in the world, righteous action, compassion, clothes that promote one's image, character, commerce, trade, business, trouble with childbearing (10th is 6th to the 5th), knees

Eleventh House—Labya Bhava, or House of Gains
Keywords: Opportunities and Cash Flow
Position: All planets are considered good here, but the ruler of this house is not well regarded by many astrologers, so this house is considered a mix of favorable and unfavorable.
Relates to: The sign of Aquarius and the planet Saturn

Signifies: Cash flow, profits, opportunities, hopes, friends, dreams, wishes, influential friends, elder sibling, paternal uncle, mother's longevity, influence of government or leaders of large institutions or corporations, wife's impact on children (5th to 7th), left ear

Twelfth House—Moksha Bhava, or House of Enlightenment
Keywords: Liberation
Position: Not favorable for material life, but good for the spiritual
Relates to: The sign of Pisces and the planet Jupiter
Signifies: Liberation, enlightenment, sexual pleasures, detention, confinement (hospitals, prisons, long-term meditation, etc.), work in places of confinement, loss, poverty, generosity, quality of sleep and beds, self-sacrifice, spiritual journeys, pilgrimages or journeys to foreign lands, wandering, trade involving long travel, life after death, the nature of one's previous incarnation, martyrs, self-sacrifice, betrayal, tapas or religious austerities, clumsiness, feet

CHAPTER FIVE

PLANETS IN SIGNS
(GRAHAS IN RASIS)

The interpretation of the Sun and the Moon in signs will reflect much of what was contained in chapter 3 regarding the ascendant or lagna—the Sun will radiate more of your external life, while the Moon will reflect more of your inner nature.

The key to understanding the placement of planets in signs is to look to the ruling planet of that sign as if it were in conjunction with the occupying planet. It is also revealing to notice which sign number, that is, which house, the occupied sign represents. You will see that the qualities of a particular sign and its ruler will "dispose" or give an inclination to its occupants to act as that ruler/sign does. What you get is a standard planet modified by the influence of the ruling planet and by the sign number that it occupies.

Another important point, relating to health matters, is that a person's health is not only identified by a planet or group of planets in a sign, but also by the indications coming directly from the opposite sign (seven houses away) in the chart. For example, Sagittarius represents the hip region, but will also indicate respiratory ailments (such as asthma) coming from the opposing Gemini, and its ruler Mercury that represents air and respiration. I have given a brief synopsis of this interpretive approach with each planet in each sign in the list below.

The quality and quantity of the influence a planet has in a sign will depend on its strength (see shadbala in chapter 12). The dasa periods, among other indications, will reflect the nature of the planet, favorable or unfavorable, as it is influenced by the sign it occupies. Transiting planets will reflect its nature and the nature of the sign transited along with its occupants (and aspects). For a more advanced evaluation of the strength of a planet as it transits a sign, an astrologer will use the ashtakavarga system (see chapter 13).

PLANETS IN ARIES

Sun in Aries
Sun is exalted at 10 degrees of Aries.

Keywords: Fiery Actions

Favorable: Leader, takes the initiative, courageous, liberal, warrior, ambitious, sharp thinker, capable of achieving fame, likes to keep busy, enjoys sports and competitions, runs around for the sheer joy of activity, acts like a father or authority figure, helps others, innovative, pioneer, can achieve wealth, strong constitution

Unfavorable: Irritable; speedy; bossy or too authoritative; dogmatic; impatient; not a team player; combative; easily excited; the desire to get things done quickly can lead to exhaustion; can be taken in by sudden emotional appeals; active but incompetent; gets overheated; can have pitta (heat) diseases such as rashes, fevers, headaches, bad circulation, or blood ailments; can get cuts, burns, wounds, and bruises, especially in the head, brain and eye area; sleep problems

Moon in Aries
Keywords: Fiery Feelings

Favorable: Agile; enjoys living spontaneously; needs to have lots of fun; able to make quick decisions, self-starter, self-assured; youthful disposition and appearance; drawn to passionate activities idealistically, emotionally, and physically; likes to travel and move around; adaptable, vibrant, popular; good resistance to disease

Unfavorable: Quick to take from others; doesn't want to take advice; short attention span; restless; pushes others too hard; bursts of anger; wants to start too soon or finish too early; good at starting but poor at finishing; will say anything to get what they want— especially sex; if bored will create a risky situation; gullible; prone to burnout, accidents, cuts, bruises and breakage, skin eruptions, eye problems, water accidents; sleep gets disturbed; headaches; females tend to be masculine and aggressive yet often seek out more docile men whom they can control

Mercury in Aries

Keywords: Fiery Thinking

Favorable: Quick thinker, clever, adaptable, quick problem-solving ability, mind keeps pushing ahead; enjoys dancing, music, and drawing; linear; gets to the point

Unfavorable: Mind wants to accomplish things too fast; talks too fast or stutters; frustrated, angry; erratic mind, poor planner; only thinks of their needs or their approach; deceitful, the ends justify the means; gets into debts, overly speculative, gambler or risk taker; uses drugs, alcohol, or food to try to calm down; troubled sleep; nervous strain and headaches; all over the map

Venus in Aries

Keywords: Fiery Love

Favorable: Romantic, idealistic, skilled in art, affectionate, charming, seductive, good at persuading, fun to be with, playful, adventurous, spontaneous, generous, believes generosity will be returned in some cosmic way

Unfavorable: Hasty, gets intimate or falls into a romance easily and quickly, likes the thrill of romance but does not sustain it, fearful of commitment, many broken relationships, strongly sexed, uses people by charming them, attracted to loose or unreliable people, will ignore common sense in the name of passion, reproductive problems, facial marks or scars, eye trouble

Mars in Aries

Mars is swakshetra, or in its own sign, in Aries. Mars is Ruchaka Yoga if in Aries on an angle, which indicates the highest manifestation of Mars's qualities.

Keywords: Fiery Fire (Strongly Fiery)

Favorable: Powerful; pioneer; gets connected to activities involving fire, "war," or manufacturing; takes the lead; pushes on through obstacles; likes to do things quickly; energetic, sportive; can organize short-term projects; very independent; generous; takes a decided point of view; strong constitution, resistant to aging

Unfavorable: Not open to listening to others; combative; not good at sustaining or maintaining; pushes aside others' emotions to get things done; rash, aggressive, doesn't think things through; gets bored if unchallenged; poor partner; not reliable; extravagant; can't sit still for long; prone to accidents and diseases involving surgery; hot blooded; head and blood ailments; clotting, strokes, headaches, overheating, cuts, wounds, breaks; has trouble settling down to sleep

Jupiter in Aries

Keywords: Fiery (Active) Expansion

Favorable: Dignified, capable of attaining good wealth and a prominent career, executive or military leadership, active yet cordial, patient, generous, good children, magnanimous, progressive, genuine, good reputation, can be strict but rules through a sense of justice and principles, overcomes obstacles through moral authority, a good partner, family is well-to-do

Unfavorable: Sense of grandness and big vision can lead to too many expenses, overly optimistic, gets indebted, can arouse jealousy in others, appears too righteous, blood sugar problems, swelling infections, liver problems, cholesterol or fat in the blood, overweight, out of balance, expects too much of others, motivated by unrealistic dreams or expectations

Saturn in Aries

Saturn is debilitated in 20 degrees of Aries.

Keywords: Focused or Obstructed Action

Favorable: Works long and hard to accomplish goals; stays focused on tasks at hand; organized; pushes their objectives through oppositions; self-reliant; things get better over time

Unfavorable: Frustrated; obstructed; faced with delays yet wants to accomplish quickly; critical; opposes people; cruel; impatient; finds it difficult to follow the norm; lack of social grace and refinement; danger from depression, violence, suicidal tendencies; might get wounded or have problems with weapons; teeth and gum ailments; blood stagnation, hearing loss, arthritis or joint problems, violent accidents

Rahu in Aries

Keywords: Destiny or Confusion in Action

Favorable: Strong desire to get things done, action-oriented, wants to achieve things quickly, pursues things with passion, success with short-duration activities; likes action, activities, sports and adventures

Unfavorable: Overextends, gets into activity without examining the consequences, gets confused and fatigued, easily bored or distracted, loses track of themselves, can get too many irons in the fire, quarrelsome, devious, self-seeking, unpleasant, blood purity problems, headaches, poor circulation, very fiery, has accidents, bodily systems get polluted

Ketu in Aries

Keywords: Quick Change in Actions

Favorable: Ability to respond quickly to events; capacity to make sudden changes; cunning in warlike activities; a spiritual warrior

Unfavorable: Sensitive to change; easily upset; unusual and sudden events come up in life; lots of change and disruption; constant surprises and unforeseen circumstances; possibility for frequent moving and job changes; makes reckless changes; accidents, head injuries, and diseases; illnesses are difficult to diagnose and might be more spiritual if not psychological in origin; pitta imbalance

PLANETS IN TAURUS

Sun in Taurus

Keywords: Persevering Activity

Favorable: Handles people well; artistic, especially music and literature; weighs what to say; love of sensuality and pleasure; considers options before acting; has stamina; stays fixed in their purpose; gets wealth prudently over time; enjoys conservative and traditional values, works best in defined, established businesses

Unfavorable: Ponderous; overly cautious or slow to take action; stubborn; takes action too late; loses by not knowing when to quit; ailments of the eyes, mouth, face, nose, and throat; mucous in throat; coughing; trouble with veins and with circulation

Moon in Taurus

Moon is exalted at 3 degrees of Taurus.

Keywords: Steady Emotions

Favorable: Fullness of life and love, popular yet quiet, generous, progressive, grounded, expanded life, active imagination, supportive, good influence over others, gets others' respect, thankful, patient, wealth builds over time, conservative, likes to accumulate things, attracted to sexual and sensual enjoyments, lives in comfortable surroundings, practical, perseverant

Unfavorable: Tendency to enjoy too much leisure time, lazy; overindulges in food, drink, pleasures and sexual activity; overly adjusting to those they love; overly self-controlled at times; lives in a fantasy; inconsistent, stubborn, reactionary, possessive, jealous, overly generous; throat problems, thyroid, sore throat, constipation, indigestion; overweight, especially the lower body

Mercury in Taurus

Keywords: Practical or Determined Thinking

Favorable: Creative with good reasoning faculty; clever; happy; good at reading, writing, or speaking; enjoys the company of learned or philosophically oriented people; mentally enjoys pleasures and amusements; playful, sense of humor, decided opinions, balanced, self-satisfied, sweet speaker, generous; likes refined pleasures, poetry, arts; accumulates wealth

Unfavorable: Might be too playful and not serious enough; lacks focus on a stable direction until later years; opinionated; lacks motivation, avoids taking responsibility, stubborn about taking advice; speech problems, ear and throat ailments, lack of fertility or potency, urinary tract troubles

Venus in Taurus

Venus is in its own sign (swakshetra). This position, if located on an angle, creates a Malavya Yoga, indicating the highest manifestation of Venus's qualities.

Keywords: Well-Developed Love and Prosperity

Favorable: Attractive, refined, good manners, educated, a pleasant person; drawn to a comfortable, elegant lifestyle with good food, clothing, and home; artistic, pursues partnerships and lovemaking; kind, generous, lives around well-placed people and circumstances; honored and respected; good finances

Unfavorable: Seeks too much leisure, overindulges, lives off the graces of others, lethargic, partnership problems, expects partner to do all the work, throat problems, phlegm, thyroid, glandular imbalance, swellings

Mars in Taurus

Keywords: Active in Enjoyments

Favorable: Charming, persuasive, seductive, fun, affectionate, youthful disposition, sensitive, caring, instinctive; likes music, dancing, sports, and amusements; sweet talker, physical and sexual, good salesperson, quick-acting executive, good earning ability

Unfavorable: Too passionate, focused on short-term pleasures, rash, overspends, wasteful, self-seeking, con artist, unreliable, a danger to those needy in love, lives for oneself, broken romances, unfaithful, throat ailments, reproductive diseases, nosebleeds or breakage, muscle ailments, lower back pain, skin eruptions, scars or marks on face

Jupiter in Taurus

Keywords: Expanded Wealth and Enjoyments

Favorable: Lawful, diplomatic, elegant, artistic, creative, wise, tolerant, knowledgeable, gentle, refined, well liked, attentive to partners; drawn to spiritual, humanitarian, and philosophic causes and ceremonies; natural educator, gets comforts and wealth, stays fixed with religious and philosophical views

Unfavorable: Indulgent, misses obvious opportunities for gain and advancement, overly optimistic, lethargic, lazy, self-gratifying, overspends on pleasure and comfort, exorbitant, stagnant, swellings in the body, overweight, throat and reproductive ailments

Saturn in Taurus

Keywords: Focused or Restricted Love and Wealth

Favorable: Self-controlled, service-oriented, reserved, inner silence, pleasures through work, devoted mate, comfortable with older or more mature persons, mate is older, monastic, economical, moderate, wealthy over the long haul

Unfavorable: Detached, mean, reserved, hesitant; muddled feelings; restricted wealth; problems with love and relationships; negligent; victim of love and work; controlled by older persons, deceitful, self-isolating, impotent or frigid, sexually unorthodox or perverse; reproductive organ problems; ailments of kidneys and lower back region; eye, ear, nose, and throat illnesses; teeth and gums could be a problem; speech or voice difficulties, eating disorders

Rahu in Taurus

Keywords: Unconventional or Confused Love and Wealth

Favorable: Displays unusual and inventive artistic skills; has a liking for foreigners; becomes an advocate and has a love for the misplaced, misrepresented, or neglected people in the world; loves the unloved; revels in solving puzzles or taking on a challenge

Unfavorable: Enjoys taking an unconventional approach; gets deceived with finances; may have an adverse or perverse attitude about love; love relationships are out of the norm; tendency toward intimacy with their own sex; difficulties with the sex organs; gets teeth and face ailments; neck and thyroid could be problematic; subject to nasal disorders

Ketu in Taurus

Keywords: Unbounded or Chaotic Love and Wealth

Favorable: Spiritually oriented, finds love in God, seeks the highest form of love, money comes unexpectedly (and goes that way as well), clever speaker, studies scriptures, ingenious at getting money

Unfavorable: Might not care enough to hold onto their finances or build up a financial base; disappointed in love; deceptive or tricky speech; family happiness is up and down; lack of libido; conflicted about sex and spirituality; reproductive problems; rare disorders of the face, mouth, and neck

PLANETS IN GEMINI

Sun in Gemini

Keywords: Clever Action

Favorable: Quick to learn, good short-term memory, charming, polite, discriminative, cheerful, can talk about anything, versatile, conservative, scientific, attracted to numbers and letters, scholarly, wants to gain knowledge quickly through books and lectures, good with the hands; could indicate twins, or basically two of anything—jobs, parents, romantic interests, etc.

Unfavorable: Not good at closing or finishing things, tends to do too many things at once, shifty, undependable, copycat, shy, not up-front, divided, torn, reluctant to take a stand, too mental, nervous, picky, hard to pin down on anything, nervous disorders, lung ailments; hand, shoulder, neck problems

Moon in Gemini

Keywords: Creative and/or Fast-Moving Mind

Favorable: Creative mind, witty, clever, sociable, good organizer; learns through writing, reading, and seminars; charming, young looking, humorous, fluent speech; may appear superficial due to their quickness of thought but are quite bright; don't like physical confrontations

Unfavorable: Too cunning, skeptical, vain, undependable when things get serious, puts too many tasks on their to-do list, mental confusion, divided, uncertain, thinks about too many possibilities and doesn't take action, flirtatious whether they realize it or not, rapid talker, emotionally overstimulated, restless, not attracted to domestic chores, lung ailments; neck, hand, or shoulder problems

Mercury in Gemini

Mercury is swakshetra (in its own sign). If Mercury is in its own sign on an angle (1st, 4th, 7th, or 10th houses) it becomes a Bhadra Yoga, indicating the highest manifestation of Mercury's qualities.

Keywords: Developed Thinking

Favorable: Oriented to mental pursuits, good speaking and communication skills, tactical, clever, inventive, resourceful, good debater, reasonable, receptive, good sense of humor, quick-witted, quick to learn; likes traveling; music, science, literature, computer skills; dual influence can lead to two of everything—mother or father, mates, children, jobs, etc.; good earning ability

Unfavorable: Talks more than accomplishes, superficial, speculates, devious, inexpedient, argumentative, not good at finishing, intellect interferes with good decision making, vacillates, moves too much, restless, conflicted, unreliable, duality prevails, breathing ailments

Venus in Gemini

Keywords: Love of the Mental. Divided in Love.

Favorable: Friendly, charming, fun-loving, love of art—especially representational art; logical, loves learning, capable of gaining wealth, respected, popular, appreciates others

Unfavorable: Gullible, vacillates about love matters, may marry later or more than once, loves two things at once, doesn't think enough about the future, too much playing around or indulging, flirtatious, charms people out of their money, lives off others by endearing themselves to them, respiratory ailments, skin troubles

Mars in Gemini

Keywords: Active or Fiery Mind

Favorable: Quick mind, good problem-solving ability, musical or literary interests, good at starting things, mechanical or scientific disposition, analytical, researcher, pushes ahead by mental energy alone at times, mind works like a military strategist, love of elegance, active with relatives, fond of change, desires to learn

Unfavorable: Sharp tongue, asocial, cynical, bitter, too clever; cuts off friends, family, and neighbors; lacks completion, active yet incompetent, restless, impatient, gets burned out or loses interest, broken education or doesn't complete classes, has attention deficit, angry, nerve damage, shoulder or neck problems, blood in the lungs, respiratory infections, speaks too fast, speech difficulties

Jupiter in Gemini

Keywords: Expanded Thinking

Favorable: Good communication and writing skills, wise, scholar, phrases weaknesses in a positive manner, good diplomat, likes novelty, can get published at some time in life, financially astute, good sense of humor, mental and emotional balance, celebrates life, good family, helpful to all

Unfavorable: Overly optimistic, nonchalant, indifferent, careless, misses opportunities by moving too slow, challenges or is critical of religious beliefs, multiple marriages, problems with fat or fluid buildup, liver ailments

Saturn in Gemini

Keywords: Focused or Immobilized Thinking

Favorable: Very focused, mentally disciplined, keeps within the proper scope of things, conservative, analytical, scientific; interest in literature, words, and numbers; systematic, exact, well-ordered thinking, good organizer, accurate, literal, follows rules to the letter

Unfavorable: Compulsive behavior, immobilized, has trouble making decisions, broken or delayed education, deceptive, rigid, gullible or takes things too literally, doesn't know where to stop, gets overly obligated, impotent, restrictions with relatives, worried, breathing or lung problems, ailments of the nervous system, mental problems; neck, shoulder, or hand troubles; paralysis or lameness

Rahu in Gemini

Keywords: Unusual Thinking

Favorable: Mind is geared toward innovating; clever, philosophical, interested in the bizarre, oddly creative, mystical adventures, offbeat humor, exceptional, unprecedented ideas and activities, unusual use of language and thinking

Unfavorable: Mental disorders, toxic problems with the nervous system, uses deception to make a living, eccentric, misunderstandings, self-isolating, troubles with siblings and neighbors, emotionally on the run; neck, shoulder, or limb complaints; breathing problems, skin ailments, diseases are hard to diagnose

Ketu in Gemini

Keywords: Unbounded and/or Chaotic Thinking

Favorable: Possesses a mind that is creative and full of new ideas; good at writing, conceiving, and presenting; thinking is oriented to the ethereal; has a quick and sensitive thought process that could be useful for astrology and any form of subtle analysis

Unfavorable: Mind is fragmented, person is conflicted and has trouble making decisions, relationship with younger siblings and neighbors is erratic, skin ailments and breathing troubles; accidents to the neck, hands, and shoulders; feels more pain than others, doctors don't know what is wrong

PLANETS IN CANCER

Sun in Cancer
Keywords: Actions Through Feelings

Favorable: Prefers to take their own advice, preference for others' support and a life of ease, can get wealth, enjoys pleasurable diversions, feminine, sensitive, economical, good memory, occupations involving water, fluids, use of light and heat, traveler, high intuition, astrologer, focus on family

Unfavorable: Tires or loses interest easily, drab, shifts moods quickly, works in subordination to others, males have feminine characteristics, often dominated, ebb and flow of career and finances, erratic life, emotional spats with loved ones, problems with digestion, swellings and water retention, fatty tissue, cancer, breast tumors, troubles with stagnation of bodily systems, oversleeps

Moon in Cancer
Keywords: Fullness of Feelings

Favorable: Sensitive, perceptive, emotionally responsible, kind, affectionate, a mother to all, loving, love of family, forgiving, humane, takes pity, high intuition, astrologer, psychic, good imagination, economizing, prosperous, comfortable life, friendly, fond of change, artistic, volunteers, has wisdom, grateful, can deal with family or emotional problems better than most

Unfavorable: Too attached, smothers their loved ones, becomes a victim or is too submissive to loved ones, impressionable, needs to be regarded by others too much, susceptible to others' troubles, lack of control, up and down emotionally, feels a lack of love, anxious, stomach ailments, trouble with digestion, anemia, too much body fat, fluid buildup, fertility problems, hypochondriac

Mercury in Cancer
Keywords: Creative or Emotional Thinking

Favorable: Fertile imagination, will say the right thing, active mind that moves quickly, sensitive, clever, can do well with artistic pursuits such as writing and music, adaptable, spiritual yearnings, mind is open to sensual enjoyments, can speculate, has many theories about life, tactful

Unfavorable: Restless, nervous, impatient, doesn't like moral constraints on their emotions, changeable, engages in a lot of different pursuits, doesn't get emotional fulfillment, too mental in love, gives undue compliments, open to flattery, impotence or lack of fertility, gas, nerve ailments

Venus in Cancer

Keywords: Fullness of Creativity and Love

Favorable: Artistic capacity, leads a comfortable life, elegant, deeply caring, treats loved ones like their children, kind, emotionally open, tries to phrase negativity in a constructive and positive manner, sensitive, cultured, great capacity to love

Unfavorable: Overly emotional, indulgent, not durable, shy, asks others for favors, full of the sorrows of the world, improper love of children, a love event turns out to be too "unbounded" and is harmful to reputation, changeable feelings, stomach ailments, swellings in the breasts and reproductive organs, irregular menstruation

Mars in Cancer

Mars is debilitated at 28 degrees of Cancer.

Keywords: Fiery or Broken Feelings

Favorable: Sharp mind, capacity to earn, ability to heal through cutting or manipulating the body, likes to give assistance to those they love, fascinated by the theoretical or academic side rather than the action side of things, wants to be independent

Unfavorable: Militant emotions, needs to be motivated to act, acts out of phase, starts/stops at the wrong time, unreliable, friction or disconnection with mother, lack of interest in family matters, neglects friendships, inconsistent earnings, fickle, infectious diseases, teeth and gum troubles, eye ailments, indigestion; accidents with fire, electricity, and cars; abortions or miscarriages, blood stagnation

Jupiter in Cancer

Jupiter is exalted at 5 degrees of Cancer. When Jupiter is in Cancer on an angle (1st, 4th, 7th, or 10th house), we get a Hamsa Yoga, indicating the highest manifestation of Jupiter's qualities.

Keywords: Expansion of Feelings

Favorable: Well educated, knowledge keeps expanding, wealthy, comfortable life, beneficial family, devoted, soft yet strong, humane, spiritual, minister, judge, person of merit, sensitive, socially active, good sense of humor, well liked, good intuition, likes to have fun, works for the public good

Unfavorable: Too optimistic, indulgent, lazy, feelings are too sensitive, given to idle chatter, overly generous; emotions keep looking for more fullness, leaving the person disappointed

Saturn in Cancer

Keywords: Stable or Obstructed Emotions

Favorable: Conservative, prudent, steady approach, consistent, succeeds over time, focused on own efforts, works for the public, gets the job done, stable family life

Unfavorable: Emotionally obstructed, problems with mother and with the family, not much comfort, undernurtured and undernurturing, not open to self-examination or suggestions from others; poor health, especially in childhood; despairing, can't feel pleasure, heartless, stomach ailments, breast and reproductive problems, cancer, poor assimilation of food

Rahu in Cancer

Keywords: Unusual and/or "Shadowed" Emotions

Favorable: Cares for the underdog and the suffering masses, benefits by living in foreign lands or working with foreigners, teaches and learns unconventional subjects, might use cosmetics and surgery to modify or improve their appearance, clever at making their home appear nice, helps people get rid of emotional toxins

Unfavorable: Finds it difficult to make full commitments, doesn't like domestic responsibilities, breaks up with others first, has affairs, emotionally conflicted, full of uncertainty, depressed, feels dominated or disregarded by their mother, unclear about educational goals, trouble with owning a home or staying in one place, car troubles or accidents, heart ailments, chest and lung problems, toxic reproductive organs, breast surgery or augmentation troubles, house gets polluted or infested

Ketu in Cancer

Keywords: Psychic or Psychotic

Favorable: Ability to "read" what is happening to others; spiritual growth is important to these people; drawn to educational, spiritual, or philanthropic efforts or organizations; strong interest in religious knowledge; emotions are sublime and unbounded

Unfavorable: Broken home (emotionally and physically), mother is not available (lots of day care or babysitting), feelings change quickly, nervous and worried, many changes in residence, lives in spiritual housing or on the campus of spiritual or religious organizations, feelings change a lot, exposure to car accidents; ailments of the chest, breast, and heart; might have surgery on the breasts

PLANETS IN LEO

Sun in Leo
The Sun occupies its own sign (swakshetra).
Keywords: Royal Action
Favorable: Leadership ability, regal, ambitious, propagandist, advocate, defender, thinks big, stands out, famous, courageous, takes command, charming, repels negativity, capable opponent, defeats opponents, sharp intelligence, independent, liberal, frank, glows when praised, stamina
Unfavorable: Grabs the spotlight, bossy, egoist, hot temper, impatient, big meat eater, doesn't listen to advice, stubborn, dominator, power hunter, finds it hard to work under others, a know-it-all, vain, self-centered, dogmatic, dictatorial, heart or circulatory ailments, spinal problems, baldness, feels a lack of praise

Moon in Leo
Keywords: Royal Emotions
Favorable: Vital, takes pride in their work, generous, affectionate, ambitious for recognition, inspiring, helpful, takes charge, obtains a prominent position, responsible; works in front of people—a politician, actor, public speaker; likes luxury and refinement, take-charge attitude, love of nature and natural surroundings, trustworthy, needs to work on their own, benefits from praise
Unfavorable: Needs to be the center of attention, selfish, too proud, irritable, arrogant, fickle, bad luck with father, takes offense easily, fits of anger, craves things intensely, social climber, tend to be too bossy or pick partners they can dominate or "fix up," inflamed colon or stomach, fevers, rashes, eye afflictions, circulatory or heart problems

Mercury in Leo

Keywords: Intelligent Action

Favorable: Bright-minded, good recall, inspiring speaker or writer, confident, good planner and organizer, well known in their field, progressive, ambitious, thinks big or with high ideals, self-reliant thinker, good earning ability, travels frequently, benefits from the government or large corporations

Unfavorable: Few children, mind moves too fast, deceptive, confused, quick temper, lack of attention to details, doesn't take sufficient action, troubles with relatives, nerve damage, heart ailments, low fertility or sexual interest, back problems

Venus in Leo

Keywords: Royal Love and Artistry

Favorable: Strong feelings, earns through the agency of art, females and feminine things; actor, or works before the public; refined, loves luxury and pleasure, strong affections, sincere; love of beauty, youth, and younger people; persuasive, wins through seduction rather than combat

Unfavorable: Conceited, complacent, self-absorbed, indulgent, troubles with sexual activities, passions turn to arguments, falls in love too fast, poor business activities; trouble with veins, heart, or circulation; back ailments, reproductive organ problems

Mars in Leo

Keywords: Energetic or Militant Action

Favorable: Self-reliant, progressive, competitive, reformer, just, aristocratic, involved in grand schemes, eager, philanthropic, hard and fast worker, stamina, strong masculine traits even for women, resistance to disease, generous in praise, skills in math and science, interested in scriptural texts; progresses through public, industry, military, defense, or security work

Unfavorable: Unconstrained, impatient, adversarial, egotistic, domineering, poor money manager, low fertility, thief, provokes others to anger, reckless, broken romances, finds it hard to sit quietly, accidents, heart ailments, problems with overheating, rashes, fevers

Jupiter in Leo

Keywords: Expansive and Wise Action

Favorable: Ability to lead or counsel others; emotionally moving; mannerly; military, strategic, or executive abilities; full of wisdom or intuitive righteousness; ethical, idealistic; actively expands in life; creative writing abilities; staying power; minister, judge, arbitrator, dependable friend, trustworthy, joyful

Unfavorable: Does not like to be shunned or rebuked, cleverly malicious when slighted, may have an overblown image of themselves, emotional, fat in the arteries, overweight, swelling or fluid buildup, heart or circulatory ailments

Saturn in Leo

Keywords: Focused and/or Restricted Activity

Favorable: Focused, dependable, hard working, persistent, life gets better later through experience, offers good service, works silently in the background, monastic inclinations

Unfavorable: Conflicted between responsibilities for themselves and for others, frustrated, obstructed fortune, takes on too much responsibility, lack of fun and pleasures, menial worker, depressed, self-isolating, problems with father or authority figures, cold, heartless, weak health, worn out, joint problems, heart ailments, spinal troubles

Rahu in Leo

Keywords: Foreign or Confused Behavior

Favorable: Capable of wealth, creative and unique approaches to business and career, works diligently to help others become wealthy and successful, helps others be more "pure" and organized, works well with foreigners and foreign activities, self-sufficient, father lives an unusual but successful life

Unfavorable: Deceptive, confused about purpose in life, will get into complications with "kings," gets taken advantage of by others, tricks others, strained relationship with father and with people who act with authority over them, toxic body, heart problems

Ketu in Leo

Keywords: Unbounded or Chaotic Life

Favorable: Spiritually advanced, interested in high forms of knowledge, able to make quick changes in life, father is religious or spiritual, gets highly enlightened guru

Unfavorable: Career is up and down, life purpose seems ambiguous or uncertain, broken relationship with father, many surprises and sudden changes in life, low or unusual blood pressure or circulation, father could have heart problems, early separation from father or father is unavailable

PLANETS IN VIRGO

Sun in Virgo

Keywords: Clever Action

Favorable: Abilities in work related to numbers, letters, and language; scientific analytical ability; good at measuring things, good organizing ability, clear comprehension, sense of service, orthodox, legal mind, healer, hard worker, outwardly reserved, wants things to be pure and their best, linear, designer, writer, mathematician, statistician, musical abilities, ages slowly

Unfavorable: Does not consider own needs enough, taken advantage of by superiors, too quick to take responsibility, sets expectations too high, wants to be happily married but doesn't know how to be happy, disappointed, depressed, angry, critical, volunteers then becomes a victim, poor self-promotion, bowel or digestive ailments, hypersensitive, lung troubles

Moon in Virgo

Keywords: Creative Mind

Favorable: Feminine, refined, defined set of standards, honest, discriminating, modest, pragmatic, capable speaker, good analytical abilities, discriminating, intuitive, astrologer, good conversationalist, sharp memory, sticks to principles, efficient worker, modest, compassionate, generous, empathetic, healing ability, counselor, likes scientific approach, philosophical, intellectual, witty, resistant to aging

Unfavorable: Too mental, nervous, depressed from unmet expectations, sets standards too high; overly monastic; critical; too many principles to be happy in life; overidealized marriage concept resulting in late or no formal contract; acts cold but can be warmed up through caring; critical, compulsive, martyr, victim, dysentery, constipation, upset stomach, mental obstructions, bad dietary habits

Mercury in Virgo

Mercury is exalted (uucha) at 15 degrees of Virgo. Mercury occupies its own sign (swakshetra). If Mercury is exalted or in its own sign on an angle (1st, 4th, 7th, or 10th houses), it forms a Bhadra Yoga, indicating the highest manifestation of Mercury's qualities.

Keywords: Precise Intellect

Favorable: Intelligent, earns through learning, resourceful, orderly, good speaker and writer, intelligent speech, analytical, scientific approach, numeric and linear mind-set, good with numbers and letters, philosopher, designer, astrologer, teacher, monk, advanced insight or intuition, explicit, works point by point, discriminating, orderly, polished, refined, interest in music and drawing

Unfavorable: Expects too much, thinks too much, tries to do too much at once, imagines negative outcomes, low libido if things aren't right, lives in a fantasy world, critical, demanding, arguer, alone, isolated, contrarian, nervous, weak physiology, diarrhea, constipation, colon ailments, dizzy

Venus in Virgo

Venus is not considered well-placed in Virgo, where it is debilitated at 27 degrees.

Keywords: Mental Love

Favorable: Focus on spiritual love; sublimates physical love for religion, art, career, relatives, pets, etc.; offers service; unpretentious, unassuming, yielding, gains through good partnerships and dedicated servants or helpers; may focus more on career than on personal interests and earn well

Unfavorable: Love interests are outside the norm; indifferent to the opposite sex; interested in the same sex; incomplete or longing for love; subservient; picks bad mates due to low self-regard; victim of love; weak; broken romances; reproductive organ troubles; impotence; fertility difficulties; blood sugar imbalances; problems with elimination

Mars in Virgo

Keywords: Active or Militant Mind

Favorable: Can get results quickly, doesn't waste time, fast problem-solving ability; strategic, militaristic approach; knows how to protect themselves, scientific or analytical skills, resistance to disease, self-reliant, craftsman, mechanic, engineer, warrior, material orientation

Unfavorable: Overactive mind, warlike thinking, doesn't know when to stop, impatient, indebted, combative and broken relationships, exaggerates, withholds information, says things that are not so, digestive ailments, accidents, wounds, cuts, fevers, nervous diseases, communicable and inflammatory diseases, hernia, torn muscles

Jupiter in Virgo

Keywords: Expansive Mind

Favorable: Enterprising, enthusiastic, sympathetic, friendly, intellectual, accepting, self-managing, methodical, insightful, conserves energy, focuses on positive and high-level activities, educated, always learning, good sense of humor, judge, minister, counselor, writer, publisher, professor, businessman, fortunate overall

Unfavorable: Overly optimistic, lazy thinking, doesn't consider options or backup plans, undirected, doesn't act in time, out of touch with practical reality, gives in too easily, liver problems, intestinal ailments, legal problems, fluid or fat buildup in tissues, ailments of the nerves and lungs

Saturn in Virgo

Keywords: Focused, Stuck, or Obsessive Thinking

Favorable: Service oriented, works better alone, productive, conservative, traditional values, focused, linear and mechanical mind, good with structured activities, administrator or analyst in health, legal, military, accounting, design, works in public sector, monastic, things are better after some experience as in later in life

Unfavorable: Dislikes change, obsessive, conflicted mind, calculating, unfeeling, mechanical, little understanding for pleasures and feelings, not romantic, discontented, foresees negative outcomes, not a people person, obstructed elimination, stagnation in nerves and intestines, headaches, mental problems and depression

Rahu in Virgo

Keywords: Innovative or Confused Thinking

Favorable: Does better in private or with sufficient alone time, thinks in unusual and creative ways, resourceful and a survivor, wants to help those in need, works well with foreigners, legally astute, knows how to provide excellent service

Unfavorable: Confused, mentally off balance, lack of ability to be of service to others, conflicting, combative, tricky, gets into debts, legal trouble; troubles with skin, breathing, digestion, allergies; social misfit

Ketu in Virgo

Keywords: Unbounded or Chaotic Thinking

Favorable: Advanced intuition, sublime thought, innovative, good at forecasting, good astrologer, very creative and quick minded, inspired and inspiring, given to a monastic lifestyle

Unfavorable: Mentally unstable, too many surprises in life, hypersensitive, allergies, delicate digestion, problems with respiration, self-isolating, feels cut adrift

PLANETS IN LIBRA

Sun in Libra

The Sun is not well placed in Libra, where it is debilitated or Neecha at 10 degrees.

Keywords: Love of Peaceful Actions

Favorable: Charming, alluring, soothing, attractive as a mate (although poor as a partner), accepting, gives the benefit of the doubt, lenient, reassuring, gives support and solace, helps the less fortunate, artistic sensibility, intuitive

Unfavorable: Out of balance, gives in too much, lacks motivation, doesn't face difficulties, avoids responsibilities, not up-front, will turn on people to suit their purposes, plays both sides, overindulges in pleasures, ineffective, poor financial management, charms others into supporting them, kidney ailments, lower back pain, sexual weaknesses, headaches, addictive behavior

Moon in Libra

Keywords: Lovely Emotions

Favorable: Diplomatic, very smooth, persuasive, seductive, gentle, will try not to hurt people's feelings, balanced, gracious, multifaceted, accommodating, good-natured, feminine, artistic, refined, pleasure loving, romantically appealing, good wealth and comforts, spiritual, guided by intuition; likes pleasant surroundings, possessions, and attire

Unfavorable: Chameleon, indecisive, devious, manipulator, runs away, torn by decisions, overly sensitive to criticism, too lenient, lack of direction or ambition, losses through misplaced affections, lackadaisical, body is out of balance or asymmetrical, open to many forms of personal relationships, lives off others, mental or emotional imbalance, kidney ailments, back problems, low and high libido, migraines, restless sleep, addict

Mercury in Libra

Keywords: Creative and Enjoyable Thinking

Favorable: fun-loving, friendly, courteous, loves philosophy, creative, idea person, humanitarian, good host, musical and artistic interests, sweet and persuasive speaker, comedic sense, likes intellectual art or the artistic side of the intellect; enjoys clubs, ceremonies, spiritual rites, and performances

Unfavorable: Youthful; not a serious friend or lover; doesn't own responsibilities until it's almost too late; agrees too much, or agrees then does what they want; doesn't finish work or thinks it's good enough; needs guidance in the early years; kidney ailments, nerve damage, reproductive weakness, lightheaded

Venus in Libra

Venus occupies its own sign (swakshetra). Venus exalted, or in its own sign on an angle, forms a Malavya Yoga, indicating the highest manifestation of Venus's qualities.

Keywords: Full Loveliness and Artistry

Favorable: Elegant, well respected, artistic, sensual, balanced in thought and deed; spokesperson, intuitive, full feelings and passions, enthusiastic, good wealth and comforts; benefits from items and activities related to women, beauty, art, and luxury; connected to spiritual and humanitarian activities

Unfavorable: Overindulgence, sets expectations too high for romance and for partnerships, extravagant, doesn't apply enough energy to things, blood sugar problems, urinary tract ailments, trouble with romance, vision problems

Mars in Libra

Keywords: Fiery Love

Favorable: Energetic, confident, charming, persuasive, self-reliant, love of beauty and romance, affectionate, friendly to all, enjoys active yet refined pursuits, passionate and likes passionate people, accomplishes quickly, strategic, enjoys challenges, mechanical artist, clever warrior

Unfavorable: Fickle, falls in love too quickly, unfaithful, broken relationships, overcome with passions, arrogant, impatient, reckless, deceptive, gullible, immature yet attractive, kidney infections, lower back trouble, headaches, heat sensitive, rashes, fevers, reproductive or venereal diseases

Jupiter in Libra

Keywords: Expanded Love

Favorable: Impartial; lawful; love of art, music, beauty, and luxury; spiritual and humanitarian base; cultured, mannerly, comforting; gains through business, art, and beauty; refined intuition, competent to lead

Unfavorable: Indulgent, takes too much leisure time; doesn't perform completely, correctly, or in time; legal problems, romantic entanglements, misunderstood intentions, doesn't explain things enough, fatigued, kidney ailments, liver troubles, blood sugar imbalances, fat or fluid buildup

Saturn in Libra

Saturn is considered well placed or exalted in Libra. If Saturn in Libra falls in an angle (1st, 4th, 7th, or 10th houses), it forms a Sasa Yoga, indicating the highest manifestation of Saturn's qualities.

Keywords: Elegant Focus

Favorable: Clever, focused, well organized, systematic, presents ideals logically, legal defender, steady in love, conventional, faithful, self-sufficient, hard worker, grows in renown, practical or traditional artist, success with foreign connections, land, agriculture, things get better over the years

Unfavorable: Restrictions in love and partnerships, delayed commitments or marriage, unaffectionate partner, little romance, ruled by loved ones, doesn't do well with ambiguity or uncertainty, wants too much definition, controlling in love, overworks, fearful of change

Rahu in Libra
Keywords: Innovative or Unusual Love

Favorable: Acceptance and love of the unusual and the foreign, able to deal in a clever manner with people, success in foreign business or with foreign people, might marry a foreigner or one who was met at a distance, material prosperity could improve after marriage

Unfavorable: Broken relationships, problems being understood or understanding others, self-centered, will take more than give, attracted to unusual sexual and sensual activities, may have a preference for relationships with their own sex, dishonest in relationships, unscrupulous in business

Ketu in Libra
Keywords: Love of the Unbounded

Favorable: Quick adaptability in business, able to deal with a multitude of personality types successfully, does not get overly attached in business, has a great love of spiritual life

Unfavorable: Broken romances; conflicts between love and spirituality; sets expectations too high regarding love, leaving the person alone a lot; desires the highest form of love but can't seem to find it; hypersensitive about their respect; may not be able to keep vows; has quick downturns in business

PLANETS IN SCORPIO

Sun in Scorpio
The Sun, indicator of one's power and action in the world, sits in the eighth sign of the zodiac, Scorpio, which is ruled by the active, aggressive Mars; and represents mystery, life, long-term health, reproduction, benefits from others, etc. Thus, we get something similar to a Sun/Mars conjunction in the 8th house (sign).

Keywords: Energetic Action and Intuition

Favorable: Competitive, capacity to act suddenly, spirited and passionate, strong will, takes decided action, leader, director, agent of control, energetic, good investigation skills, high intuition, connections with other worlds, healer, natural talents with many things, affectionate, responsive, strong seductive energy, many friends, success at a later age (when the fire cools down), resistant to aging

Unfavorable: Controlling, militant, has trouble with deciding on new things, phobic, jealous, possessive, hard to break from attachments, too blunt, scandalous behavior, cruel, provokes problems, full of crises or illness, takes from others without returning, vengeful, long-term spitefulness, reproductive problems, elimination ailments, venereal diseases, heart troubles, fevers, rashes, cuts, accidents

Moon in Scorpio

The Moon is debilitated or Neecha at 3 degrees of Scorpio.

Keywords: Fiery and Mystical Emotions

Favorable: Great innate talents, clever, prone to quick action, fixed in purpose, takes charge, self-directed, can face adversity alone, makes revolutionary changes, reformer, editor, good at correcting and guiding others, quick-witted, strong, allows a lot for those they love, open-minded yet conservative

Unfavorable: Gets intimate too early, can't break bad emotional attachments, not cautious when criticizing, strong enemy, holds on to slights, self-isolating, sexual affairs, likes the bizarre, doesn't express needs clearly, afraid of being blamed or embarrassed, reproductive difficulties, problems with elimination, marriage problems, accused in legal actions, crimes of passion, emotional rages

Mercury in Scorpio

Keywords: Quick and Fiery Thinking

Favorable: Bright mind, makes decisions rapidly; interested in research, investigation, diagnosis, detecting, and other activities that delve into the unknown. Militaristic mind-set, clever strategist, questions authority, discriminative, witty, asks for proof, interest in otherworldly activities

Unfavorable: Mind is too fast, speech can't keep up with thoughts, exaggerates, hides the truth or doesn't tell the full truth, shuns others, seeks instant pleasures, can't sustain a relationship well, impatient, broken finances, paranoid, sexually driven without much fulfillment, reproductive ailments, speech or hearing problems, inflamed nerves, problems with elimination

Venus in Scorpio

Keywords: Active Passions and Love

Favorable: Desires love but can live independently, has full expression of passions, charming, adolescent energy, protects own interests, love of action and adventure, love of debate, artistic, actor, public speaker, slow to age

Unfavorable: High passions turn to arguments; broken relationships fraught with discord; temperamental—sweet then angry; jealous; focused on their own satisfaction; think themselves devoted yet have "meaningless" affairs; little social elegance; like things rough; associate with low-class people

Mars in Scorpio

Energetic Mars is located in its own sign (swakshetra). If Mars is on an angle (1st, 4th, 7th, or 10th houses), it forms a Ruchaka Yoga, indicating the highest manifestation of Mars's qualities.

Keywords: Accentuated Fire and Energy

Favorable: Positive, "try anything" attitude, sharp mind, passionate, quick decisions, solves problems quickly, undaunted, success in dynamic enterprises, strong warrior spirit, enjoys resolving opposition, gets results, works hard and fast, excels in short-duration tasks, can beat anyone in the short run, detective, secret agent, investigator, researcher

Unfavorable: Arrogant, challenging, stubborn, impatient with slow people, partnership problems, selfish, takes things improperly, inclined to leave the job before it's finished, not good with long-duration tasks, accidents, wounds, surgeries, excessive bleeding, toxic buildup, violent responses, feverish

Jupiter in Scorpio

Keywords: Expansive Actions

Favorable: Active, competent, articulate, persuasive, always finds opportunities for growth; financial abilities, good capacity to learn and stay up to date, positive, strong sense of self and of purpose, philosophical, dignified, strong feelings or passions, interest in transcendental knowledge

Unfavorable: Gets into debt, clever backbiter, overindulges, not as holy as they want others to think, gets much criticism, legal problems, family troubles, breaks from children, financial loss through speculation, holds on to mistakes, self-absorbed, morally challenged, reproductive organ ailments, swellings, infections, liver problems, cuts, accidents, infections in organs of elimination

Saturn in Scorpio
Keywords: Focused or Restricted Activity

Favorable: Capacity to work hard and fast; powerful focus and ability to get things done; tries to remain cheerful—at least externally; shrewd; mechanical or analytical skill; orientation to defense, fire, energy, industry, etc.; follows the established path; financial success over time

Unfavorable: Subject to mistreatment or penalties, danger from weapons, angry then frustrated then depressed, high metabolism, deceptive, too clever, toxic, health is depleted from overwork, needs satisfaction but can't find it, worried, has trouble getting support from others, blood stagnation, menstrual problems, waste buildup, joint problems, nose and throat ailments, inflamed tissues and bones

Rahu in Scorpio
Keywords: Toxic Actions

Favorable: Aggressive, able to take effective action, makes money through subtle or hidden activities, highly intuitive nature, focused on material growth and personal support, driven to learn about the mysteries of life

Unfavorable: Tendency to get angry easily, easily provoked, self-serving, confused about the appropriate level of aggression, keeps grudges too long, vindictive, lives in the extremes, takes things from others, reproductive and eliminative problems, blood stagnation, allergies, rashes, cuts, wounds, accidents

Ketu in Scorpio
Keywords: Unbounded or Chaotic Actions

Favorable: Quick mind, likes to get responsibilities out of the way quickly, takes fast action, intuitive, likes researching and uncovering mysteries, gets support from surprising sources

Unfavorable: Vulnerable, hypersensitive, angry, deceptive, acts nice then strikes, loses support from others, gets illnesses that are hard to diagnose, gets sudden inflammatory ailments, trouble with elimination and reproduction, skin rashes, accidents, surgeries

PLANETS IN SAGITTARIUS

Sun in Sagittarius
Keywords: Expansive and Just Actions
Favorable: Positive beliefs, concerned for impartiality and fairness, love of philosophy, devoted to high ideals and causes, judicious, friendly, need for freedom, unrestrained, fun-loving, smiling, strong will, honest, sincere, good earning ability, fortunate, counselor, consultant, judge, minister
Unfavorable: Frustrated, willful, changes or modifies job and residence often, doesn't like to be subordinate, spoiled, will rebel if not given a good explanation, too optimistic, will say what comes to mind without thinking, doesn't take long-term responsibility, fearful of losing freedom, gets into debts, lack of review, leg ailments, liver complaints, nervous, lung ailments, hip or mid-leg problems

Moon in Sagittarius
Keywords: Expansive Feelings and Ideals
Favorable: Grateful for blessings, direct, positive attitude, brave, energetic, courteous, noble, takes a stand for their beliefs, determined, gives benefits to others, focuses on fulfilling their desires, loves independence and play, counselor, advisor, minister, charitable or humanitarian work, enjoys traveling and learning new things, love of philosophy and religion and high ideals
Unfavorable: Argues for the sake of argument, honest without consideration, blurts out, aggressive, overly sensitive, feels a lack of fairness, indulgent, insubordinate, changes jobs too often, unfixed, unreliable, restless, hip and upper leg problems, lung ailments, fat and fluid retention

Mercury in Sagittarius

Keywords: Wise and Just Thinking

Favorable: Refined thinking, enjoys learning, speaks well of others, original thinker, organized, unselfish, gifted, competent, impartial, law giver and follower, leads by example, respectable, good writer and speaker, teacher, counselor, advisor, minister, straight talker, abundant life

Unfavorable: Unmindful of the downside, blunt, lavish life, imprudent, unwary, exaggerates, thinks too much of their own point of view, superiority complex, a know-it-all, unreliable, nerve disorders, breathing troubles, hip and thigh aches

Venus in Sagittarius

Keywords: Expansive Love

Favorable: Visionary, artistic; fond of good clothes, food, and surroundings; drawn to the soothing, pleasant aspects of love; sensuous, romantic, good earning capacity, stays focused on the bright side of life, love affairs while on journeys, love of travel, loyal to loved ones, a prominent person

Unfavorable: Extravagant, indulgent, abhors the unrefined, careless investments, sluggish, misses obvious opportunities, superficial love, flirtatious, trivial, perfunctory, too frank, easily impressed, flamboyant, lung ailments, hip and thigh troubles, swellings, fluid and fat buildup

Mars in Sagittarius

Keywords: Active Fortune and Expansion

Favorable: Well spoken, jumps on opportunities, capacity for expanded knowledge, wealthy, straightforward, leadership abilities, gets things done, political savvy for government or large corporation work, unafraid, strategist, popular, sense of humor, laughs off troubles

Unfavorable: Tries too hard to succeed, honest but hurts others' feelings, expects too much too soon, legal problems, gets into debt, problems with children, broken finances, marriage trouble, conceited, impatient, manipulator, rabble rouser, overstimulated, swelling in hips and thighs, respiratory ailments, infections

Jupiter in Sagittarius

Jupiter is placed in its own sign (swakshetra). When Jupiter resides in an angle, is exalted, or is in its own sign, then Hamsa Yoga is formed, indicating the highest manifestation of Jupiter's qualities.

Keywords: Blessed Growth and Fortune

Favorable: Influential, cultured, trustworthy, humanitarian, capacity to inspire and lead others, knowledge giver, artistic, expansive attitude, well spoken, religious or spiritual bearing, socially adept, sense of humor, wise, meets commitments fully, fortunate, attached to acts of devotion, progressive

Unfavorable: Careless, poor management, indulgent, mindless investment, overly optimistic, spends too much for spiritual advancement or in seeking outer pleasures, fat and fluid retention, stagnation, lung ailments

Saturn in Sagittarius

Keywords: Structured or Restricted Expansion

Favorable: Correct, legal mind-set, humanitarian, dutiful, sense of fairness, respectful, strategist, follows the right path, structured and progressive growth, orthodox, wealth expands with age, content, speaks the truth kindly, charitable, resourceful, manager, stays on track, quietly happy

Unfavorable: Submissive, restricted growth, weak fortune, trouble with children, slow to trust, not open, frustrated, low scruples, will take what they can get, lack of honor, poor focus, lack of direction, problems with relationships, hip joint problems, lameness, respiratory troubles, liver ailments

Rahu in Sagittarius

Keywords: Good Material Destiny or Confused Growth

Favorable: Rahu can expand the financial and spiritual rewards from this position. The person is clever in legal and ethical matters; higher education may be of an unusual or foreign nature; has liking for the sublime or out-of-the-ordinary spiritual and philosophical undertakings; may travels to foreign countries

Unfavorable: Finances are low; understanding is clouded; relationship with father is troubled; speaks ill of teachers and gurus; not on a good spiritual path; takes to corrupt, unorthodox, and mysterious teachings; amoral financial dealings; lung ailments, hip or sciatica problems, liver trouble

Ketu in Sagittarius

Keywords: Mystical Expansion

Favorable: Attracted to sublime knowledge, drawn to noble causes and to high intellectual undertakings, explores many different philosophies in search of a unification of understanding, perhaps at a university or other place of higher learning, travels to mystical locales, sudden positive turns of fortune, gets a high-caliber guru

Unfavorable: Separation from father, fortunes are up and down, sudden reversals in luck, tries too many types of philosophies while never mastering any, has trouble with higher education, legal difficulties, ethics are questionable, accidents and mishaps while traveling, lung and hip (sciatica) ailments

PLANETS IN CAPRICORN

Sun in Capricorn

Keywords: Focused or Restricted Activity

Favorable: Duty oriented, silent, practical, frugal, hard worker, efficient, ambitious, responsible, thoughtful, prompt, conventional, provides good service and support, accommodating, cautious, success in monastic life, benefits from defined and established occupations, improves with age

Unfavorable: Never feels they have done enough, constrained, works too hard, used by others—especially employers, lack of pleasure, not expressive of affections, obstinate, self-centered, aloof, skeptical, humorless, depressed, self-isolating, can't tell when to stop, cruel, poor circulation, cold hands and feet, slow digestion, joint problems—especially knees, adrenal collapse, wrinkles or skin troubles

Moon in Capricorn

Keywords: Restrained or Controlled Emotions

Favorable: Dependable, reposed, long-term friend, devoted companion, performs duties constantly and completely, pragmatic, methodical approach, focus on security, orthodox; likes old and ancient things, people, and institutions; democratic; administrative and business skills; love of the outdoors and cool mountainous regions; things get better in middle age

Unfavorable: Coldhearted, unscrupulous, self-serving, lacks mercy, plays too much by the book, will do what is necessary to succeed, picks irresponsible partners or partners in need of repair, dogmatic, isolated, depressed, asexual, stubborn, insecure, odd, joint troubles, restricted hormone or blood flow, dementia

Mercury in Capricorn

Keywords: Structured or Restricted Thinking

Favorable: Purposeful, attentive to duty, logical, frugal, analytical, systematic approach, looks deeply into matters, good with numbers, orthodox designer, manages according to the rules, smart about protecting their own interests, service provider, conventional, monastic, interested in old philosophies

Unfavorable: Obsessive, loses sight of the big picture, petty, feels trapped, caught in dreary routine, morose, doubtful, speaks ill of others, seeks revenge, mean, poor finances, low self-esteem, creates a lonely life, joint problems, nerve damage, skin ailments, anxiety, poor assimilation of food, gas

Venus in Capricorn

Keywords: Businesslike in Love

Favorable: Dutiful, constant, loyal, responsible, mature in love or prefers mature love interests, love of traditions and convention, democratic ideals, gains from established enterprises, focus on love matters and the home, love of solitude, monastic, helpful to the poor and the "underdog"

Unfavorable: Slow to love, restrictions in love, frustration, lack of pleasure, may work in sexually oriented professions or perform love in a functional manner, cold, unfeeling, averse to love, slow to respond, attracted to older people, involved with the sordid, death or dying, reproductive problems, low fertility, beauty dries up, collapsed veins, emotionally drab

Mars in Capricorn

Mars is exalted or Uucha at 28 degrees of Capricorn. If Mars is exalted or in its own sign on an angle (1st, 4th, 7th, or 10th houses), it forms a Ruchaka Yoga; that is, it indicates the highest manifestation of Mars's qualities.

Keywords: Energetic and Focused

Favorable: Acts quickly and effectively, stamina, high energy, courage, warrior, won't be defeated, generous, hardworking, resists disease and aging, mechanical or technical bearing, protective, focused on results, respected, takes a calculated risk, cunning, charming, capacity for wealth

Unfavorable: Impatient, quick to anger, thinks it's okay to take things from others, deceptive, executioner, reckless, doesn't complete things, arrogant, combative, blood disorders, fevers, accidents, knee problems, inflammatory illnesses; danger from machinery, weapons, fire, poisons, and electricity

Jupiter in Capricorn

Jupiter is considered debilitated or Neecha at 5 degrees of Capricorn.

Keywords: Structured Expansion or Restricted Development

Favorable: Cares for the masses, the poor, the old, the underdog; convincing, argues for the good, legal point of view, traditional, follows the standards, accepted, slow and steady expansion, practical, organized, giving

Unfavorable: Obstructed financial growth, poor career, lack of protection, women have trouble with husbands; undeveloped, restricted, or ultraconservative religious views; lack of positivity, low energy, resentful of or depressed about others' progress, lethargic, stagnation in body, trouble with children, lack of grace, liver troubles, fat or fluid obstructions

Saturn in Capricorn

If Saturn is in its own sign on an angle, it produces a Sasa Yoga, indicating the highest manifestation of Saturn's qualities.

Keywords: Deep Focus

Favorable: Hardworking, serious, responsible, success through working with schedules and budgets, centered, makes things orderly and compact, practical, careful, thinks things through, knows what is necessary to know, deliberate, contemplative, capacity to work or be alone as required, democratic

Unfavorable: Withholds information, too shrewd, unscrupulous, not much fun, focused on the downside, cruel, disagreeable, discontented, works too perfectly, obstructed growth, low-class associations, stagnation, diseases of old age, joint problems, dryness, mental blocks

Rahu in Capricorn

Keywords: Unconventional and/or Ruthless Behavior

Favorable: Goal oriented, takes responsibility, persistent, hardworking, gets the job done, makes good money through career, inventive, practical, drawn to unusual occupations, sometimes oriented to purification or the removal of toxins, benefits from working in solitude

Unfavorable: Unscrupulous, takes advantage of others and is taken advantage of, unclear about their purpose in life, quietly intense, unkind, severe, heartless, self-isolating, gets taken advantage of at work yet can be too hard on others as well, knee problems

Ketu in Capricorn

Keywords: Sudden Success and Failure

Favorable: Able to achieve high status spiritually, innovative, quickly gets results following traditional approaches, career advances through constant renewal

Unfavorable: Career activities could seem to go up, then reverse themselves. It's good to keep away from enterprising or entrepreneurial activities, which may be too unstable for their own good. Things seem insecure or uncertain many times; possible accidents or ailments to the joints, especially the knees; circulation could be low, leaving the person feeling cold a lot

PLANETS IN AQUARIUS

Sun in Aquarius

Keywords: Innovative Activity

Favorable: Creative and intelligent, scientific, analytical, inventive, genius, caring, cordial, sympathetic, politically active, advocate, helpful to the less fortunate, dedicated, hardworking, has endurance, staying power, capacity for new realms of thinking, reserved, strength of will, monastic

Unfavorable: Secretive, low self-esteem, lack of self-promotion, undervalue their own talents, activist, low income, lack of luck, headstrong, rebel, speaks ill of others, morbid, lack of accomplishment or direction, depressed, cynical, disbeliever yet gullible, disconnected from reality, paranoid, sneaky, loner, victim, heart ailments, circulatory congestion, varicose veins, blood stagnation, eye troubles

Moon in Aquarius
Keywords: Structured or Restricted Feelings

Favorable: Creative, desires to fulfill dreams, inventive, intuitive, scientific disposition, philosopher, seer, astrologer, futuristic, thinks down to the small details, seeks the best standards and ideals, political or humanitarian perspective, mystical, ages gracefully, emotionally guarded, modest, solitary life

Unfavorable: Depressed, reluctant, shy, lack of self-referral, hard to make friends, abhor agencies of control or investigation, poor cash flow, bizarre behavior, loner, paranoid, full of self-doubt, feels "beat up" by others, guarded yet naïve, heart ailments, blood stagnation, lower leg or ankle problems, nervous disorders, poor vision, exotic or hard-to-diagnose diseases

Mercury in Aquarius
Keywords: Focused or Obsessive Thinking

Favorable: Advanced thinking capacity, looks at things in a new way, intellectual, philosopher, metaphysical interests, scientific thinker, educated, examines things deeply, focused on the pinpoint value, administrator, clever, witty, scholarly, researcher, hard worker, thinking improves with age

Unfavorable: Micromanager, critical, stuck at the small detail level, incapacitated, trouble dealing with uncertainty, out-of-step thinking, loses the big picture, worried, overexamines everything, fearful about losing control, lack of virility, nervous problems, damage to nervous system, headaches

Venus in Aquarius
Keywords: Unusual Love

Favorable: Dependable friend, faithful, classical attitudes toward love, conventional, simple in dress, desires stability in love, love for mature or older people and material things, attracted to mysteries, fantasies, unusual people and philosophies, structured approach to love, responsible to partners

Unfavorable: Delays or setbacks in relationships, love for lost causes, drawn into unusual love experiences, overly idealistic or unconventional about love and relationships, gets dysfunctional partners, partners do not reciprocate affection or finances, circulatory ailments, trouble with veins and blood flow, varicose veins, reproductive complications, sexual energy imbalance

Mars in Aquarius

Keywords: Energetic Focus

Favorable: Strong capacity to action, energetic, needs to keep busy; wins big—loses big; solves problems quickly; engineering, scientific, or militaristic nature; activist, quick to get angry yet quick to forget, good for short-duration tasks, love of adventure, propagandist, good at contests

Unfavorable: Reckless, gets into disputes, dictatorial, sets expectations too high, frustrated and conflicted, gets burned out, manic depressive, rages, cheater, clever yet dishonest, violent, gets injured or in trouble due to weapons, in too much of a rush to be courteous, cuts, broken bones, teeth and gum problems, accidents, surgeries, burns, fevers, rashes, irregularity of heart

Jupiter in Aquarius

Keywords: Expansion Through Control

Favorable: Organized, orderly, clear and convincing, oriented to lawful and democratic interests, reformer, just, caring, works hard for the good of all, philosophical, diplomatic, political skill, self-sufficient, good friend or supporter, well-behaved children

Unfavorable: Plays too much by the book, perfunctory, self-isolating, few friends, limited wealth, reluctant to expand or move into new territory, inactive, not dependable, restricted growth, gloomy outlook, restrictions with children and friends, fat or fluid buildup, swellings in the legs, heart problems

Saturn in Aquarius

Saturn is located in its own sign (swakshetra). If Saturn is exalted or in its own sign on an angle (1st, 4th, 7th, or 10th houses), it forms a Sasa Yoga, indicating the highest manifestation of Saturn's qualities.

Keywords: Stable and Structured Growth

Favorable: Focused, stable, gets results, uses a structured approach, scientific, analytical, uses time to their advantage, dependable, businesslike, sensible, deliberate, respectable, doesn't rush, philosophical, orthodox, wins in the long run, silent manner, civilized, quietly refined

Unfavorable: End justifies the means, focuses more on projects than on people, dispassionate, robotic, alienated, drawn to unhealthy foods and drink and unclean behaviors, problems with lower leg and ankles, blood stagnation, depression, heart problems

Rahu in Aquarius
Keywords: Unusual Focus or Opportunities
Favorable: Creative capacity to fulfill dreams, associates and makes friends with foreigners or people at a distance, thinks of unusual ways to make things work, cash flow is good if they refrain from getting too clever
Unfavorable: Unscrupulous behavior, cash flow and profits are hurt through deceptions, friends prove to be false and hopes are unfulfilled due to lack of clarity and purpose; this person can be taken advantage of by others, has a tendency to self-isolate, needs to socialize more to be successful

Ketu in Aquarius
Keywords: Sublime Development
Favorable: Thinks of creative ways to increase profits, oriented to a spiritual life, uses a mix of religion and politics to get ahead, cash flow increases suddenly
Unfavorable: Older siblings and friends tend to be a source of surprises and financial complications; cash flow is unsteady; person thinks of too many "harebrained" schemes that lead nowhere; can feel cut off and isolated with few friends; lacks success in pioneering-type activities

PLANETS IN PISCES

Sun in Pisces
Keywords: Supporting and Comforting Behavior
Favorable: Gives aid and support to others, emotional, respectful, peaceful, dreamer, endearing to partners, philosophical, idealistic, sociable, volunteering, inspiring, a popular leader, creative, flexible, adaptable, well liked, impressive inner life, contemplative, intuitive, cooperative
Unfavorable: Submissive, out of focus, squanders opportunities, unreliable, thinking is discontinuous and unresolved, doesn't accomplish things, puts things off, lack of confidence, volunteers too much, becomes a victim, poor financial management, has no goals or plans, disinterested in material pursuits, penalized, low vitality, foot troubles, digestive ailments, sluggish and toxic system

Moon in Pisces

Keywords: Fullness of Feeling

Favorable: Capacity to feel and comprehend deeply, intuitive, spiritual, humanitarian, empathetic, devoted, genuinely nice, a favorite friend, strong need to believe in something or someone, unpretentious, decent, expressive of feelings, loving, affectionate, idealistic, visionary, romantic

Unfavorable: Too porous emotionally, full of doubt, subservient, emotionally dependent, lazy, indulgent, gullible, poor focus on earning a living, overdrawn financial and emotional reserves, cries easily, impulsive, unreliable, doesn't complete things, feels betrayed, problems with fertility, intestinal ailments, water and fat retention, phlegm in the lungs

Mercury in Pisces

Mercury is Neecha or debilitated at 15 degrees of Pisces.

Keywords: Discontinuous Thinking

Favorable: Spiritual nature, imaginative, likeable, provides great service to spiritual and humanitarian activities, sensitive, intuitive, versatile, artistic (especially in music and writing), philosophic, analytical, mentally probing, tactful, open-minded, responsive

Unfavorable: Nervous, conflicted, spaced out, unsettled, indecisive, taken in by charlatans, discontented, pursues things of superficial value, results are mixed or insignificant, engages in many philosophical and spiritual pursuits, depressed, trouble generating thoughts that bring practical success, lung ailments, skin diseases, problems with feet, mental problems

Venus in Pisces

Venus is exalted or Uucha at 27 degrees of Pisces. If Venus is exalted, or on an angle, it forms a Malavya Yoga, indicating the highest manifestation of Venus's qualities.

Keywords: Fullness of Love and Prosperity

Favorable: Gentle, cultivated, polite, unpretentious; love of beauty, luxury, and refinement; sought after, gets promoted in all of life's affairs, knowledgeable, charming, capable of being wealthy, good sense of humor, cares deeply for others, focus on women's issues, expanded capacity to feel pleasure, donor, artistic, inspiring, full of compassion for others, intuitive

Unfavorable: Lack of capacity to earn the comforts and money they need, uses others for livelihood, unrestrained, overindulgent, loses through misplaced sympathies, taken advantage of, marriage or partnership troubles, too sacrificing, foot ailments, reproductive complaints, swellings in the intestinal area or midsection

Mars in Pisces

Keywords: Active Expansion

Favorable: Fast gains of wealth, brave outlook, active, positive goal setter, activist for legal causes, excited about life, generous, know what they want and when, dedicated to ideals, fervent, devotee

Unfavorable: Overspends, legal troubles, lives too big and fast, broken education, trouble with children, relationship problems, staggered expansion, inappropriate gains, frustrated, uneven career, doesn't keep promises or promises too much, zealot, addict, inflammatory illnesses, fractures, blood ailments

Jupiter in Pisces

Jupiter occupies its own sign (swakshetra). If Jupiter is exalted, or in its own sign on an angle (1st, 4th, 7th, or 10th houses), it forms a Hamsa Yoga, indicating the highest manifestation of Jupiter's qualities.

Keywords: Wisdom, Wealth, and Expansion

Favorable: Well-developed finances and comforts, good family life with prosperous children, astute at handling people, good education, philosophic, spiritual, supportive, highly regarded, decent, appreciates others, positive outlook, reverent, strong intuition, visionary, nurturing or healing

Unfavorable: Overly idealistic, misses obvious opportunities for success, overly indulgent, easily impressed or taken in by grandiose schemes, spends too much for spiritual advancement or charitable undertakings, puffiness, tumors, swollen feet, liver troubles, yellowing of body tissue, overweight

Saturn in Pisces

Keywords: Structured Growth

Favorable: Interested in the issues of the common man, spiritual or charitable orientation, good for their word, wealth builds up over time, respected, prudent, reliable, tolerant, best at conservative and traditional work, quiet, peaceful, gracious, a dependable friend, works from a legal framework

Unfavorable: Doesn't defend their acquisitions, family problems, delays in education, too trusting, restricted health, loner, doesn't keep track of details, hides problems, devoted to the wrong people, poor circulation, liver ailments, feet problems, joint troubles or lameness, misuse of painkillers

Rahu in Pisces

Keywords: Shadowed Growth

Favorable: Person spends money on philanthropic causes and devotes time to spiritual growth, international financing and business abroad could be profitable, profits come from foreigners and out-of-the-ordinary ways, gets support to fulfill their needs

Unfavorable: Lack of attention causes losses, ungrounded, disinterest in making money can lead to a dependency on friends and well-wishers for support, person is subject to fines and penalties for not paying attention to the rules and regulations, confused behavior in finances, poor sleep and energy due to toxic buildup and a poorly functioning liver, digestion might be poor, problems with feet

Ketu in Pisces

Keywords: Enlightened or Chaotic Behavior

Favorable: The person is naturally wise and is drawn to a spiritual life; might be a source of inspiration to others; leads a simple life yet there are many changes that turn into opportunities for growth; intuition is high

Unfavorable: Too many surprises and upheavals, finances are erratic, debts pile up due to lack of prudence and planning, might be the victim of a plot to abscond with their money through a false penalty or charge, ailments of the feet and liver might be hard to diagnose

CHAPTER SIX

PLANETS in HOUSES
(GRAHAS in BHAVAS)

In my experience, I have found that planets in houses reveal more specific information than planets in signs. Obviously, we are starting from a specific rising sign for an individual or event and not the generic Aries, as is the case for planets in signs.

A key to understanding planets in houses is to follow a few simple rules:

1. Look at the planet as if it were in a particular sign. In Vedic astrology, the sign is the house, so the first house will act like Aries, the second house like Taurus, all the way through to the twelfth house, which acts like Pisces.

2. Take the planet occupying the house and look to what planet is ruling that natural zodiac sign position. For example, if the Sun is in the first, treat it like it was in Aries ruled by Mars.

3. Since, in our example, Aries is ruled by Mars, look at the Sun as if it were in combination with Mars.

This principle of combining works throughout Vedic astrology. Follow this method with each planet in each house, and you will understand a lot about the source of the statements made for each position. The elements and qualities of the house/sign will also give you additional information regarding the nature of a planet located in a house. You can add to the simple paragraphs I have written with your own experience and knowledge, following the above approach.

The quality and quantity of influence of a planet in a house will depend on its strength (see shadbala, chapter 12). The dasa periods, among other indications, will reflect the nature, favorable or unfavorable, of the planet as influenced by the house it occupies. Transiting planets will reflect the nature of the house transited along with its occupants (and aspects).

The following list shows what specific planets in specific houses will signify. Additionally, I have included some conclusions drawn by judging from karaka planets; see chapter 4 for an explanation. You will know that a signification is drawn in this way if you see parentheticals; for example, (4th from 9th).

THE SUN IN HOUSES

Sun in FIRST House

Keywords: Hardy Physiology and Self

Favorable: Bold, adventuresome, strong-willed, regal, commanding, authoritative; help from father, government, business, or people in authority; likes to help others and do the right thing; warmhearted, generally good for wealth and health

Unfavorable: Impulsive, short-tempered, bossy or overdirecting, needs to control spending, inconsistent motivations, needs to pace their life, impatient, hotheaded, headaches, problems in the head area, fevers, burns, vision or eye problems, baldness, hyperacidity, masculine (even for females), pitta (fire) constitution

Sun in SECOND House

Keywords: Activity for Wealth

Favorable: Support or earnings from government, business (insurance, metals, gems), authority figures, and/or father; strong and regal speech, good with languages, good wealth, good education (scholarships/grants)

Unfavorable: Poor accumulation of money, can spend quickly and get into debt, friction in the family, willful, trouble with authority, exaggerates, boasts, possible speech problems, pitta (fiery) constitution, can get angry quickly; problems with eyes, face, lip/mouth area, and teeth; inclined to spicy food

Sun in THIRD House

Keywords: Determined Expression of the Self

Favorable: Brave, adventurous, determined, ambitious, quick, likes adventure, good wealth, good communicator, writer, lecturer, spokesperson, salesperson, actor, drawn to expressive arts, music, dance, drama, etc.

Unfavorable: Possible friction with siblings, close contacts, friends, or neighbors; these people may have difficulty with their own lives; need to move around, restless, lots of traveling for short distances; injuries to hands, arms, neck/shoulders; trouble through writing or printed materials

Sun in FOURTH House

The Sun occupying the 4th house is an example of judging from karaka planets. The 9th house is the house of the father. The 8th house is the house of death (or life, depending on how you look at it). If we count eight houses from the ninth, we get the fourth house in a person's chart. From the Sun's unfavorable occupation of this house, we can see a potentially negative influence on the father's health or longevity.

Keywords: Nurturing Activity

Favorable: Quick to respond; active in matters connected to clothing, shelter, homes, vehicles, education, etc.; orthodox morals; active family life

Unfavorable: Emotionally stirred up; easily agitated; discord with their mother (who represents the emotional base); Sun is the father (8th from the 9th), indicating absence or danger to father in the early years; lack of comfort; exposure to car accidents and breakdowns; interrupted education; ailments of the heart, breast, and chest region; sensitive stomach; nervous

Sun in FIFTH House

Keywords: Speculate and Contemplate

Favorable: Benefits from the momentum of good deeds of the past (purva punya), active, sportsman, traditional, romantic, proud, believes in higher values, spiritual leader, caring, acts like a father in love affairs, control of speculation, self-sufficient children

Unfavorable: Restless in meditation, friction with children or few children, abortion, miscarriage, short romances, trouble through out-dated or out-of-phase values of love, domineering, possessive, extravagant in business

Sun in SIXTH House

Keywords: Defense of the Self

Favorable: Healing, supportive, sense of service, social work, commanding, offers security and defense, wants to purify or improve people and processes around them, administrative skills, succeeds in conflicts and with adversaries, gains from lawsuits and other defensive measures, strategic planner, military or warrior mind-set, strong vital energy, works in the government or large corporations

Unfavorable: Attacker, conflicting, excessive sexual or vital energy, inflammatory ailments in digestive and respiratory system, troubles with relatives (uncles, aunts, and cousins), father is militaristic, father struggles, hardworking jobs, debts, wife is weak (12th to the 7th), possibility of divorce

Sun in SEVENTH House

Keywords: Actions for Partnering

Favorable: Supportive of partners, good business sense, travels throughout life, benefits through government contracts, partnerships strengthen success, takes the lead in relationships, attracted to take-charge and self-sufficient partners (business and personal)

Unfavorable: Delays and frictions in business, love commitments, or marriage; possessive of partner, controlled by aggressive partners, partners may have pitta (fire) health disorders, sexual energy is on and off, headaches, poor circulation in brain

Sun in EIGHTH House

Keywords: Actions for Health

Favorable: Interest in research, spiritual investigation, and other avenues into the unknown; skill in secret activities; gets money and support from others; benefits from activities related to the extension of life or the close of life; long life; strong and vital pitta disposition

Unfavorable: Problems with the father or authorities, anxious, lack of confidence, self-isolating, vulnerable, victimized, low vitality, shuts down sexually, lack of support or low visibility at work, poor self-promotion, slow advances in life, sneaky, diseases or discomforts persist over time, eye problems, circulatory disorders, reproductive weakness, etc.

Sun in NINTH House

Keywords: Actions for Righteousness

Favorable: Interest in higher levels of philosophy, religion, and esoteric thought (such as astrology), ethical, sense of justice and fair play, legal orientation, consultant, head of an educational or spiritual organization, goes on many long-distance journeys, good fortune, benefits through institutions of higher learning, success in publishing, benefits from gurus, authority figures, leaders, etc.

Unfavorable: Discord with father, guru, and authority figures; changes religion or philosophies, trouble with long travels, higher education is disturbed, legal entanglements, problems with publishing, feels unfortunate, partners have problems with siblings (3rd to 7th)

Sun in TENTH House

Keywords: Actions for Life Purpose

Favorable: Focused, orderly, purposeful, in command, courageous; authority in business, government, or religion; good career, prominent, instrumental in making things happen, good resistance to disease and to opposition, hard worker, dutiful, public servant, well informed

Unfavorable: Impatient, unsettled, problems with mother and with basic security, egotistical, troubles with authorities, obstructed career, frustrated, lack of capacity to repel opposition, knee ailments, poor digestion, joint trouble in general

Sun in ELEVENTH House

Keywords: Activities for Opportunities

Favorable: Capacity to fulfill one's desires, eager, perseverant, gets results, good cash flow, friendly, associates with well-placed people, has good friends, older brother and friends prosper

Unfavorable: Irresolute, lack of ambition, lethargic, poor cash flow, troubles with older siblings or friends, troubles with people of influence, misplaced trust in friends, obstructed dreams, lack of hope, poor circulation, heart problems, ankle weakness

Sun in TWELFTH House

Keywords: Actions for Liberation

Favorable: Works in spiritual, educational, healing, or philanthropic organizations; interested in liberating the spirit through various means, such as meditation, healing, etc.; unbounded point of view; charitable; travels abroad; benefits by time in seclusion; knowledge provider, guru; appreciation for subtle and soothing pleasures—both spiritual and sexual

Unfavorable: Lack of interest in attaining or sustaining a material existence, feels abandoned and unsupported, self-pleasuring, self-isolating, victim through volunteering, obscure life, secretive or unavailable father, time in confinement (hospital, prison, ashram), debts, penalties, fines, lives off of others' graces, weak physiology, lack of self-confidence, eye troubles, heart problems, feet ailments, breathing troubles

MOON IN HOUSES

Moon in FIRST House

Keywords: Royal and Energetic Disposition

Favorable: Playful, cheerful, curious, out-of-the-ordinary, imaginative, princely, elegant, wealthy, refined, generous, liberal, companionable, abundant life, sense of beauty, modest, easygoing, loves pleasures and comforts, seeks change and new experiences

Unfavorable: Changeable, eccentric; unbalanced spending—frugal then lavish; mood swings, both sluggish and nervous, extravagant, licentious, high tide and low tide with life in general, fertility complications, menstrual disorders, eye troubles, fluid and fat retention, lung ailments, kapha and/or vata problems depending on aspects to the first house

Moon in SECOND House

Keywords: Financial Comforts

Favorable: Comfortable life, fullness of food and financial resources, good student, family life is rich, charming, poetic, sweet speaker, gently persuasive, imaginative; liking for cosmetics, jewelry, and other fashion trimmings; pretty face

Unfavorable: Uneven finances, doesn't apply themselves diligently to gaining wealth, careless, doesn't speak up enough, poor study habits, financial losses through the mother or through misplaced sympathies; skin problems—especially the face; swollen gums and dental ailments; allergic; inclined to gain weight (either fat or water retention); sinus or nasal troubles

Moon in THIRD House

Keywords: Feeling of Adventure

Favorable: Love of change and new adventure, active imagination, quick mind, doesn't think about defeat, interest in the performing arts, artistic in general, aristocratic; love of siblings, neighbors, and close friends; good communicator, creative writer, seeks grand enterprises and noble causes

Unfavorable: Unfocused mind, wild imagination, doesn't plan enough, too much moving or traveling, lung and ear complications; swellings in neck, arm, and shoulders; speaks too much or too little, ear and throat infections

Moon in FOURTH House

Keywords: Fullness of the Home and Feelings

Favorable: Enjoys good clothing, housing, and vehicles; educated and educator, well mannered, gets emotional support from others, soothing, pleasant, motherly, nurturing, affectionate, contented, good mother and family life, fertile, expanded feelings, responsive to others, devoted, intuitive

Unfavorable: Vacillates, shy, full of uncertainty, too sensitive, emotional ups and downs, absence of nurturing, problems with mother, erratic education, submissive, disappointments and unmet expectations in domestic life, problems with chest and breast area, lung ailments, circulatory problems

Moon in FIFTH House

Keywords: Fullness of Intellect

Favorable: Spiritually refined, perceptive, intuitive, love and romance from partners; intelligent; enjoys scriptures, mantra meditation, and many other spiritual techniques; fun-loving, playful, enjoys children, fertile, good blessings from previous actions, gains from speculation, business knack

Unfavorable: Focuses on too many things, reckless, spends in anticipation of future income, loses through speculation, inconsistent, imaginary romances, fickle, inconsistent romance, fertility problems, mental imbalances, hormonal and reproductive organ problems, circulatory ailments

Moon in SIXTH House

Keywords: Stimulated Feelings and Imagination

Favorable: Good at providing service, natural healing and nurturing ability, desire to support and make things right, wants to bring things to their ideal point, protective, treats pets like children, gets support from attendants and employees

Unfavorable: Submissive, shies away from hard work, ingratiating, emotional imbalance, poor spending habits, fertility problems, discord with mother, lack of support, emotional conflicts, loss of pets, trouble with helpers, vision trouble, reproductive or hormonal imbalances, health is up and down

Moon in SEVENTH House

Keywords: Fullness of Partnerships

Favorable: Engaged in creative and artful businesses; imaginative; mother is a partner; drawn to elegance, pleasure, and comforts; relates well with others; social, affectionate, charming; benefits through partnerships and general business; desires good-looking and loving partner

Unfavorable: Many relationships, fickle, flirtatious, inconstant in affections, strongly drawn to seek pleasure from partners, partners are inconstant or changeable, back trouble, kidney disorders, reproductive problems, infertility, partner is overly sensitive, plump partner, kapha disorders

Moon in EIGHTH House

Keywords: Transcendental Emotions

Favorable: Highly responsive, highly intuitive, curious about unknown, researcher, health worker, high sexual vitality, gets support from others, gains through unearned means (insurance settlements, wills, gambling, etc.), generous, supportive of others

Unfavorable: Shy, worried, trouble expressing feelings, longs to be loved, distant relationship with mother, taken advantage of by others or abused, sexual extremes, jealous, reproduction and elimination ailments, few children, chronic watery diseases (diarrhea, lung congestion, seasick, fat buildup, etc.); danger of water accidents

Moon in NINTH House

Keywords: Fullness of Wisdom and Fortune

Favorable: Popular, public success, educated, intelligent; learned in philosophy and religion; love of God, guru, and father; travels; professor; fortunate life; respectful to older and wiser persons; idealistic, generous, success in publishing, full of devotion, pursues the highest ideals

Unfavorable: Too much traveling; incomplete higher education; not constant in beliefs and philosophies; fortunes are up and down; emotional upsets with father, guru, and/or authorities; emotional upsets with younger sibling's partner (7th to 3rd); lower back and hip problems; leg ailments; breathing troubles

Moon in TENTH House

The feeling Moon is paired with the structured and practical Saturn, the ruler of Capricorn, the 10th sign of the natural zodiac. We get a Moon/Saturn combination here.

Keywords: Nurturing and Full Life Purpose

Favorable: Responsible, emotional stability, supportive, a career of counseling and teaching others, interest in visual activities, love of traditional luxuries, nurturing in an effective and practical manner, mother prospers, good status and position in life

Unfavorable: Unsure of direction and life purpose, life is fraught with change and inconstancy, mother is unavailable or nonsupportive, emotionally and creatively blocked, little recognition or appreciation in career, slow advancements in career, troubles with knees and joints

Moon in ELEVENTH House

Keywords: Fullness of Profits and Opportunities

Favorable: Plenty of opportunities, hopeful, dreamer, inventive, imaginative, lives with high ideals, artistic, creative, friendly, generous and supportive to friends, feminine friends, well connected socially, good cash flow, very fertile, well liked, courteous

Unfavorable: Uneven cash flow, sets unrealistic goals, not practical, wild imaginations, fickle friends, lack of hope, loses their dreams from time to time, problems with older siblings, inconsistent as a friend, problems with heart valves, poor circulation, lower leg problems

Moon in TWELFTH House

Keywords: Emotions of Liberation and Self-Sacrifice

Favorable: Charitable, supportive, spiritually oriented, interested in enlightenment; capacity to heal; does well in faraway places; volunteers; works for humanitarian, charitable, health, or educational organizations; monastic disposition, yet capable of private passions; does secret work

Unfavorable: Kindness can be misinterpreted as weakness, thereby inviting the aggression of others; too self-sacrificing; lack of confidence; emotional upheavals; feels alone and confined; up and down finances; has losses, fines, insults, and penalties; self-gratifying; eye ailments, reproductive weakness, paralysis; mother is unavailable

MARS IN HOUSES

Mars in FIRST House

Keywords: Warrior Disposition

Favorable: Courageous, self-motivated, ambitious, unafraid, youthful, powerful, high stamina, best at short-term tasks, independent, successful, resistant to aging

Unfavorable: Combative, belligerent, offensive, aggressive, arrogant, doesn't complete activities, impulsive, lack of self-control, tries to get their own way, deceptive, has difficulties in relationships, accidents, head injuries, problems with teeth and gums, headaches, fevers, cuts, bumps, infectious and inflammatory diseases, high pitta constitution

Mars in SECOND House

Keywords: Active in Acquisition

Favorable: Works hard to accumulate wealth, gets money in bursts, cheerleader, full of laughter, active speaker, energetic family life, benefits with manufacturing, industrial or military activities, gives money to the needy, earns own way, charming, captivating, forceful speech

Unfavorable: Overly generous, talks too fast or too much, harsh speech, financial problems, misuse of sexual energy, blunt, lack of diligence in studies, eye ailments, mouth and teeth problems, snores, digestion off, general family conflicts, takes money without paying back

Mars in THIRD House

Keywords: Active Determination

Favorable: Clever, active mind, adventurer, courageous, determined; advocate or activist; strong persuasive skills; good at selling, marketing, or advertising; quick learner; expends high energy for short periods; accomplishes things quickly; athletic, dancer, mechanical artist, independent, warrior

Unfavorable: Rabble rouser, short fuse, will do questionable things to get what they want, conflicts with siblings and neighbors, reckless, doesn't listen to advice, burns out, education problems in early years, wounded or breaks bones in arms and upper body, travel accidents

Mars in FOURTH House

Keywords: Energetic Emotions

Favorable: Emotionally energetic, bolsters others' emotions; active home builder; benefits from vehicles, real estate, land, agriculture, manufacturing, military-style activities; teaches others quickly

Unfavorable: Car accidents and thefts, unsettled emotions, breaks in education, broken home or early separation from mother, short-term romances, deception in emotions, breast and chest inflammations and surgeries; person and/or their mother suffers from acidity, fevers, cuts, falls, cancers, and other inflammatory conditions; heart ailments, roughness for father (8th from the 9th)

Mars in FIFTH House

Keywords: Stimulated Intellect

Favorable: Strong survival instincts, quick reflexes both physically and mentally, acts spontaneously, definitive, determined, entertaining, athletic, likes to play and compete, skilled in charm and persuasion, sales and executive abilities, affectionate, sexual vitality, active children

Unfavorable: Inflexible, impatient, trouble with speculations, restless in meditation, abortions or miscarriages, broken romances, sexually overstimulated, tempted to lie, not good at focusing for long periods, doesn't like tests, problems with children, blood impurities, heart trouble, reproductive or venereal difficulties, too much heat in stomach

Mars in SIXTH House

Keywords: Warriorlike Activity

Favorable: Strong defensive, service, and protective skills; a builder or dealer in land; military and executive abilities; decides quickly; alert to take advantage; inexhaustible energy—mentally, sexually, and physically; evangelist, propagator, healer, surgeon, warrior, best at short-term tasks

Unfavorable: Overactive, drinks or takes drugs to slow down, extravagant, provokes arguments, deceptive, sexual predator, takes advantage of others, reckless, lacks long-term vision, loses through helpers, surgical operations, blood impurity, rashes, fevers, skin eruptions, heart troubles, broken bones, accidents, poisonings, trouble with relatives, hyperacidity, trouble with pets or small animals

Mars in SEVENTH House

Keywords: Stimulated Partnerships

Favorable: Clever, gets people to do their most, goal oriented, smart businessman or trader, short travels, charming, persuasive, stimulating, impressive, passionate about life, acts spontaneously or by reflex, likes strong-willed and vigorous partners

Unfavorable: Provokes fights or disputes, selfish as partner, attracts angry or aggressive partners, lacks sustaining power, impolite, inconsiderate, falls in love or gets intimate too quickly, haphazard business practices, possessive, trapper, headaches or head injuries, reproductive ailments

Mars in EIGHTH House
Keywords: A Burning Life

Favorable: High vitality, martial spirit, expressive, active; helps and gets help from others; idealistic, passionate; skills in life extension and health activities; involvement or interest in hidden matters, research, detective work, spying, etc.; love of the extraordinary

Unfavorable: Worried, vulnerable, hyperactive, aggressive yet shy, both a victim and a victimizer, lack of self-sufficiency, broken relationships, problems with siblings and neighbors, reckless with money, lack of support from others, sudden endings, scandal ridden, penalized, substance abuse, accidents, burns, poisonings, surgeries, thefts, reproductive inflammations, shortened life, inflamed body

Mars in NINTH House
Keywords: Active Fortune and Philosophy

Favorable: Active in long-distance traveling, builds a fast fortune, siblings prosper, leader in spiritual and philosophical undertakings, executive, lawyer, publishing activities, zealot, active father, free thinker, expansive vision, self-sufficient, likes adventuresome partners (3rd from 7th)

Unfavorable: Trouble with partner's siblings (3rd from 7th); friction or broken relationship with father, guru, or authorities, or they have a stressful life; illnesses for mother (6th from 4th), changes in philosophies and beliefs, skeptical, intolerant of religious differences or religious fanatic, legal troubles and expenses, fast downturns in fortune, accidents while traveling, sciatica, respiratory ailments

Mars in TENTH House
Keywords: Warrior Career

Favorable: Active leader, smart, cheerful, unafraid to innovate, tireless pursuit of goals, takes quick action to get results, self-sufficient, success in mechanical or industrial activities, warrior, best at short-term tasks, performs physical labor or uses the body in work, siblings are important in career and life, famous

Unfavorable: Forceful, pushes too hard at work, frustrated career, too much pioneering, gets into business debts, separation or distance from mother, impatient, interruptions or breaks in career, career trouble through siblings and neighbors, father's career is cut short, knee troubles, acidic, home and car problems, irregular heart

Mars in ELEVENTH House

Keywords: Active Opportunities

Favorable: Quick gains of wealth, optimistic, entrepreneur, charming, many friends and links to influential persons, inspiring, effectual, good cash flow, many opportunities, makes their dreams come true, clever, older siblings prosper

Unfavorable: Financial complications and expenditures; deception or bad advice from friends, older siblings, and people of influence; involved in a fraud or hoax; erratic cash flow, impatience and disagreements with friends and older siblings, friction or disenchanted romances (7th to 5th), ear ailments, fatigue, teeth and gum troubles

Mars in TWELFTH House

Keywords: Losses Through Speed

Favorable: Active in spiritual pursuits, generous, body worker, healer, passionate, benefits through travels and spiritual journeys, rejuvenates through solitude, spiritually innocent; secret worker; active in health, charitable, spiritual, or educational organizations; quick to give pleasure

Unfavorable: Spends too quickly, gets intimate too soon, afraid to lose freedom, repressed energies; danger of hospitalization, imprisonment, fines, penalties, and accusations; troubles in foreign lands; secretive, sleep disorders, divided about celibacy and intimacy, short-term affairs, fevers; troubles with eyes, feet, and digestion; inflammatory conditions, possible lameness, blood disorders

MERCURY IN HOUSES

Mercury in FIRST House

Keywords: Mind-Oriented Disposition

Favorable: Discriminating, cheerful, budget oriented, inventive, debates or questions the issues, conscientious, principled, ethical, religious, philosophical, mathematical or scientific approach, good speaker, resistant to aging, abilities as an astrologer, love of numbers and letters

Unfavorable: Criticizes, worried over trifles, hard to please, too much into details, gets into disputes and arguments, micromanager, takes things too literally, mentally overworked, mind goes too fast, respiratory ailments, mental afflictions, averse to showing affections

Mercury in SECOND House

Keywords: Financial Mind-set

Favorable: Student of philosophy, humorous, clever with finances, prudent, enjoys refined cuisine, pleasant speaker, diplomatic, youthful face, truthful, good with math, business, legal, administration, languages, writing, computers, communication and educational matters, enjoys music and singing

Unfavorable: Mind cannot focus on gaining wealth, unreliable, questionable finances, does not do what they say, spends a long time at the adolescent stage of life, low-paying clerical jobs, speech problems, sensitive mouth and teeth, facial blemishes

Mercury in THIRD House

Keywords: Intellectual Adventurer

Favorable: Good communicator, likes to have fun, drawn to business and clerical activities, skilled at measuring, good relations with siblings and neighbors, scrupulous and painstaking worker; writes about philosophy, religion, possibly astrology

Unfavorable: Overly detailed, loses the big picture, timid, spends too much time reading and thinking rather than acting, lack of physicality, fatigued, mind is full of chatter, worrywart, vacillates; pain in the neck, shoulders, and hands; respiratory weakness, skin ailments

Mercury in FOURTH House

Keywords: Imaginative Feelings

Favorable: Learns through books and lectures, knowledgeable, interested in educational and philosophical matters, creative, imaginative, cheerful, devoted to family and loved ones, agricultural researcher; teacher of math, music, science, languages, and other intellectual pursuits; good-humored, kind, considerate

Unfavorable: Intellect prevents expression of feelings, anxious, worrisome mother, tension or instability in the home, changes residences frequently, flat emotions, cleverness turns to unscrupulousness, not inclined to exert enough effort, nervous stomach, pain in mid region, heart pain, hypersensitive, hypochondriac

Mercury in FIFTH House

Keywords: Focused Intellect

Favorable: Good business and organizing skills, refined, philosophical mind-set, interest in spiritual advancement, concerned for children, competitive with games and intellectual challenges, good sense of humor, musical and entertainment interests, mathematical, scientific

Unfavorable: Cold, scheming, poor planning, lack of affection, worried, too mental, distant relationship with children, few children, low virility, makes exacting demands, unfeeling in business, mental or nervous system problems for children, ailments with the nervous system, low fertility, physically weak or timid, nervous stomach

Mercury in SIXTH House

Keywords: Warrior's Mind

Favorable: Outsmarts any opposition, clear-minded, executive, clever planner and strategist, provides good service, desires to purify and improve things, quick mind and speech, argues for or convinces others about their needs, industrious, dedicated, thinks about the results they want, successful

Unfavorable: Argumentative, likes to pick intellectual fights, trouble with servants and helpers, broken education, mentally violent, frustrated, skin ailments, nervous disorders, mental problems, foot problems, more mental than physical with sex, lack of fertility, disinterested in physical activity

Mercury in SEVENTH House

Keywords: Intellectual Partnerships

Favorable: Clever in getting what they want out of business and relationships, artful, follows a good business plan, respects the rules of engagement; good with math, writing, and communications; skills as an astrologer, minister, religious worker, humorous, impish, approaches relationships first from the mind

Unfavorable: Relationships serve a functional purpose, low sexual desire, angry if exact requirements are not met, too selective to get married early, critical of partners, trouble through lack of forethought in written documents and contracts; partner is weak, unstable, or anxious; bladder and kidney sensitivity, low back pain, skin ailments

Mercury in EIGHTH House

Keywords: Transcendental Thinking

Favorable: Quick mind, good research abilities, mentally vigorous; spiritual, fantasy, science fiction, and mystical interests; deep meditations and philosophical insights; psychic; astrologer; interest in the dead, dying, and afterlife; possible inheritance from relatives outside the immediate family

Unfavorable: Mentally hypersensitive, mentally abused and abusing, tormented early life, conscienceless, unethical, holds people to the letter of the law, trouble for or through relatives, deranged, disorderly, fixated on death, nervous and mental disorders, skin ailments, respiratory complications

Mercury in NINTH House

Keywords: Wise Thinking

Favorable: Legal mind, exacting, philosophical, scientific, editing, writing, publishing, judicial, involved in higher education and thinking, long travel for business, diplomat, morally correct, good fortune, innovative thinker, smart father, gets high-minded guru

Unfavorable: Immobilized from trying to be too correct or fair, lack of concentration, legal complications through bad contracts, troubles with higher education; misunderstandings with father, guru, and authorities; lacks philosophical center; doubtful, conflicted, sciatica, mental problems for father, hip problems

Mercury in TENTH House

Keywords: Intellectual Occupations

Favorable: Pursues a mind-oriented career such as writing, speaking, editing, administering, counseling, engineering, designing, science, teaching, etc.; thoughtful, discriminating, cheerful, philosophical, seeks to understand before acting, good organizer, methodical, earns through learning

Unfavorable: Indecisive, fights for meaningless details, lack of stamina, mentally exhausted, perceived by others as weak or ineffectual, unstable career, deceptive, speaks too quickly or out of turn, lack of correct foresight and planning, obsessive, stuck, nervous disorders, depressed, meek

Mercury in ELEVENTH House
Keywords: Clever with Opportunities and Profits

Favorable: Capitalizes on opportunities, friendly, cultivates contacts with influential and intellectual people, protected by alliances with powerful people, smart at managing cash flow, intelligent older sibling and friends; skills in math, science, and astrology; successful business person, politically astute

Unfavorable: Poor financial management, weak cash flow, ingratiate themselves to friends for support, unreliable, lack of responsiveness, deceitful friends or dishonest with friends, listens to wrong advice, follows wild schemes and dreams, taken in by misplaced logic and bizarre conspiracies

Mercury in TWELFTH House
Keywords: Liberation Through Knowledge

Favorable: Oriented to liberation and enlightenment; possible member of a spiritual, charitable, educational, or health organization; generous, self-sacrificing, unbounded mind, interest in philosophy and faraway places and states of mind, educated out of country, derives pleasures mentally

Unfavorable: Fooled by false gurus, gullible in general, lack of confidence, poor focus, discontinuous thinking, lack of effort or power to accomplish, worried, victimized, martyr, poor memory, narrow-minded and petty due to incapacity to think big, low sex drive, depressed, skin ailments, foot problems, mental disorders, imprisoned by own mind, paralysis both physically and mentally, clumsy

JUPITER IN HOUSES

Jupiter in FIRST House
Keywords: Expansive Disposition

Favorable: Protected, cheerful, easygoing, knows the wise thing to do, has good children or is good with children, generous, educated, natural educator, consultant, minister, conversant with all forms of knowledge, sets positive goals and attains them, uplifting, correct vision for the future, wealthy, benevolent life

Unfavorable: Overly optimistic, slow to take obvious gains, feels "bulletproof," lethargic, acts more holy than they really are, fraudulent, poor finances, problems with support, husband problems for females, blood sugar problems, liver ailments, kidney dysfunction, skin troubles, fat and fluid buildup

Jupiter in SECOND House

Keywords: Expansion of Wealth

Favorable: Prosperous, good with language, comfortable, polite, friendly, gets wealth, gourmet, humorous, good study habits, very giving; benefits from education, justice system, money handling, children, philosophy, food, precious metals, and artful endeavors; has a good family

Unfavorable: Wasteful with money, spends in anticipation of incoming money, overspends on charitable and spiritual causes, poor study habits, lazy, inactive, sluggish from too much food and drink, ailments of liver, jaundiced; swollen mouth, face, and throat; thyroid ailments

Jupiter in THIRD House

Keywords: Wise Determination

Favorable: Good writer, editor, speaker, schoolteacher, artist, consultant, salesperson, minister, philosopher; has opulent adventures and travels; siblings prosper; good neighbors; full of determination; believes in the support of nature, writes books and articles

Unfavorable: Unmotivated in general, unexcited, boring, indifferent, doesn't follow through, poor attention to details, low on energy and determination, lack of appreciation between siblings, losses through laziness, lack of resources, ear ailments, tumors or swollen neck, shoulders, fingers

Jupiter in FOURTH House

Keywords: Expansion Through Knowledge and Family

Favorable: Contented, abundant fixed assets; good home, family, children, and mother; vehicles, clothing, success in land dealings and agriculture, educator, well educated, money from things below the earth, landlord, enjoys vacations in posh resorts

Unfavorable: Trouble with children (4th is 12th from the 5th), excessive expenditures on education and home life, insufficient comfort and basic necessities, poor shelter and clothing, lack of education, inattentive mother, lack of responsibility toward home and family, heart problems, breast or chest swelling or tumors

Jupiter in FIFTH House

Keywords: Blessings of Intellect and Children

Favorable: Successful businessperson, leader, theorist; drawn to higher forms of spiritual and educational thought; noble; a guide or guru; playful; enjoys amusements and sports; affectionate, romantic, imaginative; success in speculation; good children or good with children; for women, indicates a loving husband

Unfavorable: Inattentive to children and to loved ones, religious hypocrite, disingenuous, unsound thinker, unreliable, not quick to take opportunities, careless in business, irregular in meditation, lack of romance; for women, a poor husband; liver trouble, poor digestion (especially fats and oils)

Note: Some authors say that a karaka planet in a karaka house is not good (such as Jupiter, the indicator or karaka for children, is not good in the 5th house, the karaka or indicator house for children). Other authors claim that this rule applies mainly to the Sun and Moon; whatever the case, it is not as bad as often claimed.

Jupiter in SIXTH House

Keywords: Wise in Service

Favorable: Earnings through service, expanded capacity as a healer, gets good helpers, conquers opponents elegantly, legal abilities, faces problems with optimism, humorous, clever at protecting their interests, jocular, military-type consultant or teacher, power broker, resistant to disease

Unfavorable: Dissipated, corrupt, low ethics, dishonored; lack of motivation and planning; doubtful; indistinct fortune; little optimism; low resistance to disease; troubles with relations; conflicts with helpers, gurus, and teachers; for women, problems with husband; digestive ailments; liver illnesses; fat, fluid, or swelling problems

Jupiter in SEVENTH House

Keywords: Expansion Through Partnering

Favorable: Deals well with people, able to attract and maintain good partners, good marriage, fortune building business interests, travels on spiritual quests, artistic capacity, proficient, learned, knows how to wait, gains through legal transactions and contracts

Unfavorable: Wasteful and reckless in business, lack of alignment with partners, unenthusiastic, wants wealth without effort, likes the attention of romantic or sexual partners, partner has weight problems, partners lack initiative, weak husband for women, lack of fertility, weak back and kidneys

Jupiter in EIGHTH House

Keywords: Expansion Through the Transcendental

Favorable: Earns through other people's money or support, good researcher, medical diagnostician, delves deeply into spiritual mysteries, teaches secret knowledge, military or corporate strategist, gets mystical gurus or teachers

Unfavorable: Unhappy with partner's approach to money, worried, apprehensive, feels lack of support or recognition, manipulates others for money, lack of self-promotion, timid, poor finances, lack of gracefulness, phony spiritualist, low resistance to disease, husband has financial and sexual problems, troubles with children, liver ailments, poor grooming, gets fat or puffy over time, jaundice

Jupiter in NINTH House

Keywords: Expansion Through High Knowledge

Favorable: Gains the highest forms of knowledge, gets good teachers and gurus, traveling expands fortune, good children and father, father is learned, philanthropic, compassionate, learned in scriptures and ancient wisdom, gets published, overall good fortune and personal power, optimistic, accepting

Unfavorable: Conflicted over the need for freedom and the restraints of conventional religion, extravagant, thinks too big, impractical, religious fanatic, troubles while traveling, weak fortune for father, children degrade wealth, ultraconservative, loses through charities, lack of effort to gain wealth

Jupiter in TENTH House

Keywords: Occupations of Wisdom

Favorable: Expansive career; skilled in consulting, counseling, judging, teaching, philosophy, spirituality, financial planning; father or guru as well as the person has good reputation; ethical, legal, follows the standards; contented; good children; for women, husband does well, earns through learning

Unfavorable: Overly optimistic, lack of sufficient application, poor reputation, reckless with money, problems with expansion of wealth, difficulties with children and family, low status, hurts self by being too generous, problems with the law or with following standards of behavior, father has difficulties

Jupiter in ELEVENTH House
Keywords: Growth of Opportunities and Profits
Favorable: Good cash flow; has the capacity to develop opportunities; perceives positive outcomes; friendly; benefits from older siblings or people who play that role, as well as influential people; civic-minded, altruistic, openhanded, inspiring, a dreamer
Unfavorable: Troubles with overexpansion or developing too rapidly, loss of opportunity through slow reaction or follow-up, lazy or unsupportive friends and older siblings, lack of money management, children drain resources, immoderate pleasure seeker, husband has cash flow problems (for women), ear or hearing problems, fatty heart

Jupiter in TWELFTH House
Keywords: Liberation Through Knowledge
Favorable: Seeker of liberation; benefits from monastic lifestyle; worker in a place of healing, or a correctional institution or an ashram or spiritual community; supportive; spiritual children; husband is drawn to path of enlightenment (for women), gains in foreign lands or with foreign connections, goes on pilgrimages, lives a full and simple life
Unfavorable: Lack of interest in material development, overindulgent, poor finances, educational losses, martyr, feels betrayed or unsupported, works as an underling, hypocritical show of religious interest, beggar, blood sugar problems, fat or fluid buildup, trouble with children, poor husband for a woman

VENUS IN HOUSES

Venus in FIRST House
Keywords: Disposition of Beauty and Love
Favorable: Skillful in relating to others, charming, artistic, refined, cultivated, drawn to the comforts of wealth and pleasure, good finances and fortune, naturally seductive or persuasive, expanded

sensuality and sexuality, knows how to please, strong affections, devoted, friendly

Unfavorable: Susceptible to inappropriate sensual and sexual temptations, overindulgence in gratification, unmet expectations in love, tries too hard to fulfill desires, sexually out of balance with mate, poor finances, blood sugar problems, reproductive ailments, urinary problems

Venus in SECOND House

Keywords: Refined Tastes

Favorable: Fortunate, pleasant family life, persuasive speaker, poet, musician, singer, artistic, socially adept, language skills, good study habits, nice to listen to, good manners, likes good food and sweet things, refined tastes, strong vision, money handler, makes money through the items and affairs of women

Unfavorable: Losses through feminine energy, spends too much for pleasure, social pretender, money does not build up well, family discomforts; ailments related to the mouth, teeth, and gums; facial problems, poor dietary habits, too much sugar, sweet talker

Venus in THIRD House

Keywords: Artistic Expression

Favorable: Playful, knows how to have fun, adventuresome, short travels, persuasive; good at communicating, corresponding, marketing, advertising, and sales; actor, dancer, active artistry, creative writer, gives seminars or speeches on art or women's issues, love of siblings, close friends and neighbors, journalist, computer artist

Unfavorable: Lack of motivation or self-control, finds hard work distasteful, wearisome short distance travels, lack of comfort or wealth for siblings, partner (wife) is overly motivated, dominated by loved ones, artistic ventures are obstructed

Venus in FOURTH House

Keywords: Feelings of Love

Favorable: Gracious and comfortable lifestyle, love of family and mother, nurturing, encouraging, affectionate, attentive, interest in homes, educator, well educated, artistic; drawn to elegant and luxurious homes, clothing, vehicles, etc.; well liked, patriotic, seeks love of God and the divine

Unfavorable: Insufficiency of love and comfort, inattentive mother or as a mother, yearning for love, drawn to people lacking in love, little education, car and home problems, insurance troubles, careless with love and money, reproductive problems, breast and chest ailments, heart and valve difficulties

Venus in FIFTH House

Keywords: Mind of Love

Favorable: Advisor, lawyer, business acuity, companionable, social skills, charming, persuasive, fun-loving, benefits from meditation and scriptures; connections to field of games, entertainment, athletics, and amusements; intelligent, skilled in relationships, romantic, good love of mate and children

Unfavorable: Careless in love, not watchful in business, longs for romance and personal attention, unmindful mate, troubles through romantic interludes, lack of skill or interest in love, fertility problems, flirtatious, difficulty with sweets

Venus in SIXTH House

Keywords: Stimulated to Love

Favorable: Ready to fight and defend what they love; engaged in administrative, legal, and healing activities; sense of service; keeps up to date; enjoys strong-willed partners and vigorous activities; passionate, vigilant, partnerships can improve life, loves pets and small animals

Unfavorable: Views love as a conquest, conflicts with partners, perverse enjoyment of fighting, addicted to love, likes aggressive mates, lack of dignity in relationships and in finances, blood sugar problems, poor grooming, reproductive complications, venereal diseases, kidney trouble, stagnant veins and nerves, lacking in beauty, skin ailments, pet or small animal problems

Venus in SEVENTH House

Keywords: Love of Relationships

Favorable: Capable of relating to anybody about anything; likes to have relationships—especially in terms of romance or sexual attentions and pleasures; attracts good partners, likes attractive partners, persuasive, good business skills, artistic, balanced, gains from marriage and partnerships, sexually skilled

Unfavorable: Will say anything to satisfy their desires, quick to get intimate, lack of staying power in love, financial problems, lack of love from mate, poor grooming, sexual dysfunction, reproductive afflictions, urinary tract ailments, kidney weakness

Venus in EIGHTH House

Keywords: Love of the Sublime

Favorable: Interest in secret knowledge of all forms, researcher, detective, natural about love, tantric, gains through partners and loved ones, supported, given favors, shy or modest on the outside but passionate on the inside, long life of comfort, loves solitude and the transcendent

Unfavorable: Vulnerable, secrets in love, partners do not disclose, abused in love, abusing, attracted to people disinterested in them, sexual imbalance, inattentive to loved ones or unattended by lovers, might seek attention from own sex, reproductive illnesses and surgeries, breast ailments or complications, eye afflictions, restricted sexual development, loss of loved ones

Venus in NINTH House

Keywords: Love of Higher Knowledge

Favorable: Relates well with others; legal abilities; minister; counselor; emotionally developed; drawn to people of higher learning and ethics; aided by father, guru, and people in authority; gains money and love from long distance travels; gets published; fortunate, grateful for blessings, blesses others

Unfavorable: Feels unfortunate; lack of appreciation from father, guru, and bosses; disenchanted; longs for love; overindulgent; feels bounded by life; legal complications; troubles with higher education; friction with mate's siblings (3rd from 7th); car trouble over long distances; uncomfortable in general; father has reproductive organ ailments; thigh, hip joint, and vein troubles; fat

Venus in TENTH House

Keywords: Occupations of Love and Beauty

Favorable: Good finances, comforts and pleasures, stable relationships, inspires others to success, elegant and refined occupation, nice family life, activities dealing with females and the feminine principle, artful, polite, friendly, easy to like, provides pleasure to others, loves work

Unfavorable: Troubles with females in career or with reputation, unhappy with work, obstructed finances, lack of purpose, lazy about professional life, unrefined level of art, partner obstructs career, disfigurement to knees, joint illness, respiratory ailments, reproductive troubles

Venus in ELEVENTH House

Keywords: Flow of Affluence

Favorable: Good profits and cash flow, money through artistic enterprises or the affairs and activities of women and friends, seduces people into their dreams, well liked by elder siblings and by influential people, well connected socially, creative, inventive, finances get better with experience

Unfavorable: Spends too much on pleasure, poor with money, troubles with females and things of an artful or feminine nature, jealous of others' success, longs for the fulfillment of their dreams, elder siblings and friends create financial problems, partner creates a drain on finances, swollen ankles and veins in lower legs, heart valve problems, poor circulation, obstruction in reproduction

Venus in TWELFTH House

Keywords: Love of Liberation

Favorable: Skillful in providing pleasure to others; carefree; giving; unselfish; liberal in and about love; seeks solitude for rejuvenation; drawn to work in places of healing, correctional institutions, spiritual havens, educational institutes, and charitable organizations; uninhibited in private

Unfavorable: Lack of financial motivations, morally unconstrained, sex or physical pleasure provider, secret or understated romances, lovers are distant, makes up stories to keep love alive, submissive, feels betrayed in love, many lost loves, wasteful with finances, overindulgent in pleasures, sexual diseases, reproductive problems, eye ailments, bladder and kidney troubles

SATURN IN HOUSES

Saturn in FIRST House

Keywords: Focused Disposition

Favorable: Life gets better as time goes on, benefits from working to a schedule, practical, prudent, structured approach to life, goal setter, takes a strong position, always thinking to advance their position, cunning, shrewd, honors confidences, solid and immovable

Unfavorable: Early years are the least happy, has trouble with ambiguity, controls others to diminish variables, selfish, lack of conscience, frustrated, pent-up desires, depressed, isolated, keeps things to themselves, socially inept or a misfit, joint ailments, slow physical development, low resistance to disease, vata imbalance

Saturn in SECOND House

Keywords: Attention to Finances

Favorable: Accumulates wealth over time; economical; calculating; works hard for their money; orderly speech; conservative; defined study habits; money from the old, traditional, and foreign; uses standard processes and practices; simple and traditional choice of foods; moderate family happiness

Unfavorable: Finds it hard to accumulate money, restricted or boring speech, inconsiderate, eats unhealthily, might smoke or take drugs and alcohol, dry and wrinkled face, paralysis of mouth or face, eye problems; poor teeth, lips, and gums; throat trouble, cold and restricted family happiness

Saturn in THIRD House

Keywords: Focused Determination

Favorable: Determined, deliberate, systematic, careful planner, considerate, nice in a formal way, communicates thoroughly, technical writer, conventional in art, cordial relations with siblings and neighbors, finds the best way to do something, good concentration or focus, consolidator

Unfavorable: Restrictions with younger siblings and neighbors, compulsive, plans but is immobilized about taking action, unscrupulous, has little feeling for or awareness of those close to them, communications are hard to understand or overly structured, puts in extremes of effort—none or a lot, restricted hearing or ear problems; joint pain in neck, hands, and shoulders

Saturn in FOURTH House

Keywords: Controlled Emotions

Favorable: Conservative, takes responsibility for family matters, relationship with family and mother improves over time, likes a simple and orderly home, enjoys quiet and natural surroundings, benefits from land and foreign connections, slow and steady growth of fixed assets

Unfavorable: Slow emotional growth, blocked or interrupted education, inexpressive, distressed, joyless, fearful, restrictions with family and with mother, trouble with home and vehicles, retrogressive, health problems as a child, lung and heart problems, breast ailments, cancer, reproductive problems

Saturn in FIFTH House

Keywords: Focused Intelligence

Favorable: Attentive to spiritual practices, follows a tradition-based spiritual movement or guru, drawn into the ancient scriptures, steady frame of mind, best with low-risk speculations, practical point of view, leads a simple life, unassuming, gentle, does their duty in all things

Unfavorable: Setbacks with the government (e.g., IRS) or authority figures, slow mental growth, delays and distance in romance, restrictions with children, feels a lack of fun, not agile in sports, reluctant to disclose, understates problems, obstinate, submissive, heart trouble, pain or operations in midchest or midback, weak digestion

Saturn in SIXTH House

Keywords: Steady in Service

Favorable: Great capacity to serve and do one's duty, good focus, attentive, conscientious assistant, authority on the rules and procedures, detailed, legal, contractual, administrative, healer, righter of wrongs, follows orders to the letter, perseveres to the end, hard to defeat or wear down, benefits with older relatives

Unfavorable: Inflexible, stuck, gets into too much microscopic detail, secretly slanders others, trouble with pets, poor self-promotion, trouble with helpers, respiratory ailments, mental or nervous system disorders, paralysis, digestive stagnation, accidents, slow to heal, vata imbalances

Saturn in SEVENTH House

Keywords: Controlled Partnerships

Favorable: Steady and practical in business dealings, unemotional interpersonal relationships, detached decision-making in trade, dutiful in partnerships, focused on getting the results, relationships improve over time, benefits from partnerships with foreigners and with foreign connections

Unfavorable: Obstructions and delays in forming partnerships, poor in business, restrained emotions, unfeeling, partners struggle financially, deceptive, understates, hides things, functional or businesslike response to sex, lack of libido, sexual organ problems, partner gets sick, kidney troubles, lower back pain

Saturn in EIGHTH House

Keywords: Restricted Life

Favorable: Long life; modest; focuses deeply on the mysteries of life; investigator; researcher; spiritualist; health expert; keeps secrets and confidences; benefits from traditions and old things; works with matters covering the close of life—insurance, mortuary, estate planning, probate, etc.; life is better in the later years

Unfavorable: Called Shani Ashtama (8th Saturn). Intensely possessed with a singular desire; frustrated; worried; shy; loner; lack of support; while fearing abandonment or disappointment, they abandon or disappoint others; abused and abusing; toxic system; scandals; chronic diseases; problems with elimination and reproduction; partner has restricted finances (8th is 2nd to the 7th); vata disorders; troubled early life

Saturn in NINTH House

Keywords: Focus on High Ideals

Favorable: Helps others, analytical, subtle, spiritual, sensible, organized planner, publishes, legal mind, travels to foreign countries, drawn to traditional and ancient belief systems and rituals, spiritually observant, conservative or traditionalistic father and guru, fortune builds over time

Unfavorable: Restrictions, delays, and distance with authority figures—father, guru, employer, government, etc.; resents philosophic control by others; problems with younger siblings and neighbors (6th to the 3rd); father struggles; hip joint troubles; sciatica; liver troubles;

respiratory ailments; problems traveling and in foreign countries; restricted fortune

Saturn in TENTH House

Keywords: Career Over Time

Favorable: Structured, steady, conservative, traditional approach to life, steady growth in career and finances, practical, hardworking, conscientious, benefits in foreign countries, monastic disposition increases with age; interest in old things, common people, and things connected to the earth

Unfavorable: Gets a job position but is shortly knocked out or down, lacks good reputation, uncertain or finds little purpose in life, career related to hard work and servile laboring, restrictions in family life, misfit, drops out of education, doesn't build up career or financial base, moves from place to place, knee problems, arthritic; heart, breast, or chest ailments

Saturn in ELEVENTH House

Keywords: Structured Gains

Favorable: Pursues opportunities in a structured and prudent manner; adds to existing processes and inventions; profits from traditional or established businesses; gains through older siblings, longtime friends, and mature people of influence; interest in the issues of the common man; political savvy

Unfavorable: Friends or older siblings cause obstructions to financial gain, trouble with children, unromantic partner (11th is 5th from 7th), setbacks from partner's speculations, low-level interests, questionable honesty, ear or hearing problems, trouble with children, circulatory troubles

Saturn in TWELFTH House

Keywords: Focus on Liberation

Favorable: Drawn to life in places of seclusion and reparation—hospitals, ashrams, retreats, and prisons; dedicated to the poor; charitable and humanitarian causes; stoic; lives a simple life; many relocations for spiritual reasons; visits faraway places and holy sites

Unfavorable: Lack of financial interest; weary; disinterest or lack of sexual pleasure; gives too much in charity; social misfit; gets lawsuits and personal attacks (12th is 6th from 7th); loses liberty through hospitalization, fines, penalties, or imprisonment; physical debilities involving eyes, feet, teeth, and gums; general uneasiness throughout life—especially childhood

RAHU IN HOUSES

Rahu in FIRST House
Keywords: Unusual or Innovative Behavior
Favorable: Shrewd, cautious, mystical disposition, self-sufficient, warrior energy, self-preserving, accommodating, able to thwart others' negativity, focused on developing personal power and wealth, builds success in alliance with others
Unfavorable: Lives in the shadow of other's success, confused, doubtful, low self-promotion and self-esteem, doesn't have a sense of themselves, not a dependable partner, gets diseases that confuse or mystify doctors, hypochondriac, toxic body, allergies, rashes, blood impurities, headaches and injuries, unusual accidents, odd appearance or behavior

Rahu in SECOND House
Keywords: Destiny Toward Finances
Favorable: Clever in making money, money accumulated from foreign sources, enjoys exotic dinners, uses unusual ornamentation and facial decorations, benefits from foreign languages, unusual speaking abilities, makes money from other people's money—especially partners; trader in currencies, gems, and metals; good liquid assets
Unfavorable: Devious, complains frequently, estranged family, poor study skills, bad eating habits, loses through deception or lack of mindfulness, speaks ill of others, speech problems; ailments of nose, throat, thyroid, mouth, lips, gums, and teeth; facial complaints; takes to smoking, drinking, and drugs

Rahu in THIRD House
Keywords: Innovative Determination
Favorable: Remarkable approach to activity, makes their own way in life, interested in unique forms of communication and self-expression, writer, advertiser, marketer, salesperson, actor, musician,

peculiar siblings, active, successful risk taker, unusual athletic abilities or interests

Unfavorable: Siblings are different, odd, or confused; puts effort into the wrong things or at the wrong time; takes a bizarre approach; outlandish ideas; respiratory problems; ailments to neck, shoulders, and hands; mental or nervous disorders; skin diseases

Rahu in FOURTH House

Keywords: Shadowed Feelings

Favorable: Liking for the unconventional; unusual or foreign dress and home decoration; gains through real estate, land, buildings, hotels, cars, clothing, and education; unique mother and family life; innovative educator

Unfavorable: Separation or misalignment with family, unfaithful, changeful, unsettled and confused emotions, jealous, possessive, worried, unfulfilled, disrupted education, fearful of commitment, attracted to people who aren't interested in commitment, recluse, lung and chest complaints, surgery on chest or breasts, heart problems, infertility

Rahu in FIFTH House

Keywords: Shadowed Intellect

Favorable: Spiritual being; drawn to mantras, mystical chants, and performances; interested in transcendental knowledge; attracted to foreign romances; can take care of themselves; likes unusual games, play, and amusements; exceptional intellect

Unfavorable: Deceptive, confused, shy, low self-esteem, misunderstandings in romance, poor in speculation and business, displeasure with the government (e.g., IRS), problems with children (abortions, miscarriages), trouble with studies; blocked tubes, veins, and arteries; heart troubles; poor digestion

Rahu in SIXTH House

Keywords: Clever Warrior

Favorable: Can think of a creative solution to any problem, warrior, meets opposition with courage and determination, comes out ahead in the end, provides exceptional service, uses unusual medical and healing approaches, has the stamina and intellectual resources to succeed

Unfavorable: Fiery temperament; combative, adversarial, quick to pick a fight; not trustworthy; smoking, drinking, and drug problems (to reduce stress); pets get sick; problems with mother's relatives (especially aunts and uncles); digestive troubles; inflammatory diseases that are hard to diagnose

Rahu in SEVENTH House

Keywords: Foreign Partnerships

Favorable: Benefits from nontraditional, unusual, or foreign partnerships; partner is out of the ordinary, foreign, or was met while traveling; partner works or lives far from home

Unfavorable: Drawn to foreign, unusual, even bizarre relationships; partner is deceptive and untrustworthy; confusion or secrets in relationships; gets a dysfunctional partner of lower wealth and health; loses through mistakes or deception in contracts, subject to divorce or separation, venereal diseases, reproductive problems

Rahu in EIGHTH House

Keywords: Destiny Toward the Unknown

Favorable: Capacity to investigate and understand sublime knowledge, interested in uncovering secrets, detective, researcher, good diagnostic skills, unconventional healer, can purify themselves for life extension and resistance to disease, is sexually energetic, gains money through others' support and goodwill (wills, legacies, insurance, etc.)

Unfavorable: Doubtful, disturbed, deceptive, takes money with little or no capacity to repay, overaroused, secret sexual dysfunction or perversities, body is filled with toxins (drugs, alcohol, diseases), diseases are difficult to diagnose, urinary and eliminatory ailments, has rare diseases, blood or glandular impurities, skin rashes, burns or discoloration, allergies

Rahu in NINTH House

Keywords: Innovations in Higher Knowledge

Favorable: Thinks in ingenious ways, capable of rarefied spiritual and intellectual thinking, siddha, subtle, comfortable with intangible realities, takes unusual approaches in law, education, and philosophy, educated in foreign lands, publishes esoteric knowledge, exotic travel

Unfavorable: Misunderstandings with and confusion from authorities (father, guru, boss, etc.), schemer, litigant, fugitive, outsider, acts holier than they are, desperado, keeps their bizarre philosophies private at first, liver ailments, hearing problems, hip and sacroiliac dysfunction, joint trouble

Rahu in TENTH House
Keywords: Unusual Occupations
Favorable: Success in foreign undertakings; activities associated with toxins, chemicals, pharmaceutical products, exotic energy (nuclear, turbine, etc.); waste removal; does unusual, secret, or confidential work; hard worker; resolute; career and finances grow over time; lives in remote or distant lands
Unfavorable: Lives in the shadow of others' success and reputation, confused about life purpose, family problems, weird car troubles, underpaid, lack of respect or understanding from others, devious, doesn't finish things, unscrupulous schemes, deluded, naïve, father is a stranger, knee problems, stagnant body, joint pain, nervousness, dry skin and wrinkles

Rahu in ELEVENTH House
Keywords: Innovative Profits and Opportunities
Favorable: Shrewd at cash flow management; benefits from friends—especially foreign friends; success with items that are related to chemicals, toxins, purification technology; innovative, gets unusual opportunities, develops remarkable strategies and philosophies, inspiring in a peculiar way
Unfavorable: Cleverness degrades to unscrupulousness, would rather take money than earn it, thinks up bizarre concepts, deceptive or confused friends, older sibling has problems, reproductive complications, ear ailments, problems with teeth and gums

Rahu in TWELFTH House
Keywords: Resourceful Liberator
Favorable: Works in foreign lands as an educator, healer, philanthropist, and spiritual seeker; works in secret or in confidence; capable of handling rough or unrefined people; works hard; monastic; helps others become "enlightened" or pure; spiritual journeys; manages always to succeed

Unfavorable: Gains are dashed away at the last minute, caught in unscrupulous transactions, losses through foreigners or in foreign lands, loner, disconnected from reality, lack of comforts and pleasures, asks others for help, becomes obscure, trouble from parasites, numbness or loss of sensation in a limb, eye problems, confusion, vata imbalance

KETU IN HOUSES

Ketu in FIRST House
Keywords: Quickly Changing Disposition
Favorable: Seeks a high spiritual destiny; efforts are geared toward self-liberation of any form—especially moksha; creative and action-oriented perspective; adaptable, ingenious
Unfavorable: Many surprises in life, reckless or imprudent in personal pursuits, inconsistent efforts, not open to advice, driven by desire to change, unsettled, impatient, hypersensitive, not satisfied, gets diseases that are difficult to diagnose or that defy conventional healing processes

Ketu in SECOND House
Keywords: Surprising Wealth
Favorable: Unusual ability with languages, remarkable speaking style or ability, liking for exotic or extraordinary foods, spiritually oriented family, builds up finances in peculiar ways
Unfavorable: Unsophisticated speech, ups and downs in finances, doesn't have good money-saving skills, poor study habits, deceptive, family relationships are broken, doesn't eat healthfully or eats at irregular times; ailments of the face, throat, teeth, and general mouth area; vision problems

Ketu in THIRD House
Keywords: Unbounded Determination
Favorable: Adaptable to any circumstances, daring, ready for adventure and challenges, flexible outlook on life, quick to master a multitude of pursuits, accomplishes things quickly, liking for artistic expressions, mimic, chameleon, can make friends with anyone they want

Unfavorable: Lack of determination, inconsistent, tricky, tries to do too much, poor at setting their expectations with others, problems with the siblings and neighbors, mental imbalance, ear and hearing problems; ailments or damage to neck, shoulder, arms, or hands; respiratory conditions; skin troubles

Ketu in FOURTH House

Keywords: Versatile Emotions

Favorable: Emotionally pliable, adjusts to changes in domestic life, educated in unusual subjects, spiritual base, develops curious emotional ties

Unfavorable: Changes residence or lives in remote regions, early separation from the mother, seems disconnected, lacks lasting personal emotional ties, nervous, broken education, problems or accidents with vehicles, irregular heartbeat, surgery on the breast or chest area

Ketu in FIFTH House

Keywords: Unbounded Intellect

Favorable: Benefits from scriptural knowledge, practices spiritual techniques, liking for unusual amusements, feels a spiritual love for others, spiritual destiny carried over from past lives

Unfavorable: Broken or unfulfilled romantic love, dishonest, bursts of attention, poor results with speculation, mental problems (some say from spirits), trouble with children, problems with authorities—especially regarding taxes, restless in meditation, heart ailments, poor indigestion

Ketu in SIXTH House

Keywords: Adaptable Defender

Favorable: Versatile, ingenious, deals well with ambiguity or uncertainty, intuitive, extraordinary approach to solving problems, success in conflict resolution, wins battles by subtle means, earns through teaching spiritual knowledge or providing service of a spiritual nature

Unfavorable: In and out of conflicts, gets into debts, unforeseen losses, mental instability, bizarre dreams, sleepwalking or talking, afraid of the unknown, accidents, unstable or delicate health, exotic diseases (parasites, rashes, etc.); diseases are difficult to diagnose and are often of a "psychic" or spiritual origin

Ketu in SEVENTH House

Keywords: Variable Relationships

Favorable: Has a spiritual partner and could motivate the person to go on spiritual journeys to interesting and out-of-the-way places, ingenious business strategies, does business in unusual locales, partner is flexible and innovative

Unfavorable: Unstable, ailing, or unreliable partner; unable to maintain a committed relationship; reckless or inconsistent in forming agreements and contracts with others; surprised by the advent of reproductive or venereal diseases; inconsistent libido or vitality—can swing high and low; tired from constant traveling

Ketu in EIGHTH House

Keywords: Mystical Knowledge Seeker

Favorable: Ability to comprehend subtle and esoteric knowledge, likes to uncover hidden things, gets money suddenly through unforeseen sources, benefits from solitude, clever at getting money or support from other people

Unfavorable: Depends on others, treated disrespectfully, swings between being docile and agitated, deceived and defrauded, can be both an attacker and a victim, partner has poor financial skills and saves little, serious illnesses from peculiar diseases, diseases are not diagnosed properly, accidents, fevers, burns, cuts, reproduction and elimination ailments

Ketu in NINTH House

Keywords: Unbounded Knowledge

Favorable: Adaptable perspective on life, explores many different philosophies, spiritual tendencies, travels to shrines and religious sites

Unfavorable: Unstable fortune; changes religions or philosophies throughout life; up-and-down relationship with father, guru, and authorities; doesn't finish studies at higher education level; shifts point of view to fit the circumstances; travels or changes residence too frequently; lower back and hip pain

Ketu in TENTH House

Keywords: Multifaceted Career

Favorable: Spiritual orientation, capacity to develop higher states of consciousness, travels for spiritual purposes, has the intelligence and fortitude to adapt to changing circumstances, clever, flexible

Unfavorable: Gets both respect and disrespect from others, lack of self-identity, constant change of status and career, uncertain about purpose in life, broken relationship with father, troubles with authority figures, employers don't evaluate their performance properly, knee and joint problems

Ketu in ELEVENTH House

Keywords: Multiple Opportunities and Profits

Favorable: Gets wealth by taking advantage of opportunities arising from reorganizations and chaotic situations, makes money in bursts, amuses friends, clever, partner benefits from spiritual practices, children come as a surprise (Ketu is 5th to the 7th)

Unfavorable: Variable or inconstant relationship with friends and older siblings; unreliable as a friend; loses money through risky or pioneering-type enterprises; cash flow is up and down; makes money in hidden, mysterious, or devious ways; loss of children or children are unstable; accidents and ailments of the lower leg

Ketu in TWELFTH House

Keywords: Innovative Liberation

Favorable: Has the capacity to attain enlightenment, spends time in seclusion for spiritual growth, brings a mystical element to sexual experience, travels, goes on distant pilgrimages

Unfavorable: Spends erratically, lives off others' goodwill, inconsistent, mind is disconnected from the world, unable to maintain an intimate relationship, self-isolating, appears holy but has a secret side, insufficient financial focus, peculiar ailments of the feet, ear ailments

CHAPTER SEVEN

PLANETARY RULERSHIPS
(ADHIPATIS)

Each house of the chart represents a certain set of life activities and characteristics. For example, the first house represents the body and one's general disposition, and the second house represents accumulation of money, speech, food, etc. Each house has a ruling planet, much as a house has a landlord, or a country a king, both being rulers of sorts. That ruling planet will carry much of the meaning of the house that they rule to the house that they occupy. The strength and quality of the ruling planets will influence the favorable or unfavorable manner in which the characteristics of the houses are displayed.

The linkage of one house via its ruler to another house and its corresponding interpretation is a form of a planetary yoga. Knowledge of the effects of rulership placements is a key component for correct chart interpretation. To find which planets rule which signs, see the table in chapter 2.

Once again, for more advanced readers, some of the following significations have been explained parenthetically; see Judging from Karaka Planets in chapter 4 for an explanation.

RULERS OF THE FIRST HOUSE

Ruler of First in FIRST
Keywords: Focus on the Self
Favorable: Independent, strong sense of purpose in life, self-sufficient, leader, healthy and vital, good stamina, blessed with good beginnings
Unfavorable: Selfish, egotistical, tendency to ignore others, self-seeking attitude can lead to multiple marriages or partnerships

Ruler of First in SECOND
Keywords: Financial Focus
Favorable: Individual efforts result in profits; money handler— especially skilled in accumulating money and managing liquid assets; generous with money; impressive speaker; family is a source of pride and devotion; straightforward; speaks the truth; good study habits; eats well; strong eyesight and teeth
Unfavorable: Focuses on self to detriment of family, money matters become a problem, lack of attention to studies, poor diet and teeth, eye ailments

Ruler of First in THIRD
Keywords: Determined Personality
Favorable: Siblings and very close friends and neighbors are an important part of life and contribute to progress; friendly, humorous, courageous; skills in writing, lecturing, and communicating; likes adventures and sports; good artistic expression; strong desires and motivations; strives for the highest attainments; travels a lot close to home
Unfavorable: Tries too hard to succeed; aggressive; conflicts with siblings and neighbors; frustrated; efforts don't get results; although interested, has only minor artistic and athletic skills; poor self-promotion; ailments of neck, shoulders, and hands; problems with anxiety

Ruler of First in FOURTH

Keywords: Focus on the Family

Favorable: Interest in education; success in agriculture, gardening, real estate; has good home, clothes, and vehicles; has a large amount of fixed assets (things that would take a big down payment or more than two years to pay off); emotionally balanced and strong; seeks spiritual development; does well with insurance

Unfavorable: Emotional problems; trouble with or lack of support from the mother; family problems in general; broken or insufficient education; has trouble obtaining costly possessions such as home, car, nice clothes, etc.; trouble with agriculture and related items; heart and chest problems

Ruler of First in FIFTH

Keywords: Focus on Speculations

Favorable: Has a lot of blessings carried over from previous lives, fame without effort, interested in spiritual practices and the study of scriptures, knows to do the right thing, playful, likes games and amusements, romantic, gets good children, speculations pay off, good intellect

Unfavorable: Can seem to get away with bad living but will stumble over time, feels too restless to meditate or practice spiritual methods, trouble with dating and romance, speculations fail, possible loss of child or trouble with children, dishonest, trouble with the government (e.g., IRS or taxes)

Ruler of First in SIXTH

Keywords: Sense of Service

Favorable: Strong capacity to deal with opposition and adversity, comes out ahead in conflicts, industrious, energetic, hard worker, skilled in defending and protecting, high sense of service, drawn to healing, good with animals, legal sense, benefits from mother's siblings—aunts and uncles (6th is 3rd to the 4th), good resistance to disease

Unfavorable: Struggles, adversarial, deceptive, gets into debt, has lawsuits or personal attacks; impatient, aggressive; takes special diets; weak digestion or hyperacidity; prone to inflammatory diseases, accidents, and injuries; may drink or take drugs to try to calm down; pets do not thrive

Ruler of First in SEVENTH

Keywords: Orientation to Partnerships

Favorable: Skilled in relating to people, natural ability to bring pleasure to their partners, gets help from partners, gets an attractive and supportive partner, strong desires to relate and be intimate, wealth is linked to the wealth of their partners, partner is healthy

Unfavorable: Gives in too much to please others, loses their money to partners who become a burden, encounters problems while traveling or while out of the country, sexual desires are sometimes too strong, makes many partnerships, overidealizes the partner, might become monastic in later life, partner suffers from various ailments

Ruler of First in EIGHTH

Keywords: Support for the Self

Favorable: Curious to know about hidden, ancient, mystical, and secret things; gets good support from others; may win at gambling and lotteries; gets insurance settlements, legacies, and alimonies; partner's wealth is helpful; strong sexual vitality; overall vigor; long life; healers

Unfavorable: Vulnerable; lack of support from others; abused and/ or abuser—attacker and/or victim; lack of morals; too shy; chronic poor health; worried a lot; mental imbalance; fatigued; lack of confidence in new situations or new residences; toxiphobic; reproductive and venereal diseases; turbulent endings

Ruler of First in NINTH

Keywords: Fortunate Existence

Favorable: Fortunate, ethical, good finances; interested in philosophy; truthful; gets support from father, guru, and authority figures; advanced education; does well in law and matters of justice; works at the university level of education; many long-distance voyages out of the country; has good credit from previous lives (9th is 5th to the 5th)

Unfavorable: Does not get all the fortunate breaks in life; doesn't do well in college; father struggles or has health problems; trouble with the law and with authorities; may not pay enough attention to making a living while following a spiritual path; troubles overseas or on long-distance journeys

Ruler of First in TENTH

Keywords: Works for the Self

Favorable: Independent, self-sufficient, prefers to work for himself, self-starter, good success in career, sense of life purpose or dharma, obtains a good reputation, has good character and position in life, plenty of personal power, leader, educated, good finances and plenty of valuable possessions

Unfavorable: Doesn't work well under others, does not prepare or educate themselves sufficiently to work for themselves, reputation is lowered by some unfortunate event, wants to be a leader and famous but does not rise that high, father's reputation is clouded, career troubles, might work for weak bosses

Ruler of First in ELEVENTH

Keywords: Life of Profits

Favorable: Good cash flow and profits, benefits from friends and influential persons, does well with business, fulfills their dreams, gets lots of opportunities for profit and advancement, partner's blessings are magnified through spiritual practices and the study of scriptures

Unfavorable: Defrauded or disappointed by friends and older siblings, poor cash flow, inability to fulfill desires, lack of opportunities, partner creates trouble with children and causes problems with speculations

Ruler of First in TWELFTH

Keywords: Unbounded Existence

Favorable: Seeks a spiritual life; charitable; volunteer; works in ashrams, hospitals, clinics, nursing homes, correctional institutions, and other places of confinement; travels to far-off pilgrimages; able to derive much joy from sexual experiences; possibility for enlightenment; transcends; sleeps well

Unfavorable: Poor health; many losses; financial troubles; not good in business; feels disconnected from world; gets betrayed; acts like a martyr; too generous; poor sleep; doesn't get much pleasure from sex or intimate activities; gets fines, punishments, and penalties; secretive; clumsy; problems with the feet

RULERS OF THE SECOND HOUSE

Ruler of Second in FIRST

Keywords: Money for One's Self

Favorable: Sound earning capacity and ability to handle money; makes independent efforts to accumulate money and other, more liquid assets; speaks well; influences through the voice; sings or recites; attracts others through the face; may be good with languages; good dental health; is generally happy with their family; inclined to study and gather data prior to taking action

Unfavorable: May put their own interests above those of their family, poor study habits, diet is not sound or does not eat regularly, needs to improve financial skills, tendency to not speak well of others

Ruler of Second in SECOND

Keywords: Financial Completeness

Favorable: Financial blessings are uplifted significantly by this position; has a good diet and enjoys well-prepared and luxurious meals; good eyes and teeth; benefits by family relations; studious; good speaker; adept at the use of language; money through education (earning through learning)

Unfavorable: Might have trouble maintaining support with partners (8th to the 7th); challenges for accumulating money; problems in the area of the mouth and face

Ruler of Second in THIRD

Keywords: Finances Through Personal Efforts

Favorable: Gains through activities supported by siblings and close friends and neighbors; makes money through own efforts; courageous, adventurous; benefits through artistic expression and through the voice; profits through sales, marketing, advertising, and short-distance travels

Unfavorable: Might try to gain money through aggressive or dishonest means; anxiety to get money could lead to using inappropriate methods; doesn't weigh what they say; lacks courtesy for others; impatient

Ruler of Second in FOURTH

Keywords: Finances from the Home

Favorable: Has a definite saving mentality; happy when money is saved up; benefits through voice, singing, and speaking; education; real estate; agriculture; things below the earth; vehicles; nurturing occupation; good at instruction for children and for beginners; gains through the mother and her relations; well-educated; emotionally balanced and makes others happy; good storyteller

Unfavorable: Tries to take too much for self; hoards; losses through real estate and farming (gardening); incomplete education; financial problems with mother and family; car problems; unhappy about finances; doesn't feel enough has been saved

Ruler of Second in FIFTH

Keywords: Money Through the Intellect

Favorable: Makes money through government agencies and employers, has good merit from previous lives (purva punya), develops good money-saving tax strategies, high intelligence and ethics, enjoys studying the ancient scriptures, makes money through spiritual practices, sports, entertainment, children

Unfavorable: Problems with taxes or the IRS, doesn't spend properly for fun and games, losses through speculation, spends inordinately on children and sweethearts, may speak poorly, dishonest

Ruler of Second in SIXTH

Keywords: Money Through Service

Favorable: Income generated through service occupations such as healing, protective services, armed forces, martial arts, fighting, legal trade; remains victorious after initial assaults or setbacks; makes money from enemies; makes money through perseverance and hard work; likes or works with animals

Unfavorable: Struggles to save money; gets into disputes; loses money through accidents and health problems; gets into debt; speech ailments; eye, mouth, and face diseases; bad diet; eating disorders; abrasive speech; subject to attacks and lawsuits; expenses through pets

Ruler of Second in SEVENTH

Keywords: Finances Through Partnerships

Favorable: Accumulation of money through business transactions—often foreign or out of country business, money through the partner, financial success from taking spiritual journeys and pilgrimages, more successful when in a partnership, helps others to improve and get healthy both physically and financially

Unfavorable: Subject to negativity and depressions (2nd and 7th rulers are marakas or "killers" and 2nd in 8th to the 7th), health may be weak, ailing or worried partner, trouble with foreign business transactions or foreign business partners, driven to seek multiple relationships or more than one wife

Ruler of Second in EIGHTH

Keywords: Money Through Other's Support

Favorable: Makes money as a healer and through spiritual investigations; good research and analysis abilities; money through inheritance, insurance policies, alimonies, gambling, etc.; gets good financial support for efforts; money from affairs of the elderly and the closure of life

Unfavorable: Lives off the graces of others; poor; financial problems with partner, might lose inheritance, accepts too low a payment for services; abused by family; speech problems; deceptive; ailments from food; teeth, lips, gums, and face problems; vision ailments; poor study habits; food, drug, or alcohol abuse

Ruler of Second in NINTH

Keywords: Financially Fortunate

Favorable: Financially fortunate; lucky; prosperous father and family life; earns from occupations such as professor, lawyer, philosopher, educator, guru, minister, judge, travel agent, import-export, chef, jeweler, money handler, or from organizations focused on those matters; father helps out—especially when needed

Unfavorable: Depressed about personal level of spiritual development; lack of financial fortune, money troubles abroad, bad food or food poisoning while traveling; father's finances are weak; lack of higher education hurts earning ability

Ruler of Second in TENTH
Keywords: Earns Through Career

Favorable: Income through one's own initiative and reputation; earns through money handling; precious metals; involved in food business in some way; makes living through speaking and philosophizing; income through activities related to face, mouth, teeth, throat, etc.; uses voice to influence others and to express power; involved with activities of the face; earns through constant study

Unfavorable: Problems with status and reputation decrease earning ability; lack of self-promotion hinders advancement in career; trouble with occupations related to food, money handling, dental health, or facial health; father or employer do not fare well or they suffer a loss of respect or understanding from others; loss of money through government work or with connections to big companies

Ruler of Second in ELEVENTH
Keywords: Income from Opportunities

Favorable: Very good finances; good cash flow; plenty of opportunities and good breaks throughout life; always seems to have some chance to make money; able to fulfill wishes; gets financial benefit from older siblings or from well-placed people; partner's children are a benefit (11th is 5th from 7th and is connected to the 2nd); cash flow connected to the face, voice, food, money management, family happiness, and other 2nd house matters

Unfavorable: Might be tempted to take inappropriate means to gain wealth; cash flow problems; gets into financial complications with older siblings, older close friends, or with rich people; opportunities fall out of sync; feels depressed about money; doesn't spend enough time studying how money works

Ruler of Second in TWELFTH
Keywords: Income from Enlightenment

Favorable: Earns through work with charitable, educational, philanthropic, correctional, or spiritual organizations; makes money after going on pilgrimages; speaks at spiritual conventions and gatherings; studies scriptures; makes money by working abroad; lives a simple, spiritual life

Unfavorable: Spends too much money trying to get enlightened, becomes a financial victim, many losses, takes low-paying jobs, lacks financial motivation; speech, throat, mouth, and face ailments; not very eloquent; gets bad food or has trouble feeding themselves and their family; may speak ill of others; food allergies could affect sleep and libido; vision problems

RULERS OF THE THIRD HOUSE

Ruler of Third in FIRST
Keyword: Self-Determination
Favorable: Energetic, adventuresome, courageous; successful through own efforts; quick; benefits from acting, music, and art; athletic abilities; persuasive; skilled at sales, marketing, promotions, advertising, writing; short journeys; good seminar speaker or instructor; communications specialist
Unfavorable: Impatient; doesn't take good care of their health; troubles with younger siblings and neighbors; struggles; doesn't know how to use a soft touch; tries too hard; gets into trouble through writing and other means of communication; problems with the neck, shoulders, and hands

Ruler of Third in SECOND
Keywords: Works Hard for Finances
Favorable: Efforts are oriented toward spiritual growth; determination to get wealth may pay off but after some time; younger siblings may succeed in humanitarian and charitable pursuits and have more success in foreign locations
Unfavorable: Unfavorable qualities dominate (2nd is 12th to the 3rd or the house of losses for 3rd house matters). Younger siblings have difficulties; frustrated; may resort to unlawful behavior out of desperation to get results; inability to take successful and effective action; courage is lacking; lack of artistic and musical skills; works hard with little benefit; problems with shoulders, neck, and hands

Ruler of Third in THIRD
Keywords: Successful Efforts

Favorable: Gets results with a minimum of effort; daring; love of adventure; success in field of sales, marketing, acting, art, music, athletics, dance; seminar giver; editing; gains through reading and writing; skilled communicator; younger siblings enjoy success; benefits from short-distance traveling; quick learner

Unfavorable: Could make the person overzealous and inclined to put too much effort into things; siblings may be too involved with their lives; recklessness with writing and communicating could bring problems

Ruler of Third in FOURTH
Keywords: Efforts for Happiness

Favorable: Efforts lead to happiness; active and happy family life; mother is determined and progressive; successful action in the fields of housing, real estate, hotels, transportation and vehicles, education, land and agriculture, gardening

Unfavorable: Acts out of step with rest of family; thinks activity alone brings happiness; hard to settle down and feel contented; trouble with younger siblings in the family; neighbors create conflicts in the home; discord with the mother and family, impatient about finishing education; too aggressive

Ruler of Third in FIFTH
Keywords: Intellectual Efforts

Favorable: Efforts are geared toward speculation and quick business results; not afraid to take risks; active in the field of entertainment; games and amusements; childlike enthusiasm; motivated toward acquiring scriptural knowledge; prefers action-oriented spiritual techniques such as Tai Chi

Unfavorable: Romantic tenderness is overshadowed by aggressive tendencies; younger siblings create losses in speculations; feels too active to settle down in meditation; intellect is stirred up, leading to some wrong choices or devious behavior; children are too boisterous or misbehaved; may get into tax problems from taking too many risks with the government

Ruler of Third in SIXTH

Keywords: Efforts to Serve

Favorable: Efforts eventually come to success; motivated to healing and self-improvement; interests in protective services, armed forces, police, and security work; skilled in self-defense; younger siblings succeed in medical, legal, and defense fields; protects and is protected by siblings

Unfavorable: Expends too much effort for little reward; struggles with artistic skills; overstimulated, angry, combative, deceptive; double dealer; charlatan; doesn't get along with younger siblings; trouble with law enforcement; communication and writing problems; inflammatory health problems; troubles with pets; hearing ailments (mostly right ear); accidents; pain in upper torso, arms, and hands; digestive complaints

Ruler of Third in SEVENTH

Keywords: Efforts in Partnership

Favorable: Good business transactions with younger siblings; efforts done in partnership bring success; has fun and adventures with partner; success in business related to sales, marketing, seminars, and other informative and persuasive skill activities; short travels for business

Unfavorable: Too much stimulation and antagonism for a successful partnership; sexual aggressor; partner will be exciting yet inconsiderate and self-seeking, troubles with younger siblings—especially in business matters; siblings cause troubles to marriage

Ruler of Third in EIGHTH

Keywords: Efforts with Support

Favorable: Gets support from neighbors and younger siblings; efforts are geared to research, secrets, and other worldly investigations; siblings may be in healing or an esoteric field of some form; goes on mystical adventures; long life

Unfavorable: Lack of support for efforts; little ability in music, art, and other forms of self-expression; younger siblings have chronic health problems or they create chronic problems; fear, worry; dissipated from too much sexual activity; hearing or ear problems; neck, shoulder, and hand ailments

Ruler of Third in NINTH
Keywords: Determined Ideals

Favorable: Goes on long distance adventures; gets worked hard by gurus; works diligently yet ultimately wins through luck; success as a lecturer and early education teacher; engages in both short- and long-distance travel; good travel agent; success as a writer, publisher, salesperson, advertiser

Unfavorable: Desires yet struggles to achieve high states of knowledge and spiritual development; problems with legal matters; lack of luck; father has many difficulties or is a source of conflict; employers drive person to work hard; much effort to get advanced degree; encounters strife overseas or during lengthy travels

Ruler of Third in TENTH
Keywords: Career of Self-Expression

Favorable: Good finances and career development; possible career in writing, lecturing, sales, computers, communications, Internet, or expressive arts such as dancing, acting, or music; good at instructing and giving seminars; early education or teaching beginners; works well with the hands; short travels

Unfavorable: Puts too much effort into career, siblings create problems in work, tries with little success to make it as a writer, editor, actor, artist, musician, public speaker, and salesperson; too much traveling around town

Ruler of Third in ELEVENTH
Keywords: Profits from Efforts

Favorable: Efforts lead to greater opportunities; friendly; good communicator; works diligently to fulfill desires; siblings help create greater cash flow and profits; gets benefits from artistic pursuits such as writing, acting, music, etc.; fulfills needs for adventure and excitement; leads others on quests

Unfavorable: Struggles to get money; reckless about managing cash flow; siblings hurt opportunities for inflow of cash; gets angry and resentful of others' success; ailments of the ears, neck, upper back, arms, and hands; partner struggles to bear children (11th is 5th to 7th associated to the struggling 3rd house)

Ruler of Third in TWELFTH

Keywords: Efforts for Enlightenment

Favorable: Goes on quests to faraway locales; travels on pilgrimages; seeks a spiritual destiny; writes about spiritual matters; siblings take a spiritual path; efforts are more successful in foreign countries

Unfavorable: Siblings may expect too much or be dependent; spends too much time in seclusion; not integrated; envious; lack of personal vision; fragmented; poor artistic skills; weak at communicating their needs; inept; ailments or loss of function in neck, shoulders, or hands; ear ailments; siblings get sick

RULERS OF THE FOURTH HOUSE

Ruler of Fourth in FIRST

Keywords: Focus on the Home

Favorable: Personal efforts are rewarded through constant learning; desires to secure a good home and car with comfortable living conditions; benefits through real estate; education, gets a good degree; love for the mother and the family; nurturing, intuitive; wants to have a "family" around them

Unfavorable: Focuses too much on trying to build a home and create security; emotions are too sensitive; trouble with the mother, mother runs their life; has trouble sustaining a family; problems with home and vehicles; education is incomplete; problems in chest and breast area

Ruler of Fourth in SECOND

Keywords: Money Through the Home

Favorable: Good education and emotional balance; good finances; earns in education, counseling, real estate, agriculture, gardening, hotel and housing trade, clothing, vehicles, or geological and other earth- and mineral-related activities; benefits come from the mother; has a good family; emotionally solid

Unfavorable: Emotional imbalances make it difficult to build up finances; troubles in the family through the mother; spends too much on education, clothing, housing, and cars; thinks money will make happiness; money troubles through real estate, land, and agriculture

Ruler of Fourth in THIRD

Keywords: Emotional Efforts

Favorable: Gets good fixed assets (homes, cars, etc.) through effort and perseverance; reacts emotionally and gives to the less fortunate; interested in developing Moksha or enlightenment; education in foreign countries

Unfavorable: Duress with mother and younger siblings (3rd is 12th to the 4th), emotional strife from trying too hard, worries oneself sick, lack of support and encouragement from mother or early separation from mother, insufficient education

Ruler of Fourth in FOURTH

Keywords: Fullness of Feelings

Favorable: Gets a good education, home, cars, clothes, and other blessings of comfort; emotionally well developed; prosperous; spiritually open; can feel things deeply; educator; does well in real estate, education; mother and family are very important; benefits from things that come from beneath the earth

Unfavorable: This is generally a favorable position and does not generate many negative effects. If aspected or occupied by malefics, the opposite or a lesser degree of what is expressed above will occur.

Ruler of Fourth in FIFTH

Keywords: Security Through the Intellect

Favorable: Gets support and encouragement from mother; gains through speculations; children, childlike activities (sports, entertainment, games, etc.); romantic, loving to the mate; gets emotional upliftment from the scriptures; benefits from spiritual practices; spiritual educator; good past-life credit (purva punya)

Unfavorable: Emotional strain from misbehaving children; worried about taxes; loses focus in sports and is defeated; not strong enough to handle the uncertainties of speculative activities; inconsistent with spiritual practices

Ruler of Fourth in SIXTH

Keywords: Emotional Service

Favorable: Healer; emotionally uplifting to others; intuitive (knows what's bothering others); motivated to build up good financial assets;

educator in the field of healing; law, defense, and protection services warrior; animal advocate or trainer; environmentalist

Unfavorable: Emotionally aggressive and unreliable; conflicts with or is separated from the mother; mother struggles in life; problems with home and car ownership; agricultural losses; educational difficulties or incompleteness; many residences and changes of schools; heart and chest problems; pets are aggressive or sick; fourth house can also bring serious problems (hospitalization, death) for the father (4th is 8th to the 9th)

Ruler of Fourth in SEVENTH

Keywords: Emotions from Partnerships

Favorable: Gets emotional support and happiness from partner; good marriage; earns much through partnerships; does business related to education, vehicles, and real estate, or partner is involved in these matters; partner has a strong career (4th is 10th to the 7th); very close to mother

Unfavorable: May get another mother (7th is 4th to the 4th); emotional problems in marriage; partner does not have enough equity, fixed assets, or startup capital to succeed in business; partner is poorly educated or unbalanced and nonsupportive; inappropriate relationship with mother; if fourth house is afflicted with unfavorable planets, the person will do better outside their place of birth

Ruler of Fourth in EIGHTH

Keywords: Emotional Support

Favorable: Educated as a researcher or investigator, metaphysical, intuitive, focuses on becoming enlightened, mother is a spiritual seeker, works as a family counselor, supports others' emotions, happy through inheritances and other sources of unearned income, devoted, loves the mysteries of life

Unfavorable: Emotional problems, abused or abusing, lack of attention or support from mother, mother dies or leaves family early (father could have problems as well since 4th is 8th to the 9th in the 8th), lack of libido or vitality due to psychological problems, low self-esteem, secretive, problems with fixed assets (home, car, lands, etc.), poor education, breast and reproductive ailments

Ruler of Fourth in NINTH
Keywords: Fullness of Feelings and Fortune
Favorable: Very fortunate; the mother brings luck; highly educated, stable, caring, soothing; fortunate father; emotionally stimulated by higher forms of knowledge, philosophy, and religion; gets emotional blessings and love from the guru; love of justice and fair play; benefits from long distance travels
Unfavorable: May spend too much time in spiritual and philanthropic pursuits and lose some material advantages; could submit to a charlatan spiritual teacher or lose one's own emotional discrimination; tired from too much international travel; could experience a big loss through too much optimism and lack of prudence; lackadaisical attitude

Ruler of Fourth in TENTH
Keywords: Nurturing Career
Favorable: Good combination leading to high educational benefits, career in education, real estate, vehicles, hotel business, successful businessperson, confident, upbeat, builds up others' emotions, mother plays a role in career, good status, leader, political skills
Unfavorable: Poor emotional state sabotages career, interested in too many things to get enough direction and success in one field, father's difficulties hamper career (4th is 8th to the 9th in the career house—the 10th), heart problems, knee ailments

Ruler of Fourth in ELEVENTH
Keywords: Profits from Learning
Favorable: Earning comes from learning, good profits from training one's self in the latest opportunity areas, friendly, supportive, benefits from influential friend from the mother's side of the family, happy, fulfill their dreams, get what they want, good cash flow
Unfavorable: May have a second mother (11th is 8th from the 4th), may be overly optimistic, thinks they have more time than they do and lose opportunities, undereducated to meet the opportunities at hand, emotional problems with older siblings

Ruler of Fourth in TWELFTH
Keywords: Distant Emotions
Favorable: Interested in spiritual development; giving, caring; feels more at home in foreign countries or quiet and isolated locations;

spends time in an ashram or spiritual retreat; transcends for long periods; not attached to the world; spiritual mother

Unfavorable: Not sufficiently interested to make a good living; lack of education; poor, few fixed assets; car, house, real estate, and agricultural problems; little support or love from the mother; overly generous; doesn't know how to give enough to themselves; may spend time in confinement (jails, hospitals, sanitariums, etc.); lack of good sleep; little sexual pleasure; health problems in the chest and breast

RULERS OF THE FIFTH HOUSE

Ruler of Fifth in FIRST

Keywords: Intellectual Orientation

Favorable: Success in speculative events (such as stock market); drawn to games, sports, and amusements; benefits from scriptural knowledge and practices; romantic; good children; intelligent; gets off to a good start due to credit accrued from previous actions (purva punya)

Unfavorable: Lack of intelligence; will seek unsavory allies (some say negative life forces or spirits); troubles with government and leaders of large corporations; tax problems; irresponsible with romance; has difficulty performing other spiritual practices; trouble with children or childbearing; losses through speculations; not successful in sports, entertainment, and other types of games

Ruler of Fifth in SECOND

Keywords: Money Through the Mind

Favorable: Love from mate and from children creates an atmosphere of financial success; earns well through speculation; meditation techniques; sports, entertainment, food, speech; study of the scriptures; benefits from government connections or working with handling government or corporate money; tax worker

Unfavorable: Problems with supporting children; lack of understanding and love from the mate; losses through speculation; poor in sports and entertainment field; complications with the government or large corporations; dishonest and self-seeking to the point of damaging family relations

Ruler of Fifth in THIRD

Keywords: Intellectual Efforts

Favorable: Siblings are intelligent and interested in scriptural knowledge and spiritual practices; person's efforts are focused on children, speculation, and leading an interesting and adventuresome life; benefits from writing, music, entertainment, and sports

Unfavorable: Past actions lead to struggling and expending too much effort; children are a concern; practicing spiritual techniques is not effortless; speculations don't work out well; love doesn't come easy; lack of fun in life

Ruler of Fifth in FOURTH

Keywords: Intellect Mixed with Emotions

Favorable: Well educated, educator to executives, interest in teaching beginners and/or children, attains a spiritual peace, spiritual teacher, comfortable home and family, mother is a source of inspiration, children pursue careers connected to education, real estate, and other fourth-house matters

Unfavorable: Problems with children or childbearing (4th is 12th to the 5th), losses in speculation through lack of education or understanding, difficulties or misunderstandings with mother

Ruler of Fifth in FIFTH

Keywords: Advanced Mind

Favorable: High intelligence, good at weighing the pros and cons before taking risks, successful investor or speculator, involved in spiritual practices and the study of scriptures, has good children, playful disposition, athletic interests, interest in entertainment and games, romantic, gets love from their mates

Unfavorable: Clever in deceiving people (lying, understating, withholding information, etc.), makes wrongful investments (inside trading, manipulating, etc.), charlatan spiritual person, trouble with children, lack of integrity overall

Ruler of Fifth in SIXTH

Keywords: Mind of Service

Favorable: Good skills in healing, protecting, and serving; spiritual exuberance; romantic zeal; children are active and have good resistance to disease; does well in providing service to others; pets are like children; gets healed through spiritual performances (yagyas, mantras, shantis, remedial acts)

Unfavorable: Complications or losses from children; abortion or miscarriage; fighting with children; children get sick a lot; possible adoption; lack of love or discord with the mate; trouble when dating; problems from investments; governmental problems; intellect is erratic; troubles from spiritual practices; religious fanatic; diseases are more mental and spiritual in nature

Ruler of Fifth in SEVENTH

Keywords: Love of Business and Partners

Favorable: Gets delight, friendship, and fondness from partners; good marriage; smart businessman; good relationship with children; passions are fulfilled; forms good business contracts and agreements related to speculation, sports, entertainment, and religious activities; partner is on the spiritual path

Unfavorable: Sexually overactive; partner does not meet their needs; lack of good business sense; does not correctly set up business transactions or any form of agreement; trouble with foreign business; children may be away in a foreign country or a distant state

Ruler of Fifth in EIGHTH

Keywords: Shadowed Intellect

Favorable: Accomplished scholar of books of mythology, secret knowledge, folklore, and mystery; likes fantasy and science fiction; children live long; capable of long meditations and periods of deep contemplation; profound insights from scriptures

Unfavorable: Worried or unconfident children; confused mind; loss of children; adoption of children from a foreign land or race; discontented; psychosomatic illnesses; gets ailments that are hard to diagnose; makes poor investments; trouble through dating; doesn't feel loved by the mate; both abused and an abuser; dishonest; meditations and spiritual practices seem difficult or without result

Ruler of Fifth in NINTH

Keywords: Spiritual Intelligence

Favorable: Gets fortune from merit carried over from previous actions, spiritually open and evolved, understands the subtle workings of life, publishes their philosophies, perceives love and romance on a high spiritual plane, specialist in mantras and other spiritual techniques, children are blessed, finds romance on long-distance travels, astute knowledge of law, ethics, and justice

Unfavorable: Can lose previous merits through too much optimism or lack of application; feels so lucky they don't try enough; intellect could get clouded, leading them to incorrect philosophies and loss of fortune; children travel away from home; romantic complications on long journeys

Ruler of Fifth in TENTH

Keywords: Intellectual Career

Favorable: Career activities involving fifth house matters such as speculation, investments, children and their affairs, youthful activities, games, sports and entertainment, spiritual techniques, study of scriptures and other ancient forms of knowledge, government or corporate work (possibly in politics), income generation through taxes and other forms of government, legal activities, has good status and earning ability, children and romantic interests promote career

Unfavorable: Neglects children for career, young people hamper career, trouble with romantic connections to career (office affairs), lack of results in career with basic fifth house matters (speculation, sports, entertainment, spiritual practices, etc.), government blocks career advancement (tax problems, legal rulings, etc)

Ruler of Fifth in ELEVENTH

Keywords: Profits from Good Intelligence

Favorable: Profits and good success from the grace of previous actions (purva punya); plenty of opportunities; friends are a blessing; children bring an influx of profits; cash flow associated with speculation, sports, entertainment, spiritual practices, and studies; mate contributes to earnings; older siblings are successful

Unfavorable: Cash flow is encumbered by children, romantic expenses, spending for spiritual growth, speculation, etc.; should not invest with romantic interests or "fall in love" with their business; elder siblings and friends could bring losses in investments

Ruler of Fifth in TWELFTH

Keywords: Unbounded Intellect

Favorable: Has strong drive to attain happiness and calmness (moksha); romance has a spiritual overtone to it (in love with God); children are spiritual seekers; driven by previous karmas to continue to seek enlightenment; might adopt (as amplified by partner's chart)

Unfavorable: Unsuccessful romances; afraid of having children; abortions, miscarriages; trouble with children or children get into trouble (hospitalizations, punishments, jail, etc.); suffers losses, fines, and penalties regarding speculation; losses through the government; poor results and ineptitude in the field of sports, entertainment, and amusements; mental disturbances; slow development of children

RULERS OF THE SIXTH HOUSE

Ruler of Sixth in FIRST

Keywords: Defense of the Self

Favorable: Good fighting strength; sense of service; skill in health and self-improvement fields; protector, warrior; involved in security, protecting, and defense (police, armed services, fire fighting, martial arts, security systems, etc.); prevails in conflict situations; legal abilities; great stamina and resistance to disease

Unfavorable: Works too hard; struggles; gets into debts; conflicting; inclined to take things; trickster; legal troubles; defeated; conflicts with aunts and uncles; susceptible to acute illnesses; surgeries, accidents, fevers, rashes, infections, allergies, hyperacidity, wounds, breaks, and bruises

Ruler of Sixth in SECOND

Keywords: Wealth Through Serving

Favorable: Voice carries influence; healing speech; money through medical, legal, and defense-related activities; maternal aunts and uncles have influence in the family; makes money over time through perseverance and hard work

Unfavorable: Forcible speech; family is unhappy overall; indebted; fights to accumulate money; poor study habits; eating disorders; food poisonings and allergies; rough or domineering speech; speaks ill of others; liar; speech disorders; eye troubles; ailments of teeth, mouth, face, and throat

Ruler of Sixth in THIRD

Keywords: Determined Service

Favorable: Very determined, courageous, adventure seeker; often succeeds through effort alone; common jobs related to seminars, selling, clerical, health, legal, and defense industries; younger siblings might be involved in sales, legal, healing, armed services, police, and other defense or security fields

Unfavorable: Conflicts with younger siblings and with neighbors; little aptitude in art, music, acting, dancing, etc.; reckless; trouble with short-distance travels; siblings bring debts; impatient, frustrated, dishonest; much effort to improve or maintain health; ear problems

Ruler of Sixth in FOURTH

Keywords: Combative Emotions

Favorable: Brave, thick-skinned, able to handle emotional duress; defender of the family; educated in law, defense, and military affairs; construction worker; strategic mindset, outwits their enemies; gets quick education or learns quickly; emotionally serving; animal trainer

Unfavorable: Family conflicts; emotionally stirred up; impatient learner; debts; legal problems with houses; lives in unrefined locales; car problems and accidents; troubles with education; gets sick from toxic buildings; uncles and aunts create family turmoil; garden and agricultural problems; heart and chest ailments

Ruler of Sixth in FIFTH

Keywords: Militant Mind

Favorable: Protector of children, a sports or entertainment agent, defender for spiritual organizations, natural healing abilities (from past actions—purva punya), a military strategist, affectionate, active, might seek an adoption, gets help from maternal aunts and uncles, heals illnesses from a psychological or spiritual framework, overcomes diseases (5th is 12th to the 6th)

Unfavorable: Possible miscarriage or abortion, troubles with children, trouble with cousins, losses in speculation, impatient, tries to cut corners and gets into trouble, unscrupulous, cheats in romance, gets intimate too quickly, poor success in dating, self-seeking in passions, illnesses of a psychological or spiritual origin

Ruler of Sixth in SIXTH

Keywords: Excellent Warrior

Favorable: Strong resistance to disease, highly skilled in self-defense of any form, legal and medical skills, adept office administration, provides excellent service and gets good helpers, pets stay healthy, aunts and uncles and cousins do well

Unfavorable: Gets run down from too much activity, aggressive, very hot constitution and subject to pitta (fiery) ailments, digestive problems, hyperacidity, aggressive pets, troubles with debt management, problems with maternal aunts and uncles and their families

Ruler of Sixth in SEVENTH

Keywords: Militant Relationships

Favorable: Seeks and gets dynamic partners who are responsive and vigorous in all activities (including sexual activities); partner could be involved in medical, defense, security, healing, legal, or office administration activities; partnerships with relatives

Unfavorable: Possible divorce or separation; mate is sickly or a source of conflict; drawn to aggressive and passionate partners; partners create debts and legal complications; illnesses of the external sexual organs; loses vitality through too much sexual activity; "married" to their pets

Ruler of Sixth in EIGHTH

Keywords: Defended and Supported

Favorable: Could work for secret defense organizations; medical researcher; might specialize in legal and medical activities dealing with longevity, old persons, or the affairs of their estates (inheritances); gets money from lawsuits; possible interpretation of "death to illnesses" in its best sense (since 6th is illnesses and 8th is death)

Unfavorable: Many chronic and "mysterious" illnesses; does illegal activities in secret; long-term debts; debt or legal problem due to a scandal; may be an attacker and cause harm to others; has problems with jealousy; doesn't get much support; employees or servants are abusive or disrespectful

Ruler of Sixth in NINTH

Keywords: Fighting for Fortune

Favorable: Provides service to spiritual organizations and institutions of higher education; lawyer; fortune through "blue collar" jobs and through providing service; father is involved in the health, legal, military, or defense industry

Unfavorable: Discord with boss or father or they have a rough life; lots of tiring long-distance travel; fights to get ahead; loses fortune; debts hinder advancement; breaks in college education; disagreements with gurus, philosophers, and proponents of higher education; lack of ethics; expedient; nonbeliever

Ruler of Sixth in TENTH

Keywords: Career of Service and Defending

Favorable: Career in medical, legal, business administration, defense and security fields, or as animal worker, physical therapist, exercise expert, or nutritionist; success through hard work; makes money from adversaries and by going to court; wants things to be free of impurities and performing at a high standard

Unfavorable: Struggles to find their purpose in life; gets sick or hurt at work; opponents hurt career or status; doesn't fight hard enough to keep job or position; has a low-paying and hard-working job; sometimes must ask people for money or take out loans to make ends meet; makes money hurting or attacking others

Ruler of Sixth in ELEVENTH

Keywords: Hard-Working for Profit

Favorable: Hard work pays off in terms of good cash flow; more opportunities come up over time; able to defeat opponents and come out ahead; good resistance to disease; income from animals; maternal aunts and uncles bring profit

Unfavorable: Treachery from elder siblings and friends; gets connected to sick or rough friends; ailing older siblings; lawsuits and conflicts end opportunities; struggles to maintain cash flow; setbacks; obstructions and combative attitude block fulfillment of dreams

Ruler of Sixth in TWELFTH

Keywords: Fighting for Liberation

Favorable: Ultimately overcomes problems; service brings liberation; works in medical clinics, ashrams, prisons, and other places of detention or confinement; works outside their native land; enlightenment through work and service; active sex energy; gets employees from other countries; gets spiritual healing

Unfavorable: Loses through providing service; gets into complications with foreigners; losses through medical bills, penalties, and dishonest servants or workers; goes into too much debt seeking spiritual liberation (moksha); reckless and self-defeating nature; harmful person; active yet frustrated and unpleasant sex life; tries too hard to be enlightened and gets disappointed

RULERS OF THE SEVENTH HOUSE

Ruler of Seventh in FIRST

Keywords: Focus on Partnerships

Favorable: Identifies closely with mate; mate and partnerships add power to their life; good business skills; balanced in business and daily life; astute; good relationships—skilled in relating to others; business travels bring success; good partnerships and marriage; strong and well-liked mate

Unfavorable: Has more than one mate or partner—often at the same time; partners dominate their lives; fatigued due to too much traveling; gets into sexual complications; duplicitous; too balanced or too out of balance; pretender; chameleon

Ruler of Seventh in SECOND

Keywords: Money Through Partnerships

Favorable: Money comes through partnerships and skill in business agreements; spouse contributes to their wealth; business related to money handling, food, speech, travel; makes money showing others how to be in a successful partnership; attractive; persuasive

Unfavorable: Might have more than one marriage or separations and long periods apart; mate destabilizes accumulated wealth and has speaking and eating problems; family happiness is disturbed; partner does not study well; possible depressions and negativity

Ruler of Seventh in THIRD
Keywords: Self-Expression Through Partnerships
Favorable: Determined and courageous partner; partner is involved in artistic expressions such as writing, art, music, acting, seminars, early education, and other 3rd house matters; does business with the siblings; siblings might travel or do business overseas
Unfavorable: Delays in marriage; might develop a socially unacceptable or questionable relationship with the partner of a younger sibling; partner's self-determination may create frictions and a lack of sharing in the partnership; partner seeks adventures that strain the relationship

Ruler of Seventh in FOURTH
Keywords: At Home with Partnerships
Favorable: Well-educated partner; happy marriage and family; marriage brings blessings and a sense of emotional completion; partner brings benefits to career (7th is 10th to 4th); person educates others on the basics of partnerships, contracts, and agreements
Unfavorable: Partner creates problems with the mother; family discord and problems with vehicles; partner's expression of emotions are out of balance; partner comes from a troubled home; partner is not well-educated; person loses business due to emotional problems

Ruler of Seventh in FIFTH
Keywords: Intelligence in Partnerships
Favorable: Gets good partner, romantic partner; partner is spiritual, youthful, and intelligent; has good business sense and may be involved in spiritual techniques; business with sports, entertainment, children, games, and amusement; could be an investment advisor or deal maker
Unfavorable: Immature or childish partner who lacks intelligence and spiritual content; marriage is challenged; trouble with birth of children; poor business partnerships

Ruler of Seventh in SIXTH
Keywords: Militant Partnerships

Favorable: Mate could be involved in the fields of law, medicine, protection, and defense services; animal care and office administration; mate has a high sense of service; person does business in similar fields; mate has high resistance to disease

Unfavorable: Friction in marriage; gets attracted to passionate mates who may be too fiery or conflicting; illness in external reproductive organs or inability to perform the sex act; divorce or separation; mate has poor health and may suffer from accidents, wounds, fevers, rashes, skin diseases; impatient or mean mate

Ruler of Seventh in SEVENTH
Keywords: Fullness of Partnerships

Favorable: Gets great benefit from marriage and business partnerships; person is an expert in making people feel wanted; gets others to do things for him by charming them into liking him; attractive and gets an attractive mate; wants to be married and in a relationship from an early age

Unfavorable: Too smooth; manipulates people to their end (even though they might like it); may have so many relationships that they end up with none that last; possible divorce and problems with business partnerships; mate might be too focused on themselves

Ruler of Seventh in EIGHTH
Keywords: Mysterious Partnerships

Favorable: Sexually vital mate; mate brings money to the relationship; mate lives long; mate is mystical and may be involved in research, health, investigation activities, and occupations involved with the closure or extension of life; person also may do business or have interest in these areas

Unfavorable: Marriage problems, divorce; mate is incomprehensible and isolated; mate has chronic ailments that threaten length of life; mate could have deep emotional issues surrounding support and abuse; mate is remote and unsupportive; loss of earnings through mate

Ruler of Seventh in NINTH
Keywords: Partnering with the Divine

Favorable: Good mates; might meet mate on a long-distance journey; mate brings good luck; mate is philosophical with an interest in spiritual and ethical matters; mate could be involved in legal activities; person and mate could have close partnership with a guru and with the father; luck in business

Unfavorable: Mate could be too self-interested and clashing to be a good partner; father could have misfortune and a short life (7th ruler is a maraka or killer planet, and 9th is 2nd to the 7th, and the 2nd also has a maraka ruler—so this configuration could also adversely affect the person's own wealth or fortune)

Ruler of Seventh in TENTH

Keywords: Life Purpose in Partnerships

Favorable: Person is happy; gets along well with mate's mother and family; mate has major impact on person's career; mate is career-oriented and able to achieve good status; person has good business skills; travel to distant locations for business brings good results

Unfavorable: Mate could be too career-focused; mate may want the success and activity of a career but may not be competent enough, causing expenses and strains to the relationship; the person may lose momentum in their own career due to the mate

Ruler of Seventh in ELEVENTH

Keywords: Profits from Partnerships

Favorable: Mate contributes to opportunities and the development of good cash flow; person has strong romantic feelings and passions; person has good business activities with friends and older siblings and with people of influence who bring more opportunities

Unfavorable: Mate is not affectionate enough; mate or partner make poor business decisions that affect cash flow; mate may be mentally troubled or intellectually challenged; trouble with children

Ruler of Seventh in TWELFTH

Keywords: Unbounded Partnerships

Favorable: Attracted to persons of foreign birth or customs; may meet mate while traveling in distant countries or while involved in spiritual retreats or ashrams; enjoys yet hides sexual pleasures; loves on a spiritual level (e.g., tantra); mate is a spiritual seeker

Unfavorable: Possible divorce or separation; mate brings sickness and losses; mate does not experience much pleasure from sex; person could be more mentally than physically passionate; mate is unavailable; gets involved in secret affairs or is kept as a secret lover

RULERS OF THE EIGHTH HOUSE

Ruler of Eighth in FIRST
Keywords: Mysteries of the Self

Favorable: Long life; oriented to healing and to hidden knowledge; strong intuition; good researcher, investigator, diagnostician; esoteric; gets money from unearned sources such as wills, donations, gifts, etc.; high spiritual attainments as a recluse

Unfavorable: Passionate, jealous, vulnerable; abused and gets abused; chronic health problems; reproductive and eliminatory weakness; guarded or secretive; afraid of being blamed; fearful; feels unsupported; lives off graces of others; lack of comforts, hypersensitive to pain and duress; too porous and overly sensitive

Ruler of Eighth in SECOND
Keywords: Money Through the Unknown

Favorable: Accumulates money from unearned sources such as wills, lotteries, insurance settlements, etc.; interested in healing, life extension, mystical knowledge, research, investigations, and espionage; handling the affairs for the closure of life (death); sexual topics; reproduction and elimination issues, etc.

Unfavorable: Financially distressed; does not keep secrets; secret income; problems with eating disorders, smoking, drugs, drinking; speaks ill of others; may require speech therapy; too shy to speak up at first; deceptive; family abuse; psychosomatic illnesses; food allergies; ailments of the mouth and throat areas; vision problems; reproductive and elimination ailments

Ruler of Eighth in THIRD
Keywords: Efforts with the Unknown

Favorable: Writer or speaker on mystery and the mystical; involved in the marketing and sales of products for longevity and for extended living and estate planning; uncanny communication ability; supersensory abilities in the arts, music, acting; somewhat bohemian, otherworldly, or unconventional in their approach

Unfavorable: Lack of determination, shy, jealous, too abstract; problems with younger siblings (or they have chronic health problems) and with neighbors; overactive imagination; loses through things put in writing; poor communicator; little sense of fun and adventure; ear ailments; trouble with neck, shoulders, and hands; nervous disorders

Ruler of Eighth in FOURTH

Keywords: Transcendental Emotions

Favorable: Inheritance or financial windfall from mother's side of family; supersensory emotions and intuition; interest in esoteric or hidden knowledge; involved in sale of home, insurance, securities, and estate planning connected to death or the closure of life; vital sensual and sexual feelings

Unfavorable: Loss of mother; mistreatment; hypersensitive; easily embarrassed or shamed; gets blamed; emotional problems; keeps their feelings a secret; exposure for serious auto accident; trouble with real estate; educational difficulties; might live in untidy or poor surroundings; lives in isolation

Ruler of Eighth in FIFTH

Keywords: Hidden Intellect

Favorable: Gains through sweethearts and romantic interludes; researcher for speculative activities like the stock market; benefits from inheritances, lotteries, insurance settlements, etc.; investigator, detective; benefits from deep study of the scriptures

Unfavorable: Lack of fertility; trouble with conception; children are ill, unsupportive, and a source of worry; lack of romance and love from the mate; unwanted pregnancies; too shy for dating; cloudy thinking; investments and speculations fail; lack of joy in life; sexual aberrations

Ruler of Eighth in SIXTH

Keywords: Supported and Defended

Favorable: Prevail over their problems and come out ahead; involved in military-type intrigues; expert at stealth; skill as a medical researcher, healer, investigator, detective, insurance agent (especially for disasters and accidents); unexpected wealth (perhaps from maternal relations)

Unfavorable: Trouble with defense and security operations; lack of service and support; chronic debt; serious health problems; robbed or swindled; lack of vitality; life cut short (especially by accidents and inflammatory ailments); chronic indigestion; inflammation of the organs of reproduction and elimination; constantly worried; both shy and aggressive; pets don't thrive

Ruler of Eighth in SEVENTH

Keywords: Mysterious Mates

Favorable: Mate is sexually vital and passionate; mate has fascinating spiritual and esoteric qualities; mate is more sensual than appears on the outside; mate could inherit or bring other sources of income into the relationship

Unfavorable: Subject to divorce and/or separations; chronic health problems (especially reproductive) for mate; mate could be initially shy and show a lack of confidence; loans money (which might not be paid back); loss through secret intrigues; troubles traveling; partners gamble or take too much

Ruler of Eighth in EIGHTH

Keywords: Fullness of Support

Favorable: Good health; vitality and longevity; support comes from many areas; strong intuition and supersensory abilities; interest in the supernatural and in transcendental knowledge; super secret; effortlessly sexually alluring (often don't realize their own magnetism)

Unfavorable: Vindictive; feels others owe them a living; isolated, jealous; gets into the darker side of knowledge; morbid fascination with death and the afterlife; executes heavy penalties on others; gets weak by disconnecting from the world in some way (too much sex, drugs, meditating, etc.)

Ruler of Eighth in NINTH

Keywords: Mysterious Fortune

Favorable: Inherits father's wealth; good accumulation of money from working well with authorities (bosses, leaders, etc.); guru helps person to develop finances; gets fortune through the affairs of the dead (insurance, estate planning, probates, wills, etc.)

Unfavorable: Difficulties with the father and with authority figures in general; trouble with the guru; gets employers who fail; lack of fortune; feels unhappy; thinks of negative results and gets them; poor ability to project their needs; others feel they are bad luck or don't want them around

Ruler of Eighth in TENTH
Keywords: Career of Mysteries

Favorable: Gets other people's money or support; good researcher, investigator, spy; learns secret knowledge; skilled in esoteric and mysterious activities; good psychoanalyst—knows others' feelings; works well in private; successful risk taker; interested in puzzles, magic, and surprises

Unfavorable: Never feels clear about their purpose in life; underpaid; career runs into periods of stagnation; loses visibility at work and is charged with not working correctly or completely; lack of self-promotion; less qualified people may get promoted over them; uses hidden methods to advance

Ruler of Eighth in ELEVENTH
Keywords: Profits Through the Unknown

Favorable: Cash flow from esoteric and mystical activities; makes money as an investigator, researcher, or from involvement in activities focused at the end of life; money from sex-related activities; vitality, health, and life extension; money from unearned sources (wills, games of chance, etc.)

Unfavorable: Has difficulty keeping money around; troubles and losses with elder siblings and friends; ear problems; wife has trouble with children (11th is 5th from the 7th and associated with the 8th); friends and siblings are unsupportive and even occasionally cruel (or they can be that way to their friends)

Ruler of Eighth in TWELFTH
Keywords: Liberation Through Transcendence

Favorable: This person is very spiritual and seeks out transcendental wisdom for enlightenment; may spend long times in seclusion in places of solitude (12th is 9th to the 8th)

Unfavorable: Spends time in detention, or in hospitals; financially inept; spiritual hypocrite; withdrawn yet subject to bouts of intense behavior; poor, isolated, abused, and rejected; worried; vision problems; ailments of the feet as well as reproduction and elimination; sleep disorders; problems are worse overseas or with foreigners; lack of pleasure and sensual enjoyments

RULERS OF THE NINTH HOUSE

Ruler of Ninth in FIRST
Keywords: Fortune of the Self

Favorable: Father is very supportive and helps when needed; person is very lucky; lives a life of great merit; philosophical; just; acquainted and comfortable with high levels of knowledge and understanding; might be at the head of a spiritual, educational, or philosophical organization; benefits from long-distance travel

Unfavorable: Zealot or fundamentalist; feels "bulletproof" or pushes their luck too far; ego could get in the way and become their downfall; father or guru could be too "helpful" and block the person from establishing their own identity; could be "overeducated" and not fit for practical existence

Ruler of Ninth in SECOND
Keywords: Fortune in Finances

Favorable: Makes money more easily than most; accumulates good fortune over time; father is helpful with finances and is wealthy; influences and inspires others; speaks the highest truth; studies higher forms of knowledge; charismatic

Unfavorable: Could lose money through overly optimistic financial concepts; father could lose his wealth or struggle to maintain his assets; person could quarrel with father or authorities over money; spends too much or goes into debt for knowledge and higher education

Ruler of Ninth in THIRD
Keywords: Fortune Through Efforts

Favorable: Strong courage and determination; benefits from the arts, writing, etc.; strong persuasive and speaking skills; educator, lawyer, minister, guru, and the like; expert in long-distance communications; younger siblings bring fortune and are lucky themselves; benefits through publishing; brings forth revolutionary concepts; a visionary

Unfavorable: Tries too hard to be knowledgeable; propagandist; fanatic for spiritual, educational, or ethical issues; too preposterous, aggressive, or avant-garde with writing, communicating, or publishing; wants changes and new ideas to occur too quickly; may not always reason things out before they present their ideas

Ruler of Ninth in FOURTH

Keywords: Fortune Through Family

Favorable: Lives near higher learning and spiritual knowledge; gets good knowledge from the guru, father is a teacher (if only by example); nourished emotionally by the father or guru; good fortune with cars, real estate, agriculture, education, and things that come from beneath the ground; blessings also come from the mother and the family overall

Unfavorable: Conflicts with the father and the guru, problems with father's health and longevity (4th is 8th to 9th); mother could be separated from the father by some distance or father could travel a lot; could experience a loss in agriculture or in the home by being away too much; trouble with cars on long-distance journeys

Ruler of Ninth in FIFTH

Keywords: Fortunate from All Angles

Favorable: High spiritual inclinations; benefits from mantra meditation, spiritual techniques, and philosophical knowledge; good speculations; enjoys sports, games, and other amusements; romantic; thankful for fortune; father and guru are an advantage; gets blessings from children

Unfavorable: Overly optimistic in speculations or risky ventures; loss of their fortune from issues surrounding children, entertainment and sports, and other similar 5th house matters

Ruler of Ninth in SIXTH

Keywords: Fortune Through Serving and Defending

Favorable: Connections to the defense and service field or justice system; lawyer or a medical practitioner; takes a stand against unjust or unethical behavior; will win most lawsuits; has a strong sense of service to the father and to the guru; fortune through hard work; father could be involved in similar pursuits

Unfavorable: Father has bad health, accidents, inflammatory conditions, etc.; person is hampered by legal problems and conflicts; conflicts with the father, guru, and other authority figures; challenges knowledge and knowledge givers; losses through servants, too servile, person struggles to gain their fortunes

Ruler of Ninth in SEVENTH

Keywords: Fortune Through Partnerships

Favorable: Gets lots of advantages from being married and being in a partnership; does business in foreign lands; may go overseas to seek spiritual knowledge; partner may be involved in law, higher education, and spiritual pursuits; person has good fortune overall and knows how to relate well to people

Unfavorable: Partner may be absent a lot in business in foreign locations; pursuit of spiritual knowledge may detract from business activities; father could be away on business overseas and could even die in a foreign country

Ruler of Ninth in EIGHTH

Keywords: Unearned Fortunes

Favorable: Gets support and financial benefit (possibly inheritance) from father's side of the family; spiritual knowledge from intuition and self-cognition; drawn to esoteric and secret learning; has a private relationship with teachers and gurus; fortune from partner's money

Unfavorable: Misfortune and unhappiness for father; father or guru get into a scandal; person also could have bad luck and chronic financial problems; feels abandoned or unsupported by the father; disrespectful to teachers and gurus; trouble on long-distance travels; ailments in the hip and lower back region; illnesses might be improved by spiritual methods

Ruler of Ninth in NINTH

Keywords: Fullness of Fortune

Favorable: More fortunate than most; prosperous father; success in higher education; long-distance traveling; could be a travel agent, publisher, lawyer, or philosopher; money comes easily; popular, honored for their wisdom; good grandchildren (9th is 5th to the 5th—the children's children)

Unfavorable: Excessive fortune could lead to boredom or no attempt to evolve much; could get into some trouble by pushing their luck; father is so focused on personal growth, or away on business so much, that children are neglected; father could die or leave the family early in some way

Ruler of Ninth in TENTH

Keywords: Fortunate Life Purpose

Favorable: Very lucky; good ethics; favor and wealth from career; leader, minister, political head, business person; seems to know what to do and what they do works out well; gets the best advantages; popular; supportive to others; father prospers; relationship with guru aids life purpose and career

Unfavorable: Zealot in philosophy and religion; gives too much of their wealth to leaders, politicians, gurus, educational organizations, etc.; father's lack of focus on maintaining the family wealth could create problems

Ruler of Ninth in ELEVENTH

Keywords: Fortune Through Opportunities

Favorable: Plenty of good opportunities; elder siblings prosper; good children; successful investor; makes profits from education, law, long-distance travel; natural and easy intelligence; playful, generous to gurus and teachers; is well respected and has powerful friends

Unfavorable: Friends and elder siblings could create cash-flow problems; children could drain finances; too much friendliness with associates could detract from love from the mate; speculations get too grandiose

Ruler of Ninth in TWELFTH

Keywords: Fortune of Liberation

Favorable: High interest in spiritual development; travels for spiritual purposes; finds pleasure in sensual pursuits and sexual activity; drawn to charitable and humanitarian efforts; father is a religious, spiritual, or highly educated man; gets a very good guru

Unfavorable: Lack of attention to material growth; subject to fines, penalties, and punishments; possible imprisonment or lengthy convalescence from an illness; father is either disinterested or unskilled at making money; feels unfortunate or unappreciated; distant or strained relationship with the father

RULERS OF THE TENTH HOUSE

Ruler of Tenth in FIRST
Keywords: Independent in Career

Favorable: Enjoys working for themselves; trailblazer, entrepreneur, capable of leading big projects or undertaking challenging tasks; focus is on promotion of the self; good health, strong personality, tenacious, persistent when it comes to getting what they want

Unfavorable: Pesters others until they get their way; not a team player; feels stifled working in big companies; selfish; health is compromised through putting in too much effort; wastes their savings trying to be independent

Ruler of Tenth in SECOND
Keywords: Money Through Career

Favorable: Truthful; earns through learning, food business, the face and appearance (e.g., cosmetics or beauty products); dietician, nutritionist, gourmet cook, money handler, currency trader, jeweler; does work connected to the mouth (dentist); has an influential voice; money through a family business or businesses focusing on the family; a speech or language specialist; might use or teach mantras or other chanting sounds for meditation

Unfavorable: Naive; eating disorders affect status and career; family problems ruin business; low-paying jobs; style or manner of speaking detracts from their success; does not speak the truth; may exaggerate or say things that cannot be verified

Ruler of Tenth in THIRD
Keywords: Career of Self-Expression

Favorable: Determined, persistent, adventuresome; younger siblings help the career; many short-distance travels in their job; builds their success through lecturing, selling, marketing, advertising, writing, editing, printing, communications business, computers, telephony, music, art, acting, dancing, sports

Unfavorable: Puts in a lot of effort for minimal rewards; doesn't evaluate the consequences and suffers many setbacks and delays; procrastinates; lack of determination and courage; aggressive, impatient; problems with younger siblings and neighbors; hand, neck, and shoulder injuries at work; breathing, nerve, or skin damage from occupational hazards (3rd is 8th to the 8th)

Ruler of Tenth in FOURTH
Keywords: Earning Through Learning

Favorable: Good educator; involved in housing, hotel, or real estate business; success with vehicles; mechanic, architect, psychologist; nurturing; good mother, nurse, midwife; clothing business; geologist, surveyor, agriculturist, horticulturist, florist, day-care worker, landscaper, or other land-based activities; gets a good home and car and has other valuable fixed assets

Unfavorable: Career brings trouble to mother and to family; many emotional challenges at work; lives in lower-cost housing or is always renting; home is not comfortable; does not have a reliable car; does not learn to keep up in business or career; farm worker, house servant, and other lower-wage jobs

Ruler of Tenth in FIFTH
Keywords: Intelligent Career

Favorable: Investment counselor, stockbroker, tax consultant, lawyer, government, or big corporation jobs; focused on children's affairs; teaches spiritual techniques; jobs come easily due to past-life karma (purva punya); intellectual occupations; sports and entertainment field

Unfavorable: Office romances lead to trouble; children cause complications at work; speculation careers don't pan out; does not fare well in intellectual occupations; inept or charlatan spiritual teacher; involved in dishonest transactions

Ruler of Tenth in SIXTH
Keywords: Career of Service

Favorable: Medical, legal, defense, security areas; exercise; physical or massage therapist; animal worker; paid well for tackling tough jobs; works hard for success; gets career boost from maternal relations; very good at providing service

Unfavorable: Manual laborer; struggles to keep working; low-paying occupations; disputes and enemies at work; may get fired; dishonorable discharge from the military; lawsuits at work hurt career; gets into debts, lives outside their means; work accidents and injuries; low-paying jobs in the service industry

Ruler of Tenth in SEVENTH

Keywords: Career Through Partnerships

Favorable: Expert at relationships and diplomacy; keeps in balance with others; can talk to anybody about anything; achieves maximum rapport; businessman; career could involve international travel; career counselor; mate helps with career and can advance well in their own career; good marriage and profitable business agreements

Unfavorable: Bad partnerships could hinder career; needs to draw the line between business socializing and inappropriate affairs; weakens their own career by investing too much time and money or diverting attention from their own career to help their mate; mate or partners want to pursue a career or business activity that is beyond their capacity

Ruler of Tenth in EIGHTH

Keywords: Career of the Unknown

Favorable: Good researcher and analyst, spy or detective; involved in healing or the medical fields; success with aging issues, insurance, estate planning, probate, affairs of the dead, and life extension; interest in psychological factors at work; mystical, spiritual; makes decisions intuitively; psychologist; good support and financing for work projects; a financial windfall boosts career

Unfavorable: Lack of self-promotion; too shy or fearful at work; involved in industrial espionage; scandals hurt work; doesn't ask enough for themselves; may not get the full credit for their business successes; unethical or inappropriate; has a nagging feeling that they don't know their life purpose; lack of orderliness at work; gets stress disability from work

Ruler of Tenth in NINTH

Keywords: Fortunate Career

Favorable: High level career with abundant favor and blessings; oriented to higher education, philosophy, religion, ethics, and healing of the spirit; travels in career—often for spiritual purposes; success as a publisher, lawyer, and justice of the courts; father may play a role in the person's career

Unfavorable: Could abandon their material development for spiritual growth causing concern within the family—especially the father; a well-meaning father might intervene too much or person may become dependent on father for support; has it so easy that the person loses their initiative

Ruler of Tenth in TENTH

Keywords: Fullness of Career

Favorable: Career is on the level of a "king" or top executive; highly respected and honored; becomes famous for their life's work; generous; can handle large projects and govern large groups of people; politically savvy; success in government work or with large corporations

Unfavorable: May get trapped in government jobs or positions within established companies that, while secure, do little for the person's creativity and initiative; could get into a rut or become overly dependent on their work environment for meaning or structure in life; knee injuries in career

Ruler of Tenth in ELEVENTH

Keywords: Career of Opportunities

Favorable: Good income, high status; works with people of renown; elder sibling is fortunate and helps with the person's career; plenty of opportunities throughout life; money manager; inspirational speaking, brokering, spiritual teaching; is very honorable and has a good group of friends; well connected

Unfavorable: Wrong-thinking or confused friends could bring harm to the person's career; elder sibling becomes dependent and needs support; hearing damage at work; lack of new ideas to grow much in business; political connections harm career

Ruler of Tenth in TWELFTH

Keywords: Career of Liberation

Favorable: Career related to spirituality, healing, foreign job assignments, hospitals and clinics, nursing homes and sanitariums, detention centers and correctional institutions; may volunteer or work for a spiritual, educational, charitable, or humanitarian organization; very generous, self-sacrificing; focused on enlightenment; does well with foreign business and/or foreign businesspeople

Unfavorable: Does not pay attention to responsibilities or tries to take a short cut or cheat—could lead to fines, penalties, or even imprisonment; could be detained or hospitalized in a foreign country; confidence man, swindler, charlatan healer; can't sleep or enjoy themselves due to job worries and stress

RULERS OF THE ELEVENTH HOUSE

Ruler of Eleventh in FIRST
Keywords: Opportunities for the Self
Favorable: Blessed with good financial backing and a prosperous upbringing; a winner; gets advantages and opportunities throughout life from well-placed people; creates a positive environment with fresh ideas and a hopeful vision; elder sibling prospers and could be of help
Unfavorable: Friends and associates could negatively impact cash flow; comes up with ideas that are too advanced or are out of touch with the times and loses; profit taking is minimized by lack of realistic thinking; loses money through elder siblings; lack of opportunities

Ruler of Eleventh in SECOND
Keywords: Financial Opportunities
Favorable: Good liquid assets; money handler; activities related to the voice (language, singing, speaking); diet; health supplements; food and restaurant business; facial and mouth products; eye care; has successful ventures with friends, siblings, and influential people
Unfavorable: Liquid assets and the accumulation of money is hampered by friends; elder sibling could have financial problems; family finances are strained; hearing and vision problems; bad diet and teeth

Ruler of Eleventh in THIRD
Keywords: Profitable Self-Expression
Favorable: Successful adventures; succeeds through determination and perseverance; good cash flow from communications, athletics, art, music, writing, acting, dance, computer technology, sales and marketing, seminar instructor, editor, etc.; siblings and friends contribute to financial success; person is very persuasive and friendly
Unfavorable: Friends, neighbors, and siblings could bring impediments to profits; has to work too hard to get ahead or keep a steady income; hearing problems

Ruler of Eleventh in FOURTH

Keywords: Opportunities for the Home

Favorable: Profits from education, counseling, real estate, house appraisal, hotels, buildings, vehicles, agriculture, dairy products, minerals, geological activities (surveying, mapmaking, geologist, soil test expert), architecture; mother and family create a supportive atmosphere for financial success; person is well educated

Unfavorable: Emotional problems detract from ability to generate a good income; family is financially unsupportive; elder siblings have monetary problems; loss of money through house and car problems; not enough money to finish education

Ruler of Eleventh in FIFTH

Keywords: Speculative Opportunities

Favorable: Success as an intermediary, broker, investor or gambler, teacher; sports and entertainment industry; smart, knows scriptures and mantras; good opportunities; children are a blessing; may be given the opportunity to adopt a child or works for agencies to support children

Unfavorable: Takes too many risks; may be tempted to cheat or be too clever; lack of income to properly support children's development; loss in the stock market; lack of attention to educational opportunities

Ruler of Eleventh in SIXTH

Keywords: Profits Through Service

Favorable: Income through service; may get opportunities from medicine, legal work, office administration, armed services, exercise, and self-improvement jobs; pets; maternal relations could help finances

Unfavorable: Poor money management, struggles with money, debts; income hurt by fraudulent or criminal activities; frustrated, ruins opportunities by being too eager or aggressive; sickness, accidents, or injuries disrupt cash flow; gets too involved in friend's problems

Ruler of Eleventh in SEVENTH

Keywords: Opportunities Through Partnerships

Favorable: Income is improved after marriage or from doing business in partnership; makes money traveling; mate is a friend first; optimistic, inspiring, doesn't believe in the word *can't*; makes hard things seem easy; profits through partnership with elder sibling and from people who are influential

Unfavorable: Sweet talker; opportunist; on a quest to fulfill sexual or sensual fantasies; makes business through bringing people together for pleasurable purposes; mate or partner squelches their dreams or diminishes their opportunities

Ruler of Eleventh in EIGHTH

Keywords: Opportunities from the Unknown

Favorable: Profits through health activities, affairs of the dead, estate planning, probate, research businesses; involved in secret work; gets unexpected advantages and financial windfalls; could inherit; money through sex-related business or helping people in this area; psychologist, healer, psychic, detective

Unfavorable: Older siblings have serious health problems; person lacks confidence; shy or afraid to go after new opportunities; self-isolated and without many friends; gains money through questionable means; low income; loses money through deception; passed over for advancement; gets few opportunities

Ruler of Eleventh in NINTH

Keywords: Profits and Fortune

Favorable: Large profits and a great income; father helps in some significant way; gets a very evolved and happy guru; teachers inspire the person to greatness and they continue the tradition; friends are a great blessing throughout life; makes good money through publishing, traveling, philosophy, higher education, law, and ethics

Unfavorable: Income is hampered through excess generosity; spends too much time traveling; extreme focus on spiritual life could cause loss of opportunities; father is unfriendly; trouble with finances from authorities

Ruler of Eleventh in TENTH

Keywords: Profitable Career

Favorable: Many new business ventures; friendly management style; able to fulfill their dreams; an inspiration to others; career could involve financial management, consulting; success with government and with large corporations; thinks very big and makes those visions materialize; friends and influential persons help their career; the person is politically well connected, wealthy

Unfavorable: Siblings, mate, partners, and friends could interfere with career; hearing problems resulting from work; unable to fully realize their dreams; picks a dream that is unfeasible or unlikely (for example, person is five feet tall and wants to be a basketball star—although anything is possible if not probable)

Ruler of Eleventh in ELEVENTH

Keywords: Fullness of Friends and Opportunities

Favorable: Good cash flow; financial transactions are gainful; makes and keeps friends; benefits from friends, well-placed persons, and eldest sibling—or from a person who "feels" like an older brother or sister; plenty of opportunities; abundant life with many blessings and comforts

Unfavorable: Not many unfavorable aspects with this placement, but may take gains for granted or miss opportunities due to a lack-adaisical response; might come to depend too much on friends and influential people for advancement; gets spoiled by things coming too easily

Ruler of Eleventh in TWELFTH

Keywords: Opportunities for Enlightenment

Favorable: Cash flow through foreign countries and connections; income through spiritual activities; may be involved in charitable and humanitarian activities; could generate income through clinics, prisons, hospital wards, and other places of detention; able to fulfill their desires for pleasure and comforts; income through sex-related fields; sleep expert; success in secret actions; spiritual friends

Unfavorable: Losses through friends and elder siblings; loner; cash flow troubles, debts; unable to maximize their earning potential; penalties and possible imprisonment from improper financial transactions; lacks vision; has nightmares, feelings of hopelessness

RULERS OF THE TWELFTH HOUSE

Ruler of Twelfth in FIRST

Keywords: Unbounded Self

Favorable: High spiritual content; charitable; interest in meditation, education, healing, and working for activities that benefit the world at large; generous, broad-minded; enjoys gaining for themselves by helping others to gain; pleasure seeker

Unfavorable: Many personal losses; wasteful; low vitality; poor resistance to disease; lack of confidence; has financial problems; tends to get fined, punished, or penalized; appears weak and invites the aggression of others; too forgiving; doesn't set boundaries; a victim; feels betrayed

Ruler of Twelfth in SECOND

Keywords: Finances for Freedom

Favorable: Spends money on religious or spiritual purposes; might donate money or time to feed the hungry; generous, speaks sweetly, kind; sings religious songs; makes money in foreign countries or from foreigners

Unfavorable: Does not accumulate much money; may resort to inappropriate financial strategies; family problems; unrefined, weak, or unconvincing speech; poor language skills; says the wrong thing and gets into trouble; debts, fines, and penalties; food disorders; states things that are incorrect or untrue; trouble with face, teeth, mouth, and throat; vision ailments

Ruler of Twelfth in THIRD

Keywords: Determination for Liberation

Favorable: Writes and gives seminars on self-improvement and spiritual development; religious siblings; creates spiritually uplifting art and music; determined to get enlightened

Unfavorable: Lack of courage and determination; loses through adventures; little sales or self-promotion abilities; apprehensive, timid; poor artistic and performance skills; gets into trouble through writing; uncoordinated; younger siblings and neighbors are a source of concern

Ruler of Twelfth in FOURTH

Keywords: Feelings for Freedom

Favorable: Spiritual seeker; education in foreign lands; mother may be of a different culture or race; experiences states of reverie and moksha; may work for the homeless or be an advocate for people without a home (refugees, people recovering from a housing loss or disaster, etc.); donates to schools

Unfavorable: Lives in isolated regions; low-income housing; has trouble buying or maintaining a home; could be homeless; agricultural failures; buildings are destroyed in some way; poor attire; incomplete education; loss or lack of support of mother; emotionally underdeveloped; lack of comfort; unhappy; car problems

Ruler of Twelfth in FIFTH

Keywords: Intellect of Enlightenment

Favorable: Seeks the most in spiritual advancement; studies the scriptures; teaches and uses spiritual techniques; follows a spiritual destiny motivated from previous karmas; children are spiritual; has romances with foreign-born persons or in a foreign country; might work for adoption groups

Unfavorable: Romantic problems; doesn't feel loved by the mate; children are a problem; possible miscarriage or abortion; child might not thrive; person lacks intelligence; may resort to deception; not open to spiritual writings; has trouble meditating

Ruler of Twelfth in SIXTH

Keywords: Service for Liberation

Favorable: Eventual prosperity; provides service overseas; is a devotee or volunteer; works in health, defense, self-improvement, exercise, office administration, legal matters, or animal work; active in charitable and humanitarian efforts; wins legal battles and successfully challenges fines and penalties; could do charitable work for a disaster relief organization

Unfavorable: Menial and manual labor jobs; low-level servant or hireling; has problems getting people to help or serve them; takes inappropriate approaches to solving problems; irritated; subject to punishment and detention; gets into debt; drawn to indulging in sex and self-satisfaction; problems with passion

Ruler of Twelfth in SEVENTH

Keywords: Unbounded Partnerships

Favorable: Seeks a partnership with the Divine; does foreign business; travels on pilgrimages; partners are spiritual and open to pleasures; might meet mate on foreign travels; mate and partners might do better if they live at a distance, are away on travel, or have some ability to take time to themselves; might work in marriage counseling or as a conflict mediator

Unfavorable: Divorce or separation; losses and troubles in relationships; does poorly in business; business partnerships and agreements don't work out; mate is ill, unconfident, or uncooperative; mate runs up debts (12th is 6th to the 7th)

Ruler of Twelfth in EIGHTH

Keywords: Unbounded and Transcendental

Favorable: Involved in medicine, investigation, affairs of older persons and issues at the end of life; gains from others' losses; might get inheritance and other forms of unexpected and/or unearned income; adept at spiritual matters and philosophies; very intuitive and insightful; good researcher; curious to know about the secrets of life; love of the transcendental

Unfavorable: Shy; lack of confidence; chronic financial problems; lack of vitality; doesn't focus enough on making a living; lack of pleasure; reproductive and elimination ailments; suffers in secret; lack of support and benefit from others; mate does not do well financially and might not be supportive

Ruler of Twelfth in NINTH

Keywords: Fortune in Enlightenment

Favorable: Studies abroad; interested in enlightenment and high forms of knowledge; charitable, humane; travels frequently or over long distances; looks at sex as a spiritual tool; might donate time and money to universities, churches, temples, and other places of higher learning

Unfavorable: Not much financial luck; father could lead a troubled life and end up hospitalized or incarcerated; father could leave the home early through frequent travel, divorce, or death; person and father could be at odds with each other; person might be adverse to higher learning and have little respect for the teachers associated with that level of knowledge; could have hip problems

Ruler of Twelfth in TENTH

Keywords: Unbounded Career

Favorable: Career interests center around spiritual, charitable, and humanitarian efforts; might work for one of these organizations; could also work in clinics, correctional institutions, ashrams, spiritual retreat centers, and in foreign countries; might donate money to spiritual or religious workers (monks, nuns, etc.)

Unfavorable: Career does not advance well; insufficient income; forsakes good earnings for a spiritual life and struggles too much; not much interested in working hard for a living; moves from job to job looking for purpose; subject to fines, penalties, and punishments

Ruler of Twelfth in ELEVENTH

Keywords: Opportunities with Liberation

Favorable: Income through spiritual and humanitarian activities; good spiritual activity or sensual enjoyments; has pleasant dreams—often of other worlds and levels of existence; makes profits in foreign lands or with foreigners; some say losses are destroyed since 11th is 12th to the 12th (loss of losses) and opposite the 2nd—giving increase of revenues from 2nd house matters (cash, gems, and other liquid assets)

Unfavorable: Can't seem to maintain friends and social contacts; doesn't materialize their dreams; elder siblings could lead a troubled life; relationship with siblings is distant; person doesn't have good cash flow; has low income or problems managing cash flow; feels depressed, hopeless, and frustrated

Ruler of Twelfth in TWELFTH

Keywords: Fullness of Unboundedness

Favorable: Developed spiritual nature; very generous, kind, helps the hopeless and helpless; rewarded for all their good deeds; spends on spiritual purposes; success in foreign lands; goes on pilgrimages; strong feet (grounded); enjoys the spiritual and comforting aspects of sex; sleeps well

Unfavorable: Lack of direction in life; on the run from the law and/or creditors; subject to many fines and punishments; has trouble in foreign lands; eyesight ailments; feet problems; not much joy of sex; sleep disorders; disregard for spiritual practices

CHAPTER EIGHT

YOGAS—PLANETARY COMBINATIONS

Yoga is a Sanskrit word meaning "yoke." In Vedic philosophy, it is used to signify a form of union or combination, often that of a spiritual aspirant gaining union with God. Yoga also indicates a special division in panchangas or ephemerides. In Vedic astrology, we primarily use the word *yoga* to mean a specific planetary combination that gives added effects to the chart, either good or bad.

One of the most prominent yogas is that of a conjunction, wherein two or more planets occupy the same sign or house. The degree separating the two planets is generally not much considered as long as both planets are in the same sign. If they are close by degree, but in separate signs, the planets are not considered in conjunction in Vedic astrology.

A tremendous amount of information is contained within the form of a planetary yoga. Based on my experience, I rate the importance of the aspects in this order, with the first having the highest influence: (1) conjunctions; (2) oppositions; (3) squares; and (4) trines. For example, if you have a person living in the same house as you (conjunction), their influence is quite significant. If a person lives across the street from you (opposition), their influence is less so. Some would argue that trines are more significant than squares, but in the charts that I have read, I find more influence coming from squares.

Two-Planet Combinations

In this chapter, we are going to put special emphasis on two-planet yogas. Dr. B. V. Raman has written a book detailing over 300 yogas, some of which involve three, four, or more planets. You will do well to know the 35 two-planet combinations listed in the table on page 172. Parasara indicated that there were two kinds of readings, the general one called Samanya and the specific one called Nishyaya. Knowledge of the union of planets adds greatly to your ability to give a more specific reading.

Planets, when they combine, influence each other in a synergistic manner, either favorably or unfavorably. Buckminster Fuller, the writer, brought out the idea of synergy, where the sum is greater than the parts. He used the analogy of combining two metals to get a stronger third metal. This alloy produced different characteristics than either of the contributing metals did on their own. Similarly, the combined influence of planets is distinct from any planet's individual operation. Very rarely will you see a planet acting alone, so knowing how planets work in combination is key to understanding how to effectively use Vedic astrology.

Knowledge of two-planet conjunctions is a significant tool in your astrological tool chest. While planets can combine in sets of up to seven, learning how planets combine in pairs can give you sufficient knowledge as a beginner to reasonably interpret the effects of planets in more complex combinations. Even if there are multiple planets combining due to conjunction, opposition, aspect, sign rulership, etc., you can still look at all the planets involved by analyzing them two at a time. It is important to know that the interaction between planets does not enhance both the planets. Conjunctions are not always friendly— one planet can enhance the other while it is itself diminished. You can see symbiotic, mutually supportive relationships, or you can see parasitic relationships where one planet takes more than it gives. An ant stepping on an elephant is not so bad, but the reverse is disastrous to the little ant.

After understanding two-planet combinations, you can transfer the concept to other areas of chart interpretation. For example, you can become adept at understanding the effects of the following:

1. *The ruler of one planet in another planet's sign* (e.g., for Aries rising—the ruler of the first, Mars, in the seventh sign of Libra, ruled by Venus—Mars combining with Venus)

2. *A major planetary ruler (dasa) and its combined effect with a subperiod planet (bhukti)* e.g., Mercury dasa and Sun bhukti—Mercury affiliating with the Sun (dasas and bhuktis are discussed in chapter 13)

3. *One planet being located in another planet's sign* (e.g., Jupiter in the sign of Cancer, which is the Moon's sign—Jupiter linked with the Moon)

4. *One planet transiting over another in the birth chart* (e.g., Jupiter transiting over Mercury in Cancer—a connection between the transiting Jupiter and the natal Mercury. The Moon could also participate in this yoga since it rules Cancer, giving us the effect of not only Jupiter/ Mercury, but also a Jupiter/Moon combination and a Moon/Mercury combination)

5. *Two transiting planets in combination* (e.g., transiting Jupiter becoming conjunct with the transiting Moon—a form of a Jupiter/Moon conjunction)

These combinations have the most impact when they are in the form of conjunctions and oppositions. Parivartana Yoga combinations are also significant—for example, if Jupiter is transiting over Saturn's sign and Saturn is transiting over Jupiter's sign—then Jupiter and Saturn are synergistically enhancing each other's influence.

Thirty-Five Planetary Conjunctions

	Su	Mo	Ma	Me	Ju	Ve	Sa	Ra	Ke
Su		Su/Mo	Su/Ma	Su/Me	Su/Ju	Su/Ve	Su/Sa	Su/Ra	Su/Ke
Mo			Mo/Ma	Mo/Me	Ju/Mo	Mo/Ve	Mo/Sa	Mo/Ra	Mo/Ke
Ma				Ma/Me	Ju/Ma	Ma/Ve	Sa/Ma	Ma/Ra	Ma/Ke
Me					Ju/Me	Me/Ve	Sa/Me	Me/Ra	Me/Ke
Ju						Ju/Ve	Ju/Sa	Ju/Ra	Ju/Ke
Ve							Ve/Sa	Ve/Ra	Ve/Ke
Sa								Sa/Ra	Sa/Ke

The effects of each of the above combinations is discussed in the following list.

Conjunction of SUN and MOON

Keyword: Eclipsed

Favorable: High spiritual capacity; ability to forego the world for enlightenment

Unfavorable: This is a new Moon, when the light of the Sun is blocked by the shadow of the Moon. The person's life is enfeebled by the lack of light. Endurance may be less, although the person may aspire toward self-improvement. In many cases, the birth process was difficult or protracted or had some unusual feature to it.

Conjunction of SUN and MARS

Keywords: Sun = Disposition; Mars = Fighting

Favorable: Initiative; short-duration tasks; strong resistance and stamina; competitive spirit; enjoys a spontaneous approach; reacts by reflex; stays youthful and strong; this person or the father can be in a defense/security–related enterprise; surgeon or health-related occupations involving cutting, inserting, or manipulating the body

Unfavorable: Obstinate; domineering; poor at closing; changes jobs frequently; impatient; rough or overbearing speech; expects instant gratification; subject to pitta disorders; gives females a masculine disposition; may see doctors or medical professionals frequently; self-improvement fanatic

Conjunction of SUN and MERCURY

Keywords: Sun = Activity; Mercury = Analyzing

Favorable: Called Budha Adhitya Yoga. Well organized; likes measuring and analyzing; clever or shrewd; often in the fields of bookkeeping, accounting, or business management; overall good mind for business and can keep the mind focused on the budget or money plan

Unfavorable: Mismanages money; too clever or unscrupulous; detailed and complicated

Conjunction of SUN and JUPITER

Keywords: Sun = Activity; Jupiter = Wisdom

Favorable: Comforting, enthusiastic, supportive, thoughtful, and expansive; good advisory capacities—could be consultant, minister, spiritual leader, speaker, or writer; counselor, intermediary, balances opposing viewpoints; generally a good combination for money and wealth

Unfavorable: Could be disinclined to take full action, preferring leisure or comfort

Conjunction of SUN and VENUS

Keywords: Sun = Activity; Venus = Beauty

Favorable: Charming; skilled in the arts; actor, musician, artist, etc.; entertainer, lecturer, or spokesperson; good in sales or good at promoting ideas or philosophies; an administrator in lower level government or business; could be involved with sports

Unfavorable: Manipulative; controlling in love; friction in love life; reproductive organ problems

Conjunction of SUN and SATURN

Keywords: Sun = Activity; Saturn = Focused or Obstructed

Favorable: Works hard; reliable, conventional, efficient; preference for work that is regulated and predictable; best in ordered environment with minimal uncertainties and a clear chain of command; follows their job description and work instructions precisely

Unfavorable: Averse to change; dislikes ambiguities; lack of people skills; poor in emotionally intense work; resistant to real authority figures; abhors incompetence; conflicted, speedy, and restricted; delays with finances and with their emotional lives; often mistreated

Conjunction of SUN and RAHU

Keywords: Sun = Activity; Rahu = Shadows

Favorable: Spiritual capacity; benefits from work overseas or in foreign countries; involved in unusual occupations or does normal occupations in an unusual or inventive manner

Unfavorable: Lack of confidence and self-awareness; poor self-evaluation; worried, confused, and unclear; health problems that are hard to diagnose; difficult life for the father, or relationship with father may have been distant or rough in some way

Conjunction of SUN and KETU

Keywords: Sun = Activity; Ketu = Absence of Boundaries

Favorable: Many saints and individuals with highly developed souls have this combination.

Unfavorable: Health problems, a weak or delicate constitution, lack of courage; many surprises, changes, and uncertainties; vision, circulation, and heart problems (such as low blood pressure); health problems, since father's or their own personal life has a lot of ups and downs

Conjunction of MOON and MARS

Keywords: Moon = Emotions; Mars = Energy or Fire

Favorable: Called Chandra Mangala Yoga. The emotions will be charged and easily excited, leading to bold actions and initiative. Imagination is lively and energetic.

Unfavorable: Agitated, easy to provoke, danger from acting in the midst of an elevated emotion, possibility of friction or heated interactions with the mother, mother has emotional and/or health problems; person's relationships, especially marriage, are emotionally disturbed

Conjunction of MOON and MERCURY

Keywords: Moon = Imagination; Mercury = Mind

Favorable: Agreeable, charitable, considerate; befriends others; creative in scientific or analytical methods; active imagination, innovative, good writer, theorist, playful mind

Unfavorable: Unstable if too active; scattered and fragmented; too many thoughts; overactive imagination; ineffective

Conjunction of MOON and JUPITER

Keywords: Moon = Fullness; Jupiter = Expansion

Favorable: Called GajaKesari Yoga. Overcomes obstacles and prevails; has comforts and good status in life; respected; humanitarian; likes to give advice, teach, or help others; optimistic orientation

Unfavorable: Overly optimistic; doesn't know when to quit; high expectations lead to disillusionment and dissatisfaction; lazy

Conjunction of MOON and VENUS

Keywords: Moon = Imagination; Venus = Beauty

Favorable: Good imagination, love of refinement and comfort, likes to bring comfort to others or to enrich their lives; the emotions are rich and oriented to "right brain" activities; artistic sensibilities

Unfavorable: Need to moderate one's indulgence in pleasures, extravagance, opulence, too much food, or sexual activity; routine or structure is important

Conjunction of MOON and SATURN

Keywords: Moon = Emotions; Saturn = Focus or Obstruction

Favorable: Best with moderately creative work; uses their skills in imagination or problem solving to promote themselves; efficient; good at exact processes such as technical or science writing, or the explanation of an engineering or business process

Unfavorable: Sad or emotionally withdrawn; cold; restricted emotionally; shy; indulges in their own sadness; depressed if not honored for their hard work; don't communicate their needs enough; fatigued; tries too hard

Conjunction of MOON and RAHU

Keywords: Moon = Emotions; Rahu = Unusual

Favorable: Out-of-the-ordinary creativity; able to obtain high mystical states; unusual thought processes

Unfavorable: Confused and insecure, apprehensive, vulnerable; gullible and taken advantage of; uncertainty and self-doubt leads these people to become a "jack of all trades"; may take alcohol, drugs, or a lot of food supplements to stay balanced; chemical imbalances; confusion for mother

Conjunction of MOON and KETU

Keywords: Moon = Emotions; Ketu = Unboundedness

Favorable: Highly intuitive, psychic, gives the mind a spiritual frame of reference, can experience levels of mental refinement not accessible by most people; "real" dreams

Unfavorable: High intuition and sensitivity exposes them to mental disturbances; psychotic, odd dreams, very receptive yet unable to desensitize themselves to all the inputs they are experiencing

Conjunction of MARS and MERCURY

Keywords: Mars = Energy; Mercury = Mind

Favorable: Clever, quick-witted, good speaker; has a mind for engineering, mechanical occupations, or medical work; quick problem-solving ability

Unfavorable: Very stimulated mentally; mind moves very fast; angry moods; needs to stop and think things through; driven to achieve a lot; competitive, aggressive, and ambitious; too self-centered; ruthless about attaining their goals

Conjunction of MARS and JUPITER

Keywords: Mars = Energy; Jupiter = Wealth

Favorable: This is called Guru Mangala Yoga. It brings energy, enthusiasm, and dynamism. If the person manages their assets well, this conjunction can bring good money and status. It gives the person the drive to attain a good education and a position of leadership.

Unfavorable: Expends wealth too quickly; can become impoverished for periods of time; might suffer from a negative legal settlement or incur a financial penalty involving improper management of funds

Conjunction of MARS and VENUS

Keywords: Mars = Passion; Venus = Love

Favorable: Sexually vital and appealing, enjoys a spontaneous approach to romance, has a youthful charm or charisma about them, loves action

Unfavorable: Likes sexuality but has trouble settling down, overly passionate, intimacy with heated discussions and quarreling, agitated and easily provoked, fun but not a reliable partner

Conjunction of MARS and SATURN

Keywords: Mars = Action; Saturn = Focus or Limitation

Favorable: High energy; does well with a lot of activity and physical movement; good at jobs involving aggression, risks, danger, courage, and stamina; resistant to strain; sought out for their energy; their directness and energy gives them skill in getting people to come up with results

Unfavorable: High metabolism, agitated, wants to do things too quickly; their energies are not in alignment with their environment; often thin and high strung—especially when young; rash nature; don't understand their loved one's motivations and needs all that well; drive others away with their intensity; feels alone and isolated; exhausted and depressed at times, then energetic

Conjunction of MARS and RAHU

Keywords: Mars = Fire; Rahu = Toxicity

Favorable: Generally, they have a lot of energy and take an unusual approach to action.

Unfavorable: Gets angry easily, antagonistic, vindictive; possible problems with circulation or blood purity; feverishness can lead to skin afflictions, allergies, and other inflammatory conditions in the body; can't monitor themselves; needs to cool down and not dwell on vindictive or angry feelings

Conjunction of MARS and KETU

Keywords: Mars = Energy; Ketu = Reorganization

Favorable: Can respond quickly to things

Unfavorable: Loses equilibrium; gets annoyed, irritated, easily provoked by other's negative behavior or criticism; both acts too quickly and delays in expressing themselves; emotions rise hot and quick, need to "count to ten"

Conjunction of MERCURY and JUPITER

Keywords: Mercury = Discrimination; Jupiter = Expansion and Wisdom

Favorable: Skilled speakers and counselors; good learning and insight; drawn to publishing, seminars, music, dance, art, and the "wisdom business" in general; good with children's education; wise and wealthy

Unfavorable: "Pollyanna" attitude, misses obvious opportunities for gain, lazy thinking

Conjunction of MERCURY and VENUS

Keywords: Mercury = Mind; Venus = Pleasures

Favorable: Charming manners, fun-loving disposition, enjoys the more imaginative or creative side of business or trade, fresh and original, good creative writers or musicians

Unfavorable: Shrewd if they need to be (but best to avoid hard or ruthless environment); tendency not to think much ahead in their early years or in the early stages of a job or enterprise; not serious enough; usually succeed in their forties when they begin to settle and think about the future

Conjunction of MERCURY and SATURN

Keywords: Mercury = Thinking; Saturn = Focused or Stuck

Favorable: Mind can be very focused; technical orientation; goes deeply into the detail level; good at focused and shrewd business transactions; has good business instincts and is skilled at planning; generally concise in money management and works for the improvement of a business

Unfavorable: Loses sight of the big picture, deceptive, obscuring, compulsive and obsessive, too detailed, not always open to advice, stubborn, feels stuck; subject to mental disturbances, distractions, disruptions, and depressions; in some cases, their learning ability is slow, as well as their recall

Conjunction of MERCURY and RAHU

Keywords: Mercury = Thinking; Rahu = Unusual or Toxic

Favorable: The mind may be drawn to work with foreigners or in connection with foreign lands or products. There may be a liking for the foreign or the unusual.

Unfavorable: Thinking gets clouded and toxic—especially when the pressure is on. Feels under attack, disoriented, anxious and distrustful, devious or confused in work, mean or lacking in praise or consideration; at worst this leads to criminal tendencies

Conjunction of MERCURY and KETU

Keywords: Mercury = Thinking; Ketu = Sublime or Erratic

Favorable: Subtle thinking; highly intuitive analysis; psychic; spiritual thinker; quick shifts in thinking

Unfavorable: Chaotic, frenzied and turbulent, confused, bewildered and angry; finds it difficult to process things clearly, concisely, and rationally; psychological skills are not sharp; at times can easily get disturbed or mentally off balance; mind is full of surprises and changes

Conjunction of JUPITER and VENUS

Keywords: Jupiter = Expansion; Venus = Beauty

Favorable: Counselor; skillful in attaining and giving knowledge; respected, bright, lucky, and admired; artist, social worker, devoted to a higher humane cause; political interest or ability; advisor, minister, spiritual leader; may work in the fashion or luxury trade

Unfavorable: Has a liking for leisure and comfort that could lead to loss of control; may dissipate themselves in pleasures or not actuate all their blessings; a good routine and moderate discipline will serve them well

Conjunction of JUPITER and SATURN

Keywords: Jupiter = Expansion or Wisdom; Saturn = Focus or Order

Favorable: Skilled organizer, executive or legal orientation, attracted to occupations of authority and control, tenacious, structured, concerned with law and order, advisor, psychological counselor, educator or tutor; legal type of mind, good at arguments and debates, logical

Unfavorable: Stubborn, biased, or bigoted in their opinions; extremist, fanatical about their beliefs; dwelling on suffering could lead the person to be pessimistic; might convince themselves that life is dismal and fraught with duress

Conjunction of JUPITER and RAHU

Keyword: Jupiter = Wealth or Wisdom; Rahu = Deceit or Confusion

Favorable: This person is basically friendly, and is oriented toward material pursuits.

Unfavorable: Rahu has the effect of making a normally expansive and kind "Jupiter" person a bit harder. The person is more focused on themselves; for women, this conjunction could bring confusion about their purpose and role in marriage; it also may bring confused or dishonest men into their lives

Conjunction of JUPITER and KETU

Keywords: Jupiter = Wisdom and Wealth; Ketu = Moksha and Surprises

Favorable: Mental functions are more delicate or refined; psychic or intuitive, good ability to act instinctively, knows what to do without being taught or without seemingly having had much prior experience

Unfavorable: Erratic fortunes; breaks from spiritual teachers; for women this conjunction indicates unstable partner or inability to achieve balance with the partner

Conjunction of VENUS and SATURN

Keywords: Venus = Love; Saturn = Focus or Restriction

Favorable: Stability and durability in relationships and marriage; business or technical ability; productive, hardworking; benefits from agriculture, land, iron, steel, oil, or black things; love of old and serious things, antiques, old books, older people, poor people

Unfavorable: Often abstinent or celibate, or they can go the opposite way but will probably be very functional about love; attracted to older persons or mature persons; experience delay or restriction in marriage; emotionally dry or detached; can be charming to suit the purpose; might not think the effort or responsibilities of wealth and luxury are worth it, or may not be feeling worthy of it

Conjunction of VENUS and RAHU

Keywords: Venus = Love; Rahu = Out of the Ordinary

Favorable: This person is unique and talented in some distinct, out-of-the-ordinary way.

Unfavorable: Emotional confusions, unhappy love affairs, deceit, disillusionment or disenchantment in matters of love; unconventional sexual activity or taboo behavior; problems in the reproductive organs such as tumors, prostate problems, fallopian tube blockage, etc.

Conjunction of VENUS and KETU

Keywords: Venus = Love; Ketu = Change and Moksha

Favorable: Loves the spiritual realms

Unfavorable: Up-and-down relationships; broken loves and separations from love and loved ones; often feel deceived or betrayed; surprising changes in love; don't seem to be able to hold on to love

Conjunction of SATURN and RAHU

Keywords: Saturn = Focus or Restriction; Rahu = Unusual or Foreign

Favorable: Liking for distant, remote, or foreign things; more success in foreign lands or dealing with foreign products or people; driven to obtain success

Unfavorable: Remorseless, denies or negates their feelings, mechanical or ruthless manner, uncaring and detached, depressed, emotionally unreliable, does what is necessary to serve their own needs. In some cases, this condition reverses and the person gets subjected to ruthless people.

Conjunction of SATURN and KETU

Keywords: Saturn = Focus or Structure; Ketu = Change, Unboundedness

Favorable: There is a technical orientation and the ability to focus intensely on specific things for short periods.

Unfavorable: Chaotic, fragmented, and scattered; fanatical pursuit of ideas and projects; obsessive or one-track mind; danger, disarray, losing the big picture and having a project fall apart at the seams; things start off well then fall apart

Primary Planetary Yogas

The preceding list dealt with two-planet combinations—whether combined by placement, aspect, rulership, transit, or the like. Next, we will discuss the classical astrological use of the word *yoga*, which means, as discussed, "yoke" or "union." These yogas are special combinations of planets that give results above and beyond what seems readily evident in the chart. In the past, Vedic astrologers would commit these yogas to memory, which led to very short formulas and explanations of the effects of the yogas.

With the advent of computer programs to extract data, there is now less desire and need to memorize. Many astrologers will only familiarize themselves with a few basic yogas. If they need to know more, perhaps for an important reading that requires more insight, then they might look others up in any of the many textbooks available on this subject, or they may use a computer program to look up the yogas for them.

I will discuss what I think are a good set of yogas for you to begin with. The best modern reference for learning more about yogas is B. V. Raman's book, *Three Hundred Important Combinations.*

In chapter 12, we will discuss how to weigh the positive, negative, or neutral quality of each planet in the yoga. This understanding will allow you to begin to use yogas effectively.

In general, you need to be familiar with benefic or malefic planets by rising sign, and you need to know the six sources of strength, or shadbala values, of the planets. These points will give you a pretty good approximation of the value of each planet in a yoga. If one planet is stronger, its influence will predominate. If the yoga-producing planets have mixed strengths, then the results of the yoga will be more moderate. You also have to understand that the yoga will reflect its placement in the chart, whether by house, sign, or the like, and that the yoga will give its results more noticeably during the dasa and bhukti periods or the major gochara (transits) of the yoga planets.

It should be noted that a combination of planets might qualify for more than one type of yoga, as shown below. Planets can join each other in formations that concurrently qualify as, for example, a Raja Yoga, an Arishta Yoga, and a special type such as Parivartana. The quality and quantity of each planet must be weighed to derive the net effect of these multifaceted combinations.

Raja Yogas

This name implies a combination of planets that would make a man a king (raja). In reality, there are not a lot of kings, but there could be kinglike lifestyles. The person receiving these yogas should be able to live a prosperous life and stand out in society in some notable way. It should also be understood that the Raja Yoga will occur in proportion to the person's circumstances. If a person's family karma, culture, education, income, and social status are at a high or "royal" level, then we can forecast high results from these yogas.

Generally, Raja Yoga planets increase the favorable qualities of the houses in which they are located or the houses that they rule. The effects of these yogas, as is the general rule, are most noticeable during the dasa and bhukti periods of the planets involved.

The most prevalent form of Raja Yoga arises when the ruler of a trinal, or trikona, house (1, 5, or 9) combines in specific ways with the ruler of an angular, or kendra, house (1, 4, 7, or 10). The Raja Yogas come when these trikona and kendra ruling planets form conjunctions, mutual aspects, and mutual exchanges (Parivartana).

The Basic Types of Planetary Connections

The following list gives some of the basic concepts and connections that create astrological yogas:

- **Mutual Exchange:** Two planets, as rulers of signs, are positioned in each other's signs. For example, with Virgo rising, Jupiter in Gemini (Mercury's sign) and Mercury in Sagittarius (Jupiter's sign). Mutual exchange is also called Parivartana Yoga (see below).

- **Mutual Aspect:** Two planets aspect each other, according to the basic aspect rules (see chapter 12). For example, Saturn in Aquarius aspects Scorpio by 10 (Saturn aspects houses 3 and 10 away) and Mars in Scorpio aspects Aquarius by 4 (Mars throws an aspect on houses 4 and 8 away). So Saturn aspects Mars, and Mars aspects Saturn. In general, planets can form mutual aspects if they are in a square, a trine, an opposition, or by the special aspects of Mars (4 and 8), Saturn (3 and 10), and Jupiter (5 and 9).

- **Conjunction:** Two planets "aspect" each other if they are positioned in the same sign.

In general, any relationship between the benefic rulers of the 9th and 10th and the 5th brings Raja Yoga. Some examples of these Raja Yogas are:

- From the Lagna (ascendant), the ruler of the 9th is in the 10th house, and/or 10th is in the 9th.

- 9th is in 10th and 10th in 9th from the 9th—also you can look from the 10th, from the Moon, or from the Sun.

- Ruler of the 11th house is in the 2nd and/or 2nd is in the 11th.

The impact of benefic planets in Raja Yogas are as follows:

- Ruler of the 10th house gives strong career potential and powerful life purpose.

- Ruler of Lagna creates a potent person with a strong life and behavior.

- Ruler of 2nd gives increased capacity to accumulate wealth and to speak with authority.

- Ruler of 5th generates a high intellect, expanded business skills, and capacity to.act with youthfulness and vigor.

- Ruler of 7th, which is also 10th from the 10th, increases the capacity to deal with people successfully and to promote one's own interests and influence upon others.

- Ruler of 4th gives the ability to gain through nourishing and educating others and to have fixed assets (cars, houses, etc.) at a high level.

- Ruler of 9th brings the highest of fortune and a philosophy of life that leads to success.

Basic Planetary Yogas

Pancha Mahapurusha Yoga: This formation includes the yogas introduced in chapter 5: Mars and Ruchaka Yoga, Mercury and Bhadra Yoga, Jupiter and Hamsa Yoga, Venus and Malavya Yoga, and last, Saturn and Sasa Yoga. If a planet is exalted, or in its own sign in an angle from the Lagna or from the Moon, then one of the Pancha Mahapurusha Yogas is formed. These yogas produce the highest qualities of the planets involved, especially if those planets are free from unfavorable aspects. The Moon, Rahu, Ketu, and the Sun are not members of this set of yogas.

Parivartana Yoga: This yoga occurs when two planetary rulers are located in each other's signs. This is also called an exchange of houses or signs. For example, Mercury, ruler of Gemini, is located in Leo, and the Sun, ruler of Leo, in located in Gemini. This yoga forms a tight coupling of the houses involved and gives an influence as if the ruling planets were aspecting each other. The value of this yoga is lessened if the rulers of the dusthana houses, 6, 8, and 12, are involved.

Vargottama: This is a type of planetary union that increases the influence of the planet involved. Vargottama, though not specifically called a yoga, presents itself when a planet occupies the same sign in both the rasi chart and the navamsa chart. We will discuss the navamsa chart in chapter 10; the rasi chart is the one we have been relying on throughout the book—the most commonly used, 12-sign chart.

An extension of this concept, while not given the name Vargottama, is that if a planet is debilitated in the rasi chart but is exalted in the navamsa chart, its quality improves. For example, if we find Jupiter debilitated in the rasi, but exalted in the navamsa, then in the rasi chart (the main chart), Jupiter's malefic influence will be lessened. If the reverse occurs, and Jupiter is exalted in the rasi but debilitated in the navamsa, then the quality of the exalted Jupiter in the rasi is degraded by the debilitated Jupiter in the navamsa.

Some astrologers say that you can look at Vargottama as having an effect similar to a planet in its own house or sign.

Subha Kartari: Kartari means scissors; this indicates that a planet has a favorable (subha) planet on either side of it. It's like having good neighbors living on either side of you. This "hemming in," as astrologers also call it, can be within the same sign, between three signs, or a combination. For example: the Sun in Gemini, preceded by Venus in Taurus and followed by Mercury in Cancer. Or, as another example: the Sun in 15 degrees of Gemini, preceded by Venus at 10 degrees and followed by Mercury at 20 degrees of Gemini.

Papa Kartari: The same idea as above, except that the planet is hemmed in by unfavorable (papa) planets.

Neecha Bhanga Raja Yoga: There are certain instances when the influences of a debilitated planet get canceled, or more realistically, get reduced. It might be that not all of the unfavorable qualities are dissolved by this counteracting yoga, but it does offer improvement to an otherwise disadvantageous placement. The rules for this yoga will be explained in chapter 12.

Parvata Yoga: Occurs when any favorable planet is located in an angle from the Lagna (ascendant), and the 6th and 8th houses from the Lagna are either linked with favorable planets or are empty. Or, the ruler of the Lagna (the lagnadhipati) and ruler of the 12th house from the Lagna are in an angle from each other, e.g., Lagna ruler in 4th, 12th ruler in 7th.

Lakshmi Yoga: Occurs when the ruler of the 9th house is located in its moolatrikona sign, is placed in an angle from the Lagna, and the ruler of the Lagna is exalted and favorable.

Wealth-Producing Yogas

Lakshmi Yoga, above, is one indicator for wealth, and there are many other combinations that also point to wealth. In general, combinations with the money houses bring prosperity, such as the 2nd house (liquid assets), 4th (fixed assets), 9th (general fortune), and 11th (cash flow and profits). If the first house or the Lagna is involved in these combinations as well, the wealth potential is increased further. The other trine, the 5th, can also add to wealth if connected to any of the above wealth indicators. Sometimes the 10th, the career house, can participate in a wealth-producing yoga.

Here are a few examples:

- Ruler of the 11th in 2nd and 2nd in 11th
- Ruler of 1st in 2nd and 2nd in 1st
- Ruler of 9th in 1st and 1st in 9th
- Ruler of 1st in 9th, ruler of 2nd in 9th
- Ruler of 5th in 5th, ruler of 11th in 9th
- Ruler of 2nd and 4th in 9th, ruler of 11th in 2nd
- Ruler of 1st in 10th, ruler of 2nd is exalted

Favorable Moon Yogas

The following yogas confer the best health, wealth, and happiness along with good career and relationships—overall a positive existence.

- **Adhi Yoga or Chandradhi Yoga:** Mercury, Jupiter, and Venus are located in the 6th, 7th, and 8th houses from the Moon.

- **Gajakeshari Yoga:** Occurs when Jupiter is in an angle (1, 4, 7, or 10th houses) from the Moon. This Yoga is described as giving the valor and strength of a lion (keshari) fighting an elephant (gaja). This could happen in four out of the twelve signs, or 30 percent of the time, so it is not that rare, but still good.

- **2nd and 12th houses from a favorable Moon:** If planets are close to the positive influences of a favorable Moon—in either the sign before or the sign after—then they are saturated with the moon's life-supporting energy, especially in terms of emotional blessings. This is a kind of Kartari Yoga.

- **Sunapha Yoga:** Occurs when any favorable planet other than the Sun is located in the 2nd house from the Moon (in a house bordering the house containing the Moon). Note that the planet must have high strength, since this yoga could occur frequently.

- **Anapha Yoga:** Occurs when any favorable planet, except the Sun, occupies the 12th house from the Moon.

- **Durudhara Yoga:** Occurs when any favorable planets, except the Sun, occupy the 2nd and the 12th houses from the Moon.

Unfavorable Moon Yoga

- **Kemadruma Yoga:** No planets, except the Sun, are located with or on either side of the Moon. This emotionally repressing combination can, however, be modified upward by positive offsets in the rest of the chart.

Favorable Sun Yogas

- **Subhavesi Yoga:** Occurs when any favorable planet other than the Moon is located in the 2nd house from the Sun (in a house bordering the house containing the Sun). Note that the planet must have high strength, since this yoga could occur frequently. This placement indicates favorable 2nd house matters such as food, accumulation of wealth, general family issues, speech, etc.

- **Subhavasi Yoga:** Occurs when any favorable planet other than the Moon is located in the 12th house from the Sun (in a house bordering the house containing the Sun). This combination indicates favorable 12th house matters such as enlightened behavior, freedom from constraints, goodness, etc.

Unfavorable Sun Yogas

- **Papavesi Yoga:** Occurs when any unfavorable planet other than the Moon is located in the 2nd house from the Sun (in a house bordering the house containing the Sun). Note that the planet must have high strength, since this yoga could occur frequently. This placement indicates unfavorable 2nd house matters such as lack of good food, poor accumulation of wealth, general family problems, defective or unpleasant speech, etc.

- **Papavasi Yoga:** Occurs when any unfavorable planet other than the Moon is located in the 12th house from the Sun (in a house bordering the house containing the Sun). This combination indicates unfavorable 12th house matters such as unenlightened behavior, constraints, poor health, losses, etc.

Arishta or Poverty-Inducing Yogas

One's wealth and well-being are reduced when the rulers of the dusthana houses (6, 8, and 12) combine with the rulers of the wealth houses (2, 4, 9, and 11) via conjunction, mutual aspect, or mutual exchange. There are numerous combinations with these planets. I have given a few below for you to understand the principles; you can then make your own connections.

Connections of the wealth houses to the 6th house brings debts and losses through disputes and thefts; with the 8th means the person can't seem to get the support to build their wealth—their money is "dead"; with the 12th might mean that the person is just too disinterested in earning enough money or enters events that constantly turn out to be losers. If the Sun and the Moon are located in the 12th, the person might have good finances in the early part of their lives, but end up encountering numerous losses later in life.

If there are outside favorable aspects, all negative qualities of these yogas are reduced. However, if there are negative aspects on these houses, especially if by Mars (extravagance and recklessness) and Saturn (obstructions, setbacks, and delays), then the unfavorable qualities increase.

Some examples of income-reducing yogas are:

- 2nd in the 12th and 12th in the 2nd
- Saturn, Mars, and ruler of 2nd in 12th along with ruler of the 9th in the 2nd
- 2nd and 9th in 12th
- 9th in 8th and 2nd in 12th

Vipreet Raja Yoga

This is a favorable Raja Yoga that produces good influences; it countermands and lifts the seemingly negative influences of combinations of dusthana houses and turns them into a force that creates increased possibilities for gains and comfort. This yoga occurs when there is an occupation of one dusthana ruler (6, 8, or 12) in the sign of another, following the dictum that two negatives makes a positive. For this to be effective, the dusthana ruler should be alone in another dusthana house. For example, ruler of 6th in 12th, or 12th in 8th, etc.

CHAPTER NINE

NAKSHATRAS—MOON SIGNS

The Vedic night observers divided the circle of the sky into 27 sections. These divisions, separate from the signs of the zodiac, were used in ancient times to mark the movement of planets, especially the Moon, against the main star groups that were located in or around those 27 sky sections. Each fixed star group, or nakshatra, had a bright, primary star to help observers find it. This was called the Yoga Tara. It was once believed to mark the union (yoga) or boundary between nakshatras. Due to precession, or the shifting back of the earth relative to the stars, the current orientation of the earth observers has moved back a few nakshatras from those early times. Around 4000 to 2000 B.C., Aldebaran in the sign of Taurus and in the nakshatra of Krittika was believed to mark the equinox. Today's observers, adjusting for precession, use the star Spica (Alpha Virginis) at the border of Virgo and the nakshatra of Chitra (opposite Pisces) to mark the new astrological year.

When the Moon crossed over the Yoga Tara star or its group, it designated a specific Moon nakshatra and signaled that it was time to perform certain rituals (yagyas) or to start or stop specific events (Muhurtha).

Interpreting Nakshatras

Thus far, we have relied on the rasi chart in our discussions. The rasi chart is comparable to the Western sun sign chart in that we are considering the placement of planets within the signs of the zodiac. The core understanding of personality and behavior is derived from the rasi chart, but is supplemented by a finer understanding of the Moon's effects given by the nakshatras, or Moon signs. The nakshatras are often identified relative to their position within the rasi chart—as subconstellations within the 12 signs of the solar zodiac.

There is not as much modern information in Vedic astrology on nakshatras as there is for rasis. However, you can judge the favorable or unfavorable quality of a nakshatra in a fashion similar to judging the signs and houses—that is, by the quality of the planets that aspect and occupy it. Some astrologers indicate that the placement of the "ruler" of the nakshatra will tell us if the quality of the nakshatra is good or bad. Currently, the main usage of nakshatras in India is to mark the starting point for dasa calculations (starting from Krittika nakshatra), for delineating the beginning of religious ceremonies, and for identifying a match between prospective marriage partners.

The position of the Moon in a nakshatra is also used to identify the nature of an individual. This is a more recent development, beyond the original religious ritual usage for nakshatras. Astrologers also use nakshatras for muhurtha—that is, for determining a good time to start or stop a planned activity.

Nakshatras and the Timing of Events

Vedic astrologers often want to time a specific event or activity in a way that is favorable to the nature of the event. Chapter 15 deals with this aspect of astrology, called muhurtha. The location of the Moon in a nakshatra gives the astrologer added information regarding the best time to start or stop an event. You can use a panchanga or ephemeris to locate the current placement of the Moon to determine the nature of the events at hand or you can look ahead to pick an event in tune with the rhythms of nature as evidenced by the placement of the Moon in a specific nakshatra.

Characteristics Attributed to the Nakshatras

I have listed in the section that follows many of the meanings given to the nakshatras by most Vedic astrologers. I have focused on nakshatra meanings that I believe are useful for beginners. There are many advanced descriptions and uses that we won't cover in this book. I have attempted to give you the prevalent nakshatra interpretations with a few slight modifications of meaning based on my understanding and experience. Nakshatras are a rich field for further study. As Vedic astrology continues to grow, I believe we will be finding or rediscovering even more fascinating uses for nakshatras.

On the next page, I have listed all 27 nakshatras, and given some of their characteristics. Following each of the two tables is an explanation of the characteristics.

	Nakshatra	Yoni	Gana	Sex	Disposition	Body Part	Guna
1.	Ashwini	Horse	Deva	M	Light	Knees	Tamas
2.	Bharani	Elephant	Manusha	F	Fierce	Head	Rajas
3.	Krittika	Goat	Rakshasa	F	Sharp & Soft	Hips	Rajas
4.	Rohini	Cobra	Manusha	F	Fixed	Lower leg	Rajas
5.	Mrigasira	Snake	Deva	F/N	Soft	Eyes	Tamas
6.	Ardra	Dog	Manusha	F	Sharp	Top and Back of Head; Eyes	Tamas
7.	Punarvasu	Cat	Deva	M	Moveable	Fingers	Satwa
8.	Pushya	Goat	Deva	M	Light	Mouth	Tamas
9.	Aslesha	Cat	Rakshasa	F	Sharp	Nails	Satwa
10.	Magha	Rat	Rakshasa	F	Fierce	Nose	Tamas
11.	Purva Phalguni	Rat	Manusha	F	Fierce	Genitals	Rajas
12.	Uttara Phalguni	Bull	Manusha	F	Fixed	Genitals	Rajas
13.	Hasta	Buffalo	Deva	M	Light	Hands	Rajas
14.	Chitra	Tiger	Rakshasa	F	Soft	Forehead	Tamas
15.	Swati	Bullock	Deva	F	Moveable	Chest	Tamas
16.	Visakha	Tiger	Rakshasa	F	Sharp & Soft	Arms	Satwa
17.	Anuradha	Deer	Deva	M	Soft	Breast	Tamas
18.	Jyeshta	Stag	Rakshasa	F	Sharp	Neck	Satwa
19.	Mula	Dog	Rakshasa	F/N	Sharp	Feet	Tamas
20.	Purvashada	Monkey	Manusha	M	Fierce	Thigh	Rajas
21.	Uttarashada	Mongoose	Manusha	F	Fixed	Thigh	Rajas
22.	Shravana	Monkey	Deva	M	Moveable	Ears	Rajas
23.	Dhanistha	Lion	Rakshasa	F	Moveable	Back	Tamas
24.	Satabisha	Mare	Rakshasa	N	Moveable	Jaw	Tamas
25.	Purva Bhadrapada	Lion	Manusha	M	Fierce	Sides	Satwa
26.	Uttara Bhadrapada	Cow	Manusha	M	Fixed	Sides	Tamas
27.	Revati	Elephant	Deva	F	Soft	Stomach	Satwa

Yoni: Identifies each nakshatra according to sexual nature, as exemplified by a type of animal. The animal type speaks to a certain energy emitted by each nakshatra, especially in terms of marriages or matchmaking.

Gana: Classifies each nakshatra as either: (1) Deva, or Divine, which shows high character; (2) Manusha, or Human, which shows mixed character; or (3) Rakshasa, or Demon, which shows lower character.

Sex: Male (Purusha Yoni) or Female (Stree Yoni). Some say that the nakshatras of Mrigasira, Mula, and Satabisha are sexually neutral, or eunuchs (Nampumsaka).

Disposition: Early mentions of nakshatra disposition come from Lagada's Vedanga Jyotisha and from Ramacharya's Muhurtha Chintamani. The nakshatras are grouped according to their general behavioral tendencies as follows:

- Fixed—indicates stability and perseverance
- Moveable—shows a tendency to be unstable, changeful, or to travel a lot
- Sharp—shows executive abilities and the capacity to act strongly and decisively
- Soft—indicates a tendency to indulge in pleasure and enjoyments
- Sharp and Soft—obviously, indicates a mixed nature
- Fierce—gives the ability to act in an aggressive manner, such as in wars, lawsuits, etc.
- Light—gives the ability to act quickly and with finesse, such as in business, healing, etc.

Body Part: shows which parts of the body are affected by a specific nakshatra; similarly, the rasi chart identifies parts of the body according to the Kalapurusha or body of nature (see appendix). The Narada Purana mentions nakshatra body parts.

Guna: Represents the inherent quality of a nakshatra and its influence on a house. Satwa is pure; Rajas is stimulated and energetic; Tamas is inert and lethargic.

More Characteristics Associated with Nakshatras

The following text describes some of the psychological factors attributed to each nakshatra. The realm of the nakshatras requires more research by modern astrologers. What I have listed are the general concepts covered by most Vedic observers. The nakshatras are most commonly interpreted in relation to the Moon's position in a chart. However, I believe that you can similarly associate most of these meanings to the Lagna. When the Moon occupies a specific nakshatra, the meanings of that nakshatra modify the meanings of planets in zodiac signs. As a result, you can expect a certain style of behavior to be manifest in an individual or even in an event. For example, if a person had the Moon in Libra in the rasi chart, this would indicate a softer emotional disposition from the point of view of that chart. That softness could be enhanced if the Moon is in Swati nakshatra, but could be degraded if the Moon was located in the somewhat rougher nakshatra of Visakha.

The translation of the meaning of a nakshatra is somewhat dependent upon the skill and viewpoint of the interpreter. Sanskrit can be read in multiple layers of meaning, thus giving multiple possibilities of translation. On the following pages, I have listed what seem to be the most prevalent translations used today.

I have also included a picture of the symbol associated with each nakshatra. The symbol is often a mixture between the shape of the asterism and a symbol of its meaning. The meanings and shapes have been intermixed by Vedic authors over time. The words used to describe the nakshatras seem to be more intended to invoke a feeling or concept, than to be exactly representational.

The presiding deity for each nakshatra represents an essence, force, or impulse of nature that was contacted by a devotee when the Moon passed through this nakshatra at night. As sources, I used both the Taittiriya Samhita and the Muhurtha Chintamani, which obtained a lot of its references from Varahamihira's Brihat Samhita.

Additionally, I have given the location relative to the standard sun-sign, or rasi, chart.

Finally, I have listed the dasa-ruling planets here for ease of look-up and study; in chapter 13 we will discuss the system of Vimshottari Dasa. Briefly, each nakshatra has a planet that marks the start of a dasa cycle, which is a certain span of time. The dasa-ruling planet is calibrated from the position of the nakshatra in the Moon's sign at birth. There is a controversy amongst astrologers as to whether this planet should also be used as a "ruler" for the nakshatra, much in the same way that signs or rasis have ruling planets. Many highly regarded astrologers consider the nakshatras as having rulers. It is viewed that a person is under the influence of the planet governing a nakshatra for the duration of a dasa period.

1. *Ashwini*

Translation: Swift Mover, Horseman, or Horse Harnessers

Symbol: Horse's head

Presiding Deity: Ashwinis (Health)

Location: Aries 0° to Aries 13°20'

Dasa-Ruling Planet: Ketu (7 years)

Favorable: Good, steady worker; honorable living; competent, does above-average work; intelligent, reliable, self-sufficient; good finances; light-hearted, gives upliftment and healing energy to others; spiritual tendencies; modest, moderate habits (such as eating); likes to dress well

Unfavorable: Interest in newness may cause a weakness in finishing things; naive; wants to do things their own way too much; stubborn; zealot; wild and racing about like a horse

Recommended Activities: Conveys the energy of a horse. Good for doing things that require you to "move fast" or when you need to get results quickly; good for putting in your individual effort and cleverness, taking medicine, improving health, getting more wealth, conquering enemies, starting new learning, starting the study of Vastu or building designs, setting up new religious objects, engaging in activities related to transportation such as buying or selling a vehicle, traveling, getting new jewelry. If a person gives ghee (butter) to a Brahmin during this time, their physical appearance will improve.

2. Bharani

Translation: The Bearer

Symbol: A female sex organ

Presiding Deity: Yama (Death or the setting sun)

Location: Aries 13°20' to Aries 26°40'

Dasa-Ruling Planet: Venus (20 years)

Favorable: Quick-minded; desires new experiences (especially with love affairs); prefers spontaneous behavior; gets things done quickly; dutiful; sticks by their family and friends; courageous attitude; good longevity

Unfavorable: Feels burdened; too much activity; fickle, amoral, too clever or calculating; doesn't pace themselves; resists control; unmanageable, stubborn, childlike, vulnerable; their vigor often bothers more conservative people

Recommended Activities: Conveys the energy of cutting. Good for severe activities; "bearing the burden" of those unpleasant but necessary responsibilities; doing things that have a destructive, cruel, severe, or warlike aspect to them; driving out "evil" influences; starting a lawsuit, initiating an attack, filing for divorce, entering a competition; starting a campaign against a competitor or rival; doing things that involve toxins, chemicals, fire, or any "poisonous" things (e.g., starting chemotherapy, applying pesticides, etc.); good for burning things; agricultural activities start well here; doing related things such as drilling for water

3. Krittika

Translation: The Cutter

Symbol: Axe, sharp edge, or flame

Presiding Deity: Agni (Fire)

Location: Aries 26°40' to Taurus 10°

Dasa-Ruling Planet: Sun (6 years)

Favorable: Motivated; achieves and acquires many things; bright; strong appetites (such as food and sex); goal oriented; likes to get the bottom line; goes for what they want; survivor; dignified; takes pride in what they do; will honor their commitments; good leader; straightforward

Unfavorable: Changeable, vacillating, stubborn; not open to advice; hard to please; impatient; responds too strongly to challenges; sets goals or expectations too high; burns out their health by constant and unrelenting activity; often nervous or excitable

Recommended Activities: Conveys the energy of being militaristic. This placement is good for "cutting to the chase"; being audacious, brash, and cutting straight to the point; arguing for one's point of view in a razor-sharp manner; doing any type of cutting such as carpentry work; good for seizing the initiative and being competitive; not asking for permission; taking an aggressive and combative approach; working with weapons and doing metal work; collecting monies that are due. Carefully planned strategies will be well executed when the Moon occupies this nakshatra; one's opponents will be weak to resist. Not good for travel or for driving vehicles.

4. Rohini

Translation: The Red One
Symbol: An ox cart
Presiding Deity: Prajapati (Creation)
Location: Taurus 10° to Taurus 23°20'
Dasa-Ruling Planet: Moon (10 years)
Favorable: Charismatic; a good communicator and listener; attractive; inner strength; popular and gets attention; gentle and seductive manner; comforting; oriented to truth and moral purposes; smooth talkers; sharp, steady mind; fixed in purpose; well educated; earns a good living; dutiful to the family; learns throughout their lives; helps others to grow and expand

Unfavorable: Takes advantage of the trust or belief that others put in them; manipulator; deceptive; sexually or sensually indulgent; capricious; quick to find weakness then lose interest in others; potential conflicts or lack of alignment with the mother; stubborn; overly analytical

Recommended Activities: Conveys the strength of a bull. It is deemed favorable for starting all good undertakings; even if someone has to do something unpleasant, it should turn out okay. "Be Bullish"; do things to build up your finances; develop your acquisition skills; engage in self-improvement and increase your health; get married or engage in marriage ceremonies; start construction of buildings; lay foundations; build up your spiritual wealth by placing religious objects in your home or in a temple; wear expensive jewelry for the first time

5. Mrigasira

Translation: Deer Head (some say Deer Path)
Symbol: A deer's head
Presiding Deity: Soma (Divine Nectar)
Location: Taurus 23°20' to Gemini 6°40'
Dasa-Ruling Planet: Mars (7 years)
Favorable: Curious, seeks new knowledge; mentally sharp; creative and sensitive; likes good clothing and accessories; enjoys singing, talking, and speaking; articulate in a number of subjects; enthusiastic, youthful, hopeful; rapid learning ability; satirical sense of humor; focus is more mental than physical; friendly, fun, have a number of friends and romantic interests

Unfavorable: Flirtatious, fickle, multiple partnerships (often concurrently); partners often get more attached than they do; seeks too much excitement and gets nervous or exhausted; reluctant to commit; fragmented; critical; biting conversation; immobilized; suspicious; underweight; high metabolism; need plenty of exercise and fresh, open air to stay in balance

Recommended Activities: Conveys the fleetness of a deer. Good for new beginnings. "Put your head in a new place"; marriage; making new partnerships and friends; new journeys or travel; sowing "new seeds" and starting agricultural or gardening activities; laying new building foundations or beginning to look for a new home; breaking ground on new construction; housewarming; starting the construction of spiritual buildings such as temples and churches; installing "murtis" (holy statues) and other objects in temples; receiving the "sacred thread" (for Brahmins) or taking first sacraments

6. Ardra

Translation: Moist or Perspiring
Symbol: A teardrop or drop of perspiration
Presiding Deity: Rudra (God of Storms)
Location: Gemini 6°40' to Gemini 20°
Dasa-Ruling Planet: Rahu (18 years)
Favorable: Quick-acting; good memory; skilled in physical work or work involving the body; good at getting support from the government or authorities; desires to help people who are hurting; often go through a catharsis or life conversion at some point wherein they drop many of their bad traits

Unfavorable: Arrogant; reckless; gets physically oriented jobs, often lower jobs of service and labor; self-serving, unscrupulous, ungrateful, stubborn, critical, impolite, untruthful or does not verify the facts before they speak; poor financial planning; weaken themselves through excessive indulgences; cause pain or agony to others

Recommended Activities: Conveys the concept of doing base or gross work. Good for aggressive and adversarial activities: "working up a sweat"; taking measures to subdue opponents or scare them. A time for restricting or limiting others ("tying them up" figuratively and literally); retaliating such as in lawsuits and other forms of fighting back; working with toxins, poisons, and chemicals; activities connected to fire; psychological purging (exorcisms); removing the cause of bad feelings; putting energy into learning new things. Not a favorable time for starting good actions. Marriages are deemed to struggle, if not fail, if started during this nakshatra.

7. Punarvasu

Translation: Good Again
Symbol: An arrow or arrows in a quiver
Presiding Deity: Aditi (mother of the 12 Adityas, forms of the Sun)
Location: Gemini 20° to Cancer 3° 20'
Dasa-Ruling Planet: Jupiter (16 years)
Favorable: Friendly, good-natured; simple life; lives in the moment; generous, sharing what little they may have with others; lives a spiritual life; interested in spiritual writings and philosophies; can be good writer and inspiring speaker; imaginative; strives to rid their life of any impurities or encumbrances that could slow their spiritual progress

Unfavorable: Their simple approach to life might be interpreted as a lack of mental capacity. Being oriented to an inward life, they may be disinterested and lack some of the drive and focus needed to earn a proper living. Lack of foresight gets them into complications—frequent moving, unstable relationships, multiple jobs or careers.

Recommended Activities: Good for "starting over": perhaps with self-improvement and expanding health; beginning a fast; starting agriculture (a new garden, landscaping, etc.); making new forms of transportation; taking your car (or any vehicle) in for repair; taking remedial action against an unfavorable situation or condition; traveling; making or obtaining new jewelry (ornaments); laying in the foundation of a building or starting the search for a new home; signing up for a new class; getting married. It is said that marriage during this time results in good children and happiness.

8. Pushya

Translation: Nourishing, some say a flower
Symbol: Circle, wheel, or cow's udder
Presiding Deity: Brihaspati (Guru of Gods)
Location: Cancer 3°20' to Cancer 16°40'
Dasa-Ruling Planet: Saturn (19 years)

Favorable: Intelligent, spiritual, nourishes or helps others, independent and self-sufficient, interested in education and humanitarian activities, socially adept, make good counselors and public servants, make people feel wanted, want to learn all they can about life—makes them knowledgeable in many areas, earn a good living, respected, moderate in desire, passionate about what they believe in, will come strongly to the defense of something or someone they believe in

Unfavorable: Zealot, too talkative, interested in so many things that they don't become great in any one thing, overly sensitive or emotional, their devotion can turn to submission leaving them open to being a martyr or victim; get defrauded by believing in the wrong people

Recommended Activities: Considered by some as the best nakshatra. Generally good for all "nourishing" activities except for marriage. Traditionally, herbs for Ayurvedic remedies are picked during this time. Activities meant to lift the spirits and to enliven the health do well, such as parties, celebrations, health improvement processes, and remedial measures; it is a favorable time to learn dancing and to study music; in terms of Vastu, it is good for laying the foundation stones and starting construction. This is a recommended time for travel. Any "assaults" from enemies will be weak at this time.

9. Aslesha

Translation: The Entwiner
Symbol: A coiled snake, circle, or a wheel
Presiding Deity: Sarpas (Celestial Snakes)

Location: Cancer 16°40' to Cancer 30°

Dasa-Ruling Planet: Mercury (17 years)

Favorable: Versatile, clever; makes their living in a number of ways; leader; can accomplish things when motivated and gain good wealth; puts great energy into things that interest them; can transform their lives and benefit from spiritual work

Unfavorable: Unscrupulous; dismissive attitude; impolite, tactless, unpopular, lacks social skills; doesn't like rules; hoarding mentality; secretive; talkative; lack of gratitude; fragmented and ineffective; reckless, disconnected, introspective, depressed, and isolated; lacks grace

Recommended Activities: This is a time for being "fierce"; for "tying" people up in court; using poisons and fire (inoculations, getting rid of pests, "burning bridges," etc.); entering a competition; opening a new business venture; cutting loose old and unnecessary items (and people) in your life; taking a stand for yourself in personal and public matters. Things related to snakes are recommended at this time (e.g., a type of yagya or ritual called Sarpa Homa). This is a time for hard work and for taking some chances (gambling).

10. Magha

Translation: The Mighty One

Symbol: A throne room or a house

Presiding Deity: Pitris (Ancestors)

Location: Leo 0° to Leo 13°20'

Dasa-Ruling Planet: Ketu (7 years)

Favorable: Positive, balanced, has self-respect and expects respect from others; big-hearted; goes first class; likes to be entitled and to bear titles; respects educators and spiritual people; honors traditions; likes to adhere to chains of command; does well when praised; likes to be served and given attention

Unfavorable: Arrogant, disdainful, overly demanding, indignant; has a strong dislike for those who dislike them or who treat them with disrespect; could get involved in an affair if they feel unloved by mate; can be manipulated by flattery; cruel to those who don't show them respect

Recommended Activities: Do things where you have to be bigger than your normal self; take "kingly" action, go to "war" if need be; dangerous deeds are better supported now; any activities related to water are deemed favorable. Store up your food reserves and do fire prevention. Learning music and dancing is good here. Plan to meet some influential people during this time. This is a favorable time for marriage ceremonies and for paying respect to the dead.

11. *Purva Phalguni (also called Pubba)*

Translation: The Former Red One or A Fig Tree
Symbol: Front legs of a bed, or a post
Presiding Deity: Aryaman (a form of Sun at twilight)
Location: Leo 13°20' to Leo 26°40'
Dasa-Ruling Planet: Venus (20 years)
Favorable: Bright, physically active; focus is on the body; physical approaches to healing; lively and friendly; sweet speech; likes to give; wants fame and attention; loyal; good at ministering to those in a higher position; advocate; aristocratic, cultured, and oriented to the refined; would rather "entice" someone than force them

Unfavorable: Reckless; focused too much on getting what they want; builds up debts; strong aversion to being uncomfortable; falls into bouts of gloom or depression if they do not get the praise and comfort that they feel is their right; vindictive if hurt but not in a confrontational manner

Recommended Activities: This is another nakshatra favorable for doing "fierce" or negative acts, such as having someone detained, arrested, fined, or penalized. While these deeds are of a negative nature, they should end up successful. This is not a favorable time to initiate new things, except perhaps to start a new study, to uncover hidden wealth ("buried treasure") or to gamble. This might be a time to put someone in an institution or "home." Go to "war" and use subterfuge if need be. If you need to develop schemes and strategies, then this is the time. Construction is supported now. One should take care to avoid accidents by not engaging in obviously dangerous acts. Illnesses that occur during this time might be difficult to overcome.

12. Uttara Phalguni

Translation: The Latter Red One or A Fig Tree
Symbol: The rear legs of a bed, or a post
Presiding Deity: Bhaga (the blind Sun as wealth-giver)
Location: Leo 26°40' to Virgo 10°
Dasa-Ruling Planet: Sun (6 years)
Favorable: A level-headed leader or manager; associates well with people in power and gets financial benefit from them; good communicator; loves luxury and comfort; liberal yet has fixed principles; happy, friendly, and likeable—especially popular with mates and partners; socially smart; generally fortunate
Unfavorable: May have many partners (in and out of marriage); egotistical, orders people about without due consideration for their feelings; obstinate, disdainful, vain, arrogant, takes too much for themselves (the "lion's share"); not grateful; a social climber; may be sad or angry under a "happy smile"
Recommended Activities: This is a time for new beginnings such as marriage, entering your new home for the first time, inauguration events, opening celebrations, swearing-in oaths, starting new construction of a home, taking vows and making promises, and wearing new clothes and jewelry. Performing sacred ceremonies is good now. You will succeed in tasks started now if you do careful planning, stay clever, and remain courteous.

13. Hasta

Translation: Hand
Symbol: The five fingers of a hand, or a clenched fist
Presiding Deity: Savitri (Sun's awakening rays at dawn)
Location: Virgo 10° to Virgo 23°20'
Dasa-Ruling Planet: Moon (10 years)
Favorable: Intelligent, persuasive, cordial; weighs their words to avoid expressing anger; self-motivated; in control; focused on acquisition; good at defending and promoting their own interests; understands the value of social rituals and courtesies; skilled in providing service; thick-skinned; takes advantage of opportunities in new areas or in foreign lands; dexterous, determined, hard worker, artistic
Unfavorable: Enjoys competition and conflicts; controlling, swindler, blatant self-interest, unashamed, wary; overindulgence in

pleasuring themselves; cruel; mechanical in dealing with those who provide them no advantage; may resort to alcohol, drugs, or food to deal with overwork; life of subjugation

Recommended Activities: This is a time for getting a "grip" on things or starting anew. Activities started now will have an enduring effect as long as they are positive in intent. Go on a journey; learn something new; get a new wardrobe with all the trimmings; start construction or buy a new house; get everything important set into place. Make the effort to contact important or well-placed persons if that will help your situation. They should be responsive.

14. Chitra (also Chitta)

Translation: Brilliant

Symbol: A pearl or gem, or a shining lamp

Presiding Deity: Twastri or Vishwarkarma (blacksmith, world architect)

Location: Virgo 23°20' to Libra 6°40'

Dasa-Ruling Planet: Mars (7 years)

Favorable: Elegantly restrained, dignified, discriminating; business skills; happy, well dressed and well groomed; well read; drawn to serious subjects of philosophy and social thought; motivated by opportunities outside their place of birth or in foreign countries; dexterous; inclined toward more physical expressions of art such as sculpture, printmaking, etc.; capable designer

Unfavorable: Attracted to exciting yet irresponsible mates; quarrelsome, critical, too quick to challenge someone's point of view; corrupt, amoral; supports mates who are not self-sufficient; may not focus enough on saving money

Recommended Activities: Make yourself more "brilliant." Improve your health; take corrective action on problems; buy a new wardrobe; plant something new or do anything related to gardening and agriculture; activities related to anything mechanical around the office or home do better at this time—so fix your house, mend those broken walls, install a new boiler, etc. Any spiritual rituals or performances are well received. Starting the study of music and fine arts is good.

15. Swati

Translation: The Good Goer (named after the lead goat in a herd)
Symbol: A sword
Presiding Deity: Vayu (Wind)
Location: Libra 6°40' to Libra 20°
Dasa-Ruling Planet: Rahu (18 years)
Favorable: Gentle; thinks of the needs of others; thinks before acting; much more intelligent than they appear; accurate; reduces things to their simplest components; uncorrupted; friendly; positive expectations; seeks harmony in all things; active in spiritual organizations or humanitarian causes; likes to be around holy or well-integrated people; interested in scientific and philosophical thought; modest; business skills

Unfavorable: Not alert about their debt level; lives with too many expenses; ponderous; doesn't care that much about their family members; shy, monastic, or self-isolating; secretive; hides their passions and sexual urges; gives too much away; creative thinking becomes preposterous or too far ahead of their peers; people will take advantage of them

Recommended Activities: This is considered one of the better nakshatras. Generally a good time to "cut loose" and do anything of a progressive nature. Things started during this time generally are successful, except perhaps for traveling. Sow new seeds—physically and metaphorically; help in the building of a spiritual center; get new tools and security devices—even weapons if that is part of what you need to do. If you need to be aggressive, then this is the time to go to "war."

16. Visakha (also called Radha)

Translation: Forked, or Spreading Branches; also Radha
Symbol: A decorated gateway (used in marriage ceremonies)
Presiding Deity: Indragni (Indra and Agni combined)
Location: Libra 20° to Scorpio 3°20'
Dasa-Ruling Planet: Jupiter (16 years)
Favorable: Clever; has respect for intelligent and spiritual people; enterprising; self-satisfied; determined; gets things done; can appear soft but is very powerful underneath; sexually alluring; a good mate in marriage; benefits through marriage, traveling, and through change; mathematical talent

Unfavorable: Overly talkative; nice until they get what they want; negative, speaks negatively about others, fault-finding; not open to advice; offensive and not easy to like; greedy, deceitful, aggressive, domineering, quick to take offense, militant, suspicious, possessive, envious; feels obstructed and taken advantage of by others

Recommended Activities: This is a good nakshatra for construction, land dealings, or anything related to these fields. Car repairs are best done here or perhaps the purchase of a new vehicle. The healing processes you start now, and the herbs and/or medicines you take, will be more effective. Creative construction such as jewelry making, sculpting, etc., are supported.

17. Anuradha

Translation: After Radha (Visakha, the preceding nakshatra, was called Radha); also Success

Symbol: A row or furrow

Presiding Deity: Mitra (friendship)

Location: Scorpio 3°20' to Scorpio 16°40'

Dasa-Ruling Planet: Saturn (19 years)

Favorable: Outwardly buoyant and fun-loving; attractive, hearty, popular; spiritual seeker, interested in ancient knowledge; capacity for astrology; devoted; enjoys social life and organizations; brave; benefits more if they live away from their place of birth

Unfavorable: Tries too hard to get enlightened; grieves; secretive, isolated, ethical according to the circumstances, dishonest; obstructed by envious people; doesn't understand their impact on others—especially their marriage partners who may eventually ask for a divorce; needs constant nourishment—both in terms of food and drink and in terms of their emotions; defiant; progress is hurt by submitting to bad advice

Recommended Activities: Another good nakshatra for marriage. Good for all positive events, whether they are of short duration or of lasting impact. This a time for making commitments and obligating yourself in some way, perhaps making a pledge of some sort. Activities related to travel and vehicles are good, such as going on vacation, taking possession of a new car and driving it home, etc. In terms of Vastu, this is a good time for housewarming activities.

18. Jyeshta

Translation: The Eldest (last of the best)
Symbol: A hanging earring
Presiding Deity: Indra (Chief of Gods)
Location: Scorpio 16°40' to Scorpio 30°
Dasa-Ruling Planet: Mercury (17 years)
Favorable: Most successful of their family; keeps friends and builds a good support network; generous, self-reliant, eventually wealthy; takes charge of the family; passionate response to love; acts respectable; receives fame and honors; takes control; gets things done when they want to
Unfavorable: Angry; has family frictions; too intense to keep friends; hides their feelings and intentions; religious or peaceful on the surface while impatient or immoral underneath; acts religious to get regard; scheming; makes others dependent on them to gain control in the relationship; dramatizes illnesses and troubles to gain sympathy; subject to many illnesses
Recommended Activities: "Act like an adult" and be mature. If you need to confront someone, then this is the time. Go after opponents or competition with vigor, work to settle legal disputes, and make the effort to retrieve old debts. However, if you need to ask forgiveness or express regret, then that is okay, too—just make the effort to clear the air. Any work associated with metals, designing buildings, or fuel for heating a home is good.

19. Mula

Translation: The Root
Symbol: A tied bunch of roots or a lion's tail
Presiding Deity: Niritti (Goddess of Destruction)
Location: Sagittarius 0° to Sagittarius 13°20'
Dasa-Ruling Planet: Ketu (7 years)
Favorable: Skillful in persuading or manipulating people to serve their goals and objectives; politician; tactful, clever, able to live a comfortable life with all the amenities; good fortune; determined to succeed; learned
Unfavorable: Takes with little thought of return; unstable; tells people what they want to hear to get what they want; speaks logically but makes others suspicious; too goal-focused; lacks sufficient

appreciation for others; arrogant, self-destructive, willful, sabotages their own love; has many affairs and/or marriages that don't work out

Recommended Activities: "Get to the root of things," literally—start a new garden or agricultural activity, or contribute to making some nice piece of land a park. Install new water systems, perhaps a new swimming pool, spa, or water storage reservoir. If you need to engage in a conflict or go to "war," then do so at this time. If you need to make or break an agreement or pact, then this time is also appropriate. This is a favorable travel time.

20. Purvashada

Translation: The Former Unsubdued

Symbol: A bed or an elephant's tusk

Presiding Deity: Apa (water)

Location: Sagittarius 13°20' to Sagittarius 26°40'

Dasa-Ruling Planet: Venus (20 years)

Favorable: Popular, polite, devoted to friends, intelligent; good manager but happier in service; valuable and steady worker; simple life; supportive, courageous, influential, wealthy; loves good meals; has a pleasant relationship with mate; capable of having many children

Unfavorable: Settles for less; may imagine themselves to be above others yet are regarded as unrefined or underdeveloped; not open to advice; often end up in low-paying and hardworking jobs; incompetent manager; bouts of loud and raucous behavior; lacking in education or preparation

Recommended Activities: You might take drastic action to liberate someone in some way. This could be by releasing someone who is imprisoned or detained—physically, emotionally, or financially. Pay off some debts now. You might use this time to forgive someone. Severe actions, where you have to be emotionally detached, are best done now. Economic planning should be favorable. Travel is not recommended during this period.

21. Uttarashada

Translation: The Latter Unsubdued

Symbol: A bed or an elephant's tusk

Presiding Deity: Viswadevas (all gods combined)

Location: Sagittarius 26°40' to Capricorn 10°

Dasa-Ruling Planet: Sun (6 years)

Favorable: Bright, fun-loving, popular, devoted to friends, grateful, kind, modest; has some knowledge that sets them apart; interested in learning and advocating topics that concern them—often through indirect means; enjoys reading to gain knowledge; benefits through travels; tolerant; wants fair play and justice; sympathetic ear; devoted to mate

Unfavorable: Multiple marriages or marriagelike relationships; overly concerned; takes on too many people's problems and gets stressed out; stays too long in a destructive relationship; changes residence more than most or goes on frequent journeys

Recommended Activities: "Plant the seeds of your future." Buy a new home or fix up an existing one. Redecorate—your home and yourself. This is the time to enter your new building for the first time. Start new things that will bear fruit later on. This is a favorable nakshatra for marriage.

22. Shravana

Translation: Ear or Hearing

Symbol: A trident (some say an ear)

Presiding Deity: Vishnu (the Maintainer)

Location: Capricorn 10° to Capricorn 23°20'

Dasa-Ruling Planet: Moon (10 years)

Favorable: Cordial in business; success in foreign countries; lives a prosperous, balanced, and modest life; ethical; studies scriptures and ancient knowledge; kind; drawn to working for social and humanitarian causes; helps others arrange or reform their lives; has a good marriage and a helpful partner

Unfavorable: Generosity can get excessive and lead to debts and a self-imposed poverty; overly liberal; may take an extreme stance in ethics and develop opposition or even adversaries; usually has few children

Recommended Activities: Favorable actions are well supported at this time. It's a time for hope for the future. Perform religious ceremonies; take action to improve your well-being; get a new home; set up any new devices or equipment for your work or home; take preventative measures and follow your doctor's prescriptions. Medical actions and remedial measures are more effective now.

23. Dhanistha

Translation: Wealthy
Symbol: A tabor (a type of drum)
Presiding Deity: Vasus (bright ones)
Location: Capricorn 23°20' to Aquarius 6°40'
Dasa-Ruling Planet: Mars (7 years)
Favorable: Earns a good living; believes in charitable giving; brave; does well in foreign countries; good conversationalist; enjoys music and dance; good organizational abilities; ambitious, motivated to accomplish things and develop their careers; likes old and mysterious things; could be skilled in astrology

Unfavorable: Self-seeking, aggressive; worried; capable of hurting others; makes up stories; deceptive in that they will either say what is not so, withhold information, or understate matters; don't like to be told what to do; argumentative; too talkative; select mates who often are very different in personality and outlook

Recommended Activities: Religious performances are effective at this time. Actions taken to defend oneself or to be aggressive and pro-active lead to better conclusions now. Get a new car or other means of transportation. Prepare a new garden or begin landscaping your home or business. This is a favorable travel time.

24. Satabisha

Translation: 100 Physicians for Healing
Symbol: A circle or round charm
Presiding Deity: Varuna (ocean or waves)
Location: Aquarius 6°40' to Aquarius 20°
Dasa-Ruling Planet: Rahu 18 years
Favorable: Emotionally controlled; interested in uncovering the truth; prosperous, economical, clever, capable of protecting themselves, enterprising; interested in astrology and other esoteric and philosophical realms; likes to solve mysteries and puzzles; provides good service

Unfavorable: Quiet, yet will blurt things out—often with unpleasant or unrefined expressions. Con artist; unstable or changeful; argumentative, uncommunicative, hides their true motives; miser; dependent on others or takes things from others; problems in relationships; feels intensely restrained or mentally anguished; self-isolating; relationships with children and with siblings is problematic

Recommended Activities: Negotiate and sign contracts associated with land deals. Do some auspicious spiritual performance to bring up the quality of your home or your land. Be financially aggressive with precious metals, especially silver. Curative measures started now will be more effective. Business deals should transact well.

25. Purva Bhadrapada

Translation: Former Beautiful Foot (or Ray of Light)

Symbol: Front legs of a small bed or couch

Presiding Deity: Aja Ekapad (one-footed goat, or a single ray of sun)

Location: Aquarius 20° to Pisces 3°20'

Dasa-Ruling Planet: Jupiter (16 years)

Favorable: Devoted to those who impress them; good logical skill; prosperity through cleverness; good at "reading" people; gets money from the government or from wealthy or executive people; economical; acts happy; lives a long life; could marry into a wealthy family or be born into one

Unfavorable: Skeptical; a worrier (yet still a warrior); a bit odd; pessimistic; given to grim or serious conversations; changes residence more than most; doesn't think that far ahead; dominated by their mate; penny pincher but still a poor financial planner; nervous; poor health

Recommended Activities: If you are required to do something that is dangerous, uncertain, or risky, then now is the time. Procurement activities are supported as well as any water-based actions of a mechanical nature. Land, landscaping, and agricultural undertakings are good now. Buy a new pet.

26. Uttara Bhadrapada

Translation: Latter Beautiful Foot (or Ray of Light)

Symbol: Back legs of a small bed or couch

Presiding Deity: Ahir Budhnya (the Snake of the Depths, or a stream in the lower Milky Way)

Location: Pisces 3°20' to Pisces 16°40'

Dasa-Ruling Planet: Saturn (19 years)

Favorable: Good problem-solving ability; impressive speaker; ethical, contented, generous, passive, yet financially successful; tends to make money on their own; economical, charitable, humanitarian, merciful, smart; benefits from children or beginners; drawn to the unknown

Unfavorable: Shy; reluctant; develops a set of long-term enemies or gets into disputes that take a long time to resolve; thinks too much about their own outcomes; self-centered financial focus

Recommended Activities: Most favorable activities started now will have more support to turn out well. Making promises, pledges, or commitments is good. This is another nakshatra favorable for marriage. Start construction on a new home or open escrow.

27. Revati

Translation: Wealthy

Symbol: A drum

Presiding Deity: Pushan, the "Prosperer" (a form of the Dawn)

Location: Pisces 16°40' to Pisces 30°

Dasa-Ruling Planet: Ketu (7 years)

Favorable: Fortunate, liked, supportive and gets supported; promoted quickly; skilled in pleasing; sociable, good counselor, proud, dignified presence; lively personality; brave in the face of setbacks; long life; well groomed; good hygiene; might be born into a wealthy family

Unfavorable: Spiteful—especially when hurt or jealous; overindulgent; takes on too many problems from other people (which may hurt their health); perverted or amoral attitudes; gets into debt; low fertility

Recommended Activities: Anything of a positive nature that is started now has a better chance of flourishing. Business activities involving trade and bartering are good. Marriage vows should be taken now. Build or buy a new house. Help establish or build a new church, spiritual center, or religious building. Buy yourself or commission a new piece of jewelry. Spend some time with your parents. Buy a new car, if that is in your plans.

CHAPTER TEN

NAVAMSA AND
THE DIVISIONAL CHARTS

Divisional charts are a particular feature of Vedic astrology. Some have linked the divisional chart to harmonic theory. Pythagoras, who is said to have visited India, studied harmony quite a lot and declared that when two tones sounded pleasant near each other, they were in harmony. One planet vibrating in harmony or in pleasant attunement with another brings added benefit. However, harmony can also generate destructive power—as shown by those old movies of bridges undulating in a storm's howling winds, due to harmonic frequencies of sound that ultimately caused the bridges to buckle. We've all heard how marching soldiers can create such a strong concurrent vibration with their stamping feet that they too can damage a bridge. It is interesting to note that when you pluck a string under the lid of a piano, the ninth string over vibrates—none of the others, just the ninth. Some authors hold that the divisional charts are finer resonances of major frequencies in the "music of the spheres." It's a fascinating area for further study.

The birth or rasi chart is the most well-known and most significant of the charts. However, the rasi chart sits alongside 15 sibling charts that are further subdivisions of the 30-degree rasi chart. These companion charts give further clues and nuances of meaning to each of the planets. It's the same as saying that a person is not only an American, but also a Californian, and a Southern Californian, and a Los Angeleno, and from the West Side, and from the Montana Avenue District. These are all divisions of a class of being called American.

Shodasavarga (16 Divisional Charts)

Parasara teaches us that there are 16 vargas, or divisions, of the apparent path of the Sun, which is also called the ecliptic, or the path where the zodiac resides. These 16 vargas and their meaning are listed on the next page. The center column relates each varga to the main chart division system, the rasi or zodiac sign, by indicating the further subdivisions of it. There are 15 other vargas besides the rasi. A planet's position will be refined into a further subdivision based on where it is located in the rasi, according to Parasara's rules. Each sign in the chart is subdivided, up to 60 parts within each 30-degree rasi. Vedic astrology computer programs can now do all the logic for these subdivisions and save the astrologer from the once-arduous task of calculating subdivisional planetary placements manually.

Varga Name	Rasi Division	Varga Influence
1. Rasi	Not divided (30°)	Physique, behavior, all basic indications (1st house matters)
2. Hora	2 parts of 15° each	Wealth (liquid assets), masculine/feminine tendencies (2nd house matters)
3. Drekkana	3 parts of 10° each	Happiness through brothers and sisters (3rd house matters)
4. Chaturthamsa (also called Turyamsa or Padamsa)	4 parts of 7°20' each	Wealth (fixed assets), happiness, emotions (4th house matters)
5. Saptamamsa	7 parts of 4°17'8.57" each	Family dynasty, children and grandchildren, creative energy (5th house matters)
6. Navamsa	9 parts of 3°20' each	Overall strengths and weaknesses, partner, subtle characteristics (7th house matters)
7. Dasamsa	10 parts of 3° each	Career, status, professional accomplishments, income from individual effort (10th house matters)
8. Dwadasamsa	12 parts of 2°30' each	Parents (Look to Sun and 9th for father, and Moon and 4th for mother)
9. Shodasamsa	16 parts of 1°52'30" each	Benefits and adversities from (also called Kalamsa) conveyances (e.g., car accidents)
10. Vimsamsa	20 parts of 1°30' each	Progress to be gained from spiritual practices
11. Chaturvimsamsa (also called Siddhamsa)	24 parts of 1°15' each	Learning, education, achievements gained through studies
12. Saptimvimsamsa (also called Bhamsa or Nakshatramsa)	27 parts of 1°6'40" each	Physical strengths and weaknesses, endurance
13. Trimsamsa	30 parts of 1°	Arishtas or the advent of unfavorable effects in life, integrity of the individual
14. Khavedamsa (also called Chatvarimshamsa)	40 parts of 0°45'	Auspicious and inauspicious effects in general
15. Akshavedamsa	45 parts of 0°40'	Quality of character, integrity
16. Shashtiamsa	60 parts of 0°30'	All general indications, very fine tuning

The Navamsa Chart

Among most astrologers, the navamsa chart is the next most important division after the rasi. The navamsa chart sheds further light on many things that the rasi chart (also called the birth or natal chart) only touches. Some astrologers liken the rasi chart to the branches of a tree and the navamsa to the leaves. Examination of the navamsa chart is an accepted—if not required—procedure for the study of one's partner, for marriage, and for overall general inclinations of behavior. Many astrologers will interpret the navamsa chart in the same manner as the natal chart. One key element that is considered is Vargottama (see chapter 8), which is when a planet occupies the same sign in both the natal chart and the navamsa. It is considered similar in effect to a planet being in its own sign.

How to Judge Planets in Vargas and Their Effects

Parasara, who developed this system, did little to explain its application in his work, *Brihat Parasara Hora Shastra*. He said to look for the karaka, or indicator of a life event, in the matching varga and see how it looks. So according to Parasara, we look at the navamsa for marriage and we look at the seventh "sign" in the navamsa. We can also locate which navamsa sign Venus occupies and that is about it. Much of what has been written on Shodasavarga has been by the astrologers following Parasara—extending on what they perceived to be the sage's logic.

Shodasavarga can be used to consider the strength and significance of certain life events or circumstances. Look at the rulers of the houses in the rasi and locate where they are positioned in a varga. Some astrologers indicate that you can read each varga chart in the same fashion that you read the rasi chart. This has seemed to bear out in my own experience.

It is important to give more weight to the rasi indications, but to use the varga indicators to further confirm whether the planet is strong or weak, significant or insignificant in its influence on the chart being studied.

Forecasting with Navamsa

Astrologers indicate, as a broad measure, that years 8, 32, and 59 are often critical years in a person's life. More specifically, each navamsa is said to indicate when inauspicious results might arise. If the transits and the dasa/bhukti period (see chapters 13 and 14) also indicate challenges, this navamsa technique would only add to the possibility of that happening. The navamsas would give us more notice to avoid dangers that come our way. The navamsa listed will be the navamsa for any rising sign in the rasi chart.

Navamsa	Critical Years
	(Arishtas: Disease, Injury, Trouble, etc.)
Aries	12, 25, 50, and 65
Taurus	10, 22, 32, and 72
Gemini	16, 24, 34, 40, and 63
Cancer	8, 18, 22, 31, 72, and 80
Leo	10, 20, 30, 60, and 82
Virgo	20, 50, and 60 (could live to 108 years)
Libra	3, 23, 38, 54, and 76
Scorpio	13, 18, 23, 28, 55, and 70
Sagittarius	4, 9, 16, 36, 44, and 76
Capricorn	19, 27, 34, 49, 54, and 68
Aquarius	7, 14, 20, 28, 32, and 61
Pisces	10, 12, 21, 26, 52, and 61

Additional Uses of Navamsa

There is a simple rule, which sounds complex, that you can use to get additional information from the rasi chart via the navamsa. This rule is often used to help determine profession, but can be applied to any other life event with good success. Using the example of career, the rule goes like this: Ruler of the navamsa of ruler of the tenth. To apply this, take the ruler of the 10th house in the rasi (natal) chart and look to where it is located in the navamsa. Now look at what planet is ruling that specific navamsa. That planet will have an influence on career. You can do the same for any area: marriage and partnership, education, health, etc.

SYNTHESIZING—PUTTING the BASICS TOGETHER

CHAPTER ELEVEN

RECTIFICATION OF BIRTH TIME

Before you can completely and correctly analyze a chart, you must ascertain that you have the correct birth time information. Using incorrect birth information is one of the easiest ways to deliver an inaccurate reading. In Vedic astrology, the convention is to mark the birth time as that moment when the body of the baby is outside the mother's womb. Some astrologers will say the time is when the baby draws its first breath, or when the baby touches the earth (table?), or when you first see the crown of the baby's head. In Kali Yuga (the Vedic 432,000-year grand time epoch we are currently enjoying), the convention is to mark the birth time when the child is outside the mother's womb. Be aware that the Vimshottari Dasa system will change about three or four days for every one-minute change in the birth time, and that the rising sign changes, by about one degree, every four minutes. Accurate recording is very important.

Rectification Methods

Rectifying by Dasa: One method, employed by a lot of astrologers, is to ask the client about specific dates of significant life events in the past. For example, ask about dates of marriage, divorce, birth of children, accidents, hospitalizations, etc. The astrologer will then run various birth times to locate dasa/bhukti periods that match these individual life events. This method should be verified over time to ensure that predicted life events occur within projected time frames. Some astrologers, to increase their certainty, rectify time down to the fourth and fifth levels of dasa. To make this rectification method even more useful, the astrologer should also rectify by transit.

Rectifying by Transit: Verifying the results of transits—that is, when a transiting planet passes over a certain degree in the natal chart—can tell you about the nature of the house and, correspondingly, of the ascendant. For example, let's say that a woman is unsure of her rising sign, unclear as to whether it is Aries or Taurus. Let's say she had Mars in Leo. Through questioning her, we find that she has had a miscarriage. The house of children, and any troubles with them, is represented by the fifth house, the Putra (Child) Bhava. A malefic, such as Mars, in the fifth can cause miscarriages and abortions. Let's also say we find that Mars has low shadbala strength (see chapter 12). With further examination, we also find that the miscarriage took place when, by exact degree, Saturn transited over Mars in her fifth. These transit events point to Aries rising, which puts Mars in Leo in the fifth. Use this technique with additional life events to solidify your judgment.

Additional Factors to Consider in Rectifying a Chart

Prasna: There could possibly be a correlation between the asking of a question—that is, when a person contacts the astrologer—and the time of their birth. For example, it might be that the contact time chart shows Gemini rising. When you get their birth data, if there is a question as to whether they are Gemini or Cancer, then prasna becomes a data point, indicating Gemini Lagna. (Chapter 13 further discusses prasna.)

Type of career: The career or various jobs a person has selected should be evident in the chart. When you look at the tenth house, the ruler of the tenth, and planets occupying the tenth, you should be able to recognize the career choices made by the person. To learn what types of careers are stimulated by the different planets, consult chapter 6. The Lagna and its ruling planet will also play a large role in shaping a person's skills and life interests.

Relationship to partners, family members, and their life events: The family houses are: 3rd for younger siblings, 4th for mother, 6th for mother's siblings or aunts and uncles and their off-spring, 7th for mate, 9th for father, and 11th for older siblings and father's siblings or aunts and uncles and their offspring. If the relationships and the life events of these family members are favorable or unfavorable, there should be an indication coming from positive or negative planetary aspects and occupations of these houses.

I have found that one of the best ways to rectify a person's chart, at least in determining the correct rising sign, is to compare it to that of someone they have had a close relationship with. The known chart of the mate, business associate, romantic partner, or marriage partner will show very clear interrelationships between the Sun, Moon, and rising signs. These factors present themselves in the form of conjunctions and oppositions between the charts.

Appearance and Ayurvedic body type: It takes particular skill and experience to be successful with this approach since there are so many variables that can modify appearance, but physical features as well as personality traits can be seen to a certain degree from a person's chart. Examination of Ayurvedic body type will also give you clues. Body and personality features can be used to determine the rising sign when that is in question (chapter 19 discusses Ayurvedic body type).

Body markings/wounds/organ systems: The body is divided astrologically into various sections and physical systems. These sections and systems are governed by various planets and signs. Afflicted planets in certain signs will show up as marks, moles, scars, etc. in the associated region of the body. These negative planets will also impact major bodily systems. Parasara's Brihat Parasara Hora Shastra gives details on identifying chart placements as indicated by body markings. There is an advanced system called Drekkana, also listed in Parasara's book, that gives a specific technique for determining types of physical ailments.

Navamsa Lagna: The navamsa changes about every 13 minutes or so, depending on the latitude of the chart. Adjusting the rising sign degree up or down a few degrees will give you a navamsa that should better reflect the nature of the person whose chart you are rectifying.

CHAPTER TWELVE

INTERPRETATION— HOW TO ANALYZE AND SYNTHESIZE A CHART

First, you need to determine the nature of the planets. As discussed in chapter 2, planets are, by nature and definition, either benefic or malefic. Benefic planets indicate favorable, positive, beneficial behaviors; and malefic planets indicate the tendency to act in an unfavorable, negative, destructive, fierce, or aggressive manner. The natural benefic and malefic planets are:

- Benefic (Saumya): Moon, Mercury, Jupiter, Venus
- Malefic (Krura): Sun, Mars, Saturn, Rahu, Ketu

Calling a planet benefic or malefic does not describe the degree or amount of its effect, nor does it show the ultimate favorable or unfavorable value for the chart. There are many factors to consider in determining how the basic nature of a planet is modified by its associations with other planets in a chart. We will be discussing these factors in this chapter.

After you determine that a planet is benefic or malefic, you need to decide whether the favorable or unfavorable qualities of that planet become stronger, weaker, or a mixture of both. This final judgment as to whether a planet is favorable or unfavorable comes from examining the planets in the houses, the rulers of the houses, the karaka planets, and the relationships between planets

Determining Whether a Planet Is Favorable in a Chart

A favorable planet, whether it is naturally benefic or malefic, strengthens and improves the quality of the indications (significations) of the house it occupies, rules, or aspects.

A planet is considered to bring favorable results when it is:

- exalted

- in its own sign

- moolatrikona—better than own sign, less than exalted

- in a great friend or friend's sign (mitra—discussed later in this chapter)

- located in an angle or a trine

- vargottama

- conjunct or aspected by other benefic planets

- "hemmed-in" or placed between benefics (subha kartari)

The above rules apply for navamsa and other divisional signs as well. Note that a planet in the rasi chart is influenced by its association with a planet in the navamsa and other divisional charts. Also, if the planet is in a neutral sign, it is neither strong nor weak and usually has little impact on the chart.

The following conditions also bring favorable results:

1. The **dispositor** planet of the rasi sign and the navamsa sign is strong. A dispositor, in astrological terms, is the planet that rules the sign that this planet occupies. For example, if Jupiter is in Aries (which is ruled by Mars),

then Mars is the dispositor of Jupiter—that is, Jupiter is in Mars's sign.

2. Planets in houses 1, 2, 4, 5, 7, 10, and 11 are considered to be strong and favorably placed.

3. Vipreet Raja Yoga, discussed at the end of chapter 8, states that a dusthana ruler in a dusthana house (6, 8, and 12) will do well. This offers some hope for dusthana ruling planets. The 6th is also an upachaya house, meaning that it is negative but can grow toward more positivity over time (see chapter 4).

4. The ruling planet of a house/sign should be conjunct or aspected by favorable or benefic planets.

5. It is considered good, or at least better, for rulers of angles and trines to be conjunct, even if one of the participating planets is malefic. These connections bring some financial prosperity but could still bring health problems. Planets that rule trinal houses and are located in angular houses form Raja Yogas (see chapter 4).

6. The rising sign is both an angle and a trine, so its ruler's placement is considered very favorable. Some say the ruler of the first is always good. Personally, I wouldn't say always, but there are usually good influences going to wherever the first house's ruler is placed. However, for example, it could happen that the first house's ruler benefits the house in which it is located, but is in itself drained of its full brilliance.

7. Benefic planets located 2, 4, 5, 7, 9, or 10 places from the planet being considered bring favorable results. Notice the absence of dusthana houses, and the 3rd, which is considered unfavorable, and the 11th, which is good but its ruler is not.

8. Many astrologers state that all planets are good in the 11th but that the ruler of the 11th is not good.

9. Planets that rule trines (the 1st, 5th, and 9th houses) are considered favorable. Even if the ruler is a natural malefic, it will bring some form of financial prosperity, but not necessarily good health or other nonfinancial factors.

10. Planets that simultaneously rule angles and trines are very good and are called Yogakarakas. The Yogakaraka for the rising sign brings favorable results, indicating prosperity. Mars is the Yogakaraka for Cancer and Leo; for Capricorn and Aquarius it is Venus; and for Taurus and Libra it is Saturn. Yogakarakas are defined further in the appendix.

11. Many Vedic astrologers believe that benefics ruling angular houses (1, 4, 7, and 10) become malefic. They also hold the reverse to be true: Malefics ruling angular houses become benefic. I have found that this rule is not consistently accurate and that too much is made of it. This rule is used a lot in designating functional malefics by rising sign.

Determining Whether a Planet Is Unfavorable in a Chart

An unfavorable planet, whether naturally benefic or malefic, weakens and demotes the good qualities of the indications (significations) of the house it occupies, rules, or aspects.

A planet is considered to bring unfavorable results when it is:

1. Debilitated.

2. In a great enemy or enemy's sign (satru—discussed later in this chapter).

3. In conjunction with the Sun. Planets are considered Asta (asthangatha, combust) or "burned up" by being too close to the Sun.

4. Defeated in planetary war (graha yudha). Planetary war occurs when more than one planet occupies a sign; then, the planets contend for influence, creating a warlike situation. Graha yudha is most applicable to planets co-located with Mars. The planet behind the other—that is, having less degrees—is said to win the war. However, graha yudha is a secondary influence and should not dominate in making judgments.

5. Sandhi (on the border between two signs; under one degree or over 29 degrees). This placement, if at the very beginning degree, is said to make the planet vulnerable like an infant; and if at the end, makes the planet feeble and old.

6. Located in an unfavorable house, such as a dusthana house (6, 8, or 12—see chapter 4). Most texts on Vedic astrology state that houses are "damaged" if they contain the rulers of the dusthana houses, or are aspected by them. Planets that rule other houses, if conjunct or aspected by dusthana rulers, lose a lot of their power to do good, and are weak in repelling any negative forces that fall upon them. This could be likened to a person whose immune system is already depressed by infection being less able to recover quickly, or to resist other diseases. In addition, the 3rd house indicates effort and struggling, so is also considered an unfavorable location (it is also the 8th from the 8th— see Judging from Karaka Planets, chapter 4).

7. Aspected by malefics. In this case, the favorable qualities decrease and the planet is vulnerable to problems. In addition, a malefic ruler will decrease the value of its house, so the occupants of that malefic-ruled house will also go down in value. This is the effect of dispositors.

8. Surrounded or "hemmed in" by malefics. This is called a Papa Kartari Yoga (Papa means "bad," and kartari means "scissors"). This hemming-in can occur within a sign or between signs.

How to Interpret a Planet Ruling Two Houses/Signs

In this event, the convention is to take the planet that is in its moolatrikona sign as the strength giver. Moolatrikona is a planetary position that is better than being in its own house, but not as good as exaltation (see table in chapter 2).

Strong Malefics

A natural malefic in its own house, or exalted in a favorable house, will do the good things attributed to that planet, although it will not be stopped altogether from being a potential troublemaker. For example, Mars in Capricorn in the 10th house gives very powerful career capabilities and could make the person a leader (this is a Ruchaka Yoga); however, it does not mean that the person could not use that power in a negative way—perhaps by being a powerful but mean dictator—if aspects by other malefics in the chart contribute to that. The overall, sum positive or negative quality of the entire chart will contribute to a positive use of energy or a negative one.

Are Malefics Good or Bad in Malefic Houses?

There is some controversy as to whether or not it is good to have malefic planets in malefic or dusthana houses (6, 8, and 12). My position is that malefic planets are worse in negative positions, not better. If a person is weak and hungry and enters the house of another person who has no food, there is little help available for that starving visitor. If a person has a criminal mind and is put into a prison filled with other criminally minded people, then they have little chance for rehabilitation (real-life statistics show this). One favorable note that can be gleaned from this last metaphor, however, is that the criminal's detention in the prison (the malefic's confinement to the malefic house) is good for all the other people (planets) who are outside the prison—the criminal cannot use his or her criminal mind to influence others. That might be what some astrologers are pointing to when they say it is good to have malefic planets in malefic houses.

If a malefic planet is placed in a good position, then its favorable significations increase, but at the expense of the occupied house. When Colonel Sanders enters the house of the chickens, it is good for Colonel Sanders but not good for the chickens. To succeed with strength, we need symbiotic and enlivening relationships between planets—not parasitic or draining ones.

Can Naturally Malefic Planets Be Favorable?

When naturally malefic planets (Sun, Mars, Saturn, Rahu, and Ketu) are exalted, in their moolatrikona sign, in their own sign, Vargottama, or in a friend's sign, they are considered strong, and well placed for a malefic planet. The ultimate favorable value of the malefic is stimulated. Remember, a naturally malefic planet is not all "evil" (and conversely, due to bad placements and aspects, natural benefics are not always good).

The Sun is good in that it gives us our life and vitality when well placed; however, when poorly placed, it can make us egotistical and give us health problems and conflicts with authorities. It can even cause us to be disinterested in material growth. This is fine for renunciates, who want to be detached from material urges, but if you are a householder you need to be stirred to earn a living.

Mars is good for initiating life and defending oneself. When it is well placed, you are stimulated to take effective action in life. When Mars is poorly placed, it can make you overly aggressive and impatient or it can lead you to be lazy and undirected. Mars makes leaders and dictators, givers and thieves.

We need a good Saturn for focus, structure, and the capacity to endure. When Saturn is afflicted or poorly placed, you can lose your attention and get beset with restrictions and setbacks. You don't act in time. You feel miserable because you are not living in a rhythm. Saturn can be blamed for this only partially. A lot of people are afraid of Saturn or use Saturn as an excuse for their lack of success or motivation.

A good or well-placed Rahu helps you acquire your possessions, or when poorly placed, it causes you to be confused or deceitful.

Ketu is the Moksha karaka, or indicator for enlightenment, but when weak or poorly placed it causes you to be fragmented and introduces too many variables and ambiguities. Chaos sets in.

Functional Malefics by Rising Sign

In general, planets that rule the 3rd, 6th, 8th, and 12th houses are considered to bring unfavorable results to the significations of the planet and the house/sign that it occupies. Specifically or functionally, certain planets are deemed unfavorable for certain rising signs.

I am presenting the following table to show you how many astrologers determine malefic planets for each rising sign. This information is general, is derived from many varied rules of Vedic astrology, and must be further modified by examining conjunctions and aspects from other planets—don't take malefics by rising sign as a sole source of quality! In the appendix, I have explained why each planet is considered malefic for the signs indicated in a table titled "Malefic Planets by Rising Sign." When analyzing a chart, the transit of planets and the current dasa/bhukti period must also be taken into account. No planet is unalterably benefic or malefic, either by basic nature, or functionally by position under a specific rising sign. Remember—a planet's placement in one of the houses and its association with other planets by conjunction or other aspect will modify the baseline condition of the planet, either positively or negatively. One of your skills as an astrologer is your ability to determine how good or bad a planet is within the specifics of an individual chart. Realize that in astrology, as well as in other disciplines, general rules will be modified under specific circumstances.

Rising Sign	Malefic Planets for That Specific Sign
1. Aries	Saturn, Mercury, Venus
2. Taurus	Jupiter, Moon (but Moon is still exalted)
3. Gemini	Mars, Jupiter, Sun
4. Cancer	Venus, Mercury
5. Leo	Mercury, Venus
6. Virgo	Moon, Mars, Jupiter
7. Libra	Sun, Jupiter, Mars
8. Scorpio	Mercury, Venus
9. Sagittarius	Venus, Saturn
10. Capricorn	Mars, Jupiter, Moon
11. Aquarius	Jupiter, Moon, Mars
12. Pisces	Saturn, Sun, Venus, Mercury

RELATIONSHIPS BETWEEN PLANETS

"No planet is an island"—that is, no planet's influence exists in isolation. In order to determine the strength of a planet, you have to measure the nature of that planet's relationship with other planets. Planetary indications must be modified according to the influences that fall upon them. Major influences come to planets and the houses they rule and occupy from neighboring or aspecting planets.

The standard planetary aspects are (start counting from the occupied sign as number one):

- **Conjunctions** are planets located anywhere together in the same sign of the zodiac—that is, the same 30-degree rasi. If the planets are in separate signs, even if very close by degree, a conjunction does not occur. Conjunctions occur only within the sign in Vedic astrology. There is no specific degree of proximity (orb) required to create an aspect. However, aspects by exact degree can show fairly specific results.

- **Squares** (kendra) are planets located four signs apart (again, counting the sign you start in as one).

- **Trines** (trikona) are planetary aspects that sway planets located five signs away.

- **Oppositions** are separated by 180 degrees or seven signs.

- Vedic astrology also has the following special planetary aspects (see mutual aspect).

    - **Mars** aspects other planets 4 and 8 houses away.

    - **Jupiter** throws an aspect 5 and 9 houses ahead.

    - **Saturn** casts a special glance at planets 3 and 10 houses from itself.

    - Some authors, such as Parasara, indicate that Rahu and Ketu aspect houses 5 and 9 from themselves (forming squares or kendras).

- The word *sambandha* is used to indicate that there is some mutual relationship between planets. It's like they come from the same family.

  - **Mutual exchange** means that two planets, as rulers of signs, are positioned in each other's signs (see chapter 8).

  - **Mutual aspect** (see chapter 8) is when two planets each aspect the other according to any of the rules in this list.

  - **Dispositor aspect** Dispositor planets were defined earlier in this chapter and can aspect the planet under analysis.

Grahamitra—Planetary Friendships

As already noted, a planet has defined relationships with its neighbors. These nearby planets are termed a planet's friends, enemies, or neutrals (an "even" mixture of both friend and enemy). These relationships are called either permanent or natural (*naisargika*), or temporary (*tatkalika*), depending on the influences in a specific chart.

As you will see, these calculations could become tedious, if done by hand. Many Vedic astrology software programs do these calculations automatically, so if you don't want to spend too much time with this section at first, then go on. Just make sure you know how to read the computer printout of these calculations and that you understand the effects of these relationships. I've included the following explanations so that you can understand the mechanics and logic behind the calculations. I would consider the Combined Relationships, listed in most computer programs, as the most useful; this will usually include friend, enemy, and neutral relationships.

Naisargika—Natural or Permanent Relationships

The relationships listed below are customarily the same in all charts. The relationship will either increase or decrease the qualities of the planets being examined. The rule for determining the natural relationships between planets is that the rulers of signs 2, 4, 5, 8, 9, and 12 from the Moolatrikona sign of a planet and the rulers of exaltation signs of that planet are its friends (mitra). The rest—3, 6, 7, 10, and 11—are its enemies (satru). If dual rulerships are involved and a planet is both a friend and an enemy, then it is regarded as neutral or even (samya).

Planet	Mitra (Friends)	Satru (Enemies)	Samya (Neutral)
Sun	Moon, Mars, Jupiter	Venus, Saturn	Mercury
Moon	Sun, Mercury	None	All others
Mars	Sun, Moon, Jupiter	Mercury	Venus, Saturn
Mercury	Sun, Venus	Moon	Mars, Jupiter, Saturn
Jupiter	Sun, Moon, Mars	Mercury, Venus	Saturn
Venus	Mercury, Saturn	Sun, Moon	Mars, Jupiter
Saturn	Mercury, Venus	Sun, Moon, Mars	Jupiter
Rahu and Ketu	Mercury, Saturn, Venus	Sun, Moon, Jupiter	Mars

Note that while some authors state that the Moon has no enemies, there are some who say that the enemies of the Moon are Saturn, Rahu, and Ketu. I concur. There are different opinions about Rahu and Ketu. Some say that Rahu's friends are Jupiter, Venus, and Saturn and that Sun, Moon, and Mars are enemies, while Mercury is neutral. Some consider Ketu's friends to be Mars, Venus, and Saturn; they regard the Sun and Moon as enemies and Mercury and Jupiter as neutrals.

Tatkalika or Temporary

Tatkalika or temporary relationships will vary from chart to chart. A planet placed 2nd, 3rd, 4th, 10th, 11th, or 12th from any other planet becomes a temporary friend in that specific chart. The other houses are enemies (1, 5, 6, 7, 8, 9). Remember, the counting system used in Vedic astrology means that a planet 2nd from another is next to it, 3rd has one house in between, and so on.

Combined Friendships (Naisargika mingled with Tatkalika)

Taking the rules of permanent and temporary friendships together, we will get a third kind of relationship between planets. The results of the friend and enemy relationships generally emerge as five types: friend (mitra), enemy (satru), samya (even or neutral—mixed friend and enemy), great friend (adhi mitra), and great enemy (adhi satru). The table below shows how these five are formed—for example, Adhi Mitra is formed by the combination of a planet being both a temporary and natural friend (tatkalika and naisargika mitra).

	Tatkalika Mitra	Tatkalika Satru	Tatkalika Samya	Naisargika Mitra	Naisargika Satru	Naisargika Samya
Adhi Mitra	X			X		
Samya	X				X	
Mitra	X					X
Adhi Satru		X			X	
Samya		X		X		
Satru		X			X	

ANALYZING HOUSES—STRONG OR WEAK

Now that we have determined how to identify strong and weak planets, we need to do the same for houses.

Strong houses have the power to increase or promote the significations indicated within that house. A house can be considered strong if both its ruler and the ruler of the house where this ruler is placed (the dispositor) are strong, or if it is occupied or aspected by its ruler or by favorable planets.

Weak houses are frail. They can't protect themselves from malefic aspects and they decrease or demote the value of the significations of planets within their house. A house gets weakened when it is occupied or aspected by malefic planets. For example, the fourth house is the house of the mother. If Saturn occupies the fourth, is debilitated in the sign of Aries, is aspected by Rahu, and the ruler of the fourth is in the sixth, we get a very weak house. The mother of this person will have difficulties. It will be even more unsettling for the mother if—first—the Moon, the karaka of the mother, is weak or afflicted, and—second—the sign of the Mother, Cancer, is occupied or aspected by malefics.

Consider the following matters in analyzing the benefic (favorable) or malefic (unfavorable) quality of a house. Remember that the house and sign are regarded as the same for a specific ascendant.

- What is the quality of the planets in the house?
- What is the quality of the ruler of the house? Note that the shadbala strength of the house ruler is a significant determinant of benefic or malefic quality.
- What is the quality of the aspects coming upon the house?
- What is the quality of the planets aspecting the ruler of the house?
- The ruler of a house should be strong (remember, we treat houses and signs the same).
- The house/sign itself should be naturally strong.
- The karaka or indicator of the house should be strong. For example, the second house is a money house. The indicator for money or wealth is Jupiter. If Jupiter is weak, the second house of money cannot express itself fully.

A good house is well supported. Its ruler is good and the house is well aspected. The planets that occupy that house do better. So-called malefic planets become able to act on their best behavior.

———————••꒰ 🟊 ꒱••———————

A bad house has many problems. Its ruler is not benefic or well placed. The house is afflicted by bad associations with other planets. It might even be occupied by negative planets. When a planet visits this bad house, it has trouble displaying its good features, regardless of whether it is naturally benefic or malefic.

ADDITIONAL TOOLS FOR JUDGING A CHART

Using Nakshatras and Nakshatra Rulers in Interpretation

The concept of using nakshatra "ruling" planets is a subject of scholarly debate in Vedic astrology. Parasara definitely states that each nakshatra has an association to a specific planet, but also that that planet is used to determine the starting point for Vimshottari Dasa calculations. It has been assumed by many, and has become a convention, that since Sun signs or rasis have rulers, these "dasa" planets associated with nakshatras must therefore be rulers of their nakshatras. However, it might be better to call these planets dasa rulers. Another important point to consider is that we have been given permission by the ancient sages to determine dasas starting from the Rasi Lagna (rising sign) or from the Janma Lagna (the Moon), whichever is the stronger. Thus, we have a situation where the ruler could come from either the Lagna nakshatra or the Moon nakshatra. This should be considered.

Many astrologers feel that this nakshatra "ruler" is as important as the rasi ruler. They claim that many ambiguous points in the chart are made clear by the use of these nakshatra rulers. When the planetary ruler and the nakshatra ruler indicate similar results, or when planets are placed in their own nakshatras, it is claimed that the certainty of interpretation is increased.

For a more detailed explanation of nakshatras, see chapter 9.

Using Navamsa in Interpretation and Prediction

You can use divisional charts to get additional information. You can also sum up the placement of planets in signs in the different vargas to get a wider view of the strength of a planet (Vargabala). Navamsas are used by many astrologers as yet another way to derive information from the birth chart. Many astrologers interpret the navamsa in a fashion similar to the birth chart. Chapter 10 discusses navamsa.

Using Shadbala and Vargabala Calculations

In spite of all the complexity in determining the strength of planets, Parasara was kind enough to give us a general method for analyzing planetary power. . . . There is hope for beginners! In a simple way, the strength or favorable influences of a planet can be determined by examining shadbala strength.

Most Vedic astrology programs calculate shadbala, which translates as six strengths. These six strengths are:

1. Sthana (location)
2. Dig or Dik (direction)
3. Kala (time)
4. Chesta (retrograde movement)
5. Naisargika (natural benefic qualities)
6. Drik (aspects)

However, it must be emphasized that the use of shadbala does not preclude consideration of other judgment factors such as exaltation, debilitation, friendships, sandhi, combustion, aspects, etc. These factors can add to or subtract from the general shadbala indications. You will develop the ability over time to merge these factors together.

* * *

STEP-BY-STEP GUIDE TO ANALYZING A CHART

1. Verify that you have the correct time, date, and place of birth. Rectification might be required, if there is any doubt about the time.

2. Look at the overall strength and quality of the rising sign and its ruling planet. The more negative the rising sign, the weaker the chart. People with weak rising signs tend to get into more difficulties and have more trouble extricating themselves from complicated situations.

3. Look at planetary placements relative to the Moon, the Sun, and the rising sign in the rasi, and also the rising sign in the navamsa. Good placement increases the

ability of the chart to pick up favorable indications. Bad placement brings down the chart.

4. Look at the shadbala and vargabala strengths of the rising sign ruler and of the Moon to determine which is more powerful.

5. Evaluate the strength of the Moon. Is the Moon increasing or waxing from New to Full (Shukla Paksha), or decreasing or waning from Full to New (Krishna Paksha)? See the chart in chapter 2. The Moon is considered weak and unfavorable if within 72 degrees (about 2 1/2 signs) of either side of the Sun. A weak Moon, like a weak Lagna, will drive down the quality of the entire chart.

6. Look at planets in houses, especially noting the more negative placements of 3rd, 6th, 8th, and 12th houses. Note that the 6th house is both a dusthana (negative) and an upachaya (improving) house at the same time. If malefics aspect the 6th house, then it functions as a malefic, and if benefics aspect or occupy the 6th, it eventually becomes favorable—but not necessarily 100 percent.

7. Look for the quantity or predominance of the planets' placements—are they mostly favorable or unfavorable?

8. Look at the sarvashtakavarga (see the end of this chapter) to identify the overall strength of a sign. A sign (house) with high strength points (bindus) will be able to repel negative influences that fall upon it.

9. Identify the rulership yogas—for example, ruler of the 1st is in the 9th—especially in terms of combinations with the generally unfavorable 3rd, 6th, 8th, or 12th. The quantity of negative rulership locations is significant in decreasing the overall favorable qualities of a chart.

10. Look for two-planet conjunctions, or more—signs with three or more planets will carry a tremendous amount of influence. Houses with four or more planets can be

viewed as a "pseudo lagna." Know conjunctions well—they are invaluable.

11. Identify the current dasa (see chapter 13) down to at least the 3rd level.

12. Locate the current gochara or planetary transits (see chapter 14). Note the location of the four slow-moving planets: Saturn, Jupiter, Rahu, and Ketu. Merge these transit effects with the dasa effects.

13. Identify the impact of Saturn's transit for Sade Sati (see chapter 14) on not only the Moon, but also the Sun and rising sign. Saturn's position is often more impactful in the 12th sign from these planets.

14. Locate any retrograde planets, or any planets aspected by retrograde planets. Retrogrades can negatively impact physical and emotional health. Remember, a retrograde and debilitated planet becomes almost exalted, and a retrograde and exalted planet gets degraded almost to a debilitated state.

15. Determine whether planets are weak or strong in the divisional charts (see chapter 10), especially the 9th (navamsa) for partners and overall well-being, and the 10th (dashamsa) for career and life purpose.

16. It is good to look for combust planets (see end of chapter 2), but for them to significantly impact the chart in a negative way, they must be weak to start (in bad houses, aspected by malefics, etc.) and very close to the Sun (near exact conjunction—by two or three degrees).

Planetary Strength and Benefic Analysis Chart

Fill in the blanks for each planet. I created this chart so that you can tally the favorable or unfavorable influences of the various planets, including the Lagna (ascendant), using its ruler. Total the entries at the bottom. The planet will be a favorable or unfavorable influence according to the totals.

Name of Planet:	Favorable & Benefic (+1 point)	Unfavorable & Malefic (-1 point)
Strength & Positivity Factor		
1. This planet is a natural benefic (+) or malefic (-).		
2. This planet is a functional benefic (+) or malefic (-) by current rising sign.		
3. This planet is sandhi—less than one or more than 29 degrees (-) or near the midpoint of sign—bhavamadya (+).		
4. This planet is closely combust the Sun (-).		
5. This planet is defeated in planetary war (graha yudha) (-).		
6. This planet is in its own sign (+).		
7. This planet is in a friend's sign (+).		
8. This planet is in its moolatrikona sign (+).		
9. This planet is in an enemy's sign (-).		
10. This planet is exalted (+).		
11. This planet is debilitated (-).		
12. This planet is located in a benefic (+) or malefic (-) sign.		
13. This planet is located in a benefic (+) or malefic (-) house.		
14. The planet ruling the house that this planet occupies (dispositor) is benefic or malefic—that is, the ruler has high (+) or low (-) shadbala strength.		
15. The planet ruling the nakshatra that this planet occupies (dispositor) is benefic or malefic—that is, the ruler has high (+) or low (-) shadbala strength.		
16. Planets aspecting this planet are benefic (+) or malefic (-) by virtue of being conjunct, opposite, or a special aspect.		
17. This planet is in benefic (+) or malefic (-) aspect to another sign.		
18. This planet is in benefic (+) or malefic (-) aspect to another house.		
19. This planet is in benefic (+) or malefic (-) aspect to another planet(s).		

Name of Planet:	Favorable & Benefic (+1 point)	Unfavorable & Malefic (-1 point)
20. This planet is in a benefic (+) or malefic (-) placement in the navamsa chart.		
21. This planet is overall benefic (+) or malefic (-) in the varga summary tables (available in most software programs).		
22. This planet has a benefic (+) or malefic (-) influence from the current rulers of the dasa/bhukti/antaradasa.		
23. This planet occupies a sign with high (+) or low (-) sarvashtakavarga strength.		
24. This planet has high (+) or low (-) shadbala strength.		
25. This planet is "hemmed in" between benefics (+) or malefics (-).		
26. This planet is in the same sign in the rasi and navamsa—that is, it is vargottama, similar to being in own sign (+).		
27. A debilitated planet improves through exalted placement in the navamsa (+).		
28. This planet is retrograde or aspected by a retrograde planet (-).		
29. This planet, if retrograde, is in its sign of exaltation (-).		
30. This planet, if retrograde, is in its sign of debilitation (+).		
31. The ruler of the 9th or 10th is linked to the rulers of 1, 4, 5, or 7 or is positioned in any of these houses, forming a Raja Yoga (+).		
32. This planet, though exalted, degrades since it is debilitated in the navamsa (-).		
Total Points:		

Use the form on the previous page to tally all the pluses and minuses for each planet. If the planet has more pluses than minuses, you can interpret the planet according to the "Favorable" indications that have been given throughout this book. If there are more minuses, interpret the planet according to the "Unfavorable" indicators. If the results are mixed—within approximately five points of each other—then you will get a little bit of both favorable and unfavorable qualities. For example, the person may have a mixed personality or they may have periods in their lives when favorable or unfavorable qualities surface.

You would look first at what the planet signifies generally, such as the Moon representing the mother; then you would look at what that planet signifies specifically by where it is placed in the birth chart. Let's say the Moon was favorable, so the mother would fare well, and let's say the Moon was in the second house, so we would say that the Moon would increase the significations of the second (money) and do so in terms of characteristics of the Moon (nurturing activities, soothing speech, liquids, silver, pearls, dairy products, sea or water products, visual arts, etc.).

You could also determine, from the strength analysis above, whether planetary periods will be favorable or unfavorable. In our example, with a favorable Moon in the second house, you could expect the person to do well financially within the indications promised by the Moon, so that during the Moon period (dasa) the person might expect financial aid from the mother, gains in the silver trade, success within the dairy business, etc.

The effects of gochara or planetary transits can be judged from the planetary strength. The most prevalent problem, and one that drives most clients to seek an astrologer, is when the planets functioning unfavorably in a specific chart transit over unfavorable planetary positions in the birth chart.

Cancellation of Debilitation (Neecha Bhanga)

A debilitated planet will become stronger and more positive (though it will not lose all of its negative tendencies) under the following conditions:

- The ruling planet of the sign where the debilitated planet is placed is exalted. For example, Mercury in Pisces is debilitated. However, in a specific chart, if Pisces's ruling planet, Jupiter, is placed in Cancer and therefore exalted, then Mercury's debilitation gets canceled, or at least reduced in weakness. The weak Mercury gets improved by the strong Jupiter, just like a weak child's life is improved or protected when its father is strong.

- The debilitated planet is in its own sign (in the sign that it rules).

- The debilitated planet is placed in a house whose ruler is in a kendra (square) from the Moon in the birth chart. (Some astrologers also count trikonas as giving cancellation—I only use kendras.)

- Debilitated planets in the unfavorable 6th, 8th, or 12th houses are not able to have their debility canceled.

- Debilitated planets in the more favorable houses of 1, 2, 3, 4, 9, and 11 from Lagna are not as weakened by their debilitation. They have some strength to confer good results, making cancellation of debilitation more effective.

Various Strength-Calculation Systems

Below are two systems that your computer program will calculate for you. You can use the values in the tables to find out whether or not the planetary data from the computer calculations are beneficial.

1. Shadbala

The minimum strength value is given in rupas (a strength point). If the values are greater than the numbers given below, then the planet is considered strong. Most programmers will calculate a ratio, so that if any planet is strong, a +1 value will show up, and any weak planet will show up as –1. This means the points that the planet has above 1 are good and below 1 are not good. They often call the ratio the Strength Factor, the Power Ratio, or something similar.

Sun	Moon	Mars	Mercury	Jupiter	Venus	Saturn
6.5	6.0	5.0	7.0	6.5	5.5	5.0

2. Sarvashtakavarga

Sarvashtakavarga can give strength to a sign/house that otherwise might look weak and afflicted, especially if the points exceed 30. The signs or houses with the lowest points will often signal the greatest weaknesses of that person. For example, a person having 18 points in the seventh house would most likely have relationship problems. A house with high sarvashtakavarga points, if transited by an unfavorable planet, will do better than might otherwise be expected. The capacity to prevail during Saturn's Sade Sati transit (see chapter 14) is increased when the points are high in a house. Also, negative indications have more difficulty surfacing. The strength points for this system are called bindus.

Minimum Bindu Values by House

House:	1	2	3	4	5	6	7	8	9	10	11	12
Points:	25	22	29	24	25	34	19	24	29	36	54	16

General Values—Benefic Effects from Houses
(minimum 25 points)

15–20: Poor results   25–30: Good results

20–25: Average   Over 30: Very favorable

FORECASTING
OR
PREDICTING
EVENTS

CHAPTER THIRTEEN

PREDICTING EVENTS

We start off this life with one chart. That chart is said to represent the indications and the culminating point of all our previous life actions. It is the starting point for this new life and represents where we left off in our last life. The challenging part of astrology is not just interpreting the tendencies embedded in this birth chart, or picking a good date to start or stop something. The most formidable task of the competent astrologer is this: to foresee when tendencies of behavior, as seen in the chart, might manifest over time.

The major predictive techniques that I will cover are the ones that I believe can lead a beginning or advanced student of astrology to a correct prognosis. These techniques or systems are:

- Vimshottari Dasa (planetary forecasting periods);

- Ashtakavarga (special sign transits);

- Varshaphal (birthday charts); and

- Gochara (transits; see chapter 14).

All these systems are founded on the position of planets, transiting over time and matched back to the birth chart. As the astrologer, you must be able to detect which planets are stronger or weaker in relationship to each other. You also have to know the relative strengths of planets when they form combinations, such as dasa and bhukti ruling planets. You could have a situation where you have a weak dasa ruler and a strong bhukti ruler. The bhukti ruler will show more influence, even though it is in second position.

The planets, seen at first in the cosmic "snapshot" of a birth chart, are constantly moving forward (and backward). The skill of a great astrologer is to know how to read this "moving target" of a chart. Planets change as they whirl around in their orbits, speeding through the signs in the heavens. Dasa and bhukti cycles are constantly moving forward from their natal Moon (or Lagna) starting gate. Nothing is static in a chart. It is always transforming into new realities and possibilities. This is part of the grace of God, giving us new opportunities. The Blue Ribbon Award for good astrology goes to those who can forecast events.

Vimshottari Dasa, or Planetary Periods

The position of the Moon in the chart is called the Janma Rasi, and the nakshatra in which the Moon is placed is called the Janma Nakshatra or birth star (as distinct from the rising sign or the Rasi Lagna). The Moon nakshatra is the starting point of various planetary periods. Each nakshatra has a ruling planet, which is assigned a ruling period of between 6 and 20 years. This planetary period is called a dasa. The dasa is the main planetary period; the bhukti is a subperiod within a dasa. There are further sub-subperiods within each bhukti as well, the antardasa is the third level, sookshmadasa is the fourth, and pranadasa is the fifth. This is the South India convention.

The most well-known and widely used planetary period system is Parasara's Vimshottari Dasa System. Some call this Udu Dasa or Nakshatra Dasa. Parasara says that during the Kali Yuga, this is the system to use. Kali Yuga is one of four major universal time epochs; it is 432,000 years long. We are currently about 5,000 years into this least evolved of the four major Vedic time periods (yugas). Kali Yuga started with the death of Krishna, some say on February 2, 3102 B.C. after Krishna was mistakenly shot by a hunter's arrow.

Dasa theory holds that the significations, or effects promised by planets in the birth chart, manifest mainly during the dasa/bhukti periods of those specific planets. The dasa indicates the time when the karmas linked to the planet will operate. The dasa brings out the qualities that the planet signifies in the birth chart. The quality of the manifestation depends on the functional benefic or malefic nature of the planets involved. This is according to the planetary relationships for a specific rising sign and all the interactions that occur within that chart. Many Vedic astrologers teach that examining the second level of dasa (the bhukti or sub-period) is of great significance in determining when those karmas, held by the planets in the charts, will be released.

The astrologer has the option of calculating dasas from the stronger of either the Lagna or the Moon. This is an area on which I have seen little or no commentary; currently, I don't know of many astrologers switching to the Lagna as an option for rectification, when the dasa periods don't line up with the person's birth time and life events. The use of Lagna for dasa calculations is an area open for research and discovery, but to this point the Moon is winning as the calculation method of choice (or convention).

The length of each major dasa cycle by planet in years is:

- Ketu: 7 years
- Venus: 20 years
- Sun: 6 years
- Moon: 10 years
- Mars: 7 years
- Rahu: 18 years
- Jupiter: 16 years
- Saturn: 19 years
- Mercury: 17 years

All Vedic astrology software programs that I know of calculate dasas. Since the Moon will most likely be positioned somewhere within a nakshatra, rather than at the exact start or end of one, you will get a partial first dasa period, with each succeeding dasa running its full period, until the point where you die—then, obviously, the dasa cycles are over. It is held that you start your next life where you left off in this life.

Determining the Value of the Dasa Period

Since the dasa indicates the fruition of the karmas held by its ruling planet in the birth chart, you can tell the quality and strength of the dasa by determining the inherent strength of the planet ruling the dasa. Follow the rules listed earlier for determining the strength of a planet, such as using shadbala (chapter 12).

Dasa periods will be favorable if a dasa-ruling planet is strong and favorably placed and it is participating in favorable yogas in the birth chart. The person will receive the favorable indications of the planet ruling the dasa period.

Dasa periods will be unfavorable if the dasa-ruling planet is weak and poorly placed and it is participating in unfavorable yogas in the birth chart. The person will receive the unfavorable indications of the planet ruling the dasa period.

Additional Points on Dasas

The end of a dasa period is called dasa chidra. It is considered unfavorable, like a person moving from an old house into a new house, not fully in either residence during the transition.

During this period, the dasa-ruling planet has impact, but in a more general or background mode. The bhukti, the second-level dasa, carries more weight. You will need to determine the relative strength of each of the dasa and bhukti ruling planets and merge them to get a balanced judgment. The role of the third-level dasa, the antaradasa or sub-subperiod, is to determine shorter-term events, while staying synchronized with the subperiod and main period rulers. You need to pay special attention to where the bhukti ruler is located during transit (gochara; see chapter 14).

These dasa/bhukti indications are also affected, for good or bad, by the influence coming from the current transits of planets (gochara). For a reading to be complete, correct, and timely, an astrologer must merge the results forecasted from the dasa-bhukti periods with the current gochara effects. Astrologers must pay attention to the slower-moving planets of Saturn, Jupiter, Rahu, and Ketu and merge them into the equation as well. Mars, while a shorter-duration transit, often acts as a stimulant to manifest the accumulated effects of dasas and gochara.

Reading Dasa Rulers

Treat the rulers of dasa and bhukti, bhukti and antaradasa, or any of the further subperiods as if they were conjunctions. Use chapter 8's list of significations. Look to the placement and strength in the birth chart to get the specific weight and significations of the period's ruling planets. The major, longer periods will have slower effect, while the shorter subperiods will give more immediate effects. Again, these dasa-ruling planets must also be supplemented and merged with the effects of the transiting planets (especially the slower-moving planets) to get an effective reading.

Varshaphal, or the "Birthday" Chart

According to a system called Tajaka Paddhati, an annual chart of planetary positions is drawn every birthday, which is called Varsha Phala Kundali. The key to this approach is to locate, for the current year, the day on which the Sun returns to the same degree as in the birth chart. A chart is constructed for that time and is read in conjunction with the birth chart. Some scholars say that this system came from the Muslims, most likely from Tajikastan (thus tajaka).

The Varshaphal chart, prepared for the person's birthday, will indicate favorable or unfavorable results for that specific year. There are complex interpretation rules, and a different way of using aspects and of timing planets during the year. Many computer programs make this calculation. I have found that you can get a successful reading by just calculating a chart for the return of the degree of the Sun to the natal Sun position, then interpreting it as a regular chart. You must still overlay the Varshaphal chart on the birth chart to synthesize the results with dasa and gochara predictions. The natal chart will predominate, but the Varshaphal can give additional "fruits" to the interpretation. In Western astrology, this is called a Solar Return Chart.

Ashtakavarga

Ashtakavarga is another system for forecasting specific life events. It is based on the transit of planets through the signs. Parasara created the ashtakavarga system (ashta means eight, varga means division) to help us determine the strength of a planet transiting in a specific sign. Each planet and the Lagna are given specific places where they are benefic or malefic by transit. The positive or negative value of being located in a certain sign is marked by points or bindus. If we were to take the Moon, for example, a simple chart would be drawn up for the Moon alone. Following a formula, each sign of the zodiac would be given a value from 0–8, showing where the Moon would do well or poorly by transit (most modern computer programs will do this for you).

This "value chart" is drawn up for each planet, showing where a sign has high or low bindus. High bindus—four or more—mean that the Moon will do well when transiting that sign. Under four bindus indicates that the Moon will do poorly in that position by transit, so when malefic planets transit over the sign occupied by that weak Moon, she will not be able to repel the malefic influences. If the Moon had high bindus in a sign and was transited by the same planet, that malefic planet would not be able to do too much damage to the indications of the Moon and the sign it occupies.

Using ashtakavarga can give you a very good understanding of why some planets seem to be struck by negative transits and others seem to brush off the unfavorable influences. This is a good technique to use to understand the true effect of Sade Sati.

It is held that even the best astrologers will not be able to interpret a chart fully without consulting the ashtakavarga charts for the effects of transits of planets. With the advent of computers, this once-laborious calculation can be done in seconds. It is only recently that various authors have written books explaining this process in detail. Ashtakavarga is quite detailed, but I will summarize the key points needed to effectively and simply use ashtakavarga in interpretation.

Definition of Bindu and Rekha:

- Rekha is a vertical line, minus sign (–)

- Bindu is a dot or zero, plus sign (+)

- North India: Rekha = Favorable, Bindu = Unfavorable

- South India: Bindu = Favorable, Rekha = Unfavorable (I use the South India format)

Number of Bindus	Favorable Results from Transiting Planet
7–8	100%
5–6	75%
3–4	50%
1–2	25%

Finding the Best Results

Counting the Lagna or the Moon as one, find when a planet transits its own sign, exaltation, moolatrikona, or a friend's sign. This is when the best results emerge. The results of ashtakavarga transits must be interpreted against the favorable or unfavorable nature of the planet in the birth (rasi) chart.

The planet should have good shadbala strength of at least six rupas. Planets that are malefic in the natal chart will be more malefic if they are transiting signs with low bindus

Sarvashtakavarga

Ashtakavarga is a method of understanding the effect of transits of a single planet as it moves through each individual sign. Sarvashtakavarga is a formula that judges the value of the combination of all planetary influences falling in a sign. Sarva means "all." This process summarizes all the bindus of all the planets for each sign. The resultant number will tell you the overall strength of a sign to promote good and repel bad influences. The minimum value is 25 to obtain good results (see chapter 12). Over 30 bindus is very good, and under 20 indicates that there is exposure to problems in that specific sign. I have found the sarvashtakavarga to be a very good method to determine the strength of a sign, and correspondingly, a house. Many times you will encounter a planetary position that does well in spite of the general rules to the contrary. You will want to check the sarvashtakavarga for the occupied sign. You'll probably find high bindu points that allow the sign to deflect bad influences and still exhibit its better qualities as a sign or house.

Judging When Planets Will Give Their Effects

Following are the basics of planetary effects:

1. The birth chart is the static pattern of influences.

2. The transit chart is the dynamic pattern of influences.

3. The transit chart is overlaid on the birth chart. A transit cannot give results that are not indicated in the birth chart.

4. Consider the "weight" or influence of each transiting planet. Use shadbala and other rules for determining planetary strength.

5. Summarize the total number of transits that are impacting that position at the same time.

6. Determine the overall strength of the natal chart to promote or repel favorable or unfavorable influences.

7. Take into account the counterbalancing influences.

The aspects of transiting planets can increase or decrease effects of a specific transit. For example, a Jupiter aspect by transit can reduce negative indications significantly.

How to Determine the Nature and Time of an Event

Here's a summary of many of the points you need to examine in forecasting events.

1. Examine the position of a transiting planet over a natal position.

   a. The exact degree of a transit planet over a natal planet gives very specific information. This is a simple but powerful rule. (A day on either side can still bring effects.)

   b. Look at transits relative to Lagna, Moon, and Sun passing through:
      1) houses; and
      2) signs.

3) You can also look in terms of nakshatras and lunar days (tithis).

c. Examine a planet that is transiting relative to a karaka planet.

d. Look at planets conjunct or opposite one another by transit in sign.

e. Look at the planet's strength.

2. Look at New and Full Moons against the natal chart.

a. Lunations (times of New and Full Moons)

b. Eclipses: transits over eclipse points by sign and degree give noticeable results (usually unfavorable)

3. Note at least four levels of dasas, in descending order. Determine dasa influence in relation to the dasa planet's placement in the rasi by sign, house, and aspects from and to the dasa planet.

4. Examine the ashtakavarga points for the planets involved.

5. Overlay the Varshaphal chart (as discussed earlier in this chapter) on the transits and dasas forecasts. Merge the results.

6. Look at the birthday year of impact of the planets—that is, when each planet will generically give its results. For example, Saturn age 36, Rahu age 48; see chapter 14.

7. Look at the years forecasted for significant events according to rising navamsa—for example, Pisces Navamsa Lagna: trouble at age 15, 36, and 63, etc. (see chapter 10).

Prasna—The Art of Answering Questions

Prasna is a very important tool of Vedic astrology. It is also called Horary astrology. I seriously recommend that a prasna be used along with every natal chart reading. Prasna Marga, a key work on prasna, states that the birth chart tells you your Prarabdha Karma, which is the favorable or unfavorable results from your previous lives. The prasna chart, constructed for the time of a question, tells you more about what your karmas are from this present birth. If the prasna chart is recorded exactly and the intention of the questioner is sincere, then the prasna chart can reveal a tremendous amount of detail not available in the birth chart.

Prasna charts are examined in a fashion similar to reading the natal chart. I have not given a list of the prasna effects because they can be derived from the standard explanations that I have already given for chart interpretation. Varahamihira's Shatpanchasika gives some general rules that are helpful. For example, when a benefic planet is located in the rising sign or in the navamsa rising sign, one can predict a favorable outcome to the question.

Generally, in prasna, the 1st house is the person posing the question (the querent) and the 7th house represents the people that the questioner might be asking about. If the person is asking about career, look to the 10th house of the prasna. If the questioner wants to know about the mother, look to the 4th house or the Moon, and so on.

There are other prasna systems that use very different rules, but I have found that you can use the same rules as in natal chart reading and get very good results. You will also read claims by astrologers that only one question should be asked in a prasna chart. When your skill builds, you will find that you can answer many questions pertaining to the chart constructed for the time of the call placed to you.

The prasna chart represents the questioner's environment, their universe, at any moment in time. The time when the questioner's inquiry enters into the awareness of the Vedic astrologer is the time that the prasna chart is set. The principle is that the client always approaches the astrologer.

This prasna time can be marked when:

1. The astrologer receives the call live on the phone ("live" questions give the most accurate results).

2. The questioner asks the astrologer directly, face-to-face.

3. A messenger comes, calls, or writes on behalf of the questioner.

4. A letter containing the question is read.

5. A message is taken from any recording device, such as an answering machine or service, a video or audio recording, or a fax machine or an e-mail message.

Sincerity and a strongly felt need to have a question answered are the keys to a successful prasna reading. An urge to find the answer to a personal issue should be dominant in the questioner's mind for a least a day or two prior to contacting the astrologer. This indicates that the significance of the question is strong enough to register a response that will be exact and conclusive.

Astrologers differ as to when you mark the time for a prasna chart. I always mark down the time that a person contacts me. If I get a direct call, I can be sure the prasna will work, if the person has a sincere question. I use voice mail that records the time of the person's call. I make sure my fax clock is on time, if I am contacted in that manner, and the same for e-mail contacts. I have also found that if a person calls you several times before you make a return contact, it is good to construct a chart for the time of the reading and take that into account when giving your response during your scheduled session together.

Nama Nakshatra Prasna—Using Techniques Based on Sanskrit Sounds

Every pada, or quarter of a nakshatra, represents a phoneme or sound. This sound system has been used mainly for naming babies; the nakshatra sound of the Moon is used for the starting sound of the baby's name. There are some teachers who use the sound of the person's Moon nakshatra as a meditation mantra. However, I thought there must be more to it than this. In my research, I discovered that you can use these sounds in prasna to determine the name of a person, place, or thing, according to where planets are placed in the nakshatra padas (see the Nakshatra Chart in the appendix).

I have also uncovered an additional technique: The sound or "vibration" of your name exerts a large influence on your life. You can use this nakshatra technique, Nama Nakshatra Prasna, in reverse. That is, take the first letters or sounds of your name or anyone's name and locate the nakshatra with which it is associated. Now, identify which sign of the zodiac this name/sound is occupying. Using this technique, you can tell a lot about a person merely from associating their name to a sign. For example, if a person's name is Karen, use the starting Kuh or K sound—you will find that person exhibits a lot of Gemini characteristics, since Gemini is where the Kuh sound resides.

You can also blend in the last name. Continuing with our example, let's say Karen's last name is Jones. The Juh sound or J is associated with Capricorn. So Karen would suggest friendly, bright, and quick-minded characteristics, embellished by the stable, prudent, Capricornian Jones. However, if the planets connected to these nama nakshatras were unfavorable, then Karen could be more fragmented, with a tendency not to finish things, and the Jones influence could leave her stuck and/or depressed. Also, if the prasna chart is unfavorable overall, then the participants in that question chart would exhibit more of the unfavorable or weak qualities.

This is a simple yet powerful technique that can give you information about a person that is not available through most other methods I know of in Vedic astrology. In its extremely simple form, you don't even need a chart. Just a person's name—just the sound of the first initial or syllable of their name—will reveal much useful information. Vibrations are very significant. Hearing, and being subject to, the vibration of the sound of your own name, day in and day out, is bound to generate an influence in your life. This is how I believe the technique works. If you want to change your life, then change your name. Many monks and saints of the past followed this rule.

Below, I have given a list of Sanskrit sounds in as close an approximation to English as I could develop. I have spelled each sound phonetically. You might see these sounds spelled differently in other books, but these are how they sound. I consulted with two Sanskrit experts on this pronunciation—one a university professor of linguistics, and the other a Vedic temple priest. I have been experimenting with these sounds since 1987 and find them to be accurate. Some authors include the sounds of Abhijit in Capricorn. However, since this is the 28th nakshatra, which is excluded in the modern format of 27 nakshatras, I don't use them.

Also, please note that the following sounds are not used:

- There is no true V (Vee) sound in Sanskrit. Instead, there is a blend of V and W. In English, we can interpret the V sound as also a W.

- There is also no F (Eff) sound. The closest is an aspirated P as in the Pah in Purvashada (Sagittarius).

- The Z (Zee) sound is not used. The closest buzzing sound would be the J (Juh) in Shravana (Capricorn).

- The U sound, as in university, is covered by the Y (Yoo) in Jyeshta (Scorpio).

- A beginning I (eye) is not used in Sanskrit. Names such as Eileen would be closest to the Ah in Krittika (Aries).

Remember, we are talking about sounds, not just letters of the alphabet, so the K sound is used for both Karen and Carol. Gerald starts with the letter G but is pronounced like a J. In all cases, use the pronunciation, not the letter.

Sounds by Sign of the Zodiac

As I've explained above, the sounds of people's names can be mapped to a specific sign of the zodiac. The person will generally behave characteristically for that sign, even if that sign differs from their Rasi Lagna and/or Moon sign in their natal chart. The name offers another insight into a personality.

You would normally use this technique when you want to get a quick synopsis of an individual, often in a prasna reading, if you don't have the chart of the individual that your client is asking about. I use this technique to get an indication of the person's personality, but I recommend that the client find out more about the person, and not proceed on the merits of this technique alone.

You will notice, in the table in the appendix, that when you go from the specific nakshatra to the more general rasi or sign, you get a mixture of sounds in that sign. I have found from my experience that, in most cases, you should take the letter that has the most occurrences within that sign. Your own experience will lead you.

From using this technique over the years, I have found the predominant sounds by sign. They are as follows:

- **Aries** = A as in Andy (the Ah sound is also the closest we have to the I or Eileen sound), and L as in Larry
- **Taurus** = V or W as in Victoria or Wilson
- **Gemini** = K as in Karen
- **Cancer** = H as in Harry, and D as in David
- **Leo** = M as in Mary, and T as in Thomas
- **Virgo** = P as in Peter
- **Libra** = R as in Robert
- **Scorpio** = N as in Nancy, Y as in Young, and U as in Eunice
- **Sagittarius** = B as in Brown, and F as in Fran
- **Capricorn** = J as in Jerry, and Z as in Xavier
- **Aquarius** = S as in Smith (I also see the Sh as in Shawn occurring here)
- **Pisces** = Ch as in Charles (this sound carries over to Aries, but I see it displayed mostly in Pisces)

Baby Naming

You can also use the nama nakshatra table listed above to name a person (baby), place, or thing. To use this technique, create a birth chart for the person or event in question. Next, locate the nakshatra occupied by the Moon. Refer to the nama table and locate the sound identified with the chart's Moon position. This sound can be used as the starting sound (not letter) of a person's name.

As an example, let's say the Moon is located in Bharani nakshatra in a certain chart. The sounds for Bharani all start with an L sound, so you could name the baby Larry, Linda, Lakshmi, or the like. You can also construct a chart for the incorporation of a business, and name the business in the same way. If you want to get even more specific, you can try to construct a name using the sound as the first syllable of the name, not just the start letter sound. Continuing our Bharani nakshatra example, let's say that the Moon was in the second pada or quarter of Bharani, indicating a "Loo" sound. We could then name the baby Louis, Louise, etc.

Omens

Not only do you take note of the time that a person asks a question in a prasna chart, but you can also take into account the signals that come to us from our surrounding environment. Life is an amazing matrix of influences that weave in and around us constantly. These patterns of nature have been tracked and noted for thousands of years.

Information on omens, also called Shakuna or Nimitta, was first focused on the cries of birds. In the ancient days, in a more heavily forested India, the rural inhabitants would relate the calls of birds to the nature of the event at hand.

The subject matter of omens has expanded over time to include portents signaled from earthquakes (bhauma); general catastrophes (utpata) such as drought, floods, pestilence, etc.; dreams (swapna); celestial and meteorological events (ulkapata) such as eclipses, haloes around the Moon, comets, etc.; and the throbbing of various body parts (anga). As an astrologer, you can get a sense of an omen's influence from the nature of events that occur in the course of a reading. I recall one time when a client asked if her marriage would endure. At the exact moment of her question, a gardener started up a power mower with a resounding roar. The marriage did not last.

CHAPTER FOURTEEN

GOCHARA—PLANETARY TRANSITS

This chapter describes the effect of planets transiting over houses in the birth chart. The interpretations I have given are general, but useful in giving you an idea about how to work with transits. Again, I would encourage you to re-examine the section of this book on two-planet conjunctions. By using planets in combination, you can get a pretty good idea of what happens when one planet combines with another by transit.

There are certain years of our lives when the influence of certain planets will be active. This is a separate timing factor, not to be confused with dasa periods. For example, the Sun exerts a lot of influence on a person's life at age 22, and the rest of the planets have influences as follows:

- Sun: age 22
- Moon: age 24
- Mars: age 28
- Mercury: all ages
- Jupiter: age 16

- Venus: age 25
- Saturn: age 36
- Rahu: age 48
- Ketu: age 48

You can also judge transits by counting from a karaka planet. For example, the mate is the 7th house. Transits over your 11th indicate the partner's 5th house (11th is 5th to the 7th), indicating children and their affairs and the mate's need for love and romance. Perhaps your partner could even help you with your investments and be a good companion on a meditation course.

Planet's Best Transit Position by House

What follows is a general guideline. These positions will be modified up or down by the quality of the planet in transit and how that planet is placed and aspected. Below, the x indicates that the planet is considered well placed, or in its best position, when transiting over that house.

Planets	1	2	3	4	5	6	7	8	9	10	11	12
Sun		x			x					x	x	
Moon	x	x			x	x				x	x	
Mars		x			x						x	
Mercury	x		x		x		x			x	x	
Jupiter	x			x		x		x		x		
Venus	x	x	x	x	x		x	x		x		x
Saturn		x			x						x	
Rahu		x			x						x	
Ketu		x			x						x	

Houses

Factors for Judging When Houses Give Their Effects

House:	9	10	11	12	1	2	3	4	5	6	7	8
Person's Age:	1-24	25-26	27-28	29-30	31-33	34-36	37-39	40-45	46-51	52-57	58-65	66 on

Basic Transit Rules

When a transiting planet forms a conjunction with a planet in the natal chart, life events as pledged in the birth chart are triggered—your number is called on the cosmic score card. Whether the event has a positive or negative influence, and whether it is of large or small consequence, is determined by the nature of the two planets. However, the favorable actions you have taken in this lifetime will defray a lot of negative consequences. The favorable or unfavorable quality of a planet and the amount of its influence can be determined through the standard rules for planetary strength given in chapter 12. A panchanga or sidereal planetary almanac will help you determine when the degrees of transiting planets will fall on natal positions (see appendix).

What Activates Unfavorable Events?

For an unfavorable event to occur, usually there must be multiple causative events or situations occurring simultaneously. I use the following analogy. If a person is driving in the Los Angeles National Forest and carelessly throws a lighted match out the window, then negative events can happen—namely a forest fire. However, the surrounding conditions will make the possibility of the forest fire's occurrence stronger or weaker. Was the match thrown during the rainy season or the dry season? When judging events, the astrologer has to consider all factors, judging the strengths and weaknesses and offsets by other planetary factors, such as the following:

- **Transits by unfavorable planets:** A weak and unfavorable planet in the birth chart, when transited by unfavorable planets, will give unfavorable effects. The time of effect will be the highest at the exact degree of conjunction. Effects can be felt a day or two on either side. For the slow-moving malefic planets—Saturn, Rahu, Ketu, and Mars—the effect will begin sooner and linger later than at just the exact conjunction degree. I have seen Saturn start to show its influence up to six months in advance. The situation can be likened to the following: When a person approaches a festival, they can begin to hear the music and see the glow of the party lights well before they reach the entrance to that celebration. Remember that the time of conjunction can be any time of day. Most sidereal planetary almanacs just list the planetary positions at midnight (or daybreak in some Hindu panchangas), so you might need to run charts for that day to determine the exact hour of the event.

- **Unfavorable current dasa/bhuktis** amplify unfavorable transits. If a person is in an unfavorable dasa/bhukti and an unfavorable transit occurs, the overall capacity to repel the negative transit is weak.

- **Unfavorable transits connected to the 6th house**, the 6th sign (Virgo), and the ruler of the 6th house will trigger unfavorable events related to what the 6th house represents: health, disputes, accidents, debts, etc. See the descriptions in the relevant chapters for the unfavorable effects of these positions.

- **Unfavorable transits connected to the 8th house**, the 8th sign (Scorpio), and the ruler of the 8th house will trigger unfavorable events related to what the 8th house represents: serious health problems (perhaps death if other indicators co-exist); worry; fear; loss of support; being disregarded, disrespected, or overlooked; vulnerability to mistreatment, scandal, embarrassment, etc.

- **Unfavorable transits connected to the 12th house**, the 12th sign (Pisces), and the ruler of the 12th house will trigger unfavorable events related to what the 12th house represents: loss, lack of presence of mind, disconnected thinking, clumsiness (feet are not "on the ground"), injury to feet, detention, imprisonment, fines, penalties, agony over lack of freedom or slow spiritual development, trouble with sleep, little or no sexual enjoyment, and misfortune in foreign lands.

- **Planets that are debilitated by transit** bring unfavorable results. The exception is that retrograde debilitated planets act more favorably during their transits.

- **Association or aspects by other unfavorable transiting planets** stimulate unfavorable events.

What Activates Mixed Events?

- **If the current dasa/bhukti is favorable**, but transit effects are unfavorable, then less troublesome effects will be seen overall. A general mixture of not-quite-good and not-quite-bad effects will arise. Conversely, if the current dasa/bhukti is unfavorable, but transit effects are favorable, then overall effects will be less beneficial in general—a mixture of not-quite-good and not-quite-bad effects will arise.

What Activates Favorable Events?

- **A strong and favorable planet in the birth chart** when transited by favorable planets will give favorable effects.

- **The current dasa/bhukti period is favorable.** This amplifies favorable transits.

What Makes Planets Favorable When Transiting over Unfavorable (Dusthana) Houses?

- If the 6th house, its ruler, and Virgo are strong in the natal chart, then transits over the 6th will display more positive effects—for instance, good self-defense rather than loss through attack. Resistance to disease will be stronger and the onset of illness and accidents will be less.

- If the 8th house, its ruler, and Scorpio are strong in the natal chart, then transits over the 8th will be more favorable, or at least less negative. This transit could give windfalls or unexpected income, the transfer of funds from trusts and inheritances, and insurance settlements. A trip to Las Vegas could be gainful and lottery tickets might pay off. A person should become more intuitively aware and be more astute in research matters. Actions to correct health will be more effective and doctors will be able to diagnose more effectively.

- If the 12th house, its ruler, and Pisces are strong in the natal chart, then transits over the 12th will be more positive. This transit could bring an increased sense of charity and self-sacrifice; self-sufficiency is higher; movement toward spirituality and enlightenment is on the rise; sleep improves; sex is more pleasurable; travel to foreign countries is gainful; time could be spent in a retreat or ashram; there is more protection against loss than before; legal problems leading to possible imprisonment fade away; and the person is able to leave a hospital or place of detention.

Interpreting the Effects of Transiting Planets

The following section lists the effects of each planet's transits through the houses. You can judge the transiting planet relative to the natal position of the Moon and the Lagna. Combining or merging the two is often the best approach. I give more weight to the Lagna in most cases. To use the following list, interpret, for example, "the Sun first from the Lagna" to mean that the transiting Sun is in the same house as the natal Lagna or Moon. If the Sun is second from the Moon or Lagna, then they are in neighboring houses; if third, then there is one house in between, etc.

TRANSITS OF THE SUN
Best results in houses 3, 6, 10, and 11

Sun Is FIRST from Moon or Lagna
Keywords: Dynamism of the Self

Favorable: Focus on personal issues such as health, career, and individual needs; energy levels are higher; the impulse is to take action, be aggressive (pitta), and get things done; travel and pursue actions that take more effort

Unfavorable: Not a great time for diplomacy; feelings of impatience and anger arise; selfish impulses are dominant; there is exposure to accidents, especially in the head area; headaches and heartaches could arise

Sun Is SECOND from Moon or Lagna
Keywords: Activity for Finances

Favorable: Get money from superiors and from the government; act dynamically with money—as long as prudence prevails; project your voice to get what you need; improve your diet and your money-handling skills

Unfavorable: Impulsive spending; saying things without thinking; lack of attention to studies; eating patterns might go out of balance; lack of financial prudence; money is tight; loans you give might not be given back right away (if at all); family disputes could arise; problems with the face, throat, and mouth (teeth, lips, and gums)

Sun Is THIRD from Moon or Lagna
Keywords: Determined Activity

Favorable: More determination; added energy and courage; increased will and interest to accomplish things, make commitments, and sign contracts; all activities involving communication will be good, e.g., writing, selling, and persuading; good for music, art, dance, acting, and other forms of self-expression

Unfavorable: Conflicts with younger siblings and with neighbors; exercise more to burn off any aggressive feelings; danger in short-distance travels; don't write or communicate anything while you are in a bad mood—the feelings change, but the letters don't

Sun Is FOURTH from Moon or Lagna

Keywords: Active Emotions

Favorable: Good time to be emotionally strident or aggressive; real estate matters go more easily; education and training are beneficial; try fixing up your house and repairing your car

Unfavorable: Exposure to accidents or breakdowns with vehicles and around the home; update your insurance policy; emotional disruptions within the family and with the mother; disputes with teachers; real estate transactions are risky; hard to focus on household duties; the mother could be too pitta—angry or sick

Sun Is FIFTH from Moon or Lagna

Keywords: Stimulation of the Intellect

Favorable: Good for a passionate interlude; take action in children's sports and for your own amusement; mind is sharper; insights or revelations of an intellectual nature

Unfavorable: Problems with the IRS or any governmental agency; arguments and impoliteness with sweethearts; poor dating and romance; risks with speculation, e.g., stock market; restless meditations; don't do anything that puts your children at risk and be cool because your kids might not; poor digestion; nervousness; intellect is not clear

Sun Is SIXTH from Moon or Lagna

Keywords: Service and Defense of the Self

Favorable: Deal with conflicts, enemies, lawsuits, and other activities where you have to be more aggressive; more results from healing work; get a checkup; benefits from people who provide service (helpers, attendants, etc.); good month to hire people; provide service to others

Unfavorable: More energy (pitta) this month; be patient; stay cool; watch out about getting into debt or spending too much money; don't endanger your health

Sun Is SEVENTH from Moon or Lagna

Keywords: Actions in Partnership

Favorable: Good time for business transactions and coming to agreement with others; business travel is supported; activities involved with increasing or stimulating a business or partnership is good

Unfavorable: Discord and nonalignment of the partners; don't close contracts too quickly; weariness from too much travel; don't let partners coerce you into settling for something you don't want

Sun Is EIGHTH from Moon or Lagna
Keywords: Actions with the Unknown
Favorable: Get other people's support and energy; focus on healing and strengthening; be comfortable; don't become invisible to others; if you strain you won't gain; good time for a long meditation retreat or a nice trip to a spa or health treatment; investigate into some mysteries
Unfavorable: A weak time; personal resources of health, energy, and finances might be low; try not to do too much on your own; increased fatigue and sickness is possible; speak up; don't get overlooked at work; possible embarrassment or scandal; don't let people be rude

Sun Is NINTH from Moon or Lagna
Keywords: Ethical Actions
Favorable: Take advanced training, especially in religious and philosophical areas; legal issues should resolve in your favor; do publishing, visit your father or your guru; luck is all around; use common sense and stay ethical in your transactions; long-distance travels look fruitful
Unfavorable: Realign with your boss, father, and guru—correctly set your expectations with them; stay ethical; danger on long-distance journeys; your father and/or guru could be very active if not restless and demanding at this time

Sun Is TENTH from Moon or Lagna
Keywords: Actions for Life Purpose
Favorable: Good time to change job; consider new offers; get a new home or car; self-promote; get people to take an interest in you; get some education for work; update your resume; ask for a raise; a corporate/government grant or award might be available; make Vastu plans for your dwelling or office; real estate transactions should be favorable
Unfavorable: Keep your ego in check; be patient with others as you advance; don't take all the credit; make changes thoughtfully in terms of career and home; be careful with vehicles/auto; look into things thoroughly before buying or renting a house, car, or any large asset

Sun Is ELEVENTH from Moon or Lagna
Keywords: Actions on Opportunities

Favorable: Make yourself available to new opportunities; fulfill a desire; get more public; meet some important people and make new friends; cash flow should improve and relationships with elder siblings and friends should be more cordial

Unfavorable: Don't overdo things with friends and elder siblings; protect your cash flow as you consider any new opportunities that come your way; loaning money to friends and siblings could turn out wrong

Sun Is TWELFTH from Moon or Lagna
Keywords: Activities for Liberation

Favorable: Try a long journey or a visit to a foreign land; spiritual practices should be more effective; enjoy intimate pleasures with your mate; go for a health checkup; be charitable and pay off some of your debts

Unfavorable: Old emotional issues and feelings of loss might surface; sleep and sexual activity might not be that pleasurable; shake off any gloominess with activity; watch that you are not too generous; try not to isolate yourself; resist the urge to spend; new activities will be less fruitful if started at this time

TRANSITS OF THE MOON
Best results in houses 1, 3, 6, 7, 10, and 11

A word of explanation: This next section deals with counting the transiting Moon's position relative to the natal Moon's position or from the Lagna.

Moon Is FIRST from Moon or Lagna
Keywords: Comforts for the Self

Favorable: This is the time for more comforts; creativity and optimism are up; imagination and intuition should be brighter; enjoy the company of favorite friends and indulge in private pleasures; focus on improving your appearance and behavior; get new clothes; change your appearance; do something good for you

Unfavorable: Be careful about being too lazy or unfocused; watch your expenditures and a tendency to overindulge; be responsible while engaging in sexual and sensual activities; you could worry; be emotionally more sensitive and a bit self-centered now

Moon Is SECOND from Moon or Lagna
Keywords: Fullness of Finances

Favorable: Good for general family matters; it's okay to spend some money on domestic needs; enjoy a luxury meal; buy a piece of jewelry; studying should be easier; your speech will be more influential and pleasant; money matters, bank accounts, and investment decisions should be fuller

Unfavorable: Cash could be tight or financial difficulties could crop up; watch what you say if you get caught up in strong emotions; be kind to your family; cravings for food or even smoking or drinking could crop up; watch what goes into and out of your mouth; studying may drop off

Moon Is THIRD from Moon or Lagna
Keywords: Feelings of Self-Determination

Favorable: Creative writing and communications should be favorable; physical strength, determination, and purposefulness are higher; make commitments; visit your brothers and sisters and get to know your neighbors a bit more; spend time enjoying music, art, and acting; express yourself

Unfavorable: Be careful not to send any communications that you might later regret; possible misunderstandings with younger siblings and neighbors; determination is down; artistic endeavors might be frustrating

Moon Is FOURTH from Moon or Lagna
Keywords: Fullness of Feelings

Favorable: This is a good time for more education; call your mother; spend more time with your family; do things to make your home more comfortable; take a nice trip in your car; your feelings and intuition should be higher and happier now

Unfavorable: Emotions are more delicate at this time; try not to get your feelings hurt; be kind to your mother and family; long driving is not recommended—especially if you're tired or stressed; domestic and real estate activities might not be well supported; educational energy is low

Moon Is FIFTH from Moon or Lagna

Keywords: Intelligent Feelings

Favorable: This is a time for a romantic encounter; take your mate to a nice dinner; meditations should be more subtle; it's a good time to learn a meditation technique; play a bit more and let yourself be childish; plan activities with children; since the intellect is sharper, it might be okay to follow up on an investment hunch (if your natal chart supports it)

Unfavorable: Meditations and prayers don't seem as quiet; fun things may not turn out to be so much fun; you could feel a bit cloudy mentally and emotionally; dating and romantic interludes might become complicated and a source of disappointment; this is not a good time to speculate or change your investment portfolio; children could be challenging

Moon Is SIXTH from Moon or Lagna

Keywords: Active Emotions

Favorable: Vitality is stronger; be aggressive now; if needed, develop more rapport with your employees or servants; service activities look good; check up on your health or begin a new exercise or health regimen; disputes and disagreements could calm down; visit your relatives

Unfavorable: Strive to control your impulses to spend; check your expectations with employees or service providers so you don't get into any misunderstandings; keep aggression in check; tolerance and resistance is low; emotions could be fiery, affecting your health

Moon Is SEVENTH from Moon or Lagna

Keywords: Feelings for Partnerships

Favorable: Relationships are more active, both personally and with business partners; use this time to come to a mutual agreement and set a contract; marriage or commitment is well served; enjoy pleasures with your mate; business transactions and travel look favorable

Unfavorable: There may be a desire to get a better deal in both relationships and business; try not to appear capricious or fickle; quarrels could arise in relationships; make sure you spend enough time in setting up your business plans

Moon Is EIGHTH from Moon or Lagna
Keywords: Mysterious Feelings

Favorable: Focus on being comfortable and improving your health; put your support mechanisms together; solicit help from others and try not to do so much by yourself; your intuition should be sharper

Unfavorable: Strive not to get overlooked; you might feel more vulnerable and weak at this time; don't let others be rude; take a stand for yourself and keep risks to a minimum; this is a better time for spiritual work than for material expansion; stay healthy

Moon Is NINTH from Moon or Lagna
Keywords: Fullness of Fortune

Favorable: This is a fortunate period; benefits come from legal, spiritual, and educational pursuits; take a long journey and enjoy yourself; visit your father or guru; work out your plans and strategies with employers

Unfavorable: Your boss or father might be emotionally off base in this period; worries about higher education and your overall fortune might creep in; there is exposure to complications with long-distance travel; legal issues are best deferred for a few days, if possible; stay ethical

Moon Is TENTH from Moon or Lagna
Keywords: Fullness of Career

Favorable: This is the time to catch the boss in a good mood and ask for a raise or promotion; people will be more open to your plans and strategies; build up your reputation; access experts and seminars to help develop your marketable skills; expand your advertising and promotional work; be creative

Unfavorable: Watch that you don't get too aggressive or emotional about work; pay attention to domestic matters and watch that you don't get caught in some negative publicity; guard your reputation and make sure your superiors know what you are doing and that you are aligned with them

Moon Is ELEVENTH from Moon or Lagna
Keywords: Fullness of Opportunities

Favorable: Take advantage of new opportunities; socialize with some influential people and make yourself more visible to them; be good to your friends and give your older siblings a call; your cash flow should pick up and things should be profitable; anything is possible

Unfavorable: Cash flow is weaker; problems arise when transacting business with friends and with older siblings; don't loan them money; if you hesitate to take a new opportunity, it could pass you by; be careful not to push some new concept or idea onto others

Moon Is TWELFTH from Moon or Lagna

Keywords: Feelings for Liberation

Favorable: Be charitable and volunteer for some organization; take a foreign vacation or go on a retreat; meditations will be more subtle; time spent in seclusion is beneficial; visit a spa or health clinic to keep your vitality and well-being in balance; be generous to holy people

Unfavorable: You are more susceptible to a fine, penalty, or detention at this point; be mindful not to spend too much; spending more than you can afford for spiritual advancement might not be advisable; try not to be a martyr; if you isolate too much now, you could get a bit depressed; try to enjoy

TRANSITS OF MARS

Best results in houses 3, 6, and 11

Mars Is FIRST from Moon or Lagna

Keywords: The Self as Warrior

Favorable: This period might stimulate you to accomplish many things; organize your energies; your drive will enable you to do things quickly; if you need to be aggressive and defend yourself in any way, then now is the time

Unfavorable: Watch your temper and be patient; you could be more accident prone—especially head injuries, or some burning, breaking, or cutting could take place on the body; avoid arguments and do something to stay cool; pace yourself, or you could get burned out too early; pitta is increased at this time

Mars Is SECOND from Moon or Lagna

Keywords: Financial Assertiveness

Favorable: Speech is more direct; aggressive investment strategies might work if care is taken; take preventative or restorative measures for the face, teeth, gums, and lips; good time to take rapid-acquisition learning courses and learn speed reading, memorization shortcuts, languages, and the like

Unfavorable: Don't put your financial holdings at risk; watch out for "thieves" and "get rich" schemes; care must be taken to speak politely; studies seem boring; you might not feel much like cooking; bad habits could surface (smoking, drinking, overeating, etc.); protect your face, teeth, gums, and lips; try not to get burned

Mars Is THIRD from Moon or Lagna

Keywords: Heightened Assertiveness

Favorable: Physical strength is higher; exhibit your talents in writing, art, music, dance, drama, athletics, and the like; have some fun with your siblings and neighbors; communicate; short-distance travel and some beginner's classes or seminars are good; focus on selling, self-promotion, and advertising

Unfavorable: Don't express aggression in hurtful ways; stay calm in communications; don't be a "hog" for attention; let others express themselves, take it easy with siblings and neighbors; could be exposed to accidents involving the hands, neck, and shoulders; protect your ears

Mars Is FOURTH from Moon or Lagna

Keywords: Active Emotions

Favorable: Look for real estate; look to take out loans, if required; put your house into correct Vastu; energy levels should be up; continue with your educational and family responsibilities; buy some new clothes and accessorize your home; a new car might be in order

Unfavorable: Family matters could test your patience; update your insurance policies, especially on your house, car, and mother; stay in school; take care of chest pains and overall agitation and worry; your diplomatic skill could be low so be mindful in conflicts; fix your car and be careful while driving; check the electricity and chemical or toxic waste buildup and fix any broken items around your home

Mars Is FIFTH from Moon or Lagna

Keywords: Dynamic Intellect

Favorable: Investments show an opportunity for a quick profit; do some fun things and play with the children; this is a time to show your passions; scriptural works might seem clearer to you now; you will feel sharper all round; inspire people to meditate and take delight in life

Unfavorable: Be vigilant about the well-being of your children; don't try to decide on anything until things cool down; be easy with your studies; arguments with sweethearts could get out of hand; try to be honest and agreeable; watch your investments—slow down the speculation; meditation might seem to be more agitated, but stay with it

Mars Is SIXTH from Moon or Lagna

Keywords: Definitive Self-Defense

Favorable: Take the initiative to improve and defend yourself; healing processes are better; provide service; you should get the most effective results from employees and servants; you will be more able to recapture lost items or finances at this time; court proceedings should be in your favor

Unfavorable: Pitta or heat is higher at this time, avoid engaging in any obvious, serious risks—an accident is possible; be prudent with money since you could run up some debts; quarrels won't get you anywhere; stay cool; temptations arise to take drugs, alcohol, or medication to try to calm down

Mars Is SEVENTH from Moon or Lagna

Keywords: Aggression with Partnerships

Favorable: Passions with your mate are increased by this transit; pursue business transactions that can be completed quickly; don't waste your time with people who are slow or reluctant—they will only frustrate you and impede your ability to get fast results now

Unfavorable: Disputes and conflicts could arise if patience is forsaken; encourage your partners and mate to take care of their health; could be exposed to an accident, dispute, or a "theft" during travels; pay attention to the details of an agreement or contract

Mars Is EIGHTH from Moon or Lagna

Keywords: Fighting for Health

Favorable: Money or support could come quickly; you might feel more curious and want to spend time researching matters of interest; Ayurvedic panchakarma, acupuncture, and massage would be a good idea now; your mind will be full of insights

Unfavorable: You could feel more worried, vulnerable, and irritable; your defense mechanisms might be off balance so take care of yourself and try not to overwork; if you appear too weak you might invite the aggression of others or get wrongly accused; risk-taking is not advisable

Mars Is NINTH from Moon or Lagna

Keywords: Fortune is Energized

Favorable: You will feel more lucky and inspired at this time; long-distance travel might be good; get active in spiritual work; put in some time with higher education and knowledge; fighting for an ethical cause is worthwhile; play with your dad or your boss

Unfavorable: Taking unethical shortcuts could short-circuit your future, plan ahead for any long-distance journeys, stay away from dangerous circumstances, this is not a good time to plead your case on an intellectual level, disputes or disagreement could arise with your father, guru, or boss

Mars Is TENTH from Moon or Lagna

Keywords: Motivations for Life Purpose

Favorable: Promote yourself; ask for that raise or promotion; take action and don't let your intellect get in the way of a good decision; this is a good time to take out a loan on a home or new car; Vastu activities are supported; work on career advancement or plan for a change if needed

Unfavorable: Take time to plan more for your career; gauge your employer's reactions before you make any demands; do what makes you look good and don't be reckless; don't put yourself at risk with the government or authorities

Mars Is ELEVENTH from Moon or Lagna
Keywords: Activation of Opportunities

Favorable: Cash flow should pick up; opportunities should present themselves; try to socialize and make new friends; fulfill some dream or wish you've had for awhile; your older sibling might be helpful in some way

Unfavorable: It's probably not good to make any loans to friends or older siblings. Watch out for any "get rich" schemes—someone will get rich but not you. Don't go on any spending sprees—it could all burn up quickly

Mars Is TWELFTH from Moon or Lagna
Keywords: Action for Liberation

Favorable: You could become quite busy "saving the world" at this time; put your energies into spiritual and humanitarian work; give in charity—you might lose it otherwise; pay ahead on your credit cards; revel in the transcendental wonder of life

Unfavorable: Keep your emotions and finances under control, and try not to be too clever in business—you could be fined or detained in some way; stay on your health and spiritual programs; be patient and give time to healing; sexual encounters could be frustrating or of short duration; sleep is disturbed

TRANSITS OF JUPITER
Best results in houses 2, 5, 7, 9, and 11

Jupiter Is FIRST from Moon or Lagna
Keywords: Expansion of the Self

Favorable: Optimism, cheerfulness, overall comfort, and confidence should be on the upswing; prepare for new "golden" opportunities; health looks stronger; you have a chance to move up in the world; allow yourself to grow in wisdom

Unfavorable: Watch for too much optimism and neglect of responsibilities—some degree of effort and application is still needed; avoid laziness; take action sooner not later; opportunities might slip away or be picked up and benefit someone more aggressive; keep track of your spending

Jupiter Is SECOND from Moon or Lagna

Keywords: Expansion of Wealth

Favorable: Indications are for an increase in money and other financial opportunities; this is a favorable time to buy gems, jewelry, and precious metals—especially gold; expansion of family is indicated; studying new subjects, teaching, or being a consultant is good; improve your diet and speech

Unfavorable: Don't be lazy or careless with your money at this time; wealth could be lost by slow or insufficient responses; resist extravagance and overspending on luxury items; try to be more precise with what you say and don't make promises that you know you won't be keeping; don't overeat

Jupiter Is THIRD from Moon or Lagna

Keywords: Increased Self-Expression

Favorable: Creative activities such as writing, acting, speaking, dancing, or playing a musical instrument are all good now; efforts bring expansion now; lecturing and communicating skills are sharper; grow yourself through self-promotion and marketing; enjoy time with younger siblings and neighbors

Unfavorable: You might be feeling a little lazy or disinterested in putting in sufficient effort; stay with your responsibilities; double-check what you put in writing; loans to siblings and neighbors might be slow to return; younger siblings might get into some complications or need some financial help

Jupiter Is FOURTH from Moon or Lagna

Keywords: Expanded Feelings

Favorable: Educate yourself and upgrade your marketable skills; this is a good time to enter college or start new training; do something nice for your mother and your family; buy a new car or home; make your home more comfortable; emotional blessings are on the rise

Unfavorable: Don't delay in fixing problems with your home; be mindful of the price if you sell a car or a home; emotional lethargy could set in; help your mother if she is having difficulties; spend more time building family relationships; don't dwell too long on any negative emotions

Jupiter Is FIFTH from Moon or Lagna
Keywords: Wholeness of Intellect

Favorable: Meditation; happiness with children and growth of your investments should be better; this is a good time for fun and romance; put in more time with children; you are open for spiritual education; your intellect should be running on all cylinders; take that test now

Unfavorable: If you are losing in speculations and your investments are sour, then hold back a bit; stay focused on your children's needs; this might not be the right time to add another family member; don't make any big decisions if you're feeling sluggish; think things through; romance may not be that great

Jupiter Is SIXTH from Moon or Lagna
Keywords: Wise in Service

Favorable: Provide support and service to others; expand your self-improvement goals; get healthy; straighten things out or repair some broken personal or business relationships; lawsuit has a good chance of turning out in your favor; things should proceed with more support at this time

Unfavorable: Be more frugal and conscientious about financial matters; spending on anticipation is not allowed; if you appear weak or unwary, you will increase your exposure to ill treatment from others; if your children become ill, then take care of it right away; keep up your health

Jupiter Is SEVENTH from Moon or Lagna
Keywords: Expansive Partnerships

Favorable: Form new partnerships (marriage?); business should be good; learning more about your business could increase your earnings; some travel for work is good—take your mate; diplomacy wins

Unfavorable: Don't delay starting and finishing your business transactions; keep your commitments with marriage and business partners; don't be lazy about planning your trips; show people your gratitude; for women, this transit could trigger some issues with the mate; you might be expecting too much

Jupiter Is EIGHTH from Moon or Lagna

Keywords: Support from Wisdom

Favorable: Work on those things that give the most support; be comfortable and use common sense to get things done; some monetary windfall could come your way; research should prove fascinating at this time; you will benefit by going within to build up your spiritual reserves; expand your health

Unfavorable: There could be a lack of financial support and/or discipline at this time; pay attention to your children; they could be worried and might be susceptible to some illnesses; this is not a good time to make commitments; you might be feeling unsatisfied about your progress; cheer up; eat right

Jupiter Is NINTH from Moon or Lagna

Keywords: Knowledge and Fortune

Favorable: This is one of Jupiter's best transits—there is more fortune, spiritual knowledge, and enjoyable travel. Ask for a raise or expand your fortunes; visit your father and guru; teaching is good; this is a good time to publish that book you've been thinking about; legal and ethical matters prevail

Unfavorable: There can be such a thing as "too much of a good thing"; don't be lazy; watch your finances; pay more attention to your children; there are opportunities for increased knowledge and spiritual advancement, but don't miss the boat

Jupiter Is TENTH from Moon or Lagna

Keywords: Expansive Career

Favorable: Get people to take an interest in you; educate yourself and expand your position; network with successful people at every chance—something is bound to rub off; people might regard your work more highly now; it might be worthwhile to do some teaching or consulting; be generous

Unfavorable: Your reputation could take a downturn if you don't keep up with your responsibilities; if you delay, then finance and career opportunities could pass you by; you might have to put in some extra effort to keep things going; keep busy and don't fall prey to boredom

Jupiter Is ELEVENTH from Moon or Lagna

Keywords: Wealth of Opportunities

Favorable: Cash flow should be better; have fun with your children and friends; do things with influential and wealthy persons; spiritual "wealth" should be at a high, so do things to expand your consciousness; there should be more opportunities now for expansion of prosperity; fulfill a dream

Unfavorable: It might not be a good idea to loan money to elder siblings or to friends, unless you're in no hurry to get it back; be careful about investing in "get rich" schemes; stay focused on your earnings; there are trends now to overindulge or not pay enough attention

Jupiter Is TWELFTH from Moon or Lagna

Keywords: Insights for Liberation

Favorable: Some desire for more "enlightenment" might be creeping in now; go to India, or some remote pilgrimage spot or a retreat if you feel inclined; your charitable donations will be rewarded; it's good to spend some quiet time with yourself; financial expansion should be put off until next year

Unfavorable: If you drive yourself too hard, you could end up feeling weak and worried; don't overdo volunteering or you could end up the victim; try not to impoverish yourself in the name of enlightenment; finances could be less now, so tighten your belt a bit; you could get fined, penalized, or even detained

Saturn—Sade Sati and Other Considerations

When Saturn passes the sign before, the sign of, and the sign following the Moon (12th, 1st, and 2nd houses), this is called Sade Sati, which translates as 7½ years, the duration of Saturn's passage over these three houses. It is also called Elerata by some. Although many authors don't make note of this, Sade Sati can also be applied to the Lagna and to the Sun.

Saturn's transits are often the most striking and impacting of all the transits. Much of what is happening with an individual, when they call for a reading, can be gauged from the current position of Saturn over the natal chart planets—especially the Moon, Lagna, and Sun and over dusthana houses 8 and 12. (The 6th house is considered a favorable passage for Saturn, although Saturn will still bring back old karmas if we deserve it.)

Many people get frightened, or some astrologers alarm rather than alert them, regarding Saturn's effects. However, all planets have a purpose. Saturn is the planet of responsibility and focus. During a Saturn period, it is necessary to simplify and narrow your focus. Set up a baseline of achievable goals. There is no slack with Saturn—either you do or you don't. It's the people who don't, or don't know how to work with Saturn's energy, that seem to feel the most duress during the passages of Saturn. Many times I have heard Maharishi say, "See the job, do the job, and avoid the misery." I have also seen that he puts a big emphasis on focus. These clues are key to working well with Saturn's influences.

Another important point is that Saturn does not have to be the misery-invoking planet he is so often claimed to be. People who see their responsibilities and take action to fulfill them in time can do the best that their chart has to offer—don't forget that we can improve our basic chart through right living, meditating, Ayurvedic treatments, proper Vastu, and the like. Those who don't strictly follow the rules end up more exposed to problems—that's the indifferent and factual nature of Saturn, also known as Yama, the Lord of Restraint.

Saturn's effects are also tightly linked to the transited sign/house's ability to repel negative influences and promote positive ones. Saturn's unfavorable indications will be reduced if the sign being transited has high sarvashtakavarga points. If the planet being transited also has high ashtakavarga bindus, Saturn runs more gently. For example, during Sade Sati, if the Moon's ashtakavarga is four or more bindus, then the Moon can deflect much of the unfavorable advances of Saturn.

However, even the best Saturn period can carry some challenges. Many people can do well financially during a Saturn period, but they might find that they have some physical or health problem that requires continued focus. All our recognizable boundaries start to fall off, but this is ultimately in the name of creating a new life for ourselves. We get to choose how we want it to be.

The aspect of a favorable Jupiter on Saturn will diminish many unfavorable circumstances from Saturn's transits. Also, the positive or negative nature of the current dasa/bhukti will bring Saturn's effects up or down. Furthermore, things get better regarding Saturn after a person passes age 36. So, be aware that there is grace in nature and sufficient supply, and be careful not to jump to negative judgments about Saturn right off the bat.

TRANSITS OF SATURN
Best results in houses 3, 6, and 11

Saturn Is FIRST from Moon or Lagna
Keywords: Structured Self

Favorable: A focus on individual needs is required. Use this time to get into a routine and make sure that your responsibilities are covered. A trip to the doctor might be in order to ensure everything is working right. Start creating a new life for yourself. Redefine your work habits. Use a strategy of small victories.

Unfavorable: You are in the middle of that Sade Sati period discussed above. The feeling of formlessness, while a precursor to a new shape, can fill you with ambiguity and uncertainty. There might be a lack of confidence or a reluctance to get going. Build up your health; strive to keep your agreements and commitments intact. Give enough time to things to avoid setbacks and delays. You may feel sluggish at times, if not depressed. Digestion might be off. This is not a good time to try to build a new business or get married. Partnerships might require too much of your available energy. You might have to work harder than normal to make things work. Don't isolate yourself too much.

Saturn Is SECOND from Moon or Lagna
Keywords: Focus on Finances

Favorable: Your finances could stabilize if you redirect your attention upon them. Try your hand at learning a foreign language. You'll get the most nutrition from eating simple, fresh foods at regular mealtimes. Think about what you want to say before you speak. Give your family members some more time.

Unfavorable: The Sade Sati period is starting to end, but there are still some remnants of karma to clean up. Speak the sweet truth now; thoughtless speech could give you big problems at this time. Stay focused on your studies—don't drop out. Avoid the "near occasions of sin" regarding food, drink, drugs, and alcohol. There is a possibility for problems coming from a bad diet or certain reactions to the wrong foods. A good Ayurvedic panchakarma treatment and a prescription for proper diet will be helpful. Your finances could hit the skids if you don't continue to pay attention. Visit your dentist. General family issues could seem oppressive, so try to keep your sense of humor.

Saturn Is THIRD from Moon or Lagna

Keywords: Structured Determination

Favorable: Things look to be better now, leaving you feeling more determined and stronger physically—not in terms of speed but of power. You will gain much by following a good routine and giving some structure to your efforts. Efforts should bring more rewards now. Short travels could be gainful. Work to solidify your relationships with younger siblings. Make peace with your neighbors and reevaluate what you expect from each other. Have some fun and adventures.

Unfavorable: Your efforts may not be getting the results you need. Artistic efforts could be delayed or set back. Communications might seem more encumbered, so strive to keep the lines clear and open. Speak up about what you need. Work within a plan. There could be a sense of immobilization or hesitancy to take action. Frustration could increase if you don't plan your activities properly. Be cordial with your younger siblings and neighbors. Take care regarding injuries to the neck, shoulders, and hands. It could develop into a chronic condition later on.

Saturn Is FOURTH from Moon or Lagna

Keywords: Focused Emotions

Favorable: This is a good period to move or at least remodel your home. If anything, you'll not be around your home as much as before. Use this time to get some more education. Take the safe way out emotionally and financially, and you should prosper. A new car might be in order. Your mother would appreciate some attention. Be conservative in land and agricultural dealings.

Unfavorable: Things could get boring or weary on the home front. The tedium of daily housework and responsibility may feel wearing. If you plan on moving, then think it through, or else it could be difficult to find what you want or you could get a structure that is full of problems. Get a good Vastu consultation before you proceed too far. Make sure that you arrange things ahead of time in terms of any extended care for family members, especially your mother. Education could seem like a dead-end street, but stick it out. Don't isolate yourself too much if you feel moody or depressed. Try to enjoy yourself. If you get any pain or discomfort in the chest area, see a physician right away. Give your car a checkup, too.

Saturn Is FIFTH from Moon or Lagna

Keywords: Structured Intellect

Favorable: This is a good time to stabilize and organize your investments. Take a careful look at where you want to be in a few years; then, work backward to what you have to do today. Put forth a little effort to make yourself available for dating, or spend some more time romancing your mate—this could all lead to a sense of mental and emotional ease. Long-term meditation and prolonged study of scriptures will be well rewarded at this time.

Unfavorable: The fifth house is sometimes called the house of royal displeasure (it is Leo by the natural zodiac), so it would not be wise to confront the government—especially the IRS. Don't try to get too clever with your investments. If you speculate or work too much on anticipation, you'll find that type of action is not supported by this transit. Children could be problematic. This is not the best time to try to start a family. Take it easy; your intellect will work best in a methodical manner—if you push it you could get frustrated and irritable. Socialize, or you'll be dropped from all those Rolodexes and social calendars. Romantic interludes could be few and far between (which could be good, if you're a monk).

Saturn Is SIXTH from Moon or Lagna

Keywords: Focus on Service

Favorable: This is the time to set things straight. Saturn is considered good in the 6th. Take a stand for yourself and take measures to improve yourself and your relationships with others. If you need to defend yourself in any way, then do so. Stay firm and correct. There could be some confrontations, but you'll come out ahead in the long run. You should be feeling more powerful during this time. Finances and health will pick up.

Unfavorable: Even if you're right, remember not to lose your sense of mercy. Try to be smooth with the increased sense of righteousness you're feeling. Beware of getting involved in petty disputes or acting petty in a dispute. You could be both vata (airy) and pitta (fiery) at this time. Don't expose yourself to any unnecessary, serious, evident risks.

Saturn Is SEVENTH from Moon or Lagna

Keywords: Structured Partnerships

Favorable: Some ancient karmas might make you feel like getting married at this time. If you want to make your relationship legal, and you want to go ahead, then now is okay (especially if Jupiter is aspecting Saturn as well). Strengthen your commitments to your mate and your business partner. Work to bring some structure and routine to your business. Travel to foreign countries or work with foreigners could be beneficial.

Unfavorable: There could be some restrictions creeping into your relationships. Maybe they are getting too blasé. Try to perk them up and add more delight to your life. Build in more delight in your relationships. If you've been in a relationship for a long time and feel that it is empty and colorless, try to put some of that zip back in that made you form the relationship to start with. Work to increase the friendship, fun, and fondness that got you going from the start. Help your mates cheer up and recommend that they look after their health. Don't fall prey to looking for a better deal in a relationship—you'll just get the same karma with a different face attached. Be faithful. There could be a lack of desire creeping in—make sure that this is not biological in nature. See a relationship specialist if you feel the need.

Saturn Is EIGHTH from Moon or Lagna

This transit is called Ashtami (eight) Saturn. Many astrologers regard this transit as unfavorable. As mentioned earlier, judge the chart quality of Saturn, and its association with other planets, to determine whether this transit will be favorable or unfavorable.

Keywords: Contained Support

Favorable: Focus on getting support. Make sure that others are compelled to work with you in a manner that is similar and specific to what you want. If you are planning to take action with someone but are not aligned with them, then it is best not to even start. Work with people who are happy and want to get things done. Look for commitment. Make sure you share in the results in an equitable manner. By following all this, you should be able to make the most of this transit. Do things to improve your health. Research should be profitable. Your intuition should be on the rise. Some inheritance or financial windfall could come your way.

Unfavorable: You may feel like renouncing the world and living in saintly isolation, but beware: You may be overlooked and passed by for some promotion or recognition. Focus on self-promotion. Take some planned time off to recharge your batteries. Seek the support of others before you get too far along in a project, or else you might get left holding the bag. Health concerns could be higher at this time, so engage in both improvement and prevention. Be aware that your increased sensitivity now could lead you to worry more. Keep focused and stay in a routine. If you are old and frail as you enter this period, your immunity from disease and problems is lessened. You are more vulnerable. Make sure insurance and pension plans are in order, but don't just sit around and worry. There is a saying in the East: "When you want to get rid of a snake, get rid of it when it's very small."

Saturn Is NINTH from Moon or Lagna

Keywords: Focus on Knowledge

Favorable: Concern will increase for matters of justice and ethics. There may be a rising interest in publishing and in higher education. Scriptural knowledge may seem more captivating than before. Your relationship with your bosses, guru, and father could become more defined and stable. Long-distance travel looks good. There could be a return to the roots of religion and spiritual knowledge. Fortune and finances get more established at this time.

Unfavorable: Restrictions with one's father (and authority figures in general) could set in. One's father might separate from the family in one way or another. One might feel less cordial with one's guru, or feel like challenging some scriptural position. Setbacks look possible with higher education, and attempts to get published might be thwarted. Finances are more restrained and legal issues come in, creating complications and delays. Things do not feel so divine. Problems arise on long journeys. Problems could arise in the hip area; perhaps even some chronic lung condition could pop up.

Saturn Is TENTH from Moon or Lagna

Keywords: Structured Career

Favorable: This is a good time to focus on career development and improving your reputation and character. Get all of your responsibilities into a routine as much as possible. A new job could come up, but be sure that there is some stability to it. Enterprising and pioneering work will not be as fruitful as more traditional and established work activity. Work involving land and real estate could be fruitful.

Unfavorable: Try to keep learning and work to continue the rise in your career. If you don't pay attention to work issues, you might run into setbacks, delays, and obstructions that limit your advancement.

Make sure people know you are around and work to get rewarded and honored for your efforts. Don't isolate yourself or people will think you've gone—literally and figuratively. Family problems could seem tiresome. Keep your car in good working order. Be careful not to hurt your knees or joints. Stay relaxed.

Saturn Is ELEVENTH from Moon or Lagna

Keywords: Structured Opportunities

Favorable: All planets are considered favorable as they pass through the 11th house. Saturn, the focusing planet, will bring stability to cash flow and will bring more established relationships with friends and older siblings. This placement also promises profits from the things that Saturn represents, such as favor from old, established enterprises and people. It is good to work now for democratic purposes. There could be success in gardening and agriculture, and profit from antiques and historical items. Right now, slow and steady wins the race.

Unfavorable: State your expectations with your friends and with people of influence. If you don't make it clear what your needs are in specific ways, you might find yourself misaligned with the very people you were counting on for growth and profit. You need friends at this time, so don't isolate yourself. Learn some jokes and keep your sense of humor. Be very careful about managing your cash flow. Profits could be less than you expect or may take longer to pay out.

Saturn Is TWELFTH from Moon or Lagna

Keywords: Stability of Liberation

Favorable: Go someplace where you can be a monk for a while, or at least take enough quiet time and rest for yourself. You're at a junction point of a new life. Your whole mental, emotional, and physical self might be going through a metamorphosis. Let the change come from a stable, solid, and harmonious place. Be generous and give willingly to some charitable or educational cause. Do some good for your community.

Unfavorable: This position marks the start of Saturn's seven-and-a-half-year Sade Sati voyage over the territory of your rising sign or Moon (and also Sun). I have found that the passage of Saturn over the 12th brings up a lot of issues from the past where we had felt betrayed, abandoned, or let down. This transit carries a lot more mental and emotional distress, if such is in the chart to start with. You might not feel like you can be clear enough at this time. The mind is discontinuous and unfocused at times. Debts build up. There could be loss of a job and income, or you might feel like giving up your work and moving on to something else. Family matters and issues with loved ones could be a source of conflict and unhappiness. You might feel some resentment for all the times you gave and people took advantage of you. Be mindful not to put yourself at any obvious, serious risk. You could be exposed to some form of accident, perhaps involving the feet. You might feel ungrounded or clumsy at this time. If you reduce your exposure to risks, act mindfully, and stay around positive people, this does not have to be an unpleasant time.

TRANSITS OF RAHU
Best results in houses 3, 6, and 11

Rahu Is FIRST from Moon or Lagna
Keywords: Unique Disposition

Favorable: You have the ability to get what you want during this time. Work on purifying your system and getting your affairs in order. Make things clearer in your life. Get rid of any toxic relationships or habits. Use this time for self-improvement. Business transactions with foreigners or overseas could be gainful.

Unfavorable: Some chemical or hormonal changes might occur in your system at this time. Your body might be trying to detoxify. Be alert to defend your reputation and fend off any attempts by others to take your position or finances unfairly. Pay attention to your business and to your personal safety and well-being. You might not feel that grounded or confident at this time. You might get into some misunderstandings. Check your alignment with others and make sure you are listening.

Rahu Is SECOND from Moon or Lagna
Keywords: Foreign Finances

Favorable: While you need to be careful about people who act like "snakes," you could profit well during this time. Use this transit to improve family relationships. Clean up your diet. Saying nice things about people will get you far. Try studying something related to a foreign culture.

Unfavorable: Avoid the temptation to return to some bad habits. Don't overeat—stay away from that smorgasbord—and resist any temptations to "light up." You could be exposed to bad food and drink, improper speech, and loss of money through deception, so be careful. If you are taking prescriptions, or any drugs for that matter, make sure you are taking the proper dose and are aware of the effects of drug combinations. You could be exposed to face, gum, and teeth problems as well as eye ailments.

Rahu Is THIRD from Moon or Lagna

Keywords: Unique Efforts

Favorable: Physically, you should be feeling stronger at this time. Determination should be up. This is a good time to go on an adventure to a foreign locale. Let your imagination loose for a bit—you could come up with some creative new concept. Put it in writing.

Unfavorable: If you are in a bad mood and feel you must say or write something, delay a bit. Let yourself calm down and clear up before you act, or you might be making a lot of apologies (or losing friends and business). Try to work out misunderstandings between younger siblings. Make things clear with your neighbors.

Rahu Is FOURTH from Moon or Lagna

Keywords: Foreign Feelings

Favorable: Spend some time learning more about foreign people and their customs. There could be opportunities from foreign sources. Travel and/or business in the Southwest could be good. You might even want to move there. Earnings could come from new learning. Make things more "pure" in your living environment.

Unfavorable: Responsibilities might start feeling burdensome or boring. Relationships in general could seem to be more an effort than a reward. You could be conflicted about keeping a commitment. Try to keep yourself from making any sudden, abrupt changes in your home and schooling. Keep your momentum and routine and don't get derailed by doubts. Your emotions are not at their best at this time. Get your car checked out and be careful when doing any long-distance traveling or taking trips under bad conditions. If you or your mother are experiencing any pain in the region of the chest, then go check it out.

Rahu Is FIFTH from Moon or Lagna

Keywords: Unique Intellect

Favorable: You might begin generating a love for the foreign and the unusual. Don't feel surprised if you are drawn to movies with subtitles. Do something fun, new, and beyond the norm with your kids. Use your quiet time for a good meditation session. Reading some scriptures may bring new insights into your life. Investments could be up, but pay careful attention to when to adjust them. You might feel like you want to have children, but be very careful to plan this right.

Unfavorable: This is not the best transit for romance and is usually not recommended as a time for planning a family. Issues with children could be confusing and a source of tension. You might not be clear enough now to be trying to make it big in the stock market. Speculation is not recommended. Take more time to think things through, especially if your mind is not fully lighted up. I wouldn't recommend abandoning spiritual practices, even if it feels like you're getting nowhere (you're probably getting everywhere). Your intellect could be confused or overshadowed.

Rahu Is SIXTH from Moon or Lagna

Keywords: Crafty Warrior

Favorable: While you might not be totally free of all obstructions, this should be a good time to get ahead. Make things clear and straight with someone you've had trouble or misunderstandings with. Join a gym; get Ayurvedic panchakarma (purifying) treatments; do what you can to improve your health. Enthusiasm and energy are on the rise. Don't let anyone get away with anything at this time. Service activities with foreigners should be profitable. Profits are on the upswing.

Unfavorable: Try to be clear about what service you are to provide to others. Make sure that you don't allow yourself to become the victim of someone's bad mood and be careful not to spill emotional "toxins" onto others. Keep your overhead expenses to a minimum. Stay out of debt. There could be trouble with legal matters and the possibility of cuts, wounds, burns, poisoning, and other forms of accidents. Don't put yourself at risk, especially if you're tired or feeling burned out.

Rahu Is SEVENTH from Moon or Lagna

Keywords: Different Partners

Favorable: Help your mate or partner make the best of this time. The profit picture looks up. You might start feeling love for your mate in new and unusual ways. Mutual exploring is always good. Business profits might be on the rise and there could be new opportunities overseas or with persons with foreign connections.

Unfavorable: Sometimes people feel like their relationships are no longer worth maintaining at this time. Try to clear up misunderstandings and bring some light into your life. You might be feeling jealous or possessive, so don't let this get out of hand. If you feel your partner is acting suspicious, then ask them if you have any reason to feel that way. There is some possibility of your mate or partner being involved in hidden activities. A dispute could crop up. You also should work to be honest in business. Tell your mate to go to a doctor if they aren't feeling well. You need to try to stay well while traveling.

Rahu Is EIGHTH from Moon or Lagna

Keywords: Support from the Foreign

Favorable: You might want to buy an extra lottery ticket. Opportunities for unearned income could come out of nowhere. Be alert for support and be encouraging. It's best to do things with the help of others at this time. Make sure you have good commitment and alignment for any activity you share with others. Use this time to improve your health. Your intuition should be at a high point.

Unfavorable: Try not to get overlooked, and make sure there is no confusion about what you are accountable for. You could get accused for something you didn't do, or appeared to do. Someone might take credit for what you've done. You might fall into some embarrassing, if not scandalous, situation. Perceived misdeeds can be as damaging as real ones. Your finances are subject to "downsizing," so be watchful. If you don't keep your support mechanisms intact, you will not have much to fall back on if you get hit by any gloomy moods. If you have any chronic ailments, then use this time to revisit them under the care of a competent health professional. But be aware that diseases might be hard to diagnose at this time. Get a second opinion.

Rahu Is NINTH from Moon or Lagna

Keywords: Unique Philosophies

Favorable: This is a good time to travel to a foreign country or to do business with those of foreign birth or culture. Fortune might arise in unusual ways, or might seem to come easily (at first). Take care to close all your transactions clearly to get maximum benefits. Serve your guru. Pay respects to your father. Benefits could come from publishing or higher education.

Unfavorable: Be considerate to those who have dedicated their lives to seeking spiritual goals. No spiritual grumblings allowed right now. Keep your ethics intact. It might be hard to distinguish between when you are being very clever and when you are being unscrupulous. Work to have clear understandings with your boss. If your father is not feeling well, then encourage him to visit a doctor. He should also watch his finances. There could be confusion (perhaps even theft) during long-distance travel, so be careful. You could have some misunderstandings with authorities (and your guru).

Rahu Is TENTH from Moon or Lagna

Keywords: Extraordinary Career

Favorable: Do something out of the ordinary to promote your career. Be more visible. Make yourself more marketable by learning some new or unusual skill. If you pay attention and cover the areas where things could get confused, you should come out ahead at this time. Career activities involving foreign countries should be favorable.

Unfavorable: There could be a cloud of smoke descending on you at this time—turn on the fans! Get clear about what you need to do to make a living for yourself. Mind that you take credit for what you do, or someone else might take credit for your work. Strive to present yourself in a bright manner. People could lose track of you and might feel you are not doing enough. There is some exposure to scandals and nefarious deeds. Check out what you're getting yourself into.

Rahu Is ELEVENTH from Moon or Lagna

Keywords: Unique Opportunities

Favorable: Some unusual opportunities could present themselves to you. Some deep, quiet wish you've had for a while could start to bear fruit. Fulfill your desires during this period. Associate with successful people so that their good luck can rub off on you. Take someone you admire to lunch. If your older siblings need a little help, then help. If they need a lot, then be sure about whether or not you can take that on. Money could come from the Southwest.

Unfavorable: Some clever scheme could be presented to you that might have a negative effect on your cash flow. It's not a good time to get into financial transactions with friends and older siblings. Be careful about ear infections or trouble with hearing. Maybe you just need to listen more now.

Rahu Is TWELFTH from Moon or Lagna

Keywords: Foreign Enlightenment

Favorable: This is a good time to go on that retreat to India, or perhaps a church outing in the mountains. Spend more time on inner fulfillment. Be generous in charity, but still maintain your financial wits.

Unfavorable: Try not to eat late. Sleep could be off during this period. Your libido could be off. You might not feel so grounded; in fact, there is danger to the feet, and perhaps a fall is even possible. Some unusual illnesses could crop up that seem to defy diagnosis. Transits of Rahu and Ketu carry a lot of spiritual connotations; so healing might be aided by a more spiritual approach. Try some yagyas; learn to meditate; be nice to people; give to charity; etc. There is the possibility of spending some time in isolation, so let's be smart and not make it a jail or hospital. Stay on top of your finances or you could build up debts and incur some losses.

TRANSITS OF KETU
Best results in houses 3, 6, and 11

Ketu brings a lot of change, surprises, and reorganization. It wiggles around a lot, much like the tail of a snake. Ketu, like that tail, is often detached (literally) and represents breaking away or getting separated from something. As such, Ketu is the karaka for enlightenment. Ketu is much milder a malefic than Rahu.

Ketu Is FIRST from Moon or Lagna

Keywords: Surprising Behavior

Favorable: You might be in for some pleasant surprises during this time. Spiritual energy is more available. There can be feelings about wanting to make changes for yourself, so plan to do some things that improve your personal life. If you feel like moving or switching jobs, make sure that it's not a deeper impulse to change the character of your life. A personal makeover is good. The biggest driving force is to add more spiritual content to your life.

Unfavorable: You are subject to unexpected changes at this time. There could be a move, or it might be that you do a lot of moving or traveling in general. Your job is subject to modification. Be pro-active and prepare to make a change rather than be surprised by a reorganization at work. The change energy could be so high as to make you feel erratic, or perhaps devious in that you'll do anything to make these changes. Stay on a routine and meet your responsibilities in time.

Ketu Is SECOND from Moon or Lagna

Keywords: Financial Reorganizations

Favorable: Study of scriptures and chanting holy songs is a good idea during this time. Examine your finances to make sure everything is in order. Modification of diet is recommended. Work to make positive changes in your family life. You might have a tendency to phrase things in very creative, perhaps poetic, ways.

Unfavorable: There could be ups and downs with your finances during this period. Take an active role in making sure your finances stay stable. Try to eat fresh foods and avoid eating on the run. If you are a former smoker, drinker, or drug user, try to stay away from occasions that could renew your interest in these bad habits. Make sure you know what's really wrong with your teeth. You have a possibility of doing some dental work over again. Be honest with people, but speak the truth sweetly. You might get some eye ailments and facial diseases.

Ketu Is THIRD from Moon or Lagna

Keywords: Surprising Efforts

Favorable: Go on some adventure. Have some more fun. Enlivening yourself could stimulate some exciting new changes for yourself. Be creative. Dancing, writing, acting, and playing music should all be fascinating and worthwhile. You have an opportunity to improve your relationships with younger siblings and with neighbors. Change the way you "sell" yourself. An innovative sales and marketing approach will go a long way to improve things for you.

Unfavorable: Your younger siblings might have some difficulties at this time. Their behavior could be surprising to you. Try to keep the communication lines open. If you have to write something or make an important contact, be prepared or you'll have to do it over again. Double-check that you have everything in order if you are giving seminars or instruction to others. There could be confusing interchanges with others.

Ketu Is FOURTH from Moon or Lagna

Keywords: Mystical Emotions

Favorable: Take action to reorganize your home in some way. Rearrange your furniture, or turn your den into a garage. Make the home environment more spiritual in some way. Get a Vastu consultation to ensure that your living quarters are positioned in the proper directions. Education is recommended, especially of any spiritual nature. Upgrade your job skills to make yourself more marketable. Emotional changes should be unusual but beneficial.

Unfavorable: The home life could feel unsettled at this time. Your emotions could be less stable or more sensitive, so strive to be patient and thoughtful with others. Don't make decisions if you are caught in some strong mood, whether positive or negative. Family matters might be a source of worry. Get your car checked out so you don't break down and get stranded somewhere. Work out differences with your mother in a polite yet direct manner. Stay the course in school. If you have any unusual ailments in the breast or heart area, get the consensus of several doctors. It might be hard to figure out what is wrong (it might be more psychological or spiritual in nature or it might be that you are hypersensitive at this time).

Ketu Is FIFTH from Moon or Lagna

Keywords: Versatile Intellect

Favorable: The mind might shift to more spiritual considerations. Interest could increase in meditation and reading holy works. Be mindful of your investments—it will serve you to reorganize them as necessary. Change the way you demonstrate your affection to your "intimate other." Ask them how, if you need to. Allow yourself to take more delight in life. Work to help your children make necessary adjustments. Unexpected benefits could come in due to some past credit.

Unfavorable: Your mind could feel restless and ungrounded. It might seem hard to sit quietly in meditation. This is not a good time to take risks with investments and get overly into speculating. Children might seem more erratic at this time or could be a distraction to you. Keep them on a routine. Romance might take on a more ethereal than physical form at this time. You might need to work some things out with your mate in this area. Your point of view might change regarding some spiritual teachers or some "hero." Stay positive.

Ketu Is SIXTH from Moon or Lagna

Keywords: Changes Through Service

Favorable: Things could change for the better. Use this time to reorganize and improve your life. Focus on self-improvement. Medical and healing procedures and processes usually begin to show more results during this transit. Spiritual remedies are effective as well. The change will do you good.

Unfavorable: If things change too rapidly, it could throw you off. Anger and erratic behavior could dominate if you get off your schedule. Try to avoid the "runaway train" syndrome. You are a candidate for an accident or an unexpected operation. You can avoid this by planning ahead and taking care of things when they are small. "A stitch in time saves nine."

Ketu Is SEVENTH from Moon or Lagna

Keywords: Adaptable Relationships

Favorable: This is a good time to purposely reorganize or reconfigure contracts, business conditions, and any operating terms you share with someone else. Redo your relationships so that they can grow into something larger and better. Your partner or mate might be feeling the need to make some changes. See how you can help.

Unfavorable: This is a time when some people start looking for a better deal in their relationships. You might need to face some inconsistency with partners. Try not to be too random. Strive not to make erratic changes. Discuss your needs in order to modify your relationship or contract with another. Plan your trips at this time, or you could end up wandering around a lot.

Ketu Is EIGHTH from Moon or Lagna
Keywords: Transcendental Support

Favorable: Your mind should be very sensitive at this time. This refinement could be applied to self-discovery, research, or any form of investigation. Read into the origins of religions and philosophies of different cultures. It will be revealing. Your mate could have a change in their finances. Encourage them to plan ahead for this. Some unexpected money could come your way.

Unfavorable: Guard your health at this time. You might be somewhat hypersensitive. If you see a doctor about some ailment, perhaps in reproduction or elimination, they might have trouble clearly seeing the root of your complaint. Get second opinions. Strive to keep your support network intact. You might get some surprises during this period that will be good or bad, according to the circle of support you've set up around you. Stay on a routine and don't dwell on your worries.

Ketu Is NINTH from Moon or Lagna
Keywords: Adjusting Fortunes

Favorable: Your mind could make some conceptual breakthrough in the field of religion, ethics, and higher education. Your relationship with your boss, father, or guru could take a turn for the better. Maybe it's you who has changed. Travel to a distant land could be "enlightening." Innovative learning opportunities could come your way—but make sure you don't get too "out there" (no UFO trips at this time!).

Unfavorable: You might feel like making a switch in your beliefs at this time. It might be that you feel your current spiritual path is no longer serving you. Before you abandon this track, make sure it's not just that you need to recommit to your original intentions. Your father might go through some ups and downs, so help him if you can. It's important to reset your goals and responsibilities with your boss now. Don't get creative with your ethics or scruples—you could end up with unpleasant surprises. If you have to do any long-distance traveling, make sure you have a backup plan it case things get switched at the last minute. Publishing activities might have to go through several rewrites. Don't abandon your studies at this time.

Ketu Is TENTH from Moon or Lagna

Keywords: Mystical Career

Favorable: This is a good time to explore the spiritual side of your nature. If you have the ability to take some time off for personal reflection, then that would be good. There could be a lot of coming and going and a lot of changes in your work. Use this reorganization to your advantage and jump on the new career opportunities that are created by the change. You could be recognized for unusual and creative contributions in your field.

Unfavorable: There could be a sudden and unexpected change in your work. A reorganization could shake your confidence. Keep yourself directed and on track, or you'll end up feeling fragmented and disconnected. Have a backup plan so you can make a change from strength and not end up taking only what's available. Make sure people know what you have accomplished or your good reputation could weaken.

Ketu Is ELEVENTH from Moon or Lagna

Keywords: Incomprehensible Profits

Favorable: This is a good time to consciously modify how your earn your profits. Set new goals and objectives for yourself. Take some time to dream new dreams. Meet new people. Spiritually oriented friends should prove to be a blessing.

Unfavorable: Cash flow could be erratic now. Keep on your budget and resist reckless spending. Think twice about those "amazing" opportunities that come your way, and make sure they are worth the effort. If you depend a lot on your friends and elder siblings to come through completely and on time, most likely you will be disappointed. Activity is more discontinuous and random at this time, so double-check that everything is in place before you start those new ventures. Your older siblings could be under some duress at this time.

Ketu Is TWELFTH from Moon or Lagna

Keywords: Liberation Through Reorganization

Favorable: The impulse from this transit is to disconnect from the world and to become unbounded. Spiritual expansion is a key driver at this time, so go on a retreat, or take a trip to India or some distant land. It is recommended to purify your body as well. Try to keep some form of a home base, because you might be on the road a lot. This is the time to create a new life for yourself.

Unfavorable: Your recognizable boundaries are becoming formless at this time. While the ultimate effect is a modification of behavior and the creation of a new you, the ambiguity and uncertainty of this time could be perplexing if not unsettling. Proceed in a stable manner, planning ahead a bit more to keep things more consistent around you. Finances could be irregular and you may be subject to a fine or penalty if you don't follow the rules. Travel in foreign lands could be very topsy-turvy.

TRANSITS OF MERCURY AND VENUS

For Mercury—best results
in houses 2, 4, 6, 8, 10, and 11

For Venus—best results
in houses 1, 2, 3, 4, 5, 8, 9, 11, and 12

I won't take up any space with these transits. They change signs a little less than every month and are generally second-tier contributors to life events. These planets most often show impact when they are afflicted in transit, such as retrograde or associated with a malefic planet. You can derive your own interpretation of these transits by studying chapter 5 on planets in signs. These planets, as well as the others, will display the effects described in these positions during their transits.

CHAPTER FIFTEEN

TIMING EVENTS WITH MUHURTHA

Muhurtha is a Vedic astrology tool used to determine the most auspicious or superior time to start or stop an event. Many astrologers also call Muhurtha "electional" astrology since we use it to elect or select a preferred time period. Muhurtha is not to be confused with a unit of measure equal to 48 minutes, or two ghatis. (A ghati is 24 minutes. A sidereal day [star based, not solar] is comprised of 30 Muhurthas.)

The use of Muhurtha is consistent with Vedic astrology's outlook that one can choose to live successfully and happily within time. Destiny is negotiable. Rather than look back to analyze what happened at a specific time, Muhurtha looks forward to find the best time for the nature of the event at hand and for the span of time that the person has to work within. Some people will ask an astrologer to find the best time for marriage, but they will indicate that they want to get married during the summertime. The date that the astrologer must then choose might not be the best date overall, but will be the best date for all concerned, within the constraints of the time frame selected.

If necessary, the astrologer needs to indicate to the client that there might not be any really favorable times in the next few months, and that it might be best to wait. If the client can't wait, for whatever reason, then the best available date must be chosen. The wise astrologer will set the client's expectations correctly for this situation. A person could have the very best boat, but he could elect to set sail in the winter. The best an astrologer can do, then, is pick the calmest day in that cold and stormy season.

As you will see from what follows, a key ingredient for successful Muhurtha is an accurate planetary almanac, or panchanga, and the correct birth times for the participants. Both gochara and dasa/bhukti cycles should be consulted to obtain the best time overall. You will find that there is no 100-percent best time. There will always seem to be a conflict between one time element and another. You need to synthesize the timing factors and come up with the best time overall. It takes time and good analytical skill to develop the ability to weigh and merge time factors.

Time Periods to Avoid

At minimum, try to pick a favorable day of the week and—especially—a favorable nakshatra.

Unfavorable weekdays (vara): Tuesday should be avoided, but Thursday and Friday are acceptable for any auspicious event.

Unfavorable nakshatras: Avoid Bharani (ruled by Yama, the deity for death) and Krittika (ruled by Agni, the god of fire). The last part of Aslesha, Jyeshta and Revati (gandanta nakshatras) should also not be selected. If one can strengthen the sign rising at the time chosen for an event, the nakshatra dosha can get minimized.

Solar ingress (Surya Sankranti): It is considered unfavorable when the Sun enters a new sign (16 ghatis, or 6 hours and 24 minutes, before and after entrance into a new sign of the zodiac). This time is considered good for practicing spiritual techniques, religious purification rites, and initiation into mantra meditation, but not good for any other works. Actually, it is not good to select a time when any planet is sandhi except for performing spiritual practices.

Hemmed in (Kartari): It is unfavorable when the sign rising for the start of a new enterprise is bordered on both sides by inauspicious planets. It is like being between the two knives of a pair of scissors (kartari means scissors). It is not a favorable time for any good work, especially marriage.

Afflicted Moon: In the chart constructed for the time of the event, the Moon should not be placed in the 6th, 8th, or 12th house from the Muhurtha Lagna. You should try not to associate the Moon with any other planet, either favorable or unfavorable, especially in cases of marriage.

Exceptions and "Work Arounds"

So many influences can occur simultaneously when one is attempting to select the correct time to start an event. You have to make choices that involve the highest degrees of favorable indications and try to perform some form of planetary propitiation to lessen unfavorable influences. The following are some of the combinations one could try to select in order to minimize doshas or negatives.

Overall, if the Lagna or its ruler are strong in the chart, it will counterbalance many unfavorable conditions elsewhere in the Muhurtha chart. Jupiter will remove many of the doshas from the chart, if placed in the ascendant of the Muhurtha chart. This is a key countermeasure.

1. Moon in 8th is not as bad if it is waxing (after 8th day from New Moon); or if in a benefic sign and a benefic navamsa; if there is Tarabala (occupying a strong nakshatra); or if exalted. Also the malefic effects are diminished if the Moon and the ruler of the 8th house from the Muhurtha Lagna are friends.

2. Tuesday is not as unfavorable after 12:00 noon.

3. If the ruler of the day of the week (vara) is strong in the Muhurtha chart, it will not be as unfavorable.

4. If Jupiter, Venus, or Mercury is in the Lagna in the Muhurtha chart, the malefic effects of various unfavorable combinations will be greatly diminished, if not negated in full.

5. The Moon or the Sun in the 11th will negate many of the doshas.

6. If the 1st, 4th, 7th, and 10th houses are strong, many doshas are reduced.

7. If there is an exalted planet in the Lagna, doshas are decreased.

8. If Jupiter or Venus is in an angle (1, 4, 7, or 10) and malefics occupy the 3rd, 6th, or 11th houses, the ill effects of the afflictions are diminished.

CORRECTIVE ACTIONS

CHAPTER SIXTEEN

REMEDIAL MEASURES

Vedic astrology not only reveals challenges in life or opportunity for improvement, but also gives practical procedures to improve things. These actions for improvement are what most astrologers call remedial measures, or Upayes. People want to correct, restore, or alleviate unfavorable conditions. They want to be able to live a life where they can expect positive outcomes to their actions. They want to magnify some favorable condition and let it become set within their being. Remedial measures help in this quest.

However, there is danger in not knowing the complete and correct measure of this skill.

In this book, I am only introducing you to the major areas of remedial measures. The full study should be taken up in person with an experienced Vedic astrologer. You cannot properly learn these remedial measures from books.

Yagyas are Vedic ceremonies performed to generate positive influences within the cycles of personal life. These performances must be administered by bona fide Vedic priests (pujaris) and are often performed in properly dedicated Hindu temples. The participant in the

317

yagya must know their birth star (Moon nakshatra) and preferably their Gotra, or heritage from the Seven Rishis (see appendix). The person's nakshatra helps form a connection between their personal life and their universal life—as elicited by the performance. The priest must be informed as to the right time to conduct the performance, and he must know the person's intention (better health, success in career, happiness in marriage, triumph in a dispute, etc). Most important, the priest must be told what specific Vedic deity and/or planet the person wishes to propitiate. This should be recommended by an astrologer experienced with yagya propitiations.

Mantras are sounds that have a vibrational quality of the highest level and are associated with the aspect of life you wish to improve. To be effective, mantras must be pronounced correctly and recited in a specific way. Vedic astrology associates a certain set of mantras with each planet, and with deities associated with those planets. You must contact an experienced and reputable astrologer to obtain the correct mantra and to receive instruction on how to use it properly. It is not a good idea for beginners to experiment in this area without some qualified guidance. You have a good chance of pronouncing these mantras incorrectly if you get them from books alone.

Shantis are simpler forms of corrective action that are often associated with some animate or inanimate form of nature. By synchronizing with that specific impulse of life, compelling forces of an individual's life are stimulated and made to flow in a specific, beneficial fashion. For example, iron, sesame oil, and black cloth are associated with the planet Saturn. Wearing, eating, and/or offering these items will initiate a positive or protective influence for the performer regarding the indications of Saturn—more focus, less obstruction, etc.

Dana, or charity, is an operating principle with which many are already familiar: "You get what you give," "sharing is double happiness," etc. I have found that many times a chart will indicate a period of loss, especially transits of the 12th house. The way to control loss is to lose on purpose—in this way, we help others while repaying our own karmic debt.

Vedic hymns, or Gandarvaveda hymns, are songs or musical compositions dedicated to specific deities. These deities or "impulses of nature" are related to specific planets and/or impulses in your chart.

Listening to the healing resonances of these melodies or incantations brings pleasing, protective, and reconstructive energy to the mind and body. Examples of these musical compositions are the Vishnu Sahasranam and the Sri Lalita Sahasranam. These works sing or chant the 1,000 names (sahasranam) of these deities.

Vastu Shastra (see chapter 20 on Vastu).

Gemstones (as follows).

Gems, Gem Shape, Gem Fingers, and Metals

One can placate or modify the influence of a planet by wearing the corresponding gemstone, carved in the correct shape, worn on the correct finger, and set in the correct metal. Wear it for the first time on the correct day of the week for that planet.

I have found that there are many opinions on gemstones. The standard is to wear the stone of your rising sign ruler, of the current dasa ruler, or of a specific planet that you want to improve in your chart. One idea is to wear the stone for the ruler of your current dasa more or less as a preventative measure.

Perhaps the most significant determining factor in the selection of a stone, from what I have found, is that the stone feels pleasing to the wearer.

Most astrologers recommend that a stone be at least a carat in weight and of very good quality. While I concur about gem quality, I also warn clients not to impoverish themselves in the name of improving themselves. If you really want a stone but can't afford it, I have no problem recommending an auxiliary stone, called an Upa Ratna. These stones have the same color, but are of semiprecious grade. Wearing clothing and having accessories in the color of the planet you want to improve is also recommended.

Overall, gemstones help to solidify your intention to improve yourself within the context of the planet's influence in the birth chart. Gems can impart significant coherent influences—in the same way that light, when passed through a ruby in a specific way, forms a laser beam that can cut through metal.

The following table gives you the relevant qualities for each planet.

Planet	Color	Gem	Shape	Gem Finger	Metal	Weekday
Sun	Dark red, orange	Ruby	Quadrangle	Ring	Copper	Sunday
Moon	Bright white	Pearl	Round	Little	Silver	Monday
Mars	Middle red	Red coral	Cylinder	Ring	Gold	Tuesday
Mercury	Grass green	Emerald	Triangle	Little	Silver	Wednesday
Jupiter	Golden, yellow	Yellow sapphire	Ellipse	Index	Gold	Thursday
Venus	Middle white	Diamond	Octagon	Little	Silver	Friday
Saturn	Black, blue	Blue sapphire	Tall rectangle	Middle	Iron	Saturday
Rahu	Brownish	Hessonite garnet	Line	Middle	Panchadhatu (5 metals)	Saturday (like Saturn)
Ketu	Stripes, multicolor, blue-green	Cat's-eye Chrysoberyl	Line	Ring*	Panchadhatu (5 metals)	Tuesday (like Mars)

Note: Astrologers vary as to which finger to wear a ring on. For example, some authors state that a cat's eye forKetu can be worn on the little finger.

Colors

Certain colors are healing for people and can be used to propitiate a planet. For example, wearing dark blue or black on Saturdays can help balance the influences represented by Saturn. Wearing green while taking a test could contribute Mercury's clarity to the task.

COMBINING ONE CHART WITH ANOTHER

CHAPTER SEVENTEEN

TECHNIQUES TO JUDGE COMPATIBILITY

Many Vedic astrologers indicate that, as a general rule, your mate can be determined in your chart either from the 7th house, from where the ruler of the 7th house is located, or from the strongest planet that occupies or aspects your 7th house. That 7th house position in your chart will indicate your mate's Moon sign or rising sign, or a planet that represents their personality to a good degree.

You can look for these indicators in both the rasi and in the navamsa charts. Obviously, the whole chart must support marriage for this to be applicable. These rules, while predominantly used to identify marriage partners, can also be used to determine compatibility with business partners, co-workers, bosses, family members, friends, and even pets if you want to extend these rules to all living creatures.

I have found that people find fondness and rapport with each other from the matches of the Lagna (rising sign), Moon, and Sun, as follows:

	His Rising Sign	His Moon	His Sun
Her Rising Sign	*x*	*x*	*x*
Her Moon	*x*	*x*	*x*
Her Sun	*x*	*x*	—

Look for the following connection types for rising sign and planets (both for the table above and for the planetary connections discussed below):

1. Conjunct in same signs

2. Opposite

This relationship shows up primarily in the rasi charts of the couple, but can also be seen in the navamsa chart. In fact, you can have an attraction develop between people if the match occurs between one person's rasi and the other's navamsa. One exception, which I call the "two kings in one castle" syndrome, is that egos could interfere if both persons have the Sun in the same sign or in opposition. Neither wants to give in to the other.

Initial attraction is the first of three major indicators that I have found will lead to a good relationship. However, connections of the Lagna, Moon, and Sun do not ensure durability of the relationship. A person could love someone dearly, but it might not be wise to pick that person for a partner, for the two reasons that I'll discuss next.

The second indicator is whether or not the potential partners each have the individual ability to be in a marriage at all. I have seen many cases where people have a liking for each other, but they find that they can't sustain the relationship, or that the required level of mutual commitment is lacking. Persons with afflicted 7th and 5th houses, and a weak Venus (and Jupiter for women) usually encounter troubles in sustaining a relationship.

The third indicator for a successful match is the timing of the relationship. If both parties don't have dasa and gochara indications for marriage that are around the same time, then the relationship may not endure, or might start off on rocky ground.

Guidelines for Determining Compatibility

Below, I have listed some of the basic matching categories.

General compatibility: Lagna, Moon or Sun connections. As we just discussed, this connection brings people together in ways that are beyond their initial intellectual understanding. They just feel attracted to or fascinated with each other—not necessarily just sexually—and find mutual affinities and several common interests.

"Destiny" relationship: Nodal (Rahu and Ketu) connections. The nodes draw people together karmically, whether one's nodes are associated with another's nodes or with another's Sun, Moon, or rising sign. This connection usually brings them into each other's lives to learn something from one another. It may not last, but it could bring some pleasure, or wisdom.

Sexual compatibility or enlivened passions:
Mars and Venus connections. This connection brings a level of passion that could sustain a relationship in the early stages, while more profound issues of partnering are worked out. This brings a form of married love expressed in a physical form.

Mars and Mars connections. This connection can bring sexual vigor, if not initial sexual tension. There is a common physical approach to life in general. It is not, however, any guarantee of durability. Mars brings things together quickly, but is not a sustaining planet.

Mars and Saturn connections. This connection can bring a lot of passion in the initial stages of a relationship. However, the couple has to develop a focus on kindness and politeness to make this work over time.

Good communication: Mercury connection. This connection draws people to each other on the mental or philosophical level. Couples with this combination enjoy talking to each other so much that they might not mind at first if there is not much physical activity. People in spiritual organizations sometimes get married for this reason.

Comfort. The connections listed below can all make each partner feel comfortable in the presence of the other. There is something soothing, warm, and pleasant in this relationship:

- Moon and Venus;

- Jupiter and Venus; or

- Venus and Venus.

Security: Saturn and Jupiter connections. This serves people whose charts are dominated by Saturn (with strong Capricorn or Aquarius, Saturn in the 7th, Saturn ruling 7th, or Saturn in the 1st, to name a few). These people will take on a partner who can provide them with a practical life, often in the traditional roles of provider and nest builder. The relationship will most likely endure, but it may not have much passion or delight. Marriages between older people or more conservative people may have this influence.

Determining When Marriage Might Occur

The active points for marriage often arise from movements of Jupiter, Saturn, and Venus. Additional marriage points are the 7th house, location of the ruler of the 7th, and even the rising sign. I have found, and ancient writers agree, that for a woman, the mate is represented by Jupiter, and for a man, by Venus. Some authors will state that Mars represents a husband, but I have not found this to work. Mars could represent a passionate interlude, but not a supported commitment in marriage.

The main indicators for the event of marriage can be seen from the transits. For a woman, look to when Saturn transits over natal Jupiter, or Jupiter moves over natal Saturn. This forms a larger-scale baseline that will be further activated by the transit of Venus over this Saturn/Jupiter "conjunction" of rasi planet and transit planet. You will usually find that this process works in the chart of the person who wants to get married the most, for the couple being analyzed. One person might have mostly romance indicators, such as 5th house activity, while the other has more 7th house, or marriage, planetary activity going on.

The dasa periods can also stimulate marriage. In general, these cycles are much slower-moving than the transits, but can indicate that you are in the "field." Dasas and bhuktis of Jupiter, Venus, and Rahu can bring marriage. Dasa combinations of Saturn, Jupiter, or Venus can also bring a marriage contract.

Picking a Suitable Marriage Date

Selecting the best day to get married should involve the charts of both persons in the ceremony—not just the current transits as shown in the marriage muhurtha chart. You should look at the dasas first, to narrow down the overall span of time; then, go into further detail with the transits. The finest detail is then found through the quick-moving planetary activities of the lunar day, the nakshatra, and the rising time for the day. It is very difficult to get a perfect day, so you want to get the best day within the time span available for the wedding party. Many astrologers will pick good days, but odd times such as 3:00 A.M. If the prospective bride and groom want to have an astrologically correct time, then you can select that. Another option, however, is that they get married at that time and then pick another, more appropriate time to have another ceremony where all the family and friends can comfortably come.

The following doshas (afflictions) are important to avoid in the marriage chart:

- 7th house should be unoccupied.
- Mars should not be in the 8th.
- Venus should not be in the 6th.
- Lagna should not be hemmed in between malefics.
- Moon should not be associated with other planets.
- Malefics should not be in Lagna.

Try to place the following in the wedding chart:

- Best weekdays (varas): Monday, Wednesday, Thursday, and Friday
- Moderate weekdays: Saturday and Sunday

- Bad weekday: Tuesday

- Best nakshatras: Rohini, Mrigasira, Magha, Uttara, Hasta, Swati, Anuradha, Mula, Uttarashada, Uttara Bhadrapada, Revati

- Not favorable: First pada (3°20′) of Makha and Mula and last pada (26°40′) of Revati

- All other nakshatras are not favorable

- Best rising signs: Gemini, Virgo, Libra

- Moderate rising signs: Taurus, Cancer, Leo, Sagittarius, Aquarius (the rest are unfavorable)

If a Good Time Is Too Difficult to Set

It is not always possible, in this relative existence, to find a time that is not compromised in some way. The idea is to find the best time within what is available. If you have trouble finding a good time, at least try to get the following minimal requirements in place:

- Jupiter, Mercury, or Venus should be in Lagna.

- Malefics should be in 3 and 11.

Kuja Dosha

Kuja Dosha translates as Mars affliction. If either partner has the planet Mars located in the 2nd, 4th, 7th, 8th, or 12th houses, it indicates an increased possibility of either separation or early death, or increased discord being brought upon the partner that does not have Kuja Dosha. The person with Kuja Dosha is sometimes called Manglik (after Mangala, another name for Mars). You need to be careful not to overstress the impact of Kuja Dosha. If you follow the traditional prescriptions for calculating Kuja Dosha, you will find that it occurs frequently. The best approach is to use it along with all the other compatibility techniques to form a well-rounded judgment.

Exceptions to Kuja Dosha

Kuja Dosha Samyam (Evenness) occurs when both partners have Kuja Dosha. Kuja Dosha Samyam does not necessarily cancel the unfavorable influence—more accurately, it brings it to a point of balance. This so-called cancellation of Kuja Dosha often leads to an acceptable partnership during the years of parenting and career building. However, the issues of incompatibility may still need to be addressed by the couple when children leave home and retirement sets in. At this point, the couple is left to face the core issues of their life together, hopefully with mutual cordiality and agreement.

Kuja Dosha Bhanga (Cancellation) occurs when:

- Mars occupies the following specific locations:
  - Gemini or Virgo as 2nd house;
  - Aries or Scorpio in the 4th house;
  - Capricorn or Cancer in the 7th house;
  - Sagittarius or Pisces in the 8th house; or
  - Taurus or Libra in the 12th house.
- Mars occupies Leo and Aquarius (in this case, there is no Kuja Dosha in any house)
- Mars is conjunct either Jupiter or the Moon
- the Lagna is occupied by either Jupiter or Venus
- Mars is in the 4th or 7th in the signs of Aries, Cancer, Scorpio, or Capricorn

JUDGING THE WORLD'S BEHAVIOR AND EVENTS

CHAPTER EIGHTEEN

MUNDANE or WORLD ASTROLOGY

There is a specific process to follow when analyzing world events. You construct a specific set of charts, then analyze them according to the descriptions I have listed below. World-charting can be a tricky practice. You need to have the correct time for the nation and for the president. You will find, for example, that there is a lot of controversy associated with the time of the founding of the United States. There can also be some confusion, from time to time, as to the correct chart for the nation's leader. However, you will be able to get some fascinating and useful information about your nation by constructing a chart for the nation's capital city. The most recommended starting point for the year's events is when the Sun and Moon are exactly conjunct in Pisces. This is called the Saka New Year.

Key charts to analyze are:

1. Saka Lunar Year (First New Moon after Sun enters Pisces, calculated for time and location of the nation's capital)

2. Solar Year (when the Sun enters Aries) for the nation's capital

3. President's chart for the country involved

4. National chart (use the date when the country was founded)

5. Ruler of the year (ruler of day of the week that year begins on)—this information is available in works such as the Brihat Samhita by Varahamihira

Here are some key factors to analyze:

- Against planetary placements, and what they signify in the yearly chart, look for:

  - Transits over the year's chart placements
  - Conjunctions, Oppositions, etc., of transiting planets
  - Ingresses, or when the planets enter new signs
  - Eclipses, and their transits over yearly charts

- Interpret the yearly chart much as you would a natal chart:

  - 1st house represents the general public well-being
  - 2nd is the food and money supply
  - 3rd is communications and neighboring countries
  - 4th is education, transport, and housing sectors
  - 5th is stock market, birth rate, etc.
  - 6th is diseases and armed forces
  - 7th is cooperation of businesses and marriage issues
  - 8th is death rate and serious diseases
  - 9th is travel, higher education, and ethics
  - 10th is the nation's ruler
  - 11th is cash flow and allies
  - 12th is religious issues and matters about prisons

ASTROLOGY AND OTHER VEDIC SYSTEMS

CHAPTER NINETEEN

AYURVEDA: THE SCIENCE
OF HEALTH

Ayurveda is a preventative health system developed in ancient India. Knowing how the planets express themselves in terms of the three Ayurvedic body types will give you additional clues when interpreting a chart. These types are vata, pitta, and kapha. In ancient Ayurveda, the Vaidya, or Ayurvedic practitioner ("doctor"), would consult the person's pulse, and would also review their birth chart to determine that patient's basic body constitution. The birth chart, along with the current planetary transits (gochara) and planetary periods (dasa) and the chart for the moment of arrival at the office (prasna), would give the Vaidya a greater capacity to diagnose the condition of the patient and to determine the potential severity and duration of the illness. Sometimes, people who consult with an Ayurvedic practitioner are perplexed because, due to a different pulse, the Vaidya will tell them that they have a different body type from the last visit. This can happen when the patient's constitution is evaluated solely on the pulse, without consulting the chart and its influences coming from gochara (transits) and dasa periods. The astrological diagram is a tool that shows the core constitution with temporary modifications caused by planetary effects.

How Does Ayurveda Work?

Astrologically, the planets reign over Bhutas, the elements or basic building blocks of creation. Mars rules fire, Mercury reigns over the earth element, Venus rules akasha or space, and Saturn has dominion over air. The Sun is the karaka or indicator for fire, or tejas, and the Moon who rules the tides and the fluids of our bodies is the karaka for water or jal.

As these planets and their associated elements move around their orbits in the solar system, they leave in their wake the core changes to people and events on earth. The seasons come and go, the Sun divides the day into night, and all creatures and creation are modified to some degree.

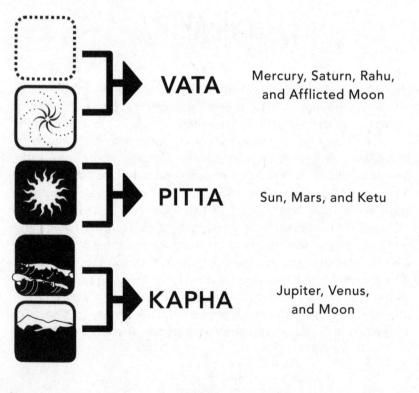

VATA — Mercury, Saturn, Rahu, and Afflicted Moon

PITTA — Sun, Mars, and Ketu

KAPHA — Jupiter, Venus, and Moon

When all the elements are in balance within our individual constitution, then individual life is good. Harmony, health, and happiness prevail. However, when the elements are deranged in some way, the microcosm of the individual is correspondingly affected, according to that person's inherent strengths and weaknesses. The current evidence (and forewarnings) are told in the chart. If the transiting planets move into unfavorable positions in a person's chart, then the possibility of ill health results. If the dasa period is correspondingly bad, the tendency toward health afflictions is more severe. As the specific elements are upset in a person's chart, particular diseases can be noted.

Ayurveda condenses the five elements into three major groups. Ayurveda's basic view is that all of life—people, food, creatures, environment, and diseases—are combinations of three elementals: air or vata, fire or pitta, and earth (with some water), which is called kapha. When these three constitutional elements are balanced, one is healthy. Illness is defined as an imbalance or excess of these elements. All health problems can be traced to defects of one or more elements or doshas.

Below is a discussion of each Ayurvedic quality.

Vata

Elementals: Air or wind (with some Akasha or space)

Planets and Signs: Mercury, Saturn, weak Moon, and Venus; also, Rahu can act like Saturn. In addition, the signs ruled by these planets: Gemini, Virgo, Capricorn, Aquarius, a weak Cancer, Libra, and Taurus.

Vata is a quality of life that is related to the air element. It governs all the activities in the body. Everything moves, or blows, on the currents of vata or air. Vata qualities are: light (as air), dry, cold, and variable. People who have a predominance of vata, as indicated by the dominant planets in their chart, are generally thin and quick-moving. They learn and forget quickly, and are subject to quick changes in feeling. Vata, when out of balance, expresses itself in poor digestion with gas, dry skin, cold limbs, cracking joints, fitful sleeping, emotional swings, exhaustion, overactivity, worry, and nervousness. Many imbalances have vata at their root. Vata people are like birds flying around.

Pitta

Elementals: Fire or heat

Planets and Signs: Sun and Mars, also Ketu can act like Mars. In addition, the signs ruled by these planets: Aries, Leo, and Scorpio.

Pitta is a life force that is related to the energy of fire. Pitta consumes. It is related to strong digestion and hunger, heat or redness in the body, clear speech and thought, motivation, and warmth of expression. Anger, frustration, exasperation, impatience, and extreme hunger are signs that pitta is out of balance in your body. Pitta people have a medium body build—not too muscular, not too thin. Pitta expresses itself in ailments such as indigestion, ulcers, rashes, fevers, cuts, wounds, bruises, redness, and other inflammatory conditions. Pittas are like lions.

Kapha

Elementals: Earth (and some water)

Planets and Signs: Moon, Jupiter, and Venus; also, the signs ruled by these planets; Cancer, Sagittarius, Pisces, Taurus, and Libra.

Kapha is a bodily constitution that is derived from the combination of earth and a little bit of the water elements. Kapha is mostly viewed as earthy, so it governs the strength and structure of the body in general. Being watery, it shows itself in imbalances such as fluid buildup, fat, colds, coughs, congestion, general stagnation, and lethargy. Kapha people are either calm and balanced or lazy and indulgent. Kaphas are strongly built and have endurance. Kaphas are like elephants.

Looking at the planets occupying the rising sign, and the signs occupied by the Moon and the Sun, gives us more specific clues as to our Ayurvedic body type. For example, a person with Aries rising, or the Moon or Sun in Aries, will have pitta or fiery tendencies. Also, if Mars is located in the first house or with the Moon or Sun, we get a similar disposition. Planets transiting the Lagna, Moon, or Sun will modify the body type temporarily. The current dasa/bhukti (time periods explained in chapter 13) will further influence the body's constitution. If a person is in Mars dasa, or if Mars is transiting over the Lagna or Moon or Sun, then the person will be more pitta (fiery) during that time. This understanding helps us know why an Ayurvedic physician can give us a different dosha reading when we get a pulse diagnosis or other Ayurvedic analysis. In general, the planets associated with the Lagna give the most information on body type. Body type is also a good tool to help identify rising signs during the process of chart rectification (see chapter 11).

The current dasa/bhukti cycle, along with the transits, will modify a person's Ayurvedic constitution according to the nature of that cycle. Vedic astrology gives value to Ayurveda by determining the current planetary cycles the patient is going through. As a general rule, the 6th house is called the Roga Bhava or the house of disease, most specifically acute or short-term diseases. The sign representing the 6th house in a specific chart will give significant clues as to the types of disease that person may be vulnerable to. You will also be able to read health significations from the planets that occupy that 6th house, and those that have a significant aspect on the 6th. This 6th sign/house will show the dosha that will be the primary culprit in disease. For example, if Saturn is in the 6th house in Capricorn, the person will have a tendency toward vata disorders. The 8th house also contributes to long-term diseases in a similar fashion.

In addition to examining the 6th and 8th houses, a Vedic astrologer and/or Ayurvedic Vaidya must look at the whole chart, noting any additional information that comes from the ascendant and any specific sign that is highly afflicted. Again, diseases tend to spring up in the dasa/bhukti periods of these planets, as well as under specific transits of these disease-inflicting planets. With the advance warning of Vedic astrology, a person can take the correct Ayurvedic preventative health measures to ward off a disease, or create a state where the disease will be of less impact and duration.

CHAPTER TWENTY

VASTU: THE SCIENCE OF SPACE

Vedic astrology is the science of time. Vastu is the science of space. The word *Vastu* comes from the Sanskrit word *Vas* (dwell). Vastu is sometimes called Stapatya Veda and is mentioned in the Atharva Veda. At the time of publication, Vastu is just gaining interest in the West. Vastu is a field of Vedic knowledge that tells us the best way to arrange the space around us to generate maximum effectiveness and prosperity. Feng Shui, the Chinese system of placement, is a cousin of Vastu.

In my studies of Vastu, my primary teacher, Niranjan Babu of Bangalore, India, told me, "Buildings have as much life as a human being. A building is a rhythmic instrument having life." Basically, a house is like a musical instrument that plays all the laws of nature. Many astrologers whom I talked to in India said they believed that up to 80 percent of the favorable or unfavorable influences on your life could be readily attributed to the good or bad influences generated by your house and its environs. Another analogy that I like is comparing the house to a seed (bija) planted in the ground (kshetra). Everything in that house/seed does well, if properly set up or planted.

It is very awe-inspiring to look at the scientific diagrams and satellite photos that give evidence of the vast interplay of solar radiation coming in from the east to the earth, mixing with the spiraling cascades of electromagnetic fields radiating north and south from the poles. The magnetosphere, produced by the earth's magnetic field, is a defensive sheath that wards off most charged particles—ions and electrons—flowing out from the Sun. The magnetosphere collects and circulates cosmic particles that are able to penetrate inside this magnetic barrier.

There are a variety of eruptions raining down from the Sun, as well as disturbances in space that can force particles and energy into the magnetosphere. These solar forces can create conditions for storms that will knock out satellite communications and even disrupt electrical power grids on the ground. When these entrapped particles descend along the lines of the earth's magnetic field and impact the atmosphere, they create the shimmering, undulating aurora borealis.

We live in an amazing matrix of forces—many of which the Vedic literature hints at but Western science has yet to discover or understand. It's easy to see that if we are in proper alignment with these forces, much like being oriented correctly with a river's current, we will benefit. If we are misaligned and out of phase with the solar and geomagnetic forces, we can imagine and experience how dysfunctional and arrhythmic our life can become.

Diagram of the Sun's solar energy (left) flowing in
and merging with the earth's magnetosphere (right)

The Shastras, or sacred texts, describe the core ingredients of Vastu as the five elements of earth (bhumi), water (jal), light or fire (agni or tejas), air (vayu), and undifferentiated space (akasha). These are the same elements that form the basis of Ayurveda, and stand at the foundations of Vedic astrology. We are made of these elements and so are our buildings. If we want to live harmoniously, the materials of our buildings should also radiate harmony. Every brick in a wall and every stone in a foundation is like a musical note in the larger symphony of our dwelling.

A person flourishes effortlessly if their planets are arranged harmoniously in their astrological birth chart. An event is fruitful when started at the time when Vedic astrology calculates the planets to be favorably placed in the sky. We can compare our bodies to planets. In Vastu, we have an edge. We get to decide where to place the "planet" of our bodies and how to set it so that it is aspected correctly by other influences. In Vedic astrology, we orient ourselves and our behavior in terms of time. In Vastu, we orient our physical bodies and their energies to their best possible positions in architectural structures and in space. It's as if we get to create our own chart—and that chart is our house with its various rooms and directions.

Home Ownership

Vedic astrology comes to the aid of Vastu in matters connected with determining the following areas:

- Capacity to finance and own a home

- The number of homes to be owned (real estate investing, managing, etc.)

- The quality, size, and best location for the home

The fourth house of a Vedic astrological chart is the house associated with real estate. (It's interesting to note the convention in astrology to call the place where a planet resides a house.) Mars is the karaka, or indicator, for loans and for obtaining buildings. Saturn is associated with large pieces of undeveloped land or land that might be used for agriculture, and Venus indicates the elegance of the land and buildings we might obtain. The overall strength of the chart would indicate the level of ownership, after we see that a house could be obtained to start with. The ruler of the 4th and the planets occupying or aspecting the 4th tell us the nature of our ownership.

A person with malefic and weak connections to the 4th will often not feel "at home" in any specific place and may move from building to building over time. If they buy real estate, they need to be careful that they buy in the right location for the right price, since they have more obstructions to the favorable ownership of a house. These persons with afflicted 4th houses might not enjoy the "burden" of home ownership and elect a lesser form such as a condominium, or may forget ownership altogether and rent or lease. In the worst case, they would be homeless.

People with the benefic planets of Venus or Jupiter in the 4th are generally home builders and nesters. Cancer is well known in astrology as a home builder. These Moon-ruled persons want the security and nurturing of a home, and they want a place where "mothering" can take place. Mars, well placed in the chart, shows a person's ability to benefit from home ownership. I have found that people with Rahu in the 4th do well with real estate for short periods of time. Ketu in the 4th often leads to intermittent stays in a location. Ketu can even cause breakage and cracks in the buildings these persons buy. In chapters 5 and 6, you can read more about planets in the 4th house and planets in Cancer to get more information about planets and home ownership.

One rule of Vedic astrology says that you can look in a chart at the house opposite the house being considered to get additional information on any indication. In this case, you can also find home information in a person's chart by looking at the 10th house, its ruler, and planets occupying or aspecting the 10th.

Questions about the Timing of Events
Associated with Home Ownership

- When should a person take out a loan, open and close escrow, start building a house, or the like?

- What time should be selected to begin the major actions for constructing a home (selecting and buying the land, breaking ground, setting the foundation, etc.)?

- When should the completed house be entered for the first time to begin residence (Graha Prevesh), or when should a building be inaugurated or opened to the public?

I have found transits of Mars over the 4th or 10th houses in a birth chart to be favorable times to buy or sell a house. I have found that transits counted from the Lagna give more results, although positions from the Moon should also be considered. Transits of the

Sun over the 4th or 10th from the Lagna or Moon are also favorable for short-term identification of a sell or buy period. Longer term, I find that most people will either move or remodel their homes when Saturn transits the 4th or 10th houses in a birth chart. A transit of Ketu over the 4th often compels a person to modify their home in some way—perhaps redecorate, or get a Vastu consultation to rearrange their living space. They might also feel the need to move.

In addition, the other planetary transits should be favorable, and the person should be in a favorable dasa period. There should also be a strong intention to buy or sell. If the person is uncommitted about moving, then nothing happens. I often find that people have difficulty selling a house if they let a relative, say a son or daughter, live there "until the house sells." Obviously, that family member is not going to be enthusiastic about the sale of the house since it means they will be out on the street following the sale. It's best to have all emotional connections to the house severed in order to sell it. Give your children a nice place to stay, or help them relocate upon the sale of the house. Things will move faster this way.

There are specific times listed in major Muhurtha works indicating when the various stages of home development should take place. I will leave it to you to consult these books, such as the *Brihat Samhita*, *Muhurtha Chintamani*, *Hora Sara*, and *Kalaprakshika* for the details. Niranjan Babu's book on Vastu contains useful information in this area as well.

Organizing Your Space

The information in the two charts on pages 348 and 349 is intended to give you a flavor of the approach to Vastu. This information can give you a beginning idea of how Vastu works, but Vastu contains much more detail that needs to be covered in a separate work. I believe that everyone should have a Vastu consultation before building, buying, or remodeling, and I think it would be wise for everyone to determine whether their current residence is set with the correct Vastu limits. A lot of improvement is possible from living within correct Vastu.

In Vastu, the ideal house floor plan is divided into 81 squares. Each of these squares represents a force of nature, otherwise known as a deity. The corners of the square are ruled by the eight directions, accompanied by a particular ruling deity. The middle of the square is the place of Brahma or the Brahma sthana. The body of the Vastu Purusha, the overall force that keeps your home balanced, is overlaid upon this diagram. The head of the Vastu Purusha points to the northeast, and his feet are located in the southwest. The house, if properly aligned to each of these quadrants and subquadrants, will be a place of peace, prosperity, and a source of happiness for all family members.

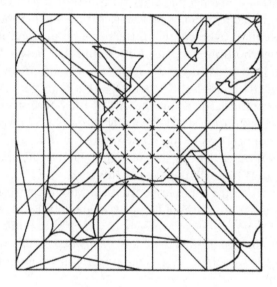

Vastu Purusha Mandala

Vastu Shastra says that everything on earth, in one form or another, is influenced by the nine planets. Every home is also under the influence of the governing planets. Different planets have beneficial influences on certain rooms. Each of the nine planets, except Ketu, guards a direction and is called the Ashatadikpalas. Each direction is ruled by a specific deity and is believed to enhance a specific element of daily living. The following diagram introduces you to the directions and their effects. To see how your dwelling compares, lay your floor plan over this diagram and see if your layout matches. If you have a lot of mismatches, then you might want to consider seeking a Vastu expert and making corrections.

Northwest Moon	*North* Mercury	*Northeast* Jupiter
Vayu, Lord of Wind	Kubera, Lord of Wealth	Eashana (Ishana), Supreme Lord
For Homes: Guests, storage , maids, garage, pets and other animals, toilet, garage, second choice for kitchen	*For Homes:* Storage of valuables, mirrors on north wall, children's room (with heads west for sleep; face east to study), living room, basement	*For Homes:* Prayer/Puja room, religious shrine, open porch, living room, no toilets, no staircases, okay for basement
For Businesses: Employee lounge, storage, toilets. Products sell faster when stored/presented in this area.	*For Businesses:* Safe, storage of valuables	*For Businesses:* Meeting rooms, money handlers, accountants, cash register; no heavy items here; final release of product
West Saturn	*Center/Brahma Sthana*	*East* Sun
Varuna, Lord of Waters	Akasha or undifferentiated space Brahma, Lord of Creation	Surya, Lord of Health, or Indra, Chief of the Gods
For Homes: Children's room (with heads west to sleep; face east to study), study area, dining room	*For Homes:* Silent area with no human activity; courtyard; area for religious shrines	*For Homes:* Bath, dining room, storage for liquids (ghee, oil, milk, etc), wash room, children's room, living room, family room, big windows, basement, mirrors on east wall
For Businesses: Build products here	*For Businesses:* No business activity; shrine for business	*For Businesses:* Storage of liquids
Southwest Rahu	*South* Mars	*Southeast* Venus
Nirriti, Lord of Dissolution	Yama, Lord of Death	Agni, Lord of Fire
For Homes: Master bedroom, storage for valuables, heavy items, no pujas in bedrooms, no toilets	*For Homes:* Dining room, bedroom, no main entrances	*For Homes:* Kitchen (face east to cook), fireplace, major electrical appliances, computers, garage (best if separate from house), weapons, exercise area, toilet (if not in NW), no bedrooms
For Businesses: Administrators, owners, business planning and development	*For Businesses:* No main entrances	*For Businesses:* Electrical equipment, furnaces, stoves, computers, power plants

Minimum Vastu Considerations

While we strive to have the best possible Vastu, it might not seem feasible to abandon our present dwelling, or our circumstances might give us limited choices in living conditions. If so, we need to try to attain at least a minimum set of Vastu requirements to help us. The minimum factors to be considered (in order) are:

1. Locate the master bedroom in the southwest or south.

2. Place the kitchen in the southeast, or second best, in the northwest.

3. Enter the house from the east or northeast. Avoid south-facing doors from other directions.

4. Keep more windows and other openings on the east and north. Put mirrors on east and north walls.

5. Sleep in the southwest corner of your bedroom, with your head to the south or east. The bed should not be up against the walls.

6. Keep the north and east sections of rooms as free and uncluttered as possible.

7. Place life-supporting and positive images, paintings, and decorations in your rooms. War masks, weapons, cactuses, and sad or grotesque pictures that depict death and negative aspects of life pull down the energy in your house.

8. Try to get a square or rectangular building on a square or rectangular plot. The house should sit square to the cardinal directions. A house at an angle greater than 10 to 12 degrees off the north/south axis is unfavorable.

There has not been enough space in this book to do much more than introduce you to some of the major concepts of Vastu. I am relaying to you what I have learned from my own research and from the knowledge that Niranjan Babu was generous enough to share with me. You will see in the next few years that Vastu will grow to be a major influence in Western home building. As a Vedic process for right and natural living, Vastu will soon join its companion systems of Vedic astrology and Ayurveda.

APPENDIX

Nama Nakshatra Prasna

The table on the following page relates to chapter 13's discussion of relating name sounds to astrological significations.

Nama Nakshatra Prasna

W.Levacy 10-12-98

Meena — Pisces

Nakshatra	Degrees	Syllable
PuBhdPd	00-00 / 03-20	Dee
Uttara Bhadra Pada (Saturn)	03-20 / 06-40	Doo
	06-40 / 10-00	Tuh
	10-00 / 13-20	Jha
	13-20 / 16-40	Jya
	16-40 / 20-00	Day
Revati (Saturn)	20-00 / 23-20	Doh
	23-20 / 26-40	Cha
	26-40 / 30-00	Chee

Mesha — Aries

Nakshatra	Degrees	Syllable
	00-00 / 03-20	Chu
Ashwini (Ketu)	03-20 / 06-40	Chay
	06-40 / 10-00	Cho
	10-00 / 13-20	Lah
	13-20 / 16-40	Lee
Bharani (Venus)	16-40 / 20-00	Loo
	20-00 / 23-20	Lay
	23-20 / 26-40	Loh
Krittika	26-40 / 30-00	Ah

Vrishaba — Taurus

Nakshatra	Degrees	Syllable
	00-00 / 03-20	Ee
Krittika (Sun)	03-20 / 06-40	Oo
	06-40 / 10-00	Ay
	10-00 / 13-20	Oh
Rohini (Moon)	13-20 / 16-40	Vah
	16-40 / 20-00	Vee
	20-00 / 23-20	Voo
Mrigashira (Mars)	23-20 / 26-40	Vay
	26-40 / 30-00	Vo

Mithuna — Gemini

Nakshatra	Degrees	Syllable
Mriga Shira (Mars)	00-00 / 03-20	Kah
	03-20 / 06-40	Kee
	06-40 / 10-00	Koo
Aridra (Rahu)	10-00 / 13-20	Gha
	13-20 / 16-40	Nga
	16-40 / 20-00	Cha
Punar Vasu (Jupiter)	20-00 / 23-20	Kay
	23-20 / 26-40	Ko
	26-40 / 30-00	Hah

Kumba — Aquarius

Nakshatra	Degrees	Syllable
Dhanishta (Mars)	00-00 / 03-20	Goo
	03-20 / 06-40	Gay
	06-40 / 10-00	Goh
Satabisha (Rahu)	10-00 / 13-20	Sah
	13-20 / 16-40	See
	16-40 / 20-00	Soo
Purva Bhadra Pada (Jupiter)	20-00 / 23-20	Say
	23-20 / 26-40	Soh
	26-40 / 30-00	Dah

Karka — Cancer

Nakshatra	Degrees	Syllable
Punarvasu	00-00 / 03-20	Hee
	03-20 / 06-40	Hoo
Pushyami (Saturn)	06-40 / 10-00	Hay
	10-00 / 13-20	Hoh
	13-20 / 16-40	Dah
	16-40 / 20-00	Dee
Aslesha (Mercury)	20-00 / 23-20	Doo
	23-20 / 26-40	Day
	26-40 / 30-00	Doh

Makara — Capricorn

Nakshatra	Degrees	Syllable
Uttara Shada (Sun)	00-00 / 03-20	Boh
	03-20 / 06-40	Jah
	06-40 / 10-00	Jee
	10-00 / 13-20	Joo
Shravana (Moon)	13-20 / 16-40	Jay
	16-40 / 20-00	Joh
	20-00 / 23-20	Guh
Dhanishta (Mars)	23-20 / 26-40	Gah
	26-40 / 30-00	Gee

Leo

Nakshatra	Degrees	Syllable
	00-00 / 03-20	Mah
Magha (Ketu)	03-20 / 06-40	Mee
	06-40 / 10-00	Moo
	10-00 / 13-20	May
	13-20 / 16-40	Moh
Purva Phalguni (Venus)	16-40 / 20-00	Tah
	20-00 / 23-20	Tee
	23-20 / 26-40	Too
UtPhgun	26-40 / 30-00	Tay

Dhanus — Sagittarius

Nakshatra	Degrees	Syllable
Moola (Ketu)	00-00 / 03-20	Yay
	03-20 / 06-40	Yoh
	06-40 / 10-00	Bah
	10-00 / 13-20	Bee
Purva Shada (Venus)	13-20 / 16-40	Boo
	16-40 / 20-00	Dah
	20-00 / 23-20	Pah
	23-20 / 26-40	Dah
UtShada	26-40 / 30-00	Bay

Vrishika — Scorpio

Nakshatra	Degrees	Syllable
Vishaka	00-00 / 03-20	Toh
	03-20 / 06-40	Nah
Anuradha (Saturn)	06-40 / 10-00	Nee
	10-00 / 13-20	Noo
	13-20 / 16-40	Nay
	16-40 / 20-00	Noh
Jyeshta (Mercury)	20-00 / 23-20	Yah
	23-20 / 26-40	Yee
	26-40 / 30-00	Yoo

Tula — Libra

Nakshatra	Degrees	Syllable
Chitta (Mars)	00-00 / 03-20	Rah
	03-20 / 06-40	Ree
	06-40 / 10-00	Roo
Swati (Rahu)	10-00 / 13-20	Ray
	13-20 / 16-40	Roh
	16-40 / 20-00	Tah
Vishaka (Jupiter)	20-00 / 23-20	Tee
	23-20 / 26-40	Too
	26-40 / 30-00	Tay

Kanya — Virgo

Nakshatra	Degrees	Syllable
Uttara Phalguni (Sun)	00-00 / 03-20	Toh
	03-20 / 06-40	Pah
	06-40 / 10-00	Pee
Hasta (Moon)	10-00 / 13-20	Poo
	13-20 / 16-40	Shah
	16-40 / 20-00	Nuh
	20-00 / 23-20	Tuh
Chitta (Mars)	23-20 / 26-40	Pay
	26-40 / 30-00	Poh

Sign letter groupings (center boxes)

- **Pisces:** T, DDDD, CH,CH, JH, JYA
- **Aries:** CH,CH,CH, LLLLL, A
- **Taurus:** E, OO, A, O, VVVVV or WWWWW
- **Gemini:** KKKKKK, CH, H, NGA
- **Aquarius:** SSSSS, GGG, D
- **Cancer:** HHHHH, DDDDD
- **Capricorn:** JJJJJ, GGG, B
- **Leo:** MMMMM, TTTT
- **Sagittarius:** BBBB, YY, DD, P
- **Scorpio:** NNNNN, YYY, T
- **Libra:** RRRRR, TTTT
- **Virgo:** PPPPP, SH, N, TT

Basic Pronunciation of Sanskrit Astrological Terms

Note that pronunciation of the planets and the signs may vary by individual astrologer and by the author of a specific Vedic astrology work. You might see the final vowel dropped off; for example, Budha may be pronounced Budh. This might be attributed to the differences in dialects between northern and southern India, and in pronunciation variances between the root language of Sanskrit and current native language pronunciations, such as in Hindi.

Also, be aware that there is no standard application of a phonetic system for describing pronunciation of Sanskrit in the English language. The letter s that sounds like sh can be represented as either an s or an sh. Originally there was a dot under the s to indicate its sh pronunciation, but frequently it is not typeset in this manner. In fact, certain words like dasa, Parasara, and navamsa are spelled with an s, but are pronounced with a sh sound, i.e., dasha, Parashara, and Navamsha. I have decided to leave things alone and just make you aware of this difference. Another phonetic variable is the use of the letters ph like Uttara Phalguni. The ph is not pronounced with an f sound as in English. This Sanskrit consonant is more like the letter p expressed with a lot of air behind it. Linguists call this a "plosive." There is no f letter or sound in Sanskrit. Nor is there a straight v sound. It is more a combination of a v and a w. In English, you can pronounce it as either v or w, and you'll see it written in these two ways in various works. Also, when the letter v is used, it is sometimes replaced by a b; for example, vasant meaning "springtime" is sometimes spelled and pronounced basant.

Translations and Pronunciations

Nine Planets:	Navgrahas	*Nahv Grah' hahs* (nine that which grasps)
1. Sun	Surya Ravi	*Soo'ree ah* *Rah' vee*
2. Moon	Chandra Soma	*Chahn' drah* *Soh' mah*
3. Mars	Kuja Mangala	*Koo jah'* *Mahng' gah lah*
4. Mercury	Budha	*Bhoo dah'*
5. Jupiter	Guru Brihaspati	*Goo roo'* *Bree huss' puh tee*
6. Venus	Sukra	*Shoo' kruh*

7. Saturn	Shani	*Shah' nee*
8. N. Node	Rahu	*Rah' hoo*
9. S. Node	Ketu	*Keh too'*

Signs:	Rasi	*Rah' shee (a heap)*
1. Aries	Mesha	*Mee shah'*
2. Taurus	Vrishabha	*Vree' shah bah*
3. Gemini	Mithuna	*Mee toon nah'*
4. Cancer	Kataka	*Kah tah kah'*
5. Leo	Simha	*Sim' hah*
6. Virgo	Kanya	*Kahn yah'*
7. Libra	Thula	*Too lah'*
8. Scorpio	Vrishika	*Vrih' shih kah*
9. Sagittarius	Dhanus	*Dhah' noose*
10. Capricorn	Makara	*Mah' kah rah*
11. Aquarius	Kumbha	*Koom bah'*
12. Pisces	Meena	*Mee' nah*

Houses:	Bhava	*Bhah' vah* (mood)
	Sthana	*Stah' nah* (place)
1. Body	Thanu	*Tah' noo*
2. Wealth	Dhana	*Dah nah'*
3. Siblings	Sahaja	*Sah hah jah'*
4. Mother	Matru	*Mah' tru*
5. Children	Putra	*Poo' trah*
6. Enemies	Ripu	*Ree' poo*
7. Partners	Vivaha	*Vee vah' hah*
	Kalatra	*Kah lah' trah*
8. Life	Ayu	*Ah' yoo*
9. Fortune	Bhagya	*Bha' gyuh*
10. Career	Dharma	*Dar' mah*
11. Gains	Labya	*Lahb' yah*
12. Enlightenment	Moksha	*Mohk' shah*

Moon Signs:	Nakshatra	*Nahk shah' trah* (not moving)
1. Ashwini		*Ahsh wee' nee*
2. Bharani		*Bhah' rah nee*
3. Krittika		*Krih' tih kah*
4. Rohini		*Roh hee' nee*
5. Mrigasira		*Mri gah sheer' ah*
6. Ardra		*Ar' drah* *Ah rih' drah*
7. Punarvasu		*Poo nar vah' soo'*
8. Pushya		*Poosh' yah*
9. Aslesha		*Ahs slay' shah*
10. Magha		*Mahg' kah*
11. Purva Phalguni		*Purvah pal' goo nee* *Purvah fal' goo nee*
12. Uttara Phalguni		*oo tah rah' pal' goo nee* *oo tah rah' fal goo nee*
13. Hasta		*Hah stah'*
14. Chitra		*Chih trah'*
15. Swati		*Swah' tee*
16. Visakha		*Vee shah' kah*
17. Anuradha		*h noor ah' dah*
18. Jyeshta		*Jaysh' tah*
19. Mula		*Moo' lah*
20. Purvashada		*Poor vah shah' dah*
21. Uttarashada		*oo tah rah shah' dah*
22. Shravana		*Shrah' vah nah*
23. Dhanistha		*Dah neesh' tah*
24. Satabisha		*Shah tah bee' shah*
25. Purva Bhadrapada		*Pur' vah bah' drah pah' dah*
26. Uttara Bhadrapada		*oo' tah rah bah' drah pah dah*
27. Revati		*Ray' vah tee*

Other Terms:

Lagna (ascendant)	*Lahg' nah*
Parasara	*Par ah' shah rah*
Dasa	*Dah' shah*
Bhukti	*Bhook' tee*
Antaradasa	*Ahn' tah rah dah shah*
Vimshottari	*Vim shoh' tah ree*
Jyotish	*Joh' tish*
Navamsa	*Nahv ahm' shah*
Prasna	*Prahsh' nah*
Ayanamsa	*Eye ahn ahm' shah*
Gochara	*Goh chah' rah*
Karaka	*Kah' rah kah*

Recommended Course for Further Study

These are the topic areas I recommend that you focus on to continue your study of Vedic astrology—now that you have mastered the basic/intermediate content of this book, you are ready to study the following. Most of these were introduced in this book:

- Lunar information, especially strong and weak moon phases
- How to use shadbala for determining strength of planets as well as favorable/unfavorable indicators such as Exaltation, Debilitation, Own Sign, and Moolatrikona
- How to use sarvashtakavarga
- Familiarization of Sanskrit astrological terms (use glossary)
- Correct pronunciation of Sanskrit terms
- Principles of forecasting
- More detail on planets, such as: Varna, Colors, Gems, Shapes, Metals, Length of Influence, Habitats, Dhatus, Senses, Cabinet, Strengths, Percent Good or Bad, Year of Influence, Deities, Height, Yagya Type, Tastes, Power Time, Body Parts, Days of the Week, Gender, Gunas, Directions, Dasa Length, Motions, Being, Yogakarakas, Ayurvedic Doshas, Rulers, Bhadaka, Planetary War, Avasthas or Planetary States, Combustion, Retrogrades
- Planetary friendships (Graha Mitra): Natural, Temporary, Combined

- More detail on signs:
  - Bhutas or Elements: Fire (Agni), Earth (Prithivi), Air (Vayu), and Water (Jala)
  - Quality of Activity: Moveable (Chara), Fixed (Sthira), Dual (Dwishwabhava)
  - Quality of Life (Guna): Pure (Satwa), Active (Rajas), Impure (Tamas)
  - Castes: Priest (Brahmin), Warrior (Kshatriya), Vaisya (Merchant), Shudra (Worker)
  - Eight Compass Directions
  - Direction of Rising: Headfirst (Sirshodaya), Feetfirst (Pristhodaya), Bothways (Ubhayadaya)
  - Types of Being: Quadrupeds (Chatuspada), Humans (Jiva), Reptile or Insect (Keeta)
  - Divisions of Kalapurusha: (From Head down to Feet)
  - Level of Being: Mineral (Dhatu), Vegetable (Mula), Living Beings (Jiva)
  - Length of Rising: Long Ascension, Short Ascension
  - Special Classifications: Twin or Double-Bodied Signs, Fruitful and Barren Signs, Odd/Even, Male/Female, Cruel/Gentle, Day/Night
- More detail on houses: Bhava Chalita chart format
- Sounds associated with signs/nakshatras
- More on rising signs: favorable and unfavorable planets by rising sign
- More on aspects: Panaphara, Apoklima, etc.
- Divisional charts (15 special chart types beyond the rasi— see chapter 10)
- Gochara or transits: transits from Lagna and Moon; Sade Sati
- Dasa to 3rd level
- Prasna or horary
- Muhurtha or electional astrology
- Chart rectification: correcting birth times
- Compatibility: matching charts
- Mundane or world astrology
- Varshaphal (birthday chart)
- Yogas or special planetary combinations
- More on Nakshatras or moon signs
- Ashtakavarga (a sign transit calculation system)
- Introduction to Ayurveda
- Introduction to Vastu
- More detail on dasas to 4th and 5th level

- Remedial measures
- Gem recommendations
- Compatibility (baby naming)
- Beginning astronomy: the solar system, ecliptic, equator, longitude and latitude, sidereal and tropical zodiac
- How to use a sidereal ephemeris or the Vedic panchanga

For Advanced Study: Good Things to Know

After you have learned the topics listed above, I suggest that you master the following. Consult more advanced books—many of which are listed in the bibliography.

- Lunar-based astrology: Tithis, Ritus (seasons), Solar months, Lunar months, eclipses
- Vimshopaka (another way of judging the favorable or unfavorable quality of planets)
- Shyanadi Bhava (an additional house system developed by Parasara)
- Sudarshana Chakra (a summary way to judge planets from the Lagna, Moon, and Sun)
- Upagrahas (Auxiliary planets or astronomical points beyond the standard 9 Vedic planets)
- Advanced use of navamsa (a one-ninth chart division)
- Kuta agreements (special formulas for verifying compatibility)
- Chandra Vasta, Velas (special states of the Moon)
- Saka New Year chart (a way to analyze trends for the coming year)
- Omens
- Advanced remedial measures
- Understanding the Ayanamsa
- Advanced planets (or grahas): myths and features of the planets
- Medical astrology
  - Onset, duration and end of disease
  - Advanced use of Ayurveda in astrology
- Finding location or direction from the dasas
- Time divisions: from yugas to ghatis
- Drekkana of Parasara
- Advanced gochara (transits); Vedha and Lata
- Additional planetary period or dasa systems: Chara, Yogini, Jaimini

- Length of life: Balarishta and Ayurdaya
- Peripheral predictive systems (at least know of them)
  - Swara or breath analysis
  - Face reading
  - Astropalmistry
  - Nadi systems: Brighu, Dhurva etc.
  - Hindu religious festivals vs. astrological date selection
- The controversies of Vedic astrology scholars (points where scholars differ)
- Animal astrology
- Stri Jataka or female horoscopy
- Concepts on development of consciousness

Subject Matter Areas for Most Frequently Asked Questions (FAQs):

The topics listed below are the types of questions most frequently asked by my clients.

- Finances: prospects for profits, when to invest, type and time of business transactions
- Compatibility: marriage, business, personal, family. Is he/she the right one?
- Health: prevention, exposure areas, onset and duration of disease
- Health of family members. (Will my mother be all right?)
- Career: starting or ending, finding new career directions, asking for raises/promotions
- Educational direction, changes in educational goals
- Type of career, or life purpose
- Times for romance; who and what to look for
- Marriage: starting, ending, or not at all (celibate or monastic life)
- Spirituality; balancing with material life
- Travel/moving/going on vacations and retreats
- Residence: Where should I live?
- When to buy or sell a home
- Vastu: layout of house
- Conception: Starting a family, adding a new member, number of children
- Remedial measures/corrective actions: How can I improve things?

Further Characteristics of Planets (see chapter 2)

Planet	Sex	Guna	Directions of Strength (Digbala)	Dasa Length (in years)	Color
Sun	Male	Satvic	South (10th)	6	Dark red or copper color
Moon	Female	Satvic	North (4th)	10	White
Mars	Male	Tamasic	South (10th)	7	Bright medium red
Mercury	Female Eunuch	Rajasic	East (Lagna)	17	Dark green
Jupiter	Male	Satvic	East (Lagna)	16	Golden or creamy
Venus	Female	Rajasic	North (4th)	20	Silvery white
Saturn	Male Eunuch	Tamasic	West (7th or descendant)	19	Coal black
Rahu	Female	Tamasic	-	18	Variegated
Ketu	Eunuch	Tamasic	-	18	Striped or spotted

Sex of planets indicates the predominance of energy—feminine, masculine, or neutral—in a chart.

Guna is the quality of a planet in terms of its purity (Satva = pure), the spur to action (Rajas = active), or inertia (Tamas = impure). The quality of a person's life will be influenced by the quantity and quality of gunas delivered by the planets in a chart.

Direction and Location of Strength (Digbala) indicates the house position where a planet gains additional strength. These directions are where the person will gain benefit in life, especially during the dasa/bhukti period or during a major transit.

Dasa Length: According to Parasara, each planet exerts an influence over a specific span of time in a person's life. Parasara tells us that a person's life cycle can be 120 years, comprised of several planetary periods or dasas (see chapter 13). The nature of this dasa span of time will reflect the favorable or unfavorable condition of the planet as seen in the birth chart.

Colors: Authors differ as to the colors of planets.

Planet	Type of Being	Length of Influence	Habitats	Yogakaraka (Rules angle & trine)	Ayurvedic Body Type (or Dosha)
Sun	Moola	6 months (ayana)	Temples and holy shrines	None	Pitta
Moon	Moola	48 minutes (muhurtha)	Wet or moist locales	None	Kapha or vata
Mars	Dhatu	1 day & night	Dry, hot, or fiery locations	Cancer & Leo	Pitta
Mercury	Jeeva	2 months (ritu or season)	Places of play & amusement	None	Vata
Jupiter	Jeeva	1 month	Banks and storehouses of money & valuables	None	Kapha
Venus	Moola	15 days (paksha or fortnight)	Bedroom and places for sex & pleasure	Capricorn & Aquarius	Kapha or vata
Saturn	Dhatu	1 year	Unclean, run-down areas	Taurus & Libra	Vata
Rahu	Dhatu	8 months	Foreign, desolate areas (remote forests, deserts)	None	Pitta
Ketu	Jeeva	3 months	Areas of mixed of influences (a bit all of the above)	None	Pitta or vata

Type of Being can be used in Prasna charts to help indicate the nature of the object held in the mind of the questioner; Moola = vegetable, Dhatu = mineral, and Jeeva = animal. Prasna charts are charts an astrologer constructs to answer a specific question; see chapter 13.

Length of Influence is used in Prasna to indicate the span of time for an event indicated in the chart constructed at the "birth" time of the person's question.

Habitats, or Abodes, of planets are used in Prasna to help identify the location of the object that is a part of the question given to the astrologer.

Yogakaraka is the name given to a planet that rules both an angle and a trine in a birth chart. This planet is said to indicate prosperity for the person, especially during the dasa/bhukti period of that Yogakaraka planet.

Ayurvedic Body Type, or Dosha: This concept is explained in chapter 19. It is held that people can be divided into three major body types or doshas, which will reflect their health and action in the world. Vata is an intellectually oriented and airy disposition. Some writers call this Wind. Pitta is an action-oriented and fiery disposition. Some writers call this Bile. Kapha is more stable and practical, and shows an earthy or grounded disposition. Some writers refer to this as Cold, Mucus, or Shleshma.

Planet	Vara	Direction	Dhatus	Signification
Sun	Sunday	East	Bones	Soul or individual ego
Moon	Monday	Northwest	Blood, Fluids	Mind or perception
Mars	Tuesday	South	Marrow, muscle	Courage and action
Mercury	Wednesday	North	Skin	Speech and discrimination
Jupiter	Thursday	Northeast	Fat	Pure knowledge and joy of wisdom
Venus	Friday	Southeast	Semen/ova	Reproductive strength and beauty
Saturn	Saturday	West	Nerves	Focus on sorrow from lack of discipline
Rahu	None	Southwest	None	Foreigners and strangeness
Ketu	None	Heaven	None	Mystics and change

Vara, or Ruler of the Day of the Week, indicates the day of the week that is ruled by a planet. Each day will carry the influence of its governing planet.

Directions, or Eight Compass Points, are useful in determining what direction a person should take. Directions are used in Prasna. They are very useful in conjunction with the dasa/bhukti period, to determine where a person should live or travel.

Dhatus, or Seven Body Elements, help us pinpoint what part of the body might be strong or weak by nature as seen in the birth chart, or by current situation as seen in the Prasna or even the Muhurtha or electional chart (see chapter 15).

Significations indicate the core essence of the planet. Authors disagree or omit data on Rahu and Ketu. Saturn is often represented as the source of sorrow and misery, but is also our ability to remain focused and structured.

Planet	Deity (According to Parasara)	Age of Planets	Shape	Body Part	Five Senses
Sun	Agni (fire)	50	Quadrangle	Head	Sight
Moon	Varuna (water)	70	Round	Face	Taste
Mars	Subramanya (Shiva's son)	16	Cylinder	Chest or trunk	Sight
Mercury	Mahavishnu (Maintainer)	20	Triangle	Hip region	Smell
Jupiter	Indra (Lord of Devas)	30	Ellipse	Belly	Hearing
Venus	Indrani or Sachi Devi (Wife of Indra)	16	Octagon	Reproductive organs	Taste
Saturn	Brahma	100	Tall Rectangle	Thighs	Touch
Rahu	(Some say Durga)	100	Line	Limbs (arms)	Touch
Ketu	(Some say Ganesh)	100	Flag	Limbs (legs)	Sight

Deity: There are many variations on the specific deity that rules over a planet. On one level, the deity can be regarded as a force of nature, or a faint feeling that we perceive within ourselves. In Vedic India, nature was classified in personal forms and with metaphors.

Age (in years): Each planet is given an age as a metaphor to describe its energy and maturity. These ages are approximate and vary by author.

Geometric Shape: In selecting and mounting gemstones, some astrologers recommend a specific shape be associated with the planet being propitiated by the stone.

Body Part: Each planet is held to rule a certain part of the body (the signs also rule parts of the body—see chapter 3). You can also use this information to interpret bodily systems. Saturn also is known to represent paralysis or lameness, often due to nerve damage. The Sun rules the head and is also associated with baldness.

Five Senses: Each of the five human senses will be amplified or reduced by the quality of their signifying planet. If the Sun, for example, is well placed by transit, then the person's eyes should be safe. It could be a good time to do elective eye surgery. A person with a weak Mercury might not have a great sense of smell.

Malefic Planets by Rising Sign (see chapter 12)

Rising Sign	Malefic Planets for That Specific Sign	
1. Aries	Saturn	Rules 10th and 11th houses—11th ruler is bad
	Mercury	Rules 3rd (8th to 8th), and 6th—a dusthana
	Venus	Rules 2nd and 7th—Marakas
2. Taurus	Jupiter	Rules 8th, a dusthana, and 11th, a bad ruler
	Moon	Rules 3rd (8th to 8th). Moon is still exalted, however.
3. Gemini	Mars	Rules 6th, a dusthana, and 11th, a bad ruler.
	Jupiter	Rules 7th and 10th—bad to rule two angles
	Sun	Rules 3rd (8th to 8th)
4. Cancer	Venus	Rules 4th (not good for benefics to rule angles) and 11th, a bad ruler
	Mercury	Rules 3rd (8th to 8th) and 11th, a bad ruler
5. Leo	Mercury	Rules 2nd, a maraka, and 11th, a bad ruler
	Venus	Rules 3rd (8th to 8th) and 10th, bad for benefic to rule an angle
6. Virgo	Moon	Rules 11th, a bad ruler
	Mars	Rules 3rd (8th to 8th) and 8th, a dusthana
	Jupiter	A benefic ruling two angles (4 and 7)
7. Libra	Sun	Rules 11th, a bad ruler
	Jupiter	Rules 3rd (8th to 8th) and 6th, a dusthana
	Mars	Rules 2nd and 7th—Marakas
8. Scorpio	Mercury	Rules 3rd (8th to 8th) and 11th, a bad ruler
	Venus	Rules 7th (benefics not good ruling angles) and 12th, a dusthana
9. Sagittarius	Venus	Rules 6th, a dusthana, and 11th, a bad ruler
	Saturn	Rules 2nd (a maraka) and 3rd (8th to 8th)

10.Capricorn	Mars	Rules 4th—benefics not good as rulers of angles. Also 11th, a bad ruler
	Jupiter	Rules 3rd (8th to 8th) and 11th (a bad ruler)
	Moon	Rules 7th; benefics not good as angular rulers
11. Aquarius	Jupiter	Rules 2nd, a maraka, and 11th, a bad ruler
	Moon	Rules 6th, a dusthana
	Mars	Rules 3rd (8th to 8th)
12. Pisces	Saturn	Rules 11th, a bad ruler, and 12th, a dusthana
	Sun	Rules 6th, a dusthana
	Venus	Rules 3rd (8th to 8th) and 8th (a dusthana)
	Mercury	Rules 4th and 7th—not good to rule two angles

Gotras and Their Use in Yagyas

A Gotra is a set of seven families descended from the original seven rishis or sages. Each gotra is represented by a specific set of nakshatras and is identified by the Moon's position in the birth chart. Each stanza of the Rig Veda is identified by a specific rishi, who is counted as the perceiver (not author) of that Vedic hymn. A priest will ask a person for their gotra when performing Vedic rituals (yagyas).

Rishi (Translation)   **Nakshatras**

1. **Marichi** (Light) — Ashwini, Pushya, Swati, Abhijit (not always used)

2. **Vasishta** (Possessor of Wealth) — Bharani, Aslesha, Visakha, Shravana

3. **Angiras** (the Fiery one) — Krittika, Magha, Anuradha, Dhanistha

4. **Atri** (One who Devours) — Rohini, Purva Phalguni, Jyeshta, Satabisha

5. **Pulasthya** (One of Smooth Hair) — Mrigasira, Uttara Phalguni, Mula, Purva Bhadrapada

6. **Pulahu** (Connector of Space) — Ardra, Hasta, Purva Ashadha, Uttara Bhadrapada

7. **Kratu** (the Inspirer) — Punarvasu, Chitra: Chitta, Uttara, Ashadha, Revati

What Is a "Panchanga"?

A panchanga is a planetary almanac, also called an ephemeris. *Panchanga* is a Sanskrit word meaning "five (pancha) branches (anga)." It describes five ways that we can break down the element of time in daily life. Thus, a panchanga gives a person the ability to act correctly, at the proper times, and to refrain from action at the proper times.

By consulting with the panchanga each day, a person can get an idea of the types of influences that may arise, both for the current day and for a particular day to come. By referencing one's birth chart, one can begin to see patterns emerging. One will begin to notice that certain characteristics emerge in life events, as marked by each of the five divisions of time. There is a basic tendency for events to unfold in a certain direction under the conditions indicated by a certain panchanga time factor. We can use the information of the panchanga and our experience to make projections that will lead us to promote action at the right time or to defer that action to a time where the conditions will generate more success and fulfillment.

Vara

The first category of time covered by a panchanga is the vara, or day of the week. Certain days of the week are better for certain types of activities than others. This is basically determined by the planet that rules that day. For example, Sunday is the "Sun's day," or Ravivara, and is beneficial for starting or ending events that carry the indications of the Sun, such as activities related to employers, one's father, health, and so forth. Each weekday should be evaluated according to the nature of its ruling planet.

Nakshatra

The second category of the panchanga is the nakshatra, or "Moon sign." There are 27 nakshatras, each with its own territory of influence. The referenced literature on nakshatras will give you insight into how to pick an auspicious event according to the nature of a particular nakshatra.

Nakshatras mark the amount of time the Moon spends in one of the 12 sun or zodiac signs. Each nakshatra counts for 13°20' of the 360° annual "path" of the Sun. Each nakshatra is further divided into four subsections of 3°20', called a "pada," or foot of a nakshatra. A pada is similar in length to a navamsa or one-ninth division of a 30° Sun sign. Nine nakshatra padas make one Sun sign.

Tithi

A third division of time is the lunar day or "tithi." This is the span of time that the moon will cover in 1/30 of a lunar month (New Moon to next New Moon). Mathematically, a tithi marks the daily spread of the distance between the Sun and the Moon, which is approximately 12 degrees. The New Moon marks day one or the first tithi and culminates on the 14th day at the full moon, or Purnima. The waning cycle of increasing darkness begins for another fortnight ending in the Amivasa, or next New Moon. The cycle repeats again and again. The individuality of your personal birth chart and the events at hand are the variables with which to judge the effects of a lunar day. Outside of the realm of Vedic astrology, the tithis have been used primarily for timing religious festivals, but they also offer additional insight into the nature of the planetary influences being generated at any one time. Again, the classical literature explains tithis in detail. An ancient Vedic text, the Narada Purana, indicates that one counts a tithi from its end point to be in tune with the forces of nature (devatas).

Karana

By cutting the lunar day or tithi in half, we come up with the fourth temporal division in the panchanga, known as the karana. Since there are 30 lunar days or tithis, there are 60 karanas. This portion of time gives us a more exact description of the nature of the favorable or unfavorable influences occurring around us at a specific time of a day.

Yoga or Nityayoga

The fifth and last division of time in the Vedic astrology system of trend analysis is the yoga or nityayoga. In this instance, the word *yoga* means "the union or spatial relationship between the longitudes of the Sun and the Moon." There are 26 yogas and a specific interpretation is allotted for each of them.

Pisces/Meena		
SAd	6-03-95 / 7-06-95	
SAr	7-07-95 / 8-09-95	
	back to Aquarius	
SAd	2-17-96 / 7-18-96	
	return from Aquarius	
SAr	7-19-96 / 12-03-96	
SAd	12-04-96 / 8-01-97	
SAr	8-02-97 / 12-16-97	
SAd	12-17-97 / 4-17-98	
JUd	5-26-98 / 7-18-98	
JUr	7-19-98 / 9-10-98	
	back to Aquarius	
JUd	1-13-99 / 5-26-99	
	return from Aquarius	
RA	2-23-05 / 11-08-06	

Aries/Mesha	
SAd	4-18-98 / 8-15-98
SAr	8-16-98 / 12-29-98
SAd	12-30-98 / 8-30-99
SAr	8-31-99 / 1-12-00
SAd	1-13-00 / 6-06-00
JUd	5-27-99 / 8-25-99
JUr	8-26-99 / 12-20-99
JUd	12-21-99 / 6-02-00
RA	8-29-03 / 2-22-05

Taurus/Vrishabha	
SAd	6-07-00 / 9-12-00
SAr	9-13-00 / 1-24-01
SAd	1-25-01 / 9-26-01
SAr	9-27-01 / 2-08-02
SAd	2-09-02 / 7-23-02
SAr	1-09-03 / 2-22-03
	from Gemini
SAd	2-23-03 / 4-07-03
	back to Gemini
JUd	6-03-00 / 9-29-00
JUr	9-30-00 / 1-25-01
JUd	1-26-01 / 6-16-01
RA	3-01-02 / 8-28-03

Gemini/Mithuna	
SAd	7-24-02 / 10-11-0:
SAr	10-12-02 / 1-08-03
	back to Taurus
SAd	4-08-03 / 10-25-0
	return from Taurus
SAr	10-26-03 / 3-07-04
SAd	3-08-04 / 9-05-04
SAr	1-14-05 / 3-22-05
	from Cancer
SAd	3-23-05 / 5-26-05
	back to Cancer
JUd	6-17-01 / 11-02-0
JUr	11-03-01 / 3-01-02
JUd	3-02-02 / 7-05-02
RA	8-31-00 / 2-28-02

Aquarius/Kumbha	
SAd	... / 6-02-95
SAr	8-10-95 / 11-21-95
	from Pisces
SAd	11-22-95 / 2-16-96
	back to Pisces
JUd	1-09-98 / 5-25-98
JUr	9-11-98 / 11-13-98
	from Pisces
JUd	11-14-98 / 1-12-99

Gochara Transits
of
Saturn, Jupiter, Rahu

1995-2005

(Greenwich Mean Time)

Cancer/Kartaka	
SAd	9-06-04 / 11-08-0
SAr	11-09-04 / 1-13-0:
	back to Gemini
SAd	5-27-05 / 11-22-0
	return from Gemir
SAr	11-23-05 / ...
JUd	7-06-02 / 12-04-C
JUr	12-05-02 / 4-04-0
JUd	4-05-03 / 7-30-03
RA	12-18-98 / 8-30-0

Capricorn/Makara	
JUd	12-27-96 / 6-10-97
JUr	6-11-97 / 10-08-97
JUd	10-09-97 / 1-08-98

Leo/Simha	
JUd	7-31-03 / 1-03-04
JUr	1-04-04 / 5-05-04
JUd	5-06-04 / 8-27-04
RA	6-20-97 / 12-17-98

Sagittarius/Dhanus	
JUd	12-08-95 / 5-04-96
JUr	5-05-96 / 9-03-96
JUd	9-04-96 / 12-26-96

Scorpio/Vrishika	
JUd	11-12-94 / 4-01-95
JUr	4-02-95 / 8-02-95
JUd	8-03-95 / 12-07-95

Libra/Thula	
JU	9-28-05 / ...
RA	... / 12-24-95

Virgo/Kanya	
JUd	8-28-04 / 2-02-05
JUr	2-03-05 / 6-05-05
JUd	6-06-05 / 9-27-05
RA	12-25-95 / 6-19-9

GLOSSARY

Abhijit — a nakshatra referred to in early Vedic works, later removed to make 27 nakshatras. Still used in some prasna (horary) charts.

Adhi — first

Adhimitra — a planet that is a "good friend" (see chapter 12)

Adhipati — owner, ruler. The planet ruling over a particular sign.

Adhisatru — a planet that is a "great enemy" (see chapter 12)

Afflicted — in a weak state due to the presence of or association with unfavorable planets, or due to unfavorable location

Agni — deity of fire

Akasha — undifferentiated space; ether. One of the five elements.

Altitude — elevation or distance of a celestial object (star, planet, etc.) above the earth's horizon. A celestial object is measured according to its angular distance from 0 to 90 degrees above the horizon line.

Amavasya — New Moon day. The following day (the first crescent or "Shiva Moon") marks day one of the waxing (or Shukla Paksha) part of the monthly lunar cycle.

Amrita — enlivening beverage drunk by the Devas (gods), which grants them immortality. Also gives Yogis higher consciousness through its production during meditation; see Soma

Amsa — longitude of planet; part of a sign; a division, as in *Nav amsa*

Anga — part of the body, a branch or limb, as in *Ved anga*, limb of the Veda

Antaradasa — sub-subperiod (3rd level) in Parasara's Vimshottari Dasa system

Antya — last

Anupachaya — houses other than 3rd, 6th, 10th, and 11th from ascendant

Anuradha — seventeenth nakshatra

369

Apa (also Apah) — water. One of the five elements.

Apachaya — houses 1, 2, 4, 7, and 8 (some add 12)

Apoklimas — houses 3, 6, 9, and 12; the Western term is cadent houses

Apourusheya — not of human or earthly origin. The Vedas are *apou rusheya* in that they exist beyond time and space and were *perceived* (shruti) by rishis but not created by them.

Ardra — 6th nakshatra

Arishta — a defect or a danger to life (*bal arishta* is death before age 12)

Artha — material wealth (houses 2, 6, and 10). One of the four aims of the ideal Vedic life.

Arudha — rising sign in a prasna chart

Arudha rasi — sign as far from the ruler of the ascendant as ascendant is from ruler

Ascendant — the zodiac sign and its degree rising on the eastern horizon at the time and place of a person's birth (or for prasna, of the "birth" of an event); related to 1st house, also *Lagna, Kundali, rising sign*. Vedic astrology counts the degree of the ascendant as the midpoint (bhava madhya) of a house and extends 15 degrees on each side to form a 30-degree sign or house.

Ashadha — fourth Hindu lunar month (June 15–July 15)

Ashta — the number 8; also *combust*, or a planet located within a few degrees of the Sun

Ashtakavarga — Parasara's formula/system to determine planetary strength in transits

Ashtama rasi — 8th sign. *Sani Ashtami*, or Saturn transiting 8th from the Moon or Lagna; not counted as good

Ashtami — tithi or lunar day #8

Ashubha (also Asubha) — inauspicious

Ashwina — seventh Hindu lunar month (September 16–October 15)

Ashwini — first nakshatra; the Ashwinis were the celestial twin physicians that healed the world (also *Asvini*)

Aslesha — ninth nakshatra

Aspects — one of the methods used by astrologers to determine how planets influence each other

Asta — setting; combust

Astangata — combustion. Planets are considered combust when they are within a few degrees of the Sun.

Asterism — a nakshatra or subconstellation

Asura — a type of "demon"; negative life force or energy

Atmakaraka — planet occupying the highest degree in a chart; said to carry a lot of influence

Autumnal equinox — occurs each September; marks the starting point of the sign of Libra in the Western systems, although due to precession the Sun is actually positioned in about 6 degrees of Virgo. The second of two points (the first being the vernal equinox) that mark the intersection of the Celestial Equator and the Ecliptic when the Sun crosses from North to South.

Aya — income or profits; 11th house; also *Ayaya*

Ayana — course; half of a year; the Sun's northern course is Uttarayana, from Capricorn through Gemini; the Sun's southern course is Dakshinayana, from Cancer through Sagittarius

Ayanabala — one of the shadbalas

Ayanamsa — the angle (about 24 degrees) separating the Vedic and Western starting points of the sign of Aries. The Western system marks 0 degrees Aries at the vernal equinox. The Vedic system adjusts for precession and marks the vernal equinox at about 6 degrees of the sign of Pisces.

Ayurbhava — 8th house, the house of *Ayu*, or life (some call it the house of death)

Ayurveda — Vedic preventative health system individualized by special body types: vata (air), pitta (fire), and kapha (a mix of earth and water)

Ayushthana — 3rd and 8th houses (the life-giving, or life-taking, houses)

Bala — strength; also means "infant"

Bandhu — family relations; brother or sibling

Benefic — gives favorable results. The amount of favorableness is determined by separately measuring the planet's strength (bala)

Benefics — unafflicted Moon, Venus, Jupiter, and unafflicted Mercury are the natural benefic or favorable planets

Bhadra — sixth Hindu lunar month (August 15–September 15)

Bhagya — fortune, luck, destiny, prosperity; 9th house, also *baghya*

Bhamsa — 27th divisional chart of Parasara's *Shodasavarga* chart system

Bhanga — cancellation, usually used in terms of cancellation of negative influences, i.e., *neecha bhanga*

Bharani — second nakshatra

Bhava — one of the 12 astrological houses. Translates as "house, mood, or state of existence." Astrology divides the heavens into 12 sections based on earth's 24-hour rotation, thus houses in one's chart are sensitive to one's birth time. Houses signify certain traits of behavior.

Bhava Chalita — chart system where the rising degree is considered the beginning point or cusp of the house. Has unequal houses. Also *Bhava Chakra*

Bhava Madhya — considers the ascending sign to mark the midpoint of a house, placing 15 degrees on either side; traditionally used by most Vedic astrologers

Bhu — earth (as in *Bhuta*); one of the five elements; also *Bhoo*

Bhukti — sub-period (2nd level dasa)

Bhumi — earth, or the Earth Goddess; also *Bhoomi*

Bhuta — element. The five basic elements or primordial building blocks of nature are: akasha (ether), vayu (air), agni or tejas (fire), apa (water), and prithivi (earth); also *Tatwa*.

Bindus — strength points in ashtakavarga indicating favorable position of a transiting planet

Brahma — the Vedic or Hindu god of Creation (part of the Trinity; see also *Shiva* and *Vishnu*)

Brahman — the highest level of consciousness; also the all-encompassing force of life; also the spiritual/philosophical caste; also *Brahmin*

Brihaspati — the planet Jupiter

Budha — the planet Mercury

Celestial equator — an imaginary great circle, extending out from earth's equator into space; used to help mark the location of celestial objects in the heavens

Celestial meridian — another imaginary great circle, running north and south of the celestial equator, cutting through the poles, the zenith and nadir, and the north and south points of the horizon

Chaitra — first Hindu lunar month (March 13–April 12)

Chakra — a name for the birth chart; also a wheel or cycle; also one of seven energy centers of the body

Chandala — lowest caste/class Vedic societal structure

Chandra — the Moon; also *Soma*

Chandra Lagna — the Moon counted as a special or alternate 1st house or ascendant

Chandra Masa — lunar month

Chandra Varsha — lunar year, 360 days long

Charana — phase or section; one fourth of a nakshatra; also *pada*

Chathurhamsa — 4th divisional chart of Parashara's *Shodasavarga*

Chaturdashi — tithi or lunar day #14

Chaturthi — tithi or lunar day #4

Chaya Grahas — shadowy planets; names for Rahu and Ketu, which fall in the shadow of eclipses

Chitra — 14th nakshatra; also *Chitta*

Combust — weakened because the planet is too near the Sun (distance varies)

Common Signs — have qualities "common" to both moveable and fixed signs: Gemini, Virgo, Sagittarius, and Pisces. See *Dual*

Conjunction — two planets residing in the same sign (regardless of degree or distance apart)

Constellation — $1/27$ division (13°20') of the zodiac. Also *nakshatra* or *asterism*; used in astronomy to describe *any* grouping of stars. Those star groups close to the ecliptic have the same names as the astrological signs but do not exactly occupy the same space in the sky.

Cusp — the line of demarcation or the point where one sign is divided from another: used to mark the boundary between a sign or a house

Daiva — past karma, the impulses generated from previous actions that compel us to act again in the same manner

Dakshina — south

Dana — charity

Daridra — poverty; certain planetary combinations or yogas indicate lack of prosperity

Dasas — planetary periods employing nakshatras, as grouped in the Vimshottari Dasa system; the ruling constellations determines the ruling Dasa

Dasa Chidra — end of a Dasa, considered an unfavorable period

Dasamsa — 10th divisional chart of Parashara's *Shodasavarga* system

Dashami — tithi or lunar day #10

Declination — angle of the distance of a celestial object as measured from the Celestial Equator

Devas — Gods or celestial beings

Dhana — wealth; 2nd house

Dhanakaraka — Jupiter, the indicator of wealth

Dhanistha — 23rd nakshatra; also called *Sravista*

Dhanus — Sagittarius

Dharma — duty; one's life purpose; righteousness

Dharmabhava — 9th house; also *Dharmasthana*

Dharma Karmadhipati Yoga — combination of the rulers of the 9th and 10th houses

Dhatus — bodily constituents represented by planets: Sun = bones, Moon = blood or fluids, Mars = marrow, Mercury = skin, Venus = semen/ovum, Saturn = muscles

Dhruva — the pole star

Dig or Dik — direction

Digbala or Dikbala — directional strength of a planet according to house location ("best" house)

Dina — a day, measured from sunrise to sunrise; averaged at 5:30 A.M. in some Hindu planetary almanacs (panchangas)

Dosha — an affliction; for example, Kuja Dosha is an affliction to marriage

Drekkana — one third of a sign

Drik — aspect; also *drig*

Drishti — aspects (planets influencing or "glancing at" certain other planets and houses)

Dual Signs — indicate flexibility, balance, and the capacity to adapt and integrate (Gemini, Virgo, Sagittarius, and Pisces); also called *Common Signs*

Dusthanas — malefic houses 6, 8, and 12; also called *trik*

Dwadashi — tithi or lunar day #12

Dwipada rasis — two-legged signs (common/mutable)

Dwirwadasa — type of aspect where planets are in 2nd and 12th houses from each other

Dwiteeya — tithi or lunar day #2

Ecliptic — apparent path of the Sun around the earth; the planets all tend to orbit within a few degrees north or south of this imaginary track in the sky

Ekadasamsa — 11th divisional chart of Parasara's *Shodasavarga* system

Ekadashi — tithi or lunar day #11

Ephemeris — a planetary almanac containing the daily positions of planets and the various tracking systems for the Moon; an essential tool for calculating transits of planets and, in the absence of a computer, for calculating astrological charts; also *panchanga*

Equal House System — all houses are equally counted as having 30 degrees each; there is no adjustment for "compression" of house space due to latitude (the distance above or below the earth's equator), as in the Bhava Chalita system

Even signs — earth and water signs (same signs as female or gentle)

Exaltation — most favorable sign position for a planet; also *deeptha; uucha*

Female signs — earth and water signs (same signs as even or gentle)

Friends — positive or mutually supportive planetary relationships

Gandanta — the point where a nakshatra and a sign of the zodiac end concurrently; also the junction point (cusp) of water and fire signs; considered unfavorable

Ganita — astronomical calculations; the mathematical part of Vedic astrology

Gentle signs — earth and water signs (same signs as even or female)

Ghati — a unit of time. One ghati = 24 minutes (= 60 palas); 2 ghatis = 1 muhurtha; 60 ghatis = 1 day; also *Ghatika*

Go — Taurus, bull, ray of light

Gochara — planetary transits, or the location of any planet at a particular time. The planet's moving positions, especially over natal chart positions, are located to help determine future events. Also indicates the movement of planets in general through their orbits.

Gotra — set of seven families descended from the original seven rishis or sages. Each gotra is represented by a specific set of nakshatras. A priest will ask a person for their gotra when performing Vedic rituals (yagyas).

Grahas — planets; literally translates as "that which grasps"

Graha yudha — planetary war. Some astrologers consider all planets to be "at war" when they are conjunct, the winner being the planet with the lower degree in a sign. However, some contend that the higher degree wins.

Gulika — an auxiliary or *upagraha* planet; a mathematical point

Guru — Jupiter; a spiritual teacher

Hasta — 13th nakshatra

Homa — a Vedic spiritual ritual or performance involving fire

Hora — planetary hour; each hour of the day is ruled by a specific planet. In the Divisional charts, a hora is one-half a sign.

Hora Lagna — planetary ruler of the hour for a specific day

Horary astrology — see *prasna*

Hora Shastra — science of time (astrology)

Ishtadeva — one's personal deity, sometimes identified by the planet ruling the 5th or 9th house, or by a strong and favorable planet located in the 5th or 9th house. Some astrologers feel that their attunement with their personal deity allows them to function clearly and correctly as an astrologer.

Jaimini — author of a system of astrology that contains different rules from the system developed by Parasara. It is used by a small group of astrologers in India, but merits further study and support.

Jala — the water element; also *Jal*

Janma Lagna — the "rising sign" counted from the position of the Moon in the chart

Jataka — the field of astrology dealing with interpreting birth charts

Jeeva — living things (insect to human); life; individual soul

Jyeshta — 18th nakshatra; also the name for the third lunar month

Jyotish — Vedic astrology. Derives from *Jyoti* (light) and *Ishwara* (God or all-encompassing nature); also Jyotisha

Jyotishi — a Vedic astrologer

Kala — time; a unit of time; 30 kalas = 1 ghati (24 minutes)

Kala Bala — temporal strength (of a planet)

Kala Purusha — the embodiment of time; time identified as a "person." The planets, signs, houses, and nakshatras are identified with parts of his body.

Kalatra Bhava — 7th house; the house of the wife or mate, or partnerships

Kali Yuga — the current epoch of the four major Vedic universal time epochs; 432,000 years long

Kama — desire; 7th house

Kanya — Virgo; a young girl or a virgin

Kapha — a mix of water and earth; one of the three Ayurvedic doshas or body types. A stable constitution when healthy, sluggish when ill.

Karaka — indicator. The characteristics exhibited by a planet, sign, or house.

Karana — half of a tithi or lunar day (each has a name recycled eight times per month)

Karka — Cancer; also *Karkata, Karkataka, Kataka*

Karma — action; also from the doctrine of reincarnation, "What you sow is what you reap"; also career; 10th house

Kartari — planets "hemmed-in" by planets on both sides; literally means *scissors*

Kartika — 8th Hindu lunar month (October 16–November 14)

Kartikeya — son of Shiva; associated with Ganesh, Skanda

Keeta — Scorpio; insect

Kendra — type of aspect; angular or quadrant houses (1, 4, 7, and 10). Squares.

Ketu — lunar south node, used astrologically as one of the nine planets. Mythically, a demon's dragon tail.

Kranti — celestial declination

Krishna Paksha — the dark fortnight of the Moon; starting from the full Moon (purnima) and waning or decreasing to the new or dark Moon (amavasya)

Krittika — 3rd nakshatra

Krura rasis — cruel or aggressive signs; also masculine; also *asubhas*

Kshatriyas — warrior caste

Kshetra — field or placement, e.g., house

Kuja — Mars

Kuja dosha — Mars located in houses 2, 4, 7, 8, or 12 (some also say 1); creates discord, separation, or "death" in a marriage

Kumbha — Aquarius

Kundali — horoscope or birth chart; map; diagram

Kutas — special set of astrological criteria used for making marriage matches

Kutumba — family; 2nd house

Labha — gain or profits; 11th house

Lagna — ascendant or 1st house; literally, "attached to"

Lagna Adhipati — ruler of the ascendant or rising sign

Lahiri — created the official ayanamsa approved by the government of India

Lakh — a Hindu unit of measure for 100,000

Lunar mansion — a nakshatra

Lunar month — averages 29 days, 12 hours and 44 minutes: one orbit of the Moon through all 12 signs of the zodiac, or the orbit of the Moon around the earth

Madhya — middle; midpoint of 10th or any house

Magha — 10th nakshatra; also the 11th lunar month. Also *Makha*

Maha Dasa — primary planetary period in the Vimshottari system of Parasara

Mahapurusha Yoga — a planet located on an angle occupying its own sign or sign of exaltation. Gives extra strength to planets, bringing out the very best qualities of the planet. The Sun, Moon, and Nodes are not included in this set.

Maharishis — great Vedic sages, seers, or wise men

Makara — Capricorn

Male signs — the fire and air signs

Malefic — unfavorable, negative, destructive, or fierce in effect

Malefic planets — Sun, afflicted Moon, Mars, Saturn, Rahu, Ketu, and afflicted Mercury if with Mars or Saturn

Manda — Saturn

Mandi — son of Saturn, sometimes said to be the same as Gulika, an unfavorable upagraha or auxiliary planet

Mangala — Mars

Mangala Dosha — see *Kujadosha*; also *Manglik*

Mantra — a sound or vibration used in meditation techniques; said to be a "seed" (bija) to elicit higher states of consciousness

Manushya — human

Maraka — so-called killer planets: the rulers of 2nd (money) and 7th (sex) houses. Said by some to kill the "spiritual" essence, more than the life essence.

Margasira — 9th Hindu lunar month; also *Mrigashirsha*

Masa — lunar month

Matru — mother; 4th house

Meena — Pisces

Meridian — imaginary great circle on the Celestial Sphere that cuts through the poles, zenith, and nadir; corresponds to the earth's longitude

Mesha — Aries

Misra — mixed (i.e., common or dual signs)

Mithuna — Gemini

Mitra — friend, in planetary relationships; a form of the Sun

Moksha — enlightenment, spiritual liberation

Moolatrikona — a benefic planetary position. Planets are good in their own sign, but better still in Moolatrikona positions. The next highest position for planets is when they are Uucha or exalted in position.

Moveable (signs) — signs indicating change or movement (Aries, Cancer, Libra, Capricorn)

Mrigasira — fifth nakshatra

Mritya — death

Muhurtha — electional astrology. A chart constructed for giving the best outlook for the future start or stop of an event. Also, a unit of time equal to two ghatis.

Mula — 19th nakshatra; also minerals; plants, roots

Nadi — a nerve channel; branch of astrology often predicting or discussing events using palm leaf "documents" to guide the conversation, such as *Brighu Nadi*

Nadir — the point in the sky that is opposite the zenith (the point on the celestial sphere directly above an observer on the earth; 90 degrees from the horizon)

Naisargika — permanent or natural, as in permanent planetary friendship

Naisargikabala — natural strength

Nakshatra — constellation based on the Moon's position in the sky. The nakshatra divides the ecliptic into 27 sections of 13°20' each. Originally the nakshatras were used to determine the best time to perform specific religious rituals and when to time events. Modern Vedic astrologers are exploring using the nakshatras in ways similar to the signs of the zodiac, that is for interpretation of personality. Also called an asterism, constellation, Moon sign, or lunar mansion.

Nava — nine; 9th house, also *Nav*

Navami — tithi or lunar day #9

Navamsa — 9th divisional chart dealing significantly with relationships; the most frequently used divisional chart next to the standard rasi or birth chart

Neecha — debilitated planet; a planet located in its most unfavorable position by sign

Neecha Bhanga — cancellation of debilitation, or almost so

Neecha Sthana — the planet's sign of debilitation

Nirayana — Vedic astrological year, adjusted for precession of the equinoxes; Sun currently rises at about 6° Pisces on the equinox day. In contrast, Western astrologers, using the sayana system, don't adjust for the backward shift of the earth and say, on that same equinox day, that the Sun is rising in zero degrees Aries, as it has been counted since the 3rd or 4th century A.D.

Odd signs — same as male signs

Oja — odd

Own sign — when a planet is positioned in its own sign (the sign that it rules) it is not as good as moolatrikona or uucha; also *Swakshetra and Swabhava*

Pada — one-fourth part; foot; each nakshatra is divided into 4 subsections called padas, or *charan*

Paddhati — specific system of astrology. Some more advanced astrologers, such as Krishnamurti, feel compelled to structure a system of astrology built on their own knowledge and experience.

Paksha — half a lunar month, a fortnight

Panchami — tithi or lunar day #5

Panchanga — Vedic sidereal planetary almanac. Gives data in terms of positions of planets according to day of the week, nakshatra, tithi (lunar day), karana (half a lunar day), and yoga (a special calculation for the separating distance of the Sun and Moon). Also *ephemeris.*

Papa — malefic (planet); also sin (papi means "sinful")

Papakartari — a planet "hemmed in" between malefics

Parasara — ancient rishi and author of the most popular astrology system

Parasari — Parasara's system of Vedic astrology

Parivartana — exchange of places (signs/houses), e.g., Jupiter in Gemini and Mercury in Sagittarius: the rulers of each of these signs are located in each other's sign

Paryaya — cycle; there are three sets of nine nakshatras, comprising 27 total; each set is called a Paryaya

Phala — the fruits or effect of something

Phalguna — 12th Hindu lunar month

Poornima — tithi or lunar day #15, the full Moon day; also *Purnima*

Prana — 5th-level dasa; also life breath or vital energy

Prasna — horary astrology; a chart constructed for the time of a question and interpreted similar to a natal chart

Pratipada — first day of a lunar month, the day *after* the new or full Moon; also *Pratipat*

Precession — the slow backward shifting motion of the earth as it rotates; causes the ayanamsa

Prithivi — earth; also *Prithvi*

Puja — Vedic ritual performed by a priest for the benefit of a person; often used interchangeably with *yagya*

Punarvasu — seventh nakshatra

Punya — merit, as the cumulative effects of good actions from current or previous life

Puranas — Vedic knowledge written more in a more easily accessible story form, aimed at giving knowledge to the general masses, rather that a select groups of priests or philosophers (Brahmins)

Purnima — Full Moon day. The following day marks day 15 and the second fortnight (waning or Krishna Paksha) of the 30-day lunar cycle or month.

Purusha — Cosmic Being: the universe personified

Purva Bhadrapada — 25th nakshatra

Purva Phalguni — 11th nakshatra

Purvapunya — past-life credit, represented by the 5th house

Purvashadha — 20th nakshatra

Pushya — 8th nakshatra, considered the most favorable

Putra — son; 5th house; children

Quadrants — see *Kendra* (the four angular or square houses)

Radha — alternate name for 16th nakshatra; see *Visakha*

Rahu — lunar north node, used astrologically as one of the nine planets. Mythically, a demon's dragon head.

Rakshasa — demon, negative force, or unfavorable impulse of nature

Raja — king or executive

Raja Yogas — combinations of planets, usually involving an association of rulerships of trines and squares. Said to confer "kingship" or good financial blessings to the chart holder. Also *royal yogas*.

Rajas — vigorous, aggressive or agitated; one of the three gunas or qualities of life

Rasa — taste, flavor

Rashmi — ray or power emanating from a planet

Rasi — zodiacal sign

Rasi chakra or natal chart — birth chart, natal horoscope; the zodiac diagram. The main 12-sign chart used most prevalently. Also *rasi kundali*.

Rasi Lagna — the rising sign or ascendant counted from the first house of a chart

Ratna — gem or precious stone; each planet has a specific stone that is regarded as pleasing to that planet, which allows the planet's best influence to operate.

Ravi — Sun

Ravivara — Sunday

Rectification — adjustment of birth time to match more closely to the indications in the person's life. Many birth certificates show times that were incorrectly recorded.

Rekna — malefic points in Ashtakavarga

Retrograde — apparent backward motion of a planet

Revati — 27th nakshatra

Right Ascension (R.A.) — the distance measured from the first point of Aries eastward to some part of the ecliptic; used along with declination to measure the position of planets

Rishis — ancient Vedic seers

Ritu — season; India has six seasons to the West's four

Rohini — 4th nakshatra

Rupas — units of strength measurement (planet/house) used in shadbala calculations

Sade Sati — literally, "7½ years." Saturn's transit of 12th, 1st, and 2nd from Moon. Can also be considered from the Lagna and the Sun; happens every 30 years and is considered unfavorable by some, yet can bring improvements for better living. Also *Elerata*.

Sahaja — siblings; 3rd house

Samya — neutral

Sambandha — a strong planetary relationship where planets reinforce each other's influence

Samhita — as astrological text dealing with subject matter beyond the basic birth chart

Samsaptaka — opposition; planets aspect each other by 180°

Sandhi — junction point between signs or houses: a planet located in less than one degree or over 29 degrees. Considered a weak and unfavorable position for a planet.

Sani — Saturn; also *Shani*

Sankranti — the point where the Sun moves from one sign into the next; a type of sandhi

Sanskrit — ancient language of Vedic astrology and of ancient India Although a "dead" language in that it is not a language of everyday conversation, it is still very much used in Vedic philosophy and rituals.

Sanyasa — renunciate who wanders about taking what comes along unasked; also *sanyasi*

Saptami — tithi or lunar day #7

Saptamsa — seventh divisional chart of Parasara's *Shodasavarga* system

Sapta rishis — the seven rishis of ancient Vedic philosophy; also the constellation Pleides

Shadbalas — six sources of strength gained by each planet

Satabisha — 24th nakshatra

Satru — enemy

Satrukshetra — unfriendly house

Satruvarga — an unfavorable divisional chart

Satva — purity, one of the three gunas or basic qualities of life

Satvic — spiritual or pure in nature and influence, also *satwic* or *sattvic, sattwic*

Sayana — tropical zodiac, used by Western astrology. Starts the sign of Aries at the time of the vernal equinox, without compensating for precession. See *nirayana*

Setting — the Descendant (the 7th house)

Shadbala — Parasara's system that generates six kinds of planetary strengths

Shadow planets — Rahu and Ketu; see *Chaya grahas*

Shadvargas — six main divisional charts

Shakuna — omens, also called *nimritta*

Shaniwara — Saturday

Shanti — Vedic astrology remedial act aimed at correcting some perceived defect in the chart

Shashtashtaka — type of aspect: 6th and 8th from each other

Shashthi — tithi or lunar day #6

Shastra — teachings, books of Vedic learning, science, ancient scriptures, also *sastras*

Shastyamsa — 16th divisional chart of Parashara's *Shodasavarga*

Shiva — Vedic or Hindu god. Called Shiva the Destroyer. Part of the Trinity; see Brahma and Vishnu.

Shodasavargas or vargas — 16 kinds of divisional charts

Shukla Paksha — the bright fortnight (two-week period) of the Moon. Starting from the New Moon (amavasya) and waxing or increasing to the Full Moon.

Shukravara — Friday

Siddhamsa — 24th divisional chart

Siddhanta — mathematical treatise, often used to expound astronomical formulas and concepts, such as the *Surya Siddhanta*

Siddhis — special powers or perfections of yogis and saints, indicating a high degree of mental and spiritual coherence leading to effortless fulfillment of desires, as explained in such works as Patanjali's *Yoga Sutras*

Sidereal (zodiac) — zodiac based upon the relationship of the earth to fixed star positions, see *Nirayana*

Sign — a geometric division of space constructed by dividing the apparent path of the Sun into 12 equal segments, each located and named by the constellations that reside near them (but are not fully apportioned to them). In Vedic astrology, if someone were to ask you your sign, it would be more appropriate and meaningful to tell them your rising sign and/or Moon sign, rather than the less detailed Sun sign.

Simha — Leo

Solstice — occurs around June 23 (summer solstice or longest day for the northern hemisphere) and December 23 (winter solstice or shortest day for the northern hemisphere); the points where the Sun is farthest from the equator on its apparent journey around the earth

Soma — the Moon, also a beverage or fluid said both to grant immortality to the Gods and to give Yogis higher states of consciousness; see *Amrita*

Somavara — Monday

Sravana — 22nd nakshatra; also 5th lunar month

Sthana — position or location (also used to describe a house)

Sthanabala — positional strength of a planet

Sthira — fixed or unmoving signs: Taurus, Leo, Scorpio, and Aquarius

Sthirabala — strength due to one or more planets in a sign

Subha — auspicious (factor); benefic (planets); 9th house

Sudras — the working-class caste, such as farmers and laborers; Mercury and Saturn; air signs

Sukra — Venus

Sukshma — 4th-level time period of the Vimshottari Dasa system (after dasa, bhukti, antaradasa)

Surya — Sun

Sutra — short statement on a subject constructed to facilitate memorization and to trigger simple understandings of a topic of study, such as the *Yoga Sutras* of Patanjali. Literally translates as "a stitch."

Swakshetra — planet located in its own house (the house it rules)

Swami — ruler; owner

Swati — 15th nakshatra

Swavarga — a planet in its own division; also *Svavarga*

Synodical — a planetary cycle beginning and ending at the same point, as a synodic or lunar month is comprised of one New Moon to the next

Tajika — an astrological system for forecasting the upcoming year based on the degree of the Sun around the birthday; also called *Tajaka*

Tamas — one of the three Gunas or qualities of life; represents laziness, inertia, lethargy, low energy, and lack of cleanliness

Tanu — body; 1st house, also *Thanu*

Tapas — "heating up," austerity, penance

Tatwas — see *bhutas*

Thula — Libra; scales

Tithi — lunar day or $1/_{30}$ of a lunar month, calculated according to the fortnight. Used when selecting auspicious times for religious ceremonies.

Transits — see *gochara*

Trik — see *dusthana*

Trikona — type of aspect: trine or angular houses (1, 5, and 9)

Trimsamsa — 13th harmonic chart comprised of 30 parts of 1 degree each; shows the potential for unfavorable effects in life; indicates personal integrity

Triteeya — tithi or lunar day #3

Triteeya-Ekadasa — type of aspect: 3rd and 11th from each other

Tropical (zodiac) — Western zodiac based on the earth's relationship to the Sun and the four seasons. The Sun is observed to move through these seasons in relationship to zones on the earth (the Tropics), rather than "fixed" stars in the sky (the Vedic or *sidereal* zodiac). Tropical astrology starts each new astrological year at the spring equinox. See *sidereal*.

Turyamsa — another name for the 4th divisional chart

Udu dasa — another name for the Vimshottari Dasa system developed by Parasara

Upachaya — houses 3, 6, 10, and 11; called "growing houses" because unfavorable indications can get increasingly better over time

Upa grahas or auxiliary planets — though called secondary or auxiliary planets, these are actually mathematical points without any observable mass

Upaya — corrective action to appease a planetary affliction; see *Shanti*

Uttara Bhadrapada — 26th nakshatra

Uttara Phalguni — 12th nakshatra

Uttarashadha — 21st nakshatra

Uttarayana — northern course of the Sun (as it moves from Capricorn through Gemini); considered a favorable time of year and called a "day" of the Gods

Uucha — exaltation

Uuchabhanga — cancellation of exaltation

Vaisakha — second lunar month (April 13–May 14)

Vaisyas — the merchant caste

Vara (Wara) — weekday; each day of the week is governed by a specific planet and reflects the nature of that planet. Rahu and Ketu do not rule any day of the week, but Rahu is associated with Saturn (Saturday) and Ketu with Mars (Tuesday). The planets are usually listed in the order of the days of the week.

Varga — a divisional/Shodasavarga chart (16 total), sometimes called an *Amsa*

Vargottama — planet is in the same sign in both rasi and navamsa; regarded as a positive indicator somewhat similar to the effects of a planet in its own sign

Varna — social class or caste. Some researchers feel that British colonial rule distorted the caste system, which originally measured one's nature and disposition more than inherited social level.

Varsha — year, also the rainy season

Varshaphal or Birthday Chart — many astrologers construct and interpret an annual chart based on the birthday of a person, and matched to the exact time when the Sun returns to the same degree as in the natal chart

Varshapravesha — solar return

Vasanta — spring; also *Basanta*

Vasanta Sampat — vernal equinox

Vastu — dwelling, or the science of space in Vedic studies; akin to Feng Shui

Vata — the Ayurvedic dosha or constituent associated with the wind element

Vayu — air element, or the God of Air; there are eight Vayus or "wind" currents in the body

Veda — the ancient knowledge of India; the purest form of knowledge: knowledge itself without the knower. A set of four works compiled by Vyasa, including the Rig, Samya, Atharva, and Yajur Vedas.

Vedanga — a branch of the Veda

Vedanta — philosophy of knowing one's self; self-realization

Vernal equinox — the point where the ecliptic intersects the equator; the Sun crosses this point around March 23. See also *precession, ayanamsa*.

Vimshottari Dasa — the 120-year-long, nakshatra-based planetary forecasting system developed by Parasara

Visakha — 16th nakshatra

Vishnu — the Maintainer of the Universe; part of the Hindu trinity (see *Brahma* and *Shiva*)

Vivaha — marriage

Vrishika — Scorpio

Vrishabha — Taurus; also *Vrishabha*

Vyasa — son of Parasara; wrote the epic story of India called the *Mahabharata*, and also compiled the Vedas (with Ganesha's assistance, according to legend)

Vyaya — loss and expenditure; 12th house

Watery signs — Cancer, Scorpio, Capricorn, and Pisces

Yagya — type of Vedic performance often recommended by Vedic astrologers to help remedy or improve some circumstance observed or forecasted in the birth chart

Yama — God of death, control, and restraint

Yantra — symbol or diagram used for visual meditation and for protective purposes

Yoga — specific planetary combination that gives added effects to the chart, good or bad

Yogakarakas — indicators for union (integration of life); a positive planet due to good ownership conditions, identified, by specific rising sign, as planets that rule both an angle and a trine

Yoni — the birth source, the external form of a woman's reproductive organs

Yudha — war between planets

Yugas — four major time epochs constituting a Maha Yuga

Yuga — even

Yuti — conjunction

Zenith — the point on the celestial sphere directly above an observer on the earth; 90 degrees from the horizon

Zodiac — from a Greek word meaning "band of animals." A circle or band measuring about 8° on either side of the ecliptic; the planets visible by the naked eye can be seen moving along this belt. For astrological measurements the zodiac is divided into 12 equal sections (signs) that are named after constellations located in the vicinity, but these star groups do not always cover a full 30 degrees each; also *Bhachakra*

BIBLIOGRAPHY

The Agni Purana, J. L. Shastri, Delhi: Motilal Banarsidass, 1985

Ancient Hindu Astrology for the Modern Western Astrologer, James Braha, North Miami, Florida: Hermetician Press, 1986

The Astrological Magazine, B. V. Raman, ed., Bangalore: Raman Publications

The Astrology of the Seers, David Frawley, Salt Lake City, Utah: Passage Press, 1990

Astronomy and Mathematical Astrology, Deepak Kapoor, New Delhi: Ranjan Publications, 1995

Astronomy for Astrologers, John and Peter Filbey, Kent, Great Britain: The Aquarian Press, 1984

Ayurvedic Cures for Common Diseases, Dr. Bhagwan Dash, Delhi: Hind Pocket Books Ltd.

Ayurvedic Healing, Dr. David Frawley, O.M.D., Salt Lake City, Utah: Passage Press, 1989

Bhrigu Sutram, Sage Bhrigu, New Delhi: Ranjan Publications, 1992

(Varahamihira's) Brihat Jataka, B. Suryanarain Rao, Bangalore: Moltilal Banarsidas, 1986

Brihat Parasara Hora, Maharishi Parasara, Bombay: Chowkhamba, 1963

Brihat Parasara Hora Sastra, Maharishi Parasara, New Delhi: Sagar Publications, 1994

Brihat Parasara Hora Sastra, G. C. Sharma, New Delhi: Sagar Publications, 1994

Chamatkar Chintamani, S. S. Sareen, New Delhi: Sagar Publications, 1991

The Circle of Stars, Valerie J. Roebuck, Rockport, Massachusetts: Element, Inc. 1992

Deva Keralam, R. Santhanam, New Delhi: Sagar Publications, 1992

Doctrines of Suka Nadi—Retold, R. Santhanam, New Delhi: Ranjan Publications, 1984

Dots of Destiny, Vinay Aditya, New Delhi: Systems Vision, 1996

Encyclopaedia of Indian Medicine, S. K. Ramachandra Rao (Ed.), Bombay: Ramdas Bhatkal, 1985

Essentials of Horary Astrology or Prasnapadavi, M. Ramakrishana Bhat, Delhi: Motilal Banarsidass Publishers, 1992

Essentials of Medical Astrology, Dr. K. S. Charak, New Delhi: Vision Wordtronic, 1994

Fundamentals of Astrodynamics, Bate, Mueller, and White, New York, N.Y.: Dover Publications, 1971

Fundamentals of Astrology, M. Ramakrishna Bhat, Delhi: Motilal Banarsidass Publishers, 1992

Fundamentals of Hindu Astrology, S. Kannan, New Delhi: Sagar Publications, 1981

The Garuda Purana, J. L. Shastri, Delhi: Motilal Banarsidass Publishers, 1990

Graha and Bhava Balas, B. V. Raman, New Delhi: UBS Publisher's Distributors, Ltd., 1991

The Handbook of Ayurveda, Dr. Shanta Godagama, London: Kyle Cathie, Ltd., 1997

Handbook of Vastu, B. Niranjan Babu, New Delhi: UBS Publisher's Distributors Ltd., 1997

Heal Yourself, Heal Your World, Brian Rees, M.D., M.P.H., Pacific Palisades, California: Manu Publishing, 1997

The Healing Power of Gemstones, Harish Johari, Rochester, Vermont: Destiny Books, 1988

Hindu Astrological Calculations, Usha-Shashi, New Delhi: Sagar Publications, 1978

Hindu Astrology Lessons, Richard Houck, Ed., Gaithersburg, Maryland: 1997

Hindu Gods and Goddesses, A. G. Mitchell, New Delhi: UBS Publishers, 1997

Hinduism Today, Acharya Palaniswami (Ed.), Kapaa, Hawaii: Himalayan Academy Publishers

Hindu Omens, C.D. Bijalwan, New Delhi: 1977

Hindu Samskaras, Dr. Rajbali Pandey, Delhi: Motilal Banarsidass Publishers, 1991

Hindu Symbology and Other Essays, Swami Swahananda, Madras: Sri Ramakrishna Math, 1983

Hora-sara, Prithuyasas son of Var hmihira, New Delhi: Ranjan Publications, 1982

How to Judge a Horoscope, B.V. Raman, Delhi: Motilal Banarsidass Publishers, 1991

Issues in Vedic Astronomy and Astrology, Pandya, Dikshit, and Kansara (Eds.), Delhi: Motilal Banarsidass Publishers, 1992

Jataka Parijata, V. Subramanya Sastri, New Delhi: Ranjan Publications

(Mahadeva's) Jataka Tatva, S. S. Sareen, New Delhi: Sagar Publications, 1987

Kalaprakasika, N. P. Subramania Iyer, New Delhi: Asian Educational Services, 1991

Light on Life, Hart Defouw and Robert Svoboda, Middlesex, England: Penguin Books, 1996

Light on the Yoga Sutras of Patanjali, B.K.S. Iyengar, London: Thorsons, 1993

The Linga-Purana, J. L. Shastri (Ed.), Delhi: Motilal Banarsidass Publishers, 1973

Minor Vedic Deities, J. R. Joshi, New Delhi: University of Poona, 1978

Muhurtha, B. V. Raman, Bangalore: IBH Prakashana, 1979

Muhurta Chintamani, G. C. Sharma, New Delhi: Sagar Publications, 1996

The Myths and Gods of India, Alain Danielou, Rochester, Vermont: Inner Traditions International, 1991

Nakshatra, K. T. Shubhakaran, New Delhi: Sagar Publications, 1991

The Narada Purana, J. L. Shastri, Delhi: Motilal Banarsidass, 1980

The Penguin Book of Hindu Names, Maneka Gandhi, New Delhi: Penguin Books, India, 1992

Perfect Health, Deepak Chopra, M.D., New York: Harmony Books, 1991

(Mantreswara's) Phala Deepika, S. S. Sareen, New Delhi: Sagar Publications, 1992

The Practical Astronomer, Brian Jones, New York, NY: Simon and Schuster, Inc., 1990

Practical Horary Astrology, Gayatri Devi Vasudev, Bangalore: Raman Publications, 1992

Prasna Marga, B. V. Raman, Delhi: Motilal Banarsidass Publishers Pvt. Ltd., 1991

Prasna Marga, J. N. Bhasin, New Delhi: Ranjan Publications

Predictive Astrology of the Hindus, Pandit G. K. Ojha, Bombay: Taraporevala Sons & Co., 1990

Puranic Encyclopaedia, Vettam Mani, Delhi: Motilal Banarsidass Publishers, 1989

Rectification of Birth Time, Prof. P. S. Shastri, New Delhi: Ranjan Publications, 1992

Sama Veda, S.V. Ganapati, Delhi: Motilal Banarsidass Publishers, 1992

Saravali, K. Varma & R. Santhanam, New Delhi: Ranjan Publications, 1983

Satya-Jatakam, Sage Satyacharya, New Delhi: Ranjan Publications, 1979

Siva Sutras, Jaideva Singh, Delhi: Motilal Banarsidass Publishers, 1991

Sri Sarwarthachintamani, B. Suryanarain Rao, Delhi: Motilal Banarsidass Publishers, 1996

Studies in the Puranic Records, R.C. Hazra, Delhi: Motilal Banarsidass Publishers, 1987

The Surya Siddhanta, P. Gangooly (Ed.), Delhi: Motilal Banarsidass Publishers, 1989

Surya the Sun God, Shakti M. Gupta, New Delhi: Somaiya Publications, 1977

Swara Chintamani, S. Kannan, New Delhi: Sagar Publications, 1991

A Textbook of Varshaphala, Dr. K. S. Charak, New Delhi: Bharatiya Prachya Evam Sanatam Vigyam Sanstham, 1993

Three Hundred Important Combinations, B. V. Raman, Delhi: Motilal Banarsidass Publishers, 1994

The Times of Astrology, Rajeshwari Shankar, ed., Rajeshwari Shankar Associates, Publishers

Uttarakalamrita (of Kalidasa), S. S. Sareen, New Delhi: Sagar Publications, 1993

Varshaphal, Prof. B. V. Raman, Bangalore: IBH Prakashana, 1982

Vedic Astrology, Dr. K. S. Charak (Ed. of magazine), New Delhi: Systems Vision, Publishers

Vedic Astrology, Ronnie Gale Dreyer, York Beach, Maine: Samuel Reiser, 1997

Vishnupuranam, M. N. Dutt, Varanasi-1, India: Chowkhamba Sanskrit Series Office, 1972

The Yajurveda, Devi Chand, New Delhi: Munshiram Manoharlal Publishers, 1994

Yoga Philosophy of Patanjali, H. Aranya, Calcutta: Calcutta University, 1981

ABOUT THE AUTHOR

William R. (Bill) Levacy held a B.A. in English, an M.S. in the science of creative intelligence with a concentration in Vedic science, and a Ph.D. in education. The Indian Council of Astrological Sciences (ICAS) awarded him the titles of Jyotish Kovid, Jyotish Vachaspati, and Jyotish Medha Pragya. Bill began his practice in Vedic astrology in 1983 and grew a community of thousands of clients from around the world. He authored the books *Beneath a Vedic Sky, Beneath a Vedic Sun*, and *Vedic Astrology Simply Put*. A dedicated teacher, Bill conducted workshops on Vedic astrology across the globe and served as the president of the American College of Vedic Astrology (ACVA) for almost a decade. His books continue to inspire new generations of readers and enlighten lovers of Jyotish everywhere.

We hope you enjoyed this Hay House book. If you'd like to receive our online catalog featuring additional information on Hay House books and products, or if you'd like to find out more about the Hay Foundation, please contact:

Hay House, Inc., P.O. Box 5100, Carlsbad, CA 92018-5100
(760) 431-7695 or (800) 654-5126
(760) 431-6948 (fax) or (800) 650-5115 (fax)
www.hayhouse.com® • www.hayfoundation.org

———

Published in Australia by: Hay House Australia Pty. Ltd.,
18/36 Ralph St., Alexandria NSW 2015
Phone: 612-9669-4299 • *Fax:* 612-9669-4144
www.hayhouse.com.au

Published in the United Kingdom by: Hay House UK, Ltd.,
The Sixth Floor, Watson House, 54 Baker Street, London W1U 7BU
Phone: +44 (0)20 3927 7290 • *Fax:* +44 (0)20 3927 7291
www.hayhouse.co.uk

Published in India by: Hay House Publishers India,
Muskaan Complex, Plot No. 3, B-2, Vasant Kunj, New Delhi 110 070
Phone: 91-11-4176-1620 • *Fax:* 91-11-4176-1630
www.hayhouse.co.in

———

<u>**Access New Knowledge.**</u>
<u>**Anytime. Anywhere.**</u>

Learn and evolve at your own pace
with the world's leading experts.

www.hayhouseU.com